Rice Wars in Colonial Vietnam

ASIA/PACIFIC/PERSPECTIVES
Series Editor: Mark Selden

Crime, Punishment, and Policing in China
edited by Børge Bakken
Woman, Man, Bangkok: Love, Sex, and Popular Culture in Thailand
by Scot Barmé
Making the Foreign Serve China: Managing Foreigners in the People's Republic
by Anne-Marie Brady
Marketing Dictatorship: Propaganda and Thought Work in China
by Anne-Marie Brady
Collaborative Nationalism: The Politics of Friendship on China's Mongolian Frontier
by Uradyn E. Bulag
The Mongols at China's Edge: History and the Politics of National Unity
by Uradyn E. Bulag
Transforming Asian Socialism: China and Vietnam Compared
edited by Anita Chan, Benedict J. Tria Kerkvliet, and Jonathan Unger
Bound to Emancipate: Working Women and Urban Citizenship in Early Twentieth-Century China
by Angelina Chin
The Search for the Beautiful Woman: A Cultural History of Japanese and Chinese Beauty
by Cho Kyo
China's Great Proletarian Cultural Revolution: Master Narratives and Post-Mao Counternarratives
edited by Woei Lien Chong
North China at War: The Social Ecology of Revolution, 1937–45
edited by Feng Chongyi and David S. G. Goodman
Prosperity's Predicament: Identity, Reform, and Resistance in Rural Wartime China
by Isabel Brown Crook and Christina Kelley Gilmartin with Yu Xiji, edited by Gail Hershatter and Emily Honig
Little Friends: Children's Film and Media Culture in China
by Stephanie Hemelryk Donald
Beachheads: War, Peace, and Tourism in Postwar Okinawa
by Gerald Figal
Gender in Motion: Divisions of Labor and Cultural Change in Late Imperial and Modern China
edited by Bryna Goodman and Wendy Larson
Social and Political Change in Revolutionary China: The Taihang Base Area in the War of Resistance to Japan, 1937–45
by David S. G. Goodman
Rice Wars in Colonial Vietnam: The Great Famine and the Viet Minh Road to Power
by Geoffrey C. Gunn
Islands of Discontent: Okinawan Responses to Japanese and American Power
edited by Laura Hein and Mark Selden
Masculinities in Chinese History
by Bret Hinsch
Women in Early Imperial China, Second Edition
by Bret Hinsch
Chinese Civil Justice, Past and Present
by Philip C. C. Huang
Local Democracy and Development: The Kerala People's Campaign for Decentralized Planning
by T. M. Thomas Isaac with Richard W. Franke

Hidden Treasures: Lives of First-Generation Korean Women in Japan
by Jackie J. Kim with Sonia Ryang
North Korea: Beyond Charismatic Politics
by Heonik Kwon and Byung-Ho Chung
Postwar Vietnam: Dynamics of a Transforming Society
edited by Hy V. Luong
From Silicon Valley to Shenzhen: Global Production and Work in the IT Industry
by Boy Lüthje, Stefanie Hürtgen, Peter Pawlicki, and Martina Sproll
Resistant Islands: Okinawa Confronts Japan and the United States
by Gavan McCormack and Satoko Oka Norimatsu
The Indonesian Presidency: The Shift from Personal towards Constitutional Rule
by Angus McIntyre
Nationalisms of Japan: Managing and Mystifying Identity
by Brian J. McVeigh
To the Diamond Mountains: A Hundred-Year Journey through China and Korea
by Tessa Morris-Suzuki
From Underground to Independent: Alternative Film Culture in Contemporary China
edited by Paul G. Pickowicz and Yingjin Zhang
Wife or Worker? Asian Women and Migration
edited by Nicola Piper and Mina Roces
Social Movements in India: Poverty, Power, and Politics
edited by Raka Ray and Mary Fainsod Katzenstein
Pan Asianism: A Documentary History, Volume 1, 1850–20
edited by Sven Saaler and Christopher W. A. Szpilman
Pan Asianism: A Documentary History, Volume 2, 1920–Present
edited by Sven Saaler and Christopher W. A. Szpilman
Biology and Revolution in Twentieth-Century China
by Laurence Schneider
Contentious Kwangju: The May 18th Uprising in Korea's Past and Present
edited by Gi-Wook Shin and Kyong Moon Hwang
Thought Reform and China's Dangerous Classes: Reeducation, Resistance, and the People
by Aminda M. Smith
Japan's New Middle Class, Third Edition
by Ezra F. Vogel with a chapter by Suzanne Hall Vogel, foreword by William W. Kelly
The Japanese Family in Transition: From the Professional Housewife Ideal to the Dilemmas of Choice
by Suzanne Hall Vogel with Steven K. Vogel
The Korean War: An International History
by Wada Haruki
The United States and China: A History from the Eighteenth Century to the Present
by Dong Wang
The Inside Story of China's High-Tech Industry: Making Silicon Valley in Beijing
by Yu Zhou

Rice Wars in Colonial Vietnam

The Great Famine and the Viet Minh Road to Power

Geoffrey C. Gunn

ROWMAN & LITTLEFIELD
Lanham • Boulder • New York • Toronto • Plymouth, UK

Published by Rowman & Littlefield
4501 Forbes Boulevard, Suite 200, Lanham, Maryland 20706
www.rowman.com

10 Thornbury Road, Plymouth PL6 7PP, United Kingdom

British Library Cataloguing in Publication Information Available

Library of Congress Cataloging-in-Publication Data
Gunn, Geoffrey C., author.
Rice wars in colonial Vietnam : the Great Famine and the Viet Minh road to power/Geoffrey C. Gunn.
pages cm — (Asia/Pacific/perspectives)
Includes bibliographical references and index.
ISBN 978-1-4422-2302-8 (cloth: alk. paper) — ISBN 978-1-4422-2303-5 (electronic)
1. Vietnam—History—20th century. 2. Vietnam—Economic conditions—20th century. 3. Famines—Vietnam. 4. Vietnam—Colonization. I. Title. II. Series: Asia/Pacific/perspectives.
DS556.8.G86 2014
959.704—dc23 2013040484

∞™ The paper used in this publication meets the minimum requirements of American National Standard for Information Sciences—Permanence of Paper for Printed Library Materials, ANSI/NISO Z39.48-1992.

Printed in the United States of America

Contents

Tables

Maps

Preface

Alongside the names and places that stud this book, an authorial presence hardly figures. Yet it docs obliquely. Lacking patronage or protection (neither diplomat, soldier, journalist, nor spy), I first set foot in the Mekong Delta in 1974, a deceptively peaceful interlude between US president Richard Nixon's face-saving "peace with honor" formula signed at the Paris Peace Accords in 1973 and the communist "liberation" of Saigon in April 1975. At Vung Tau, the colonial French beach resort, banners and assembled black-clad peasants heralded president of the Republic of Vietnam Nguyen Van Thieu's "land-to-the-tiller" program, an ambitious attempt to eliminate land tenancy. On the American-built highway, southwest across the southern delta, matters were being contested militarily as "support artillery" boomed overhead. Still, the landscape was famously yellow-green with foliage matching the picture of natural richness, just as the *nhaque* (rural dwellers) went about their labour, much as described in this book. At Long Xuyen in the western delta, making a closer foray into the countryside, young Hoa Hoa boys from that religious sect pelted me with stones—it could have been worse—warning me that contestation was everywhere. A month later, across the border in the western Cambodian provinces of Battambang-Siem Reap, I was delivered by my Peugeot taxi escort into the maelstrom of a Khmer Rouge rocket attack, with roadside houses smoldering and refugee columns fleeing the other way. Relocating upstream the Mekong River to Vientiane in Laos, I was also present in the capital at the moment in December 1975 when the Pathet Lao movement took over by stealth, abolished the six-hundred-year-old monarchy, and ushered in a new and militant age of socialist transformation and austerity.

From participant observation in Long An Province in the southern delta in March 2012, a period coinciding with the winter-spring harvest and the storage and transport of newly harvested rice, I could observe certain continuities with the past and certain radical changes. In the ricefields, mechanized harvesters/threshers dominated. Alongside small-scale roadside and canal-side rice-sacking and rice-mill operations, hard by the Cambodian border I observed a large modern rice collection, storage, and processing factory. Throughout Long An Province, roads generally follow canals of some size and undoubted antiquity, just as settlements are linear, befitting the description of a "frontier." Motorized barge and "junk" traffic was heavy and the ubiquitous cargo was rice, bulk—not sacked. The role of Chinese brokers, merchants, or capital in rice distribution networks in present-day Vietnam—if at all—has obviously been long eclipsed, especially as state-owned enterprises dominate this area. Yet one legacy of the past is the hybrid hull style of the motorized "junks" with their prominent and distinctive Chinese-style prow "eyes." As observed in mid-2013 along the "typhoon coast" of central Vietnam, the rural scene was very different. Here the encircling mountains virtually reached to the sea. But wherever the narrow coastal plains opened up, intricate systems of flooded rice fields, small-bunded squares of emerald green, reached flush to the sea. Recalling the past, water buffaloes idled, just as field labour was by hand—female by the looks.

As with much history writing, the composition of this book is separated by time and place from the real events it describes, especially as I seek to distill some broader truths through more recently released documentary evidence. I am also aware that the writing of history can be a highly subjective and selective exercise. To add a research note, the reader will observe a preponderance of archival sources, especially French. Since the early 1980s, when I first initiated archival study on Indochinese nationalism and communism, I have worked in several French archives, some more systematically than others, and sometimes with a view to breadth rather than depth. Returning to Paris, Versailles, and Aix-en-Provence in the new century, I have still consulted only a fraction of these Indochina-related archives. The uninitiated should be aware that, lined up, the corpus of French documents on Indochina runs to several linear kilometers. Nevertheless, there are serious lacunae in these records, as with missing dossiers or the underdocumentation of otherwise important events and issues (the Great Famine of 1945 a case in point). I do not feel obliged to individually announce the authenticity of the documents I have perused or cited as that would deaden the story. Still, I acknowledge a wide variation in provenance, whether police, military intelligence, diplomatic, or more bland administrative correspondence. Each is loaded in special ways and, as the interpreter of this diverse set of documents, I am simply responsible for the selection, appraisal, and translation. Allowing that I have tracked over ground long staked out by many esteemed specialists of Indochinese history, my debt is well acknowledged. Even so, every historical interpretation produces something new. Although I have only sampled remaining French-language archives in Vietnam, I believe that the crucial French high-level decision-making documents on the Great Famine were indeed repatriated to France, especially as I have replayed in chapters 7 and 8.

One might rightly question the legitimacy of this "history from above" approach. In theory, indigenous documentation should be better, but, as others have alluded, official Vietnamese histories—many now in translation—should be treated with much caution. In my view, even more pitfalls await the reader of officialized sources than the raw and "corrupt" colonial documentation. Where possible I have also sought to match official histories (in translation), and there are many, with alternative sources, including the colonial version. There must be some merit in this approach as, over the years, I have encountered many Algerian, Moroccan, Vietnamese, and other researchers from France's former colonial world, *including* officials working in these archives. Needless to say, I have not conducted famine "survivor" field research—the passage of time, language, and research permissions all mitigate against this kind of investigation—but, where others have attempted this in the northern delta, I have incorporated their research. Although not a Vietnamese reader, I have sought to identify key Vietnamese language sources reflecting on the famine, and they are few. I have duly acknowledged and, with assistance, interpreted key Japanese scholarly works relating to the 1944–45 famine, certain of which have been translated into Vietnamese. However, the notion that Japanese "archives" yield a hitherto untapped source on close events relating to their occupation of Indochina does not hold up to scrutiny with the possible exception of broad planning documents, alongside testimonies collected by war crimes investigators.

Still, I have also sought to capture a sense of place in northern, central, and southern Vietnam. For research leave I am obliged to Nagasaki University. Inside Vietnam I especially acknowledge the assistance of development worker and Indochina specialist (Bac) Shane Tarr, along with individual Vietnamese who would prefer to remain nameless. For broad bibliographical help, especially relating to modern China, I acknowledge Vincent Ho of University of Macau. For expert assistance on geographical sources and interpretations, I acknowledge both Mark Cleary and Frédéric Durand. I also thank Frédéric Durand for drafting certain of the maps. For running commentary on excerpts published online on Japanfocus.com, I thank Mark Selden and Martin Murray. I also thank two anonymous reviewers of the entire manuscript, whose advice I have mostly, though not entirely, heeded. I also thank Susan McEachern of Rowman & Littlefield for her careful reading and judgment.

On orthography, I have pinyinized Chinese names except in quotations. The names Chiang Kai-shek and Sun Yat-sen are also exceptions, as is Kuomintang and Whampoa. Because I am dealing with the colonial period, I have retained the French nomenclature for Tonkin, Annam, and Cochinchina, although I also refer to northern, central, and southern Vietnam as, respectively, Bac Bo, Trung Bo, and Nam Bo, in line with official Vietnamese parlance. The dollar sign ($) is used to represent the Indochina piaster. Vietnamese diacritics are lacking on my keyboard.

Abbreviations

AGAS	Air Ground Air Services
ATC	Air Transport Company
AN	Archives Nationales (Paris)
AOI	Asie Océanie Indochine
AOM	Centre des Archives d'Outre-Mer
AP	Associated Press
ADB	Asian Development Bank
BAAG	British Army Aid Group
BCRA	Bureau Central de Renseignements et d'Action
BEI	*Bulletin Economique de l'Indochine*
BI	Banque de l'Indochine
BR	Bulletin de Renseignements
CCP	Chinese Communist Party
CIA	Central Intelligence Agency
Comindo	Comité interministériel de l'Indochine
COMINT	Communications intelligence
CLI	Corp Léger d'Intervention
DGER	Direction générale des études et recherches
DMH	Dong Minh Hoi
DRV	Democratic Republic of Vietnam
EFEO	Ecole Français d'Extrême-Orient
EMGDN	Etat-Major général de la défense nationale
FAO	Food and Agricultural Organization
FEA	Foreign Economic Administration
FEC	Far Eastern Commission

GG	Gouverneur Général (de l'Indochine)
GBT	Gordon, Bernard, Tan networks
GPRF	Gouvernement Provisoire de la République Française
ICL	International Communist League
ICP	Indochina Communist Party (Don Duong Cong San Dang)
ICCR	International Committee of the Red Cross
IFEFEO	Forces Expéditionnaires Françaises d'Extrême-Orient
JACAR	Japan Center for Historical Records
KMT	Kuomintang
KWIZ	Kweilin Weekly Intelligence Summary
MAAG	Military Assistance Advisory Group
MAE	Ministère des Affaires Etrangères
MDA	Military Defense Assistance
NAA	National Archives of Australia
NF	Nouveau Fonds
NM	Note Mensuelle
NP	Note Periodical
NTCIP	Note Technique de Contre-Ingèrence Politique
OCI	Office of Coordinator of Information
ONI	Office of National Intelligence
OSS	Office of Strategic Services
PCF	Partie Communiste Français
POW	Prisoner of War
PRC	People's Republic of China
PRO	Public Record Office (London)
PRO HK	Public Record Office (Hong Kong)
PSF	Partie Socialiste Français
RPF	Rassemblement du Peuple Français
RS	Résident Supérieur
RST	Résidence Supérieur Tonkin
SCAP	Supreme Commander of the Allied Powers
SEAC	South-East Asia Command
SEH	Service d'études historiques
SFIO	Section Française de l'Internationale Ouvrière
SHD	Service Historique de la Défense (Vincennes)
SHM	Service Historique de Marine (Paris)
SLFEO	Section de Liaison Français en Extrême Orient
SLOTFOM	Service de Liasion de Originaires des Territoires Français d'Outre-Mer

SREO	Service de Renseignement en Extrême-Orient
SWNCC	State, War, Navy Coordinating Committees
Tél.	Telegram
UK	United Kingdom
UNDP	United Nations Development Programme
UNRRA	United Nations Relief and Rehabilitation Administration
Viet Minh	Viet Nam Doc Lap Dong Minh (Vietnam Independence League)
VNDCD	Viet Nam Dan Chu Dang (Vietnamese Democratic Popular Party)

Introduction

A common and picturesque image of Vietnam is that of an elongated country represented by a bamboo shoulder or carrying pole balancing two rice baskets, one representing the northern delta and the other the southern. This depiction does carry some geographical verisimilitude, but it should also be understood that there is no balance between the regions of Vietnam in either productivity or demography. Through modern history, the southern delta has mostly proved capable of producing a rice surplus, whereas the overcrowded north-central and northern regions—the traditional political centers through most of Vietnamese history—are frequently in deficit. As this book explains, more or less coincident with the Japanese overthrow of French colonial rule in March 1945 and the largely unexpected Viet Minh seizure of power in Hanoi six months later, the Great Famine of 1945 afflicting the northern delta region—dubbed Nan Dói 1945 in Vietnamese—left between one and two million victims. Yet, at this time, the southern harvest was bountiful, with surplus rice literally rotting on the docks.

How can we explain this conjuncture of events? In French Indochina, peasant subsistence or livelihood came to the heart of social and political debates throughout the colonial period, reaching a climax in the depression year "rice rebellions" of 1930–31 in north-central Vietnam (Nghe-Tinh), especially under the impetus of the nascent Indochina Communist Party (ICP). We need to know the context in which colonial France developed and exploited Indochina's rich agricultural potential, especially rice production in both the northern and southern deltas, as well as the power plays over this resource between, variously, the French, the Japanese, and the victorious Viet Minh. Especially given the nature of the "hydraulic pact" entered into between France and the millions of peasant producers who traditionally looked up to the state to protect them from natural disasters, we also need to know how—to the advantage of anticolonial rebels—this "bargain" unraveled in the throes of the Great Famine. Stated another way, did the Great Vietnamese Famine spell a loss of the "mandate of heaven" for the French colonial rule in Vietnam, and was the overall dire human condition a determining factor in facilitating communist victory in late 1945?

As this book explains, colonial capitalism drew larger and larger numbers of mostly landless Vietnamese peasant farmer-producers, alongside a nascent working class, into a colonial cash economy. The vicissitudes of nature in the form of floods and drought and the rising demographic pressures, alongside the vagaries of the international rice trade economy, frequently threw this mass of people back to a subsistence level. While the colonial state also developed ameliorative measures, as with hydraulic control and agricultural credit, the system—at least in northern Vietnam—did not survive the major external shocks of war and capricious nature. Without ignoring the rural roots of resistance dating back to the French conquest, as well as the colonial agro-economy as it developed, this book also seeks to situate the Viet Minh ascendency within the context of the socioeconomic crisis of 1944–45 climaxing with the Great Famine.

Allowing that the Viet Minh triumph in August–September 1945 was contingent on a multiplicity of factors, I am not offering a deterministic view of agrarian crisis and communist success. Neither do I view the August Revolution as a purely momentary or opportunistic affair. Revolutions seldom are. Neither, accordingly, is the scope of the book narrowly restricted to the events of March–August 1945, however crucial they were to final outcomes. Rather, looking back to the 1930s and earlier, I have sought to scrutinize French colonial policies and actions affecting rice production and distribution alongside demographic, social, and ecological understandings crucial to the management of agrarian crisis. Alongside the long history of agrarian-based rebellion in Vietnam, I have also sought to trace the origins of Vietnamese anticolonialism in both its intellectual and mass dimensions. I am especially concerned to trace the formative activities of the ICP in Vietnam in mass peasant actions, such as demonstrated during the depression years of 1930–31, down to the ICP's transformation into an essentially peasant-based guerrilla army in 1944–45.

In reaching back to the "rice rebellions" of 1931–32, I am attracted to the analysis of Vietnamese scholar Hy Van Luong (1986, 153) who argues that "without an in-depth analysis of the ambiguities and contradictions in structural principles and ecological parameters, neither the Nghe-Tinh movement, nor the Vietnamese revolution, nor agrarian unrest in general can be fully understood." I am also in line with the reasoning of one who witnessed the Viet Minh August Revolution in Hanoi firsthand, the American Archimedes Patti (1980, 188), who argues that the many years of ICP preparation "did not count for nothing," especially as Ho Chi Minh "could not have succeeded if his ICP had not been well organized and prepared for seizing power." I also heed the remarks of historian Nguyen The Anh (1998a, 224) that it would be erroneous to view the conditions of instability surrounding the 1944–45 famine as the sole factor facilitating Viet Minh success. Nevertheless, he continues—and I also seek to demonstrate—that "the repercussions of this catastrophe on subsequent events were momentous."

Engaging the labor of millions in its cultivation, rice can also be construed as a multivalent factor in this narrative, whether as the means of subsistence on the part of the population or benefiting mostly big landlords along with Chinese and French entrepreneurs, whether as the key source of colonial taxation or forced procurement in the hands of the Japanese or as a strategic reserve in the hands of mostly rural-based communists or their Western-backed adversaries. As the principal export of colonial Indochina and the major source of livelihood, rice and its production connotes a range of contests and struggles in this work. In a word, rice becomes a metaphor for war or, more accurately, struggles or contestation besetting a range of actors, not excluding the peasant producer. Where others have given short shrift to politics at the expense of economics or vice versa, this work seeks to offer a correlated political economy approach to social revolution in a colonial setting. Neither should such an approach ignore the broader geopolitical context, not only Japan's wartime claims on Indochina's strategic resources—rice especially—but also French right to rule and prestige, China's proprietary historical interest, and the quixotic role of the United States, variously in defense of self-determination for former European colonies and as future defender against internationalist communist threats.

Reaching its grim climax on the cusp of the Viet Minh August Revolution of 1945, the famine which crippled northern Vietnam begs for greater understanding. More broadly, I view famine as a catastrophic subsistence crisis ("unheard of among living men") or an extreme event involving a wide spectrum of shortages of food and leading to starvation and mass death (see Jordan 1996, 7). More than that, in line with Amartya Sen's (1981) analysis of famines, I share a concern to highlight the mismanagement of food distribution, not only food shortage. Famously, in his independence proclamation of September 2, 1945, Ho Chi Minh laid direct blame on both the French and the Japanese for causing the deaths of, specifically, two million Vietnamese. Yet alongside the near-contemporaneous Bengal famine of 1943, the subject of an official inquiry, and the Honan famine of 1949, covered on the ground by *Life Magazine*,[1] the Great Vietnamese Famine of 1944–45 remains an understudied event even in the voluminous literature on the French and American wars.

Although rare in the flow of history, extreme famine events are not one of a kind. Insofar as the French administration tended to view the northern delta region of Vietnam as portending a Malthusian crisis, it also took ameliorative measures to postpone this event. In this light, it remains to be seen whether the Great Vietnamese Famine fitted the mold of a crisis brought about by population increase and limited by the means of subsistence or whether it stemmed from failed human interventions. In other words, we also need to know what measures were taken by the colonial state to stave off famine once the warning signs became evident, as with the onset of drought, floods, or crop failure. Both regional and temporal examples are not lacking, even setting aside the episodic chronicle of floods and famines in Vietnam reaching back to dynastic times.[2] Unexpected weather events do count as well, and they can be both unseasonal and damaging.

But locally in the northern Red River delta of Vietnam in 1944–45, the conjunction of natural and political events was epochal and is acknowledged as such. Notably, as Vietnamese communist ideologue and architect of the disastrous 1953–56 land reform, Truong Chinh (1977, 31), underscored, the focal issue of the August Revolution was the famine just as communist actions in seizing government granaries eased the development of the revolutionary movement. Summarizing a range of writings, historian George McT. Kahin (1987, 13) concluded that it was "this early and very palpable championing of the famine-ravaged peasantry, together with the Viet Minh's unequivocal anti-Japanese and anti-French stance, that was chiefly responsible for its rapid increase in popular backing." The Great Famine of 1944–45 would also emerge as a subject of recriminations engaging the French, the Vietnamese, and the Japanese, respectively, at least when the question of war reparations was raised in the 1960s (Gunn 2012). "Rice wars," or the contest for control over the rich rice-producing zones of the northern and southern deltas of Vietnam (and Cambodia), did not, of course, disappear with the August Revolution and would become integral with the French and, in turn, the American wars in Indochina.

It should not be ignored that bloody postwar French reoccupation in the face of armed Viet Minh usurpation of power likewise redounded on French right to rule at a time when the "free French" had recovered their own liberation from German occupation and when international sentiment had turned against old-style colonialism. No less challenged by homegrown socialists and communists, the French war would be fought out not only in the Red River delta and the "high country" of northern Vietnam but also in the French capital, in the boardrooms in Lyon, on the waterfront in Marseilles, as well as in the metropolitan and international press. To take up a refrain voiced by French scholar-diplomat Paul Mus and, as reprised in chapter 7, there was *crise morale* at every twist and turn in the story leading up to the events of August 1945, complicated by the advent of the Cold War, which recast Vietnam (and Laos) as keystones in a global theater.

FRENCH KNOWLEDGE PRODUCTION ON INDOCHINA

Writing in 1979, French historian of Vietnam Pierre-Richard Féray (1979, 9–11) commented on the "massification" of information and "inflation" of publications on Vietnam. In part, he was justifying yet another book on Vietnam in an obviously saturated marketplace of ideas. Still, as he also pointed out, the 1920–45 period remained a lacuna in studies on Indochina at least until access to French colonial archival materials became freely available. It is also true that thirty years later, these archives are still being harvested in the interest of a better comprehension of this watershed period standing between colonialism and decolonization and also ushering in the Cold War.

But French knowledge production on Indochina was always integral with colonial strategy. As suggested, the French project was not only an act of physical conquest but, following metropolitan rationalizations, created its own discourses such as promoted by colonial lobbies, associations, sections of the colonial press, and officially sponsored research institutes. Notable in this sense was the celebrated Ecole Français d'Extrême-Orient (EFEO) set up in Hanoi in 1898 alongside more scientific activities conducted under French rule. Today, the genealogy of such grand ventures becomes part and parcel of a postcolonial studies agenda.

Possibly no other activity was more challenging for the French than mastering knowledge of agriculture, a vast subject embracing land, tradition, seasonality, hydrology, soil conditions, markets, financial credit, demography, and disaster management. As geographer Michel Bruneau (2005, 307–8) has revealed, although embedded in colonial discourses of environmental determinism and culturalist paradigms, Indochina emerged as major locus of research by French geographers and agrarian studies practitioners. Among them we can identify close student of the northern delta peasantry and village community, Pierre Gourou (1931, 1936, [1940] 1945), economist Paul Bernard (1932, 1934), agronomist and pioneer environmentalist René Dumont ([1935] 1995), geographer Charles Robequain (1929, 1935, 1944) also known in the English-speaking world, Louis Lotzer (1933, 1941), and colonial inspector general of agriculture Yves Henry (1932; Henry and Devisme, 1928).[3]

Although not all these individuals could be painted with the same brush, the work of Gourou, especially, has given impetus to present-day critiques of French colonial "*tropicalisme*."[4] Author of the critically detached and now classic *Việt Nam, sociologie d'une guerre* (1952), Paul Mus would also help popularize the view that the northern village was the basic unit of Vietnamese society and even nation (Kleinen 2005, 346).[5] While Mus would attribute these ideas to Gourou, the purely scientific as opposed to ideological character of such works of tropical geography should also be questioned (Claval 2005, 299–300). In other words, according to Bruneau (2005, 304), through their scientific understandings of "monsoon Asia," French colonial administrators sought a way of overcoming nature—both forest and disease—to make these territories more amenable to colonization. In Indochina, the arriving French colonial regime quickly grasped the human condition stemming from the vulnerabilities of irrigated rice production in the two delta regions alongside rising population densities and the cycles of famine and poverty.

On the other hand, the youthful Truong Chinh, together with Gourou collaborator Vo Nguyen Giap, would plunder French-era scholarship to script their own class analysis of the peasant condition (Truong Chinh and Giap 1974). Other young Vietnamese attracted to French intellectual and political life, as with Ho Chi Minh, his "Stalinist" rival Tran Van Giau, and their mutual enemy, Trotskyist intellectual Ta Thu Thau, would literally transform the nature of Vietnamese collaboration as their revolutionary careers advanced. A generation removed, beneficiaries of the Sihanouk government's scholarship program in Paris, namely Hou Yuon, Hu Nim, and Khieu Samphan (1979), would likewise defend doctoral theses engaging Cambodia's peasant society and underdevelopment. Variously, the intellectual prodigy of the French project would command the victorious armies and communist parties that would not only expel the French and their successors but would radically remake both tradition and peasant society in cataclysmic ways, the effects of which are still playing out.

While French colonial academic traditions are now viewed in Vietnam in a more neutral manner, we still seek to know how these narratives played out, not only politically but through famine relief, flood control, and migration programs. We also seek to know how the colonial project came to be challenged or rejected by a range of local constituencies and, in the ultimate act of denouement, subverted by the Japanese militarists and, on their shirttails, the communist Viet Minh. More than anything, by adopting a broad historical-sociological approach, this book seeks to identify the rural roots of insurrection in colonial Indochina (1930–45), a period coinciding with world economic depression, a major cycle of floods and famine, Japanese militarist demagoguery, mass peasant political awakening and rural banditry, armed insurrection, and mass starvation. The world described by Robequain, Gourou, or Mus would never be quite the same.

HYPOTHESIS AND QUESTIONS

In the general literature on French colonialism in Indochina, we cannot ignore a range of discussions turning on two major considerations. These may be summarized as whether (a) the dissolution effects of French colonial capitalism on peasant structures in Vietnam overwhelmed social life and traditional safety nets or (b) colonialism actually reinforced precapitalist and feudalist structures, arresting social change and deadening the rise of indigenous industry or even import-substitution. In the first case, we might hypothesize an activist peasant riding with the new market forces unleashed by colonialism as with the rise of a cash economy. In the second case, we might hypothesize a reactive risk-averse and defensive peasantry, victim of the new market forces and an intrusive colonial state making new and unreasonable claims on livelihoods. Insofar as these are contrived, modern-day social science perspectives on historical social reality and not readily testable given the range of historical circumstances and numbers of variables at play, my method is also descriptive-analytical.

We also wish to investigate the degree to which economic crisis triggered political action in Indochina as in 1930–31 and again in 1944–45, at least alongside other variables at play, as with demography, natural environment, leadership, and mass mobilization. Inter alia, we need to know whether the evidence supports a case of economic deprivation driving mass peasants' actions alongside the proactive role of the Communist Party in harnessing anticolonial resistance. Neither, as suggested, can we ignore more subjective factors at play, as with the crucial immobilization of the French administration on March 9, 1945, by the Japanese military and the concomitant French loss of legitimacy or right to govern as popularly perceived. Granted that the northern communists did not sweep all before them, that large segments of the population remained outside their sway, and that the returning French and Allied forces commanded disposable rice surpluses and other resources, we need to ascertain the capability of armed peasant-rebels in both filling the administrative vacuum at the point of the Japanese surrender and in coping with local rural contingency against the backdrop of mass famine.

Three periods in this study lend themselves to this kind of analysis and comprise the basis of three key chapter-episodes, namely, as mentioned, the Nghe-Tinh or so-called depression rebellion of 1931–32; the near-famine event of 1937 in northern Annam and its amelioration; and the Great Famine and August Revolution of 1945 conjuncture, scarcely a generation after the Nghe-Tinh events. In all this, we know that colonial subjects were capable of striking alliances, were both calculating and risk averse, and were manipulated by all kinds of false prophets, both religious and secular. Such understandings undoubtedly defy even the best social science inquiry as to causal links and outcomes, but the devil is in the detail and in making sense of this truly veiled and mostly inaccessible and fading historical reality. In a word, this book is not just a reading back of a single event, the near conjuncture of the Great Famine and the Viet Minh triumph but, for the patient reader, seeks to offer maximum historical context to that event.

The foregoing raises a number of interrelated questions I seek to answer across a number of chapters. As heirs to a long imperial tradition of hydraulic control and oversight over land and agriculture, what special features did the French colonial state adopt in Indochina, especially in the management of agrarian crises? What were the main contours of village and rural life under colonialism, and how did Vietnamese people respond to the new demands and encroachments of the colonial state? What was the nature of Vietnamese political resistance to colonialism, especially its international communist currents? Given the scale of human suffering stemming from the famine, how important was the agrarian factor in the eventual Viet Minh victory, following repeated setbacks and missteps as with the earlier Nghe-Tinh rebellion? Alongside wartime Japanese economic pressures, how effective was French economic management during the 1944–45 crisis? Also taking into consideration the Allied bombing of vital infrastructure, how do we attribute blame for the Great Famine? To be sure, these are big questions and an ambitious agenda, but all help to throw light on the main storyline of this book, agrarian crisis in modern Vietnam, French colonial administrative practices, as with disaster management, and the climactic political events of August 1945 in conjuncture with the Great Famine and immediate aftermath.

NOTES

1. See "Millions Die in China's Famine," *Life Magazine*, May 13, 1946, 29–34. Graphically illustrated by New Zealand–born photographer George Silk and subtitled "Millions Are Starving in the Once-Rich 'Rice Bowl,'" the narrative continues, "From the Great Wall to French Indochina, wherever Chinese lands were gripped by occupying Japan, the story is virtually the same. . . ." Two-thirds of farmland in Henan lay untilled, "like an idiot's tale that has suddenly taken on terrible meaning."

2. Relevant comparable events include the Great Leap Forward Famine of 1958–62 in China; grand hydraulic projects gone wrong and falsification of data in the face of failing communization of agriculture (Dikötter 2010; Thaxton 2008; Zhou Xun 2012); the "killing fields" famine in Cambodia in the late 1970s, unending labor, too little food, rudimentary health care, terror, and mass executions (Kiernan 1996; Ponchaud [1976] 1978); and land reform conducted in North Vietnam between 1953–56 and rapid-paced communization (Hoang Van Chi 1964; Moïse 1983).

3. Robequain (1929), who conducted fieldwork in Thanh Hoa under EFEO sponsorship, made clear distinctions between the slash-and-burn (*rai*) culture of the slopes and the rice culture of the plains. Gourou, as suggested, conducted his fieldwork-based studies of the northern village between 1931 and 1935. By contrast,

Yves Henry (1932) researched the material conditions of rural life in the southern delta during a time of social unrest.

4. As Kleinen (2005, 46) clarifies, the term *tropicalité* dates to a 1955 polemic by Martiniquan writer Aimé Césaire in his *Discours sur le Colonialisme* (1955).

5. For an intellectual appraisal of Paul Mus, see David P. Chandler and Christopher E. Goscha, eds., *Paul Mus (1902–69): L'Espace d'un Regard* (Paris: Les Indes Savante, 2005).

Chapter 1

The Agrarian Setting

With its overwhelming agrarian character, no work on revolutionary change in Vietnam can ignore the overwhelming mass of peasant cultivators and their livelihood. Just as the land question would engage the infant Communist Party, so the colonial administration was also obliged to intercede in rural questions, as with the Nguyen and Trinh dynasties before them. More than that, the colonial state would emerge as the major arbitrator and provider of last resort in the macromanagement of hydraulic systems, the collection of rural taxes, and facilitation of the smooth deliveries of rice surpluses that practically sustained the colonial economy, including its commercial centers and ports. In describing the system as it worked, we also anticipate failure when it came in 1944–45, which is explained in a concluding chapter.

As Virginia Thompson (1937, 123) wrote in her pre-World War II classic on Indochina, rice made the colonial economy a virtual monoculture. Rice formed three-fifths of the agriculture, four-fifths of the native diet, and 60 percent of the export trade. For the vast majority of the peasants, Thompson underscored, rice was the sole product, "the only article for both consumption and as a medium of exchange, the condition of the country's prosperity, the keystone of Indochina's economy." Indochina has been and probably always will be an essentially agricultural country, she predicted, with the cultivation of rice in the hands of its people. Only the conditions of production are different across the regions as the varieties of rice differ with soil and climate.

We recall as well the multivalent character of rice across Asian traditions, not excluding anthropological understandings of rice in Vietnamese, Cambodian, Lao, and ethnic minority societies. Rice can also be valued as both an item of consumption as well as a good fit for the development needs of the state (Shepherd and McWilliam 2011). It follows that rice has one valence in a subsistence society, another in a setting bound by reciprocal relations between landlords and tenant farmers (*ta dien*), and yet another in a situation of capitalist agribusiness. Mostly in this work we are concerned with irrigated rice, which is rice grown on rice fields flooded by drawing water through canals and dikes to the point of entry to rice paddies or rain-fed lowland rice, which may also be drought prone at higher elevations, and upland rice, that grown where there is no natural flooding of the land and where rice may be grown in conjunction with other crops such as maize or legumes (Greenland 1997, 53–54). To be sure, as Féray (1979, 219) has written in his own general study, it would take a voluminous work to treat on agrarian issues in Vietnam. Accordingly, what follows is highly summary.

This chapter divides into six sections. A first backgrounds the historical adaptation of rice culture in the Red River delta area alongside the role of the state in hydraulic management. A second focuses on the major rice-growing areas of Indochina with particular emphasis on the Red River delta region. A third describes the climatic and hydraulic regime, especially as it touched the northern (Red River) and southern (Mekong River) deltas of Vietnam. A fourth examines the colonial rice regime with respect to hydraulic control and management. A fifth touches the land question. A final section examines the demographic-agrarian crisis with examples from Japan and Java, alongside famine protection measures as they panned out in late colonial Indochina.

THE HISTORICAL ADAPTATION OF RICE CULTURE AND THE IMPERIAL PROJECT

With its source in the Tibetan-Yunnan massif, the Red River (as with the Mekong) shares the common characteristic of all "tropical rivers" of alternating summer floods with periods of winter dryness. As Thompson (1937, 215) long ago pointed out, and a fact not always obvious in the literature, the gradient of the Red River is ten times that of the Mekong, so it falls precipitously into the sea. Over time immemorial this has obliged the construction of dikes in the northern delta to prevent the flooding of towns and rice fields. While the torrential Red River must be held in check "as the price of survival," on the other hand, the overflowing of the Mekong is of a "beneficent nature" to local agriculture, especially as it annually deposits rich alluvial soil. Therefore, while hydraulic agriculture in Cochinchina takes the form of dredging, in Tonkin it takes the form of dike construction, meaning variant adaptations of the two rivers to forms of flood control and irrigation. In sum, the rivers of the lower Mekong basin are of low gradient, those in the north of the country are steep and faster flowing, and those in the center, where there is also annual flooding, are both short and very steep.

Understanding that the "true" domestication of rice began in the lower Yangtze River valley in China some 7,500–8,500 years ago, the earliest evidence of rice cultivation by village communities in Vietnam comes from the Neolithic Phung Nguyen culture of the middle Red River valley dating from the late-third to mid-second millennium BCE, or several millennia after the Yangtze River pioneers (Higham 2002, 84). Innovations in rice-field bunds to control water movement, leveling of fields to even the distribution of water, and construction of rice fields at higher levels followed, as did the practice of river diversion irrigation and the construction of dams or water-holding tanks (see Greenland 1997, 24).

The Imperial Project

Emerging out of the prehistoric Hoabinhian culture, known for its stone assemblages dating to ca. 10,000–2,000 BCE, along with Dong Son culture, associated with prehistoric bronze castings as with bronze drums, the Dai Viet state emerging from the tenth century, with its basis established in the Red River valley, also adapted and perfected the techniques of irrigated rice, including the transplantation of seedlings. Dating back one thousand years, Thang Long (Hanoi), under the later Ly dynasty (1009–1225), initiated hydraulic works essential for both food security and the accumulation of a surplus by a centralized state system with extensive Chinese borrowings. The Tran dynasty from the thirteenth century and, in turn, the Nguyen dynasty from the sixteenth century onward would build on this legacy of protective dike construction, creating a veritable hydraulic society in the Red River delta from upstream Hanoi to the construction of sea dikes in the vulnerable lower delta.

The overall vulnerability of the delta populations during imperial times is starkly demonstrated by the research of Japanese scholar Sakurai Yumio. As he has documented, twenty-two natural disasters occurred in Tonkin between 1634 and 1693, variously floods and droughts. Drought was almost invariably followed by epidemics and famines, as in 1634 and 1681–83. While famines were relatively rare events, a natural disaster could occur every other year, compounded by man-made disasters including wars, mutinies, and other social unrest of considerable frequency over the same period (cited in Iioka 2011, 126, 129–30). As explained below, the need for central-level hydraulic control in the interest of protecting the population from flood as much as for ensuring food security increasingly engaged the imperial state over long time.

Alongside disasters, as historian Victor Lieberman (2011, 936–63) elaborates, local records point to growing land constraints under Dai Viet. After 950 or 1000, reclamation moved from hilly regions north and west of the Red River basin into the coastal and delta regions to the south and east, where peasants built polders, drainage systems, and irrigation works. Aided by court-sponsored hydraulic projects, the population of the delta rose from 1.2 million in 1200 to 2.4 million in 1340. But from the late 1200s, reclamation stalled and, beginning in 1343, dynastic annals refer repeatedly to peasant uprisings. By 1400, owing to disturbances, emigration, drought, disease, and Cham attacks mounted by the Hinduized coastal kingdoms prior to Vietnamese annexation and absorption, the delta population decreased to perhaps 1.6 million.

As Andrew Smith (2003, 95, 154) interprets, under Emperor Minh Mang (r.1820–41), especially in the first decades of the nineteenth century, flood control and irrigation infrastructure were combined to help the Nguyen court ensure stable food production and establish political control. Two major projects exemplified the integration of the "protective and productionist" hydraulic infrastructure, namely the construction of the Cuu Yen canal in Hung Yen Province in the lower Red River delta and the creation through land reclamation of two new districts, Tien Hai and Kim Son. But, lacking engineering equipment and skills, by the late nineteenth century the dikes began to collapse amid uprisings and rural unrest. According to local informant Hoang Cao Khai (1915), under Tu Duc (r.1847–83), the dikes were breached, leading to studies on the dike system by the *kinh luoc* (viceroy) of Tonkin, especially as the bed level of the river had already increased its height above the surrounding plain. From this time, the Duong River, known to the French as the Canal des Rapides, was constructed in the mid-lower delta to better evacuate accumulated water. Essentially, this swift-flowing channel redirects water from the Red River due eastward into a network of rivers toward Haiphong and the sea with the main channel of the Red River entering the Gulf of Tonkin in Nam Dinh Province. Working from imperial annals, Olivier Tessier (2011, 45) concludes that concerted efforts by the Nguyen just prior to the French intervention essentially set the dike system in place and laid the foundations of a rational system of water management in the delta. Even so, echoing Smith, he explains that there were also periods of withdrawal alongside engagement on the part of the imperial state, frequently leaving peasant communities to take over, as with private dike construction.

But was this a hydraulic state, such as drawn by Marx and tested by Karl Wittfogel against the experience of imperial China? Relative to China, as Alexander Woodside (1988, 137) points out, Vietnamese water control was "miniature, but probably more highly developed." He also allows a far greater role for provincial officials in oversight over dike construction than with Chinese counterparts. As Smith (2003, 14, 18, 47, 57, 74) argues, on many levels the state in Vietnam at the beginning of the nineteenth century appeared to have been a hydraulic state, at a time when both the state and the water users of the Red River valley managed the hydraulic systems. Although the state had played a key role in establishing flood-control systems, as with dike and drainage canal construction, historically, irrigation had been the responsibility of individuals. Notably, as many as 42 percent of all dikes in the Red River delta were nonstate. Typically, precolonial irrigation was based on pond and creek irrigation without intervillage cooperation. Smith found no true comparison with the mobilizational capacity of the Chinese state alongside that of big landlords, absent in the Vietnamese setting. However, he also allowed that elements of Wittfogel's hydraulic state as well as ad hoc self-organized hydraulic systems, such as those discovered by anthropologist Edmond Leach in upper Burma, both applied. But what is important in this discussion—elaborately extended through numerous literatures—is that in Vietnam, the priority of the state was on flood control, not irrigation, a bias that continued through most of the colonial period, with its emphasis on gravity-fed irrigation systems in the middle delta. As a consequence, irrigation systems remained at the village or commune level throughout the Red River delta prior to 1954. As such, Smith argues, "the colonial state and the peasantry never established a thoroughgoing hydraulic bargain in the Tonkin delta." But how did the colonial state and the water users cooperate, and how did the nature of the "hydraulic bargain" or pact differ from that of the Nguyen predecessors?

THE RICE-GROWING REGIONS

More generally, four major rice production zones were acknowledged in colonial Indochina; first, the northern Red River delta along with northern Annam; second, the southern Mekong River delta including lower Cambodia; third, central Annam; and fourth, central and western Cambodia, along with some surplus produced in southern Laos. With the exception of Laos, the rice production zones also coincided with the major populated areas as well as optimal ecological factors. Although largely dismissed in colonial studies, upland rice, or the "slash and burn" or swidden-cultivated rice of the southern highlanders should also be included in this enumeration.

The Red River Delta of Northern and North-Central Vietnam

Taken together, the major focus of irrigated rice cultivation in the north is in the Red and Thai Binh River deltas, along with the Chu and Song Rivers for Thanh Hoa Province and the Ca River for Nghe An (south of Thanh Hoa). Through late colonial times, fields were mostly diked to defend against floods. Certain fields were irrigated by gravity or pumping. The soils were plowed and prepared. All the rice was transplanted. Three types of rice field can be identified. According to harvest, these were those of the fifth month;

those of the tenth month (in line with the lunar calendar); and rice fields capable of two harvests (*Riziculture en Indochine* 1931).

As described by French agronomist and pioneer environmentalist René Dumont (1995, 17–19), 1,200 kilometers long with a basin of 130,000 square kilometers, the descent of the Red River from its source in Yunnan is rapid as far as Lao Kay and progressively weakening toward the delta. At Viet Tri, 220 kilometers from the delta, it is at ten meters altitude. Floods can be caused by heavy rains falling in the catchment basin, not necessarily coinciding with rain falling in the delta area. Occasionally, as in 1915, such a "discordance" resulted in floods in the delta but a failure of upland rice owing to an insufficiency of water. Contrariwise, in 1926, floods coincided with strong rains in the delta. The Red River also divides into several branches, notably the Day River with weak flow. In the lower delta, two great rivers, the Canal des Rapides, below Hanoi, and the Canal des Bambous at Hung Yen join the Thai Binh River and the Tra Ly River before flowing directly into the sea.

Topographical variation along with differential sediment accumulation has resulted in a great diversity of terrain in the Red River delta, permitting the northern delta to be divided into several regions. The first, including the fringes of the delta in the north and northeast, comprise poor sand-clay soils, including land of different elevations, as in valleys, thus presenting a particular economy based on the single harvest of rice in the tenth month, with the exception of an irrigated perimeter where a fifth-month harvest is possible. With a reduced population density, this region was deemed capable of exporting a surplus of rice to overpopulated areas. A second region, that of the northwest border of the delta, offers more clay soils along with more irrigation resources. Owing to the presence of *cuvettes* (basins), it was possible to harvest rice over a large area. But it was impossible to irrigate in the sixth month because the ground was too hard, having been left fallow during winter. The third is the central delta region formed from abundantly rich alluvium recently accumulated from the Red River. The western part of the great basin permits only a single harvest, in the fifth month. The boundary of the basin, the major bed of the Red River bounded by the Canal des Rapides to the north and the Canal des Bambous to the south, generally yielded a mixed harvest of rice and maize, or two harvests of rice in the east. The Thai Binh River zone was less rich (regions of two harvests). Fourth, the lower delta comprising the maritime littoral region was capable of producing two harvests, except for the saline region. The Thanh Hoa (or Ma River) delta offered a similar division. We can thus see that the agricultural economy of the different regions was very particular (Dumont 1995, 17–19).

As René Dumont (1995, 201) pointed out, with its alternation of ridges and depressions alongside a vast zone of low-lying land, the Red River delta is, in fact, a delta still in the making. However, the actions of human beings in channeling the excess water through dikes have also arrested its natural evolution, especially toward the southwest. As evidence, Dumont offers the example of the deltaic part of Thanh Hoa Province, developed later than the rest of the delta and which, accordingly, remained less populated. The result of this man-nature intervention, he observed, is a far more easily managed hydraulic environment.

Land Parcelization in the Red River Delta

As suggested, the imperial and subsequent colonial stake in assuming responsibility for hydraulic control was great, even a measure of state legitimacy, and, in Sino-Vietnamese conceptions, a veritable "mandate of heaven" governing the lives of millions. The entire Red River basin, the zone including that covered by the Red and Thai Binh Rivers, comprises an immense alluvial area of 155,000 square kilometers (today supporting a population of fifteen million). With a population density of more than 1,200 per square kilometer, it hosts one of the highest concentrations of rural dwellers in the world. Cultivated like a huge garden, as described by René Bouvier (1937, 1–9), its landscape required a prodigious labor of 363 days a year. As such, the rice fields and hydraulic works literally represented the accumulated labor of millions over history.

According to a 1936 Rice Office report, the northern delta differed from its southern counterpart in one important respect: it had twice fewer rice fields while supporting an extremely large population. In certain cantons in the Red River delta, the population density reached 1,500 per square kilometer. To support this population density required the intensive cultivation of all available rice fields, of which only one-third were capable of producing two harvests a year. Paddy exports were weak, reaching only 25,000 tonnes a year (1918–30), falling to 4,500 tonnes in 1934 following the Great Depression crisis (AOM Indo NF 2234/263 "La condition de la production de rizière Cochinchinois et au Tonkin établi avec la collaboration de l'office de riz," Hanoi, April 1936).

Further highlighting the importance of the Red River delta, as Dumont (1995, xii) pointed out, although comprising just 2 percent of the area of Indochina, by the late 1920s it hosted one-third of the population (6.5 million rural inhabitants alongside town dwellers) and probably increased its population by one million between 1901 and 1929. Moreover, owing to the population density, the land in the northern delta was—and is—intensely parceled. By the late 1920s, the cultivable land was in the hands of 1,300,000 rural landowners, 98 percent of whom possessed less than 5 hectares, with 66 percent possessing between 0 and 0.5 hectares and 32 percent from 0.5 to

5 hectares. Thus, small owners possessed around 40 percent of the total of rice fields, with a similar percentage of the delta rice lands in the hands of the middle and big landlords (possessing more than 5 hectares), along with French *colons*. Although certain of the middle landlords (not the majority) directly cultivated their land, among the big landowners, direct cultivation was unknown. In their case, the land was divided up among a great number of peasant share croppers, each cultivating land rarely surpassing six to ten *mau* (about one-third of a hectare). Additionally, 20 percent of the total area of rice fields constituted communal rice lands, divided among numerous village taxpayers albeit to the benefit of the communal budget. In sum, rice fields were worked by a near totality of small owners, farmers, sharecroppers, and registered taxpayers, in part benefiting from communal land. All the locals practiced a family cultivation without recourse to extended labor during time of great agricultural works (transplanting, harvest, etc.). The practice of mutual assistance, exchange of workdays of labor, was limited. But all of this—ownership, use of manpower, and so on, differed from north to south. It is certainly striking, as Dumont (1995, 17) observed, that the population density of the northern delta closely matched soil fertility.

The Mekong Delta

With its source in China and also fed by westward-flowing tributaries from the central or Truong Son cordillera, the Mekong River supports an intricate ecological and economic system depending on the seasonal ebb and flow of the waters and, even in the flat, low-lying lower delta, the tide. This is a reference not only to the fertile alluvium seasonally flushed down the river but to the biodiversity which the river supports, notably wild-catch fish and other aquatic life. Dating back to the first century AD, centralized states emerged in the lower delta, as with Hinduized delta civilization of Oc Eo, thriving as a transit point for long-distance east-west trade as well as benefiting from trade up and down the Mekong River. The early Oc Eo state also initiated canal construction in the southern delta, both for irrigation and transport. Rice was then a staple, although probably a variety of "floating rice," still grown in the western delta and known for its resilience to flooded fields (cf. Higham 2002, 236–38).

The Nam tien Movement

Evocatively dubbed Cuu Long, or "Nine Dragons" in Vietnamese, historically the lower Mekong delta was a zone into which, from 1700 onward, Vietnamese frontier settlement expanded as the Nguyen consolidated political control over what had been an integral part of the ancient Khmer kingdom (and with significant Cham outliers to the north). With good reason, Nola Cooke and Li Tana (2005) describe the southern delta as a "water frontier," a virtually stateless zone where Chinese merchant groups staked out trading interests and where the Nguyen initiated reclamation works vastly expanding the land frontier through canal construction and reclamation of marshes, centuries before the present-day coastline even took shape. In lower Cochinchina, where Saigon (Gia Dinh), on the bank of the Dong Nai River, existed in embryo in the early seventeenth century, it remained the largest conglomeration of people in the south, with an estimated population of one hundred thousand under Emperor Minh Mang (r.1820–41) (Osborne 1969, 24).

Germane to this history is an acknowledgment of the Vietnamese southward movement, or *Nam tien*. As Michael Cotter (1968, 12–24) explains, the *Nam tien* movement both reproduced and altered traditional Vietnamese social relations in both complex and subtle ways. Allegiance to family and loyalty to one's village remain features of Vietnamese society. Wet-field rice and settlement on lowlands also remain important characteristics, even though village settlement patterns became more spread out and with the size of landholdings larger in the south. Vietnamese frontier society along the central coast retained the basic elements of northern society—wet-rice agriculture, densely settled villages, and local self-sufficiency. However, geographic constraints, as with the narrow coastal plain girded by mountains to the west and with the plains interrupted by "lowland pockets," hindered the development of coastal trade. Such constraints also kept the villages more or less isolated behind their bamboo hedges, as befitted the general description of northern villages. The new environment also facilitated the development of maritime activities. Notably, rice fields were laid out on terraced banks, and village settlement patterns were adapted to allow for the sea. In contrast to northern villages, often sited far from the floodplains of rivers, villages of the center were frequently located along riverbanks. Certain agricultural techniques may have also been learned from the Cham, as with terracing. Still, the village hierarchy continued under control of the elders, the mandarins, and the village officials. Further south in ancestral Khmer lands, as indicated, the Vietnamese entered a zone of extensive waterways and arable land. Villages here were seldom settled as compactly as in the north but, practically to this day, were strung out along waterways, the major transportation routes. According to Cotter, such a linear settlement pattern reflected in part "not only the influence of the environment but also the breakdown of village traditions over the years." Unlike the self-contained villages of the traditional areas, the southern village not only was more open to outside forces but eroded family traditions and weakened family hierarchy. Houses—straw or wood rather than straw and mud—became more of a shelter than an ancestral temple.

With time, the Mekong delta became the granary of Vietnam. But, as more land was reclaimed, more land concentration took place. The trend was exacerbated after the Nguyen defeat of the Tay Son (1778–1802), leaving the mass of peasant cultivators landless. Nevertheless, vast areas of fertile land remained outside of cultivation. According to colonial statistics (Henry 1932, 272–73), the total cultivated area in the south in 1868 was only 215,000 hectares. Although population density was rising, it was still far behind that of the north and center of Vietnam. Even prior to the French conquest, the big landowners in the south were producing surpluses of rice for export. Under the Nguyen, certain canals were also constructed using local peasant labor. In the 1790s, Chinese traders in the south were annually selling 12,000 tonnes of rice to other countries, just as Chinese traders were entering the marketplace in materials, silk, and other commodities in local demand (Tran Ngoc Dinh 1979, 82).

More generally, rice cultivation in central Vietnam was concentrated in the deltas spread along the coastal littoral otherwise differing little from the rice field regime in the north. But where the terrain was fertile and the commencement of the rainy season variable, then the cultivator preferred sowing *en place* instead of transplanting. Two rice harvests a year were rare, with farmers preferring to follow a rotation where sugarcane alternated with rice. There were cultivators who followed the third-, fifth-, eighth-, tenth-, and twelfth-month cycles. Undoubtedly a Chinese introduction, a long tradition of sugarcane farming existed in the central-south (*Riziculture en Indochine* 1931).

THE NATURAL OR CLIMATIC-HYDRAULIC REGIME

As well understood, the seasonal alternation between the winter and summer monsoon deeply affects human activities across this broad equatorial and subequatorial zone, especially agriculture, as with the length of the growing season and the need for irrigation. Understanding the "monsoon system" also helps to explain the key elements of the typhoon-flood and drought regime to which all of Indochina is subject. The term *monsoon* (from the Malay term *musim*) applies to both the prevailing wind direction (respectively, northeast from October to early April and southwest from April to September) and the rainfall regime. But the length of the dry season also varies with latitude. With distance from the equator, variation in the climatic regime increases, with the monsoon becoming more pronounced and with the length of the dry season prolonged. In northern Thailand and Laos, the dry season can extend for as much as five months but is less than four months in central and southern Vietnam. Obviously, a prolongation of drought can impact negatively on agriculture and food security. Altitudinal variations also influence precipitation and temperature. Rainfall variability can have a major impact on rice cultivation systems, just as rice varieties and cultivation techniques have traditionally been carefully adjusted to the climatic regime. Obviously, wet-field rice—especially new hybrid rice varieties—requires a more even annual rainfall regime than dry-field rice (See Cleary 2004a, 453–59; 2004b, 908–9).

The Typhoon Regime

Typhoons generated in the Luzon area and moving northwesterly across the South China Sea are an annual feature along the southern Chinese and Vietnamese coasts, especially between July and October. Less frequent in the south than in the north, and occasionally even making their impact felt across the central cordillera in Cambodia and Laos, the rains the typhoons unleash break the drought and replenish irrigation systems. Nevertheless, as indicated below, they are frequently devastating as well. While several typhoons make landfall each year (four to six on average), records suggest that the northern delta is the most vulnerable. Typically, typhoons generate high waves and raise the water level of the sea, inundating coastal settlements and agricultural land with saline water. Such typhoons and storm surges often overtop and frequently destroy sea dikes, flooding lowland coastal areas. Intense rainfall also causes flash floods, landslides, and mud flows in the mountains, along with erosion and siltation of riverbeds and water-retaining structures further downstream. The colonial state was well aware of the risks of typhoons and other meteorological events, and the Service Météorologique de l'Indochine was not backward in data collection and analysis, as with the work of Bruzon and Carton (1930). Even today, as Vietnamese disaster specialist and flood management official Dang Quang Tinh (1999) points out, annual losses from water disasters in Vietnam, both human and material, are large.

Notably, Haiphong was the site of one of the most catastrophic natural disasters in history and the third-deadliest tropical storm ever recorded. On October 8, 1881, a typhoon set off tidal waves that flooded the port city, causing widespread destruction and killing an estimated three hundred thousand inhabitants, with more believed to have subsequently died of disease and starvation (*Encyclopedia Britannica* online). According to Dang Quang Tinh (1999), the most damaging typhoons of the twentieth century were the 1904 typhoon in the south, which caused death and injury to five thousand people, and the September–October 1985 typhoon centered on Hue, which killed nine hundred people. On November 5, 1930, a typhoon wreaked havoc on the prison island of Poulo Condore (Con Son) off the southern tip of Vietnam, leaving some hundreds of the penal population dead (AOM Indo NF 1848–59 227/1853 tél. à Colonies, Hanoi, Sept. 6, 1930).

At least the most serious typhoon damage in the immediate prewar period were the floods of August 1937, simultaneously afflicting both the north and the south of Vietnam along with Cambodia, a rare event. Lashed by rains of "extreme violence," harvests were destroyed, and the populations of entire regions were reduced to "atrocious misery." In the Red River delta alone, the material losses were 160 million francs, with the number of victims reaching 750,000 persons. In Cochinchina, 232,000 hectares were flooded, with five hundred thousand people requiring assistance. Touching off a wave of support and solidarity for the victims, the French parliament voted a special line of credit for the tragedy, although still not allowing a moratorium on victim debts and taxes such as popularly demanded (AOM Indo NF 227/1858 Des Deputés à Colonies, Paris, Feb. 21, 1938).

As Dang Quang Tinh (1999) elaborates, between 1900 and 1945 there were eighteen years in which dikes failed in the Red River delta, translating into one dike failure with crop losses every two to three years on average. In the September 1945 flood, as described in the epilogue, the dike system failed in seventy-nine places, flooding eleven provinces over a cultivated area of 312,000 hectares and affecting some four million people. The 1971 flood caused the dikes to fail in three large sections, inundating 250,000 hectares and seriously affecting 2.7 million people. At the time of the 1986 flood—the fifth-largest of the twentieth century—a section of dike along the Red River was destroyed, and a sluice under the Can River collapsed. Nevertheless, as broached in the epilogue, my concern is with the late August 1945 flood, following hard on the floods of September–October 1944 and the Great Famine reaching its climax in early 1945.[1]

The Flood and Drought Cycle

Some sense of the agricultural cycle set against seasonal conditions is also necessary. As Gourou (1931, 74) explained in one of his earlier studies, the Red River delta is seasonally threatened with floods from June to October. Correspondingly, typhoons attain their maximum frequency in Tonkin and northern Annam in July, August, and September (later still in Annam and Cochinchina). Being both the hot season and the rainy season, it is also the peak time for agricultural work. More generally, rice cultivation in the delta follows a fixed sequence. The first harvest takes place in June (or the fifth month of the lunar calendar) and the second in November, although preparation work commences in June. Notably, the rice seedlings are transplanted in July. This means that the two harvests can be destroyed by the flood, especially as rice plants submerged for over a four-day period will die. Between 1884 and 1923, there were twenty severe floods in the northern delta prior to June 20, of which eighteen lasted longer than four days, resulting in the destruction of the crop in the flooded regions just before the harvest. On the other hand, over the same timeframe, there were fifty-nine major floods after September 1, of which forty lasted longer than four days and destroyed the transplanted seedlings. On average, the first harvest was destroyed one year out of three, and the second, just about every year.

Relative to the south, north-central and northern Vietnam are more vulnerable to drought, which, from the historical record, often follows after a year of floods. Citing a missionary source, Martinez (2007, 84) states that 1857 was a famine year in Tonkin, with the price of rice four times higher than at any time over the previous twenty-five years. But when eight hundred persons died of famine in Hai Duong Province in 1865, the imperial government imposed bans on rice exports, especially entering the Chinese junk trade. Again, in the summer of 1895, a drought affecting Tonkin led to a "disastrous" famine. From 1898, in response to these events, Governor General Paul Doumer initiated the construction of a canal leading from the Red River with the goal of irrigating three thousand hectares of riceland in Hanoi Province. Fed by gravity during the rainy season, the canal system was mechanized during the dry season (with the entrepreneur taking one-third of the harvest as dues). As Doumer's successor, Jean Baptiste Paul Beau, reported, canal construction was then underway but not unproblematic (Beau 1908). Irrigation for food security reasons was not unknown under imperial rule, although under colonial rule, as pointed out below, flood control would be prioritized over big irrigation projects also allowing for gravity-fed irrigation.

Then came the drought of the spring of 1906, leading to famine in northern Vietnam. As Nguyen-Marshall (2008, 34–41) observed, while small compared with the Great Famine of 1945, the famine breaking out in March 1906 caused several thousand deaths, leaving 100,000 out of 250,000 people at risk in Nam Dinh Province. Reminiscent of the Great Famine, a series of natural disasters had preceded the 1906 famine, such as the drought in the summer of 1905, subsequent floods, and the rupture of the Co Lieu dike in Ha Dong Province, damaging thirty-six thousand hectares of rice fields across Ha Dong, Ha Nam, Ninh Binh, and Nam Dinh Provinces, and yet another dike rupture in Bac Ninh Province in August, leading to the flooding of a further thirty thousand hectares in Bac Ninh, Hung Yen, and Hai Duong, and then, in late September, torrential rains and a typhoon, which caused further crop damage in the Red River delta. Nguyen-Marshall uses this example (and the example of "the subsistence crisis of 1915–17") to demonstrate that the French administrators did not share the people's expectations of a right to subsistence but rather, as victims, they had to prove their worthiness as loyal and "deserving poor." To be sure, as discussed below, the floods (and drought) of 1937 and their management would become a major test case for the Popular Front government and even the legitimacy of the French presence in the eyes of peasant victims across Indochina.

Seasonal Variations in the Northern Delta

Seasonal conditions offer another major variable in the Red River delta, again with wide regional variation. Drought ruins the cultivations on higher irrigated land but tends to advantage the cultivations on lower ground. The reverse also holds when an excess of rain occurs. Wherever the level of water prevents the cultivation of rice in the tenth month, then the peasant-farmers transform themselves into fishermen. And wherever irrigation was not possible, and wherever the soil was without excess clay, then the cultivators would plant such crops as maize, potatoes, soybeans, and beans. But these crops required intensive labor. If the family members were without work, then this activity contributed greatly to the family budget. If the soil was too hard, then a certain number of cultivators would become inactive during winter, drifting toward employment in public works (throughout the dry season) or in the mines. Other members of the family, especially women and children, were constantly engaged in commerce, as with cattle raising, small industry (rice polishing), handicrafts, and so on. The family budget was also complemented by loans, in cash or *en nature*, through moneylenders, merchants, big landowners, speculators, or Chinese exporters, inexorably leading to peasant indebtedness (Nguyen-Marshall 2008, 34–41).

Seasonal Variations in the Southern Delta

As French Vietnam specialist Pierre Brocheux (1995, 6) outlines in a dedicated study, with a mean temperature of 27°C, average humidity between 60 and 90 percent, and abundant and regular rains, the climatic zone of the southern delta is entirely propitious for wet-rice cultivation. Rainfall distribution ranges from 1,000–2,000 millimeters in the eastern part, to 1,200–1,500 millimeters in the center, to 2,000–2,500 millimeters in the western and southern part. The rainy season (the southwest monsoon) lasts from April to October in the western part of the delta (dubbed the Transbassac by the French) and from May to November in the rest. Notably, during the southwest monsoon, the Mekong breaches its banks and spreads its waters over thousands of square kilometers through the lower delta, overwhelming the region's starkly linear features. As rice fields, canals, and other features disappear beneath the inundation, the inhabitants take to houseboats and sampans. However, delayed rains during the "little dry season" of August–September can be particularly risky for transplanting rice seedlings. Unlike the Red River delta, the flooding increases slowly owing to the buffer effect of the upstream Tonlé Sap in Cambodia. Nevertheless, during the rainy season, the flood can reach more than four meters for a two- to three-month period (starting in July to August and lasting until

November or December and even January in poorly drained, depressed areas). Additionally, a high tidal effect reaches upriver as far as the border with Cambodia. Both salinity and acidity constraints apply. Historically, different adaptive practices have been employed to deal with the water and flooding in the southern delta, as with the expansion of "floating rice," a less coveted but adaptable variety of rice. While nature may be taken as a given, the man-nature balance has also been dramatically modified over time in both deltas. Setting aside deliberate defoliation in the south practiced by US forces during the American war, the effects of defoliation in the Red River basin were already palpable during colonial times. In even earlier centuries, logging and mining in Yunnan also transformed the watershed of the Red River for the worse.

COLONIAL HYDRAULIC CONTROL AND MANAGEMENT

Having examined the ecological setting of the two deltas, we detour to explain French colonial understandings of the "monsoon Asia" agricultural regime. As mentioned in the introduction, the academic discipline of tropical geography also drew impetus from research conducted in Indochina by such individuals as Pierre Gourou, René Dumont, Charles Robequain, and Yves Henry. In this context, a shared understanding by French colonial administrators to harness knowledge production in this part of the world also came into being. The importance of rice cultivation was quickly grasped by the arriving French colonial regime both to sustain livelihoods as well as to lay the foundation of viable export production. But, as with the Nguyen before them, the French had to confront the vulnerabilities of irrigated rice production in the two delta regions, alongside rising population densities and natural calamities, including long droughts and raging floods, as well as concomitant cycles of famine and poverty.

It would take decades to work through, but the French administration was also obliged to recreate some version of the Nguyen's hydraulic state if it was to overcome the forces of nature, as with dike construction, but also, and moving beyond the provision of protective infrastructure—a Nguyen priority—seeking to expand irrigated land. As suggested, agricultural modernization was not only an act of overcoming nature—both forest and disease—but also part of the colonial state project to make the region more amenable to colonization. But the success of such a venture also called down a pact or bargain between the state and the peasantry who, if piqued or pushed too far, quite obviously had the wherewithal to derail the best intended colonial projects implemented without their consent (as well demonstrated in the events of 1930–31).

The Colonial Hydraulic "Bargain"

Needless to say, there was wide variation in this state-community "bargain" between Tonkin and Annam and on the frontier in Cochinchina. It is pertinent, as Brocheux (1995, xvi) remarks, that nearly every feature of the southern delta during colonial times stood in contrast to its northern counterpart. He cites ethnic diversity, the untamed hydrological environment, the absence of established villages, greater scope for mercantile activity and, under colonial rule, greater integration into the world market. By contrast, as famously depicted by Gourou, the *xa* or village of the northern delta remained sequestered behind its bamboo hedge, a legacy of ancient defensive responses to the outside world but also suggestive of autonomy vis-à-vis the reach of the state.

It is also true, as Dumont (1995, 18) boldly states, that without the protection of the dikes, the Red River would flood the major part of the delta. Having breached the dikes, floods also dump enormous quantities of sand, which diminishes the fertility of the soil, sometimes leading to entire village evacuations from the affected areas. But fine sand mixed with silt can actually increase the fertility of the soil and the value of the land. Good irrigation by canals allows the sand to settle and the silt to flow. At the same time, the lower delta has to be protected from sea invasion and salination, especially the conjunction of weak river flow and the action of tides of the Gulf of Tonkin reaching a maximum amplitude of four meters. Owing to seawater invasion along the Thai Binh River, large expanses of rice fields, as in the maritime province of Kien An, cannot be cultivated in the dry season owing to lack of fresh water.

However, according to Smith (2003, 108), colonial advance in hydraulic management was delayed by several decades owing to a hesitation stemming from what he describes as the "siltation hypothesis." In this understanding, first entering French reports in 1886 and also given voice by certain traditional authorities, because dikes were eroding, siltation was pushing up the heights of riverbeds and raising water levels above dikes. Between 1896 and 1926, the French administration worked to reduce water levels in the Red River rather than attending to the dikes. In line with the siltation theory, dikes would have to be raised ad infinitum to accommodate the rising river bed. In the event, the decision to dike the Red River delta was made only in 1923 and only after the French had convinced themselves through the accumulation and analysis of data. Only then could they remain unassailable in the face of local—and skeptical—Vietnamese knowledge.

As the French engineer Gauthier (1930) explained, a major dike construction program that was kicked off in 1926 also necessitated a strict surveillance regime against potential ruptures. With dikes in place and as a second step, the focus shifted to the construction of irrigation canals and sluice gates and the general modernization of infrastructure. As approved by Gourou and others, wet-field rice agriculture was at the centerpiece of agricultural development and modernization, just as improved productivity depended on water control. Basically, as Smith (2003) confirms, the postcolonial state has not deviated from this strategy and, by the end of the twentieth century, every major waterway in the Red River delta had been diked.

French Colonial Hydraulic Works

The question of protecting Hanoi and the lower reaches of the delta also exercised French planners from an early date, just as the subject became the object of three commissions, each convened after the floods of 1894, 1904, and 1915, respectively. For instance, as the "Commission Supérieur du Digues" reported (*Rapport de la Commission* 1896), the total suppression of dikes in the north would produce a negative impact on cultivation and this solution should be rejected. In the meantime, works to improve water flow and other works should be undertaken.

Generally, a consensus developed among French administrators that hydraulic control helped to tame nature just as other engineering works—as, indeed, with hydropower—also served to display colonial mastery. But dike maintenance and the progressive raising of the riverbed over the surrounding countryside was also a trap in the way of exposing the entire system to inundation, whether by breach during a serious flood or even deliberately, as in the time of war, such as exposed in chapter 7. By the 1930s, various commissioned studies debated the question of dike management, but by then there was no retreat. Statistics are hard to come by, but, according to Dang Quang Tinh (1999), from 1884 to 1945, the Vietnamese people placed eighty-seven million cubic meters of earth fill while, since 1945, 255 million cubic meters of earth fill and 4.2 million cubic meters of rock revetment was used. In short, the capacity of dikes has been constantly strengthened by widening and raising at an accelerated rate. However, Dang Quang Tinh also allows that the existing river dikes built long ago by hand using local materials and in the absence of sound geotechnical principles left them highly vulnerable to erosion.

Red River Floods and the Hydraulic Control Debate

Speed and preparedness was obviously of the essence in managing flood disaster in Vietnam, especially when the dikes were breached. Facing down a massive flood risk in September 1909, Beau's successor, Governor General Antony Klobukowski, alerted Paris as to the dangers. As he telegraphed, "Red River Hanoi 11.2 m.; the flood of 1893, the strongest we have seen and the consequences of which were disastrous, was only 10.94 m." Further injecting a note of urgency, "Dikes which have held up to now threaten to give way, notably in the province of Ha Dong neighboring Hanoi. Tuyen Quang completely flooded. Provinces of Hung Yen, Vinh Yenet, Phuc Yen, threatened. Very serious damages, no human losses so far. All immediate dispositions taken" (AOM Indo NF 1848–1859 227/1853 tél., Klobukowski, Hanoi à Colonies, Paris, Sept. 1, 1909). Almost fifty years later, as mentioned in the epilogue, Klobukowski's urgent words would be echoed by none other than Ho Chi Minh, warning of a breach in the dikes in the northern delta as floodwaters reached an unprecedented high.

The flood of 1909 also gave way to public discussions as to cause and remedies. Writing in 1911, a Hanoi Chamber of Commerce report noted that although the Vietnamese themselves had realized a system of dikes reaching an impressive 1,200 kilometers in length, they lacked a general plan. Nevertheless, by protecting cultivated areas against floods, they proved their utility over the long term in staving off mass famine. While indigenous mapping certainly also existed, the Service Géographique de l'Indochine moved ahead with the production of maps of Tonkin and Annam (1:100,000), alongside a 1:25,000 map of the Tonkin delta. Cadastral survey would follow. By the time of this report (1909), some 5,500 hectares of new land had been brought under cultivation by French engineers. The Chamber of Commerce report identified three problems in hydraulic management of the northern delta (Tonkin and northern Annam): first, that involving gravity irrigation (rainfall); second, the need for pumping devices; and third, preventing the invasion of saline water into the freshwater zones on the coastal littorals (*Rapport de la Chambre* 1911).

Periodic and devastating famine afflicting northern Vietnam was yet another component of the hydraulic control debate. Characteristically, a famine would break out in late January and last until April, when the spring crop was harvested. During this period, the price of rice and potatoes would shoot up as stocks began to erode. A parallel argument engaging French administrators and planners was how much weight to accord precolonial accounts of drought and its effects. By way of illustration, Smith (2003, 47, 51, 103) hails the work by Edmond Chassigneux (1913) as seminal in seeking to prove the absolute necessity of irrigation in the delta to alleviate the cycle of suffering caused by a history of droughts.

One body of opinion held that defoliation of the watershed inside Tonkin was a primary cause of major flooding. But certain authors, such as A. Normandin, French head of public works, writing in *Cahier de la Société de Géographie de Hanoi* (1923) argued the contrary. Although he was also not against the reforestation of the watershed, he held that the floods were simply the outcome of violent storms, correctly noting as well that deforestation of the watershed on the Chinese side of the border was of some antiquity. Otherwise, Normandin was one of the most influential supporters of pump irrigation and drainage as opposed to the "primitive" use of scoops and baskets to lift water. A technology introduced from China to Vietnam in the thirteenth century, it is also one that survived the French "productivist" revolution.

Other experts, such as A.A. Pouyanne (1931), argued that in order to manage the entire delta region, the uplands should be irrigated to ensure a successful fifth-month harvest of rice in the dry winter season. Correspondingly, the thoroughly flooded lowlands should be allowed to dry out to facilitate the tenth-month harvest during the rainy summer. This view of a coordinated delta management policy was not without validity, especially in the light of the Great Famine of 1945. Upland rice, generally secure from floodwaters, then offered a reserve to balance the deficit experienced in the flooded lowlands. To some extent, the upland rice regime also succored the early Viet Minh guerrilla units in the highlands who literally lived off the land.

The Brévié or Popular Front Approach

From 1931, as Robequain (1944, 224–25) elaborates, attention was directed toward improvement of the large "checkerboard" which covers most of the Tonkin delta formed by dikes paralleling the Red River's divergent streams as well as traverse streams, "which isolate each section like bits of cloissoné." Within the checkerboard, and to end this isolation without increasing the risk of floods, it was decided to cut a network of canals which would either carry off excess freshwater or bring in water for irrigation. Dams (as with the Day River dam) and dam and canal networks, as in Annam, were also constructed to provide gravity irrigation.

More generally, as discussed in chapter 4, the Popular Front ushered in a more ethical policy, albeit motivated by the need to neutralize the threat exposed by the Nghe-Tinh uprisings of the early 1930s or, at least, not to lose control over the colonial project to radicals. In 1938, as Smith (2003, 189) elaborates, Governor General Jules Brévié outlined a plan to construct hydraulic agriculture infrastructure capable of irrigating 500,000 hectares throughout the Red River delta with a view to increase rice production from 500,000 to 600,000 tonnes. In this plan, irrigation, migration, cooperatives, and low-interest loans would all play their part. As Smith (2003, 190) comments, the difference with the Brévié plan from past practice was not just a productionist push but sought to use irrigation and modern techniques in order to establish—in modern terms—food security while also maintaining political control. Nevertheless, the Brévié plan was also specifically critiqued by Truong Chinh and Vo Nguyen Giap (1974) in their study on the peasant question for its failure to address landlord rent oppression, the seizure of peasant land, and high taxes (Smith 2003, 189–90).

As Brévié exulted on the occasion of the inauguration of the Do Luong barrage in Nghe An in 1937, this was one of the most important works achieved in Indochina, notably in facilitating the irrigation of a "particularly disadvantaged" region and the "theater of serious and prolonged troubles in 1930." Speaking in the company of Emperor Bao Dai, he also remarked on the historical works undertaken by the emperors of Annam and the mandarins of Tonkin in introducing hydraulic works, "We find ourselves at a unique moment," he intoned, "to demonstrate with some *éclat* to the entire population the superiority of our techniques over those of the Annamites." Prudently, he added, "Our engineers must avoid failure" (AOM Indo NF 263/2280GG à Colonies, Dalat, June 27, 1937). Much hung on those words, just as failure risked everything in the eyes of the peasant masses. Precisely, Brévié was reaching out to establish the kind of "hydraulic bargain" espoused by Smith (2003).

Summarizing the general trend, Brévié declared that between 1920 and 1936, Indochina had dispersed around seventy million piasters on agricultural hydraulic works (or approximately 750 million in 1928 values). The figure was higher if expenses related to inland navigation were added (eight hundred million francs), of which six hundred million was from the Indochina budget. The general concept in Annam, he explained, was to irrigate the deltas and the valleys from the central cordillera to the sea. As he explained, the existing systems in place, such as spread out along the coastal littoral, were fragmentary and compartmentalized in a geographical, climatic, and even social sense, a reference to extreme localism or regionalism such as existed in Annam over a long time (Smith 2003).

But the colonial state was also presented with a dilemma. As the governor asked rhetorically, once the barrages, canals, and so on are constructed, who will maintain them? For certain, the locals will not pay voluntarily, he acknowledged. The evidence for this understanding was all too clear in the light of past campaigns against the personal tax and the *régies*, or government monopolies over salt, alcohol, and so on. "The agitators know that they have an assured ear of the public." To be sure, this was an obstacle to be overcome. Even so, Brévié was struck that in the case of works under the "*aide à la rizière*" (rice fields support) program, "the peasant spontaneously brings his money and labor to establish the works." For him, this proved that the peasant was not irremediably hostile to such works when self-interest was also involved (Smith 2003).

Setting aside the standard communist critique of the age, as with Truong Chinh and Giap's study on the peasant condition in southern Indochina, Smith (2003) views French social engineering as carrying the seeds of failure as well. In any case, by 1937, the bulk of French investment in irrigation and drainage was still concentrated in the Tonkin midlands, where extensive pumping was not necessary in conditions of gravity-fed irrigation. The center and south, where pumping was required, was untouched. It should also be emphasized, as Smith (2003, 133) points out, that despite the influence of such New World introductions as potatoes and corn in precolonial Tonkin, paddy was prioritized in the colonial schema. Even in an era before the introduction of fast-growing rice varieties (such as embraced by the DRV in the 1960s), the French sought to encourage double cropping in the northern delta.

Indigenous Perspectives

Without neglecting the colonizer's need to know, along with the mapping, the drawing of boundaries, and categorizing that accompanied European scientism of the age, we should not neglect indigenous knowledge as well, to the extent that we can recover precolonial understandings of local economy and ecology. Exemplary in this sense is the small study on rice written by Nguyen Khac Vi (1904), *tong doc* (governor) and member of the protectorate council of Tonkin. More generally, his study describes forty-four rice types found in northern Vietnam, although he conceded that older people could easily identify some one hundred varieties (in fact, many hundreds). As such, he identified each rice type with two Chinese characters, offering the *quoc ngu* version, along with a short description in French. Written in classical Chinese, certain of these Chinese descriptions invoke color or fragrance, for example. He offered two broad distinctions, namely between rice of the *cuongdao* type, or rice whose grains are separate when cooked, and rice of the *nhudao* type, or rice grains which, when cooked, adhere to each other (sticky or glutenous rice). But within this distinction he allowed that certain types of rice were better adapted for the lowlands, while others were found on higher terrain. He indicated wide regional differences in variety, as between Quang Nam, Annam, and Tonkin. Some types of rice were adapted by season, as with an autumn rice. All in all, he described rice varieties of different colors, odors, and tastes. His emphasis appears to be on the quality of grain as opposed to the rice plant itself. Obviously, indigenous understandings of rice ecology and seasonal variations long preceded the classical colonial studies of rice cultivation, even if little is attributed. Long preceding Gourou and others, Nguyen Khac Vi explained that there were generally two harvests a year, the harvest of the fifth month (known as *luachien* in the Vietnamese lunar calendrical method of counting) and the winter harvest (harvest of the season, or *luamua*). In Quang Binh and Quang Tri in central Vietnam, the rice fields were sown in the eleventh and twelfth months, yielding a harvest in the third and fourth months of the following year, when the rice reached its maturity. But the two

Rice market in Saigon-Cholon, the traditional center of the rice trade in Vietnam.
Source: Author 2012.

harvests were not equal in importance; that of the summer was inferior to that of the winter. Obviously, local knowledge extended across a range of practices from irrigation, dike, canal, and hydraulic techniques, certain of them understood by the French and, in turn, the Japanese, but many undervalued, ignored, or overridden, as will be developed in subsequent chapters.

Paddy Collection

As in the present-day Philippines (Wong 2011, 594), where translocal grain-trading routes connect rice farmers with Chinese traders, millers, and officials, so Chinese middlemen dominated the colonial rice trade in Indochina at least until interrupted by the Japanese intervention. Essentially, the Chinese of Saigon-Cholon and Haiphong controlled the all-important milling of rice, a highly capitalized operation involving the use of imported machinery and with most of the mills located adjacent the still-extant French-built Cholon market in the "Chinese arroyo" and its tributary, the Canal des Potèries (Robequain 1944, 277). Just as Chinese networks reached the most remote rice-producing villages, so they were connected by canals and waterways with an elaborate and finely-honed procurement system.

As described in a colonial-era report, rice was generally sacked in the fields before being collected by the Chinese broker or agent. But during sacking, grain was mixed from various fields. The peasant was indifferent as to whether the crop was sold in advance. The sacks were not even marked as to origin. Before being laden on junks bound for, respectively, Cholon, Battambang, or Phnom Penh, the sacked rice was often damaged by water en route, in which case it would be dried on the ground, broken, and then mixed again for resacking. Otherwise, only the better-off landlords conveyed their rice directly to the point of export. By contrast, in northern Indochina, where the extreme parcelization of land and the quantities of grain involved hardly justified a visit by a broker, the sale was done by a neighboring merchant, sometimes Vietnamese, usually Chinese, and with the paddy taken to a rudimentary market set up at a crossroads or near a lading point for junks (plying the inland rivers and arroyos). The broker was not concerned as to the mixing of grains. The lot was sacked and transported away to one of the major ports, Nam Dinh, Hanoi, or Haiphong, and sold either to a (Chinese-owned) rice mill or a distillery (*Riziculture en Indochine* 1931).

LAND DISTRIBUTION AND OWNERSHIP

With its economic and cultural values dominated by a peasantry, as geographer Mark Cleary (2003, 356) demonstrates, metropolitan France "provided a mirror and model for the reshaping of the colonial periphery." By this he means that the small family-owned and occupied farm such as underpinned the stability of the French Third Republic was mirrored in early colonial reform of land legislation in colonial Indochina. For the French, indigenous property systems as with shifting agriculture typically practiced by the mountain- and slope-dwelling populations were viewed as inimical to the social and economic development of the colony, especially the export economy based on the rice and, with even greater impact, the development of the rubber plantation economy from the 1920s.

Under the Nguyen kings, a concept of private ownership of land had already developed in southern Vietnam alongside collective land pioneered by the soldier-settlers otherwise vested with the state. According to French geographer Frédéric Durand (Durand, Fortunel, and Pham Viêt Hà 2005, 122), the appearance of private property in a Vietnamese context is testified in administrative documents dating from the twelfth century. Land (rice fields) would become codified under Gia Long legislation, but it is also important to recall the cosmological significance of land in Confucianized societies. With the sky, land represents one of two cosmological points of reference. With the four other elements, metal, water, wood, and fire, land occupies a special place in a system of correspondence with humans, seasons, cardinal points, and the heavens. In other words, far outside of Western legal concepts and understanding, land in Vietnam was always vested with a cultural-civilizational quality.

Notwithstanding colonial codifications on communal organization in Cochinchina reaching back to 1907, as Durand, Fortunel, and Pham Viêt Hà (2005, 122) confirm, a colonial land regime made its debut in Cochinchina only in 1925, including the precincts of urban areas in Tonkin, Cambodia, and Laos. Between 1929–30, however, Governor General Pierre Pasquier launched a major study to determine the lands that could be opened for colonization and "*mise en valeur*" (development). Under this dispensation, large swathes of prime land, including the mountainous zone of northern Vietnam (the military regions excepted), the coastal lands of Annam, a leopard's spot of concessions in Cochinchina, and most of lowland Cambodia were—theoretically—open for colonization (Durand, Fortunel, and Pham Viêt Hà 2005, 122).

In practice, large tracts of land, especially in the prime Transbassac region of Cochinchina, situated south of the Bassac River, was ceded outright to French settlers who, in turn, sublet tiny parcels to Vietnamese tenants. Substantial tracts of land were also granted to Vietnamese who demonstrated a willingness to operate within the colonial framework. The collaborators were often Vietnamese Catholics or members of local pro-French militia and occasionally disaffected mandarins alienated from the court of Hue. As a consequence, the *colon* gained a permanent stake in Cochinchina, becoming, as discussed in chapter 4, a local political factor often at loggerheads with metropolitan opinion. Second, a previously nonexistent class of local merchants and landowners emerged owing political allegiance to the French, even converging in interest and values with the previous category (Murray 1980, 57–61).

Land Ownership

The unequal distribution of land and ownership was not only exacerbated by French colonialism but, as discussed below, would come to the heart of the communist and subsequent Viet Minh understanding of the "agrarian question," essential in the contest for the hearts and minds of the peasantry, or the "rice war" of our study. Pioneering studies on land allocation in both Cochinchina and Tonkin were produced by Yves Henry (1932) such as encoded in table 1.1.

As Féray (1979, 217) interprets this data (table 1.1), if we take the population of Vietnam in 1930 as numbering seventeen to eighteen millions, 90 percent of whom were peasants, then the 1,874,880 landlords (including French) scarcely represented 50 percent of peasant households (averaging four persons per household). Thus, one-half of the peasantry was landless.

Table 1.1. Land Ownership in Vietnam, 1930

Size of Holding	*Number of Landowners*	*Percentage of Landowners*	*Area (ha)*	*Percentage of Total*
Under 5 ha	1,176,200	94.8	1,225,000	28.5
5–10 ha	92,150	4.9	1,210,000	28.1
>50 ha	6,530	0.3	1,355,000	31.5
Communal lands			510,000	11.9
Total	1,274,880	100	4,300,000	100

Source: Henry (1932), cited in Féray (1979, 217).

While this picture illustrates the importance of small landlords and the parcelization of land, it does not indicate the degree of concentration of holdings, such as prevailed in Cochinchina.

From table 1.1, we can also observe that, whereas the vast majority of landowners (97.5 percent) worked plots of land smaller than ten hectares, a mere 2.5 percent of big landlords controlled over 45 percent of the land. According to Féray (1979, 218), concentration of land ownership in the hands of French owners (missionaries included) in the middle regions of Cochinchina, along with the "landed bourgeoisie," was further accentuated at the provincial level. In Transbassac, big owners dominated up to 70 percent of the land. At Bac Lieu, 7.2 percent of owners owned 65 percent of rice fields. Small owners predominated only in the zones of old settlement at Can Tho, with an important Khmer participation at Chau Doc, at Soc Trang, and in zones of "poor development" such as at Ha Tien. Communal land, where possession was collective and the allocation was decided democratically and in an equitable manner, had practically disappeared (3 percent) relative to central Vietnam (Annam) with 25 percent communal land or 195,000 hectares and in the north (Tonkin) with 21 percent or 235,000 hectares. In other words, the most fertile communal lands had been appropriated by the notables, affirming their arbitrage positions. As Féray (1979, 219) further comments, it was these landlords who faced the brunt of revolutionary violence following the August Revolution of 1945.

From table 1.2 we can extrapolate that while in Tonkin communal lands still represented a decent percentage (25 percent), French, church, and big landlords combined (26.5 percent) dominated the lion's share of the land and, undoubtedly, the prime land with the largest average land holding per family, with the reverse for the peasantry. Although the categories of rich, middle, and poor peasantry would undergo much hairsplitting in the throes of communist land reform, together they shared progressively smaller parcels of family land.

At the peak of the Great Famine of 1945, as glossed in an epilogue, the size of land mattered when subsistence was threatened by external shocks. Whatever the complexities of the agrarian regime, as Féray (1979, 220)

Table 1.2. Land Ownership in Tonkin, 1945

Ownership	*Area (ha)*	*Percentage of Total*	*Average Area Appropriated by Family Member (m²)*
French-owned land	15,952	1	
Church-owned land	23,928	1.5	
Big landlords	390,825	24.5	10,093
Communal lands	398,801	25	
Rich peasants	113,259	7.1	3,972
Middle peasants	462,609	29	1,372
Poor peasants	159,520	10	432
Waged peasants	17,547	1.1	124
Others	12,761	0.8	236

Source: Féray (1979,219).

demonstrates, the facts remain that overall, given the trend to land concentration in Vietnam, big landlords (*dienchu* in Vietnamese) representing 5 percent of the population controlled 60 percent of cultivated land (including so-called communal land), while 90 percent of the peasantry possessed only 30 percent of the land.

Loans and Credit: Case of the Indian Chettiars

Bank loans, usury, and peasant-farmer indebtedness is another side of the story, with French banks and government-linked credit organizations dominating alongside Indian, Chinese, and rich Vietnamese moneylenders (Brocheux 1995, 71–81). Generally speaking, large concentration of lands led to mass bankruptcy on the part of peasant-farmers, turning them into field hands or tenant farmers. As of 1930, there were 3,623 landowners holding from 50 to 100 hectares, 2,449 holding from 100 to 500 hectares, and 224 holding more than 500 hectares. The very big landlords (accounting for 2.46 percent of the total) owned 45.5 percent of the total cultivated area. In general, the largest concentrations of land were found in the central and western parts of Cochinchina. Altogether, Cochinchina hosted 255,000 landowners in a population of four million, meaning that the vast majority of the people did not have their own land (see table 1.2). High rents imposed by the landlord class on tenants further robbed them of their land. Added to that, farmers were obliged to pay personal and land taxes and, to gain money to redeem the tax, the farmers were obliged to sell rice on the market. Poverty and bankruptcy became generalized (Robequain 1944, 194).

The Chettiar case exploded in 1932 at the height of the recession. According to head of the Land Office P. de Feyssal (1933), over a long period the Chettiars had been lending at rates of up to 26 percent. This was sustainable at a time when the economy was booming, just as farmers borrowed heavily in order to extend their cultivations. But the Chettiars took advantage of the margins of security left to the farmers after they had already borrowed from the Société de Credit Agricole. Taking advantage of certain legal advisers, they thus lent to mostly indebted landlords. But in the crisis, the debtors could no longer pay up, and neither could the Chettiars redeem their loans short of seizing property. In September 1932, the richest Chetty in Saigon, A.R.M. Soccalingnam-chetty, said to have accumulated a fortune of 2–3 million piasters (20–30 million francs), "pitilessly" seized the property of an indigent Vietnamese. Emotions ran strong among the indigent farmers of the Transbassac. Mindful of concurrent events in British Burma, where rebellious acts occurred alongside a massacre of Chettiars, the French authorities sought to defuse the situation. Certain Chettiar were duly expelled, Soccalingnam among them (AOM Indo NF 2280–2295 "Expulsions des Banquiers Indiens-dits 'Chettys', sujèt Anglais," P. de Feyssal, Saigon, April 20, 1933).

Although some Chettiars were bankrupted by the Depression, their prosperity soon returned and, in spite of French attempts to increase credit for the rural areas, the Chettiars remained lenders of last resort to large numbers of improvident landowners. In 1937, there were 120 Chettiar establishments in Cochinchina, owning an estimated 22,204 hectares of riceland in the Mekong River delta. Unlike the Chinese, the Chettiars repatriated most of their profits home, around 65 percent in 1939 (Le Manh Hung 2004, 73). Even if they did not act alone, as journalist Nayan Chanda (1993, 33) sums up, Chettiar businessmen earned notoriety as "exploitative and usurious moneylenders." As French agricultural banks and official credit organizations lent money only on first-class security, over half the farmers in Indochina borrowed from Chettiars with the result that by the mid-1940s, their outstanding loans amounted to nine million piasters.

THE DEMOGRAPHIC-AGRARIAN CRISIS AND ADMINISTRATIVE RESPONSES

Within a century of the French conquest, the population of Vietnam had increased by a factor of six and cultivated surface by two (and, we dare say, in the absence of a productivist revolution). The balance of population and grain production therefore became extremely uncertain, just as the peasant cultivators were periodically wracked by agro-ecological crisis. Public health and vaccinations did control mortality stemming from terrible cholera epidemics through the colonial period. In 1937, there were from two to three million agricultural day laborers and more than a million unemployed in the Red River delta (Brocheux and Hémery 2009, 263–65).

Alongside a rising class of Chinese-style big landlords, there was also extreme parcelization of landownership. Already apparent before 1930, vast areas of rural misery expanded in the regions where the ratio of population to cereal production was most strained, namely the Red River delta, along with Nghe An, Ha Tinh, and Quang Ngai Provinces. All things considered, a classic Malthusian situation imposed itself in the northern delta in the real sense of population growth outpacing increases in food production. The demographic-agrarian crisis, such as it was in Vietnam, might usefully be compared with the case of Japan and Java, two other densely populated wet-rice cultivation zones.

As taken up in chapter 5, a reverse trend in rice under cultivation and production also set in during the war years, which would have major consequence for rice availability across Indochina, especially at a time when the cycle of drought and floods once again sapped away at human sustainability in the most vulnerable regions of the Red River delta and coastal Annam, leading to the Great Famine. According to an Allied intelligence report, in January–March 1945 rice deliveries (in Cochinchina) amounted to only 11,617 tonnes, versus 104,000 tonnes for the previous year. As the report commented, the decrease in production began ten years earlier, although not as serious as the recent declines. Noting that the flight of peasant farmers coincided with the drastic reduction in rice shipped to Japan and the inadequate means of internal transport, it had to be said, the report concluded, that a more convincing explanation of rural-urban flight was the desperation of farmers left bereft of surplus or cash following the strict procurement regime imposed at the bequest of Japan by the Vichy French regime (MAE AOI 31 Far Eastern Bureau, New Delhi, June 1–15, 1945).

According to Nguyen The Anh (1998a, 213), the condition of the rural population in northern Vietnam had been growing more and more distressing. Long before the Pacific War, the agricultural economy of the northern delta already showed signs of "grave deterioration." Between 1919 and 1922, Tonkin yielded an average 2,100,000 tonnes of paddy per year from a tilled area of 1,54,000 hectares. However, from 1930 onward, the level of production decreased regularly, albeit rising somewhat in the early 1940s, but undoubtedly under intense pressure from the Japanese and Vichy French for procurements (see table 1.2).

To be sure, yields per hectare and production per inhabitant were highly variant across regions. In 1943, outputs were estimated at thirteen quintals per hectare in Tonkin, unchanged since the beginning of the century; eight in Cambodia; fourteen in Cochinchina; and, in Annam, falling away from thirteen (up to 1922) to an average of ten quintal in 1942–43. As Brocheux and Hémery (2009, 259) interpret, "The stagnation of agrarian cultures also played a part in the slow, regional deterioration in the peasant economy's food-producing capacities." As a result of export demands, the majority of farmers were left with only a small part of the agricultural product.

Comparisons with Japan

From a reading of E.H. Norman (1975, 263–73), the parallels between the Japanese tenant farmer of late Tokugawa–early Meiji and his Vietnamese counterpart some decades later are quite analogous, allowing that the historical trajectory of the two countries was obviously quite different. On the side of parallels, the peasant in Japan was not a capitalist entrepreneur but paid a large percentage of produce in kind. Vietnam, too. The Japanese tenant farmer resembled an agricultural day laborer. The wage of this semi-proletarian was not a money wage but payment in kind which depended on the size of the harvest and fluctuations in the prices of agricultural products. As in Vietnam, the tenant was also hostage to the international market in buying back industrial goods. As Norman found in Japan, in a year of poor crops, the price of cereals may rise but scarcely any surplus remain, and the tenant may be obliged to buy back the cereals which he grew. (This is precisely what happened during the Great Famine in Vietnam.) The Japanese tenant farmer was thus Janus-headed: he was a capitalist tenant who took risks, and he was also an agricultural proletariat since the landlord extracted high rent and accumulated profits. There are striking analogies with Vietnam here as well. Norman also commented on the extreme parcelization of land in pre-Meiji Japan that preempted mechanization or a revolution of agricultural technique. Again the analogy with Vietnam is tempting, although Japan would trump Vietnam in raising crop yields and in modernizing agricultural techniques. In both countries, surplus labor was also forced off the land, but one would have to concede that in Japan, the process of proletarianization—both male and female—proceeded at a much faster pace (and several decades earlier than in Vietnam), as indeed did urbanization and, to a far greater degree, the rise of domestic industry, as with textiles. Added to that, the rice market in Japan was already in an advanced state of commercialization prior to the Meiji Restoration. And when Japan outgrew its domestic market, famously it expanded overseas. Indochina, by contrast, was cocooned inside colonial tariff walls, its domestic market was small, industrialization was deliberately restricted by France, and it was metropolitan French and, to a lesser extent, Chinese business that expanded, not Vietnamese. Japan's early industrialization was not only a first in Asia but gave Japan the wherewithal for its peasant armies to secure stunning military victories over Korea, China (Taiwan), and Manchuria in the space of thirty-five years. Setting aside strikingly different geographic regimes between the fragmented Japanese archipelago and the crowded deltas of Vietnam, we might have to allow for an even more interventionist state in Japan than even the French in Indochina.

Comparisons with Java

As Brocheux and Hémery (2009, 262) point out, the situation in the northern delta resembled the case of "agricultural involution" as described by Clifford Geertz (1963) of late colonial–early postwar central Java. But how does Geertz's study relate to colonial Tonkin? More generally Geertz found a basic distinction between *sawah* (wet-field rice) and swidden (or dry-field) cultivation, the former supporting dense population in Java and Bali, the latter common in more sparsely populated zones across the Indonesian archipelago, arguably categories also fitting French geographical understandings of the irrigated delta and the rain-fed uplands, respectively. From his historical understandings of colonial state pressures (external demands) on the populations—increasing production and tax deliveries—alongside a concomitant rise in population or an intensification of labor (internal pressure), Geertz spelled out his now famous concept of "agricultural involution" or ecological stasis in a situation without major innovation or change and without a concomitant increase in per capita yield. The collectivity just sinks into poverty. In this construct, there is little incentive for technological innovation. Notably, tradition-bound Javanese peasants harvest with a small handheld *aniani* blade, not even a sickle. Following Geertz, "agricultural involution" applied to cognate situations became over decades a byword for nonevolutionary-nonrevolutionary change. Statistics provided in table 1.3 as to land-population ratios starkly showcase the Tonkin case with approximately double the population of Cochinchina but with half the hectarage of riceland.

Looking back, as famed agronomist and pioneer ecologist René Dumont wrote in *Famines, le retour* (1997), having conducted studies in Tonkin in 1929–32, he came to the realization before others that the population of the northern delta increased more quickly than the supply of food. In *La culture du riz dans le delta du Tonkin* (1935), he underscored the necessity of birth control, a concept "shocking to both Catholics and even Marxists." Through his publishing career, he dwelled on the demographic factor. Working under

Table 1.3. Rice Land (Hectares) versus Population by Region, 1936

Regions	*Hectares*	*Population*
Tonkin	1,180,000	8,000,000
Northern Annam	295,000	2,000,000
Cochinchina	2,200,000	4,484,000

Source: AOM Indo NF 2234/263, 1936; Robequain (1944, 220).

Yves Henry in the Rice Office, the young Dumont came to understand the value of phosphate fertilizer in increasing rice yields. For his efforts he was criticized by lower-echelon staff and resigned his position (though his disdain for the French colonial repression of the peasantry was another reason). But in seeking to improve on traditional farming techniques, he also carefully documented and explained the old ways, as, for example, the methods of maintaining the water level in the ricefields.

CONCLUSION

As with the establishment of the Rice Office, agricultural modernization under French colonial auspices not only sought to overcome nature but also was part of a colonial state project to make the region more amenable to colonization. In this sense—and Indochina was different from French colonies in west and north Africa only in the degree of its natural and human endowments—colonization also called down the exploitation of a range of agricultural exports. In Indochina, rubber amply fulfilled this role, alongside rice and other local productions. There were obviously dividends for peasant producers of rice and maize and other crops from increased yields, better access to markets, and some embryonic agricultural extension. At the same time, however, cultural practices were also deeply embedded, notably landowning patterns, the system of credit and moneylending, and the Chinese-dominated rice procurement system. To be sure, easier government credit could have offered compensation to some, but the peasant producer was also exposed to the full gamut of French-imposed taxes, not to mention communal obligations at the hands of mandarins where that counted, as in Annam. A scrutiny of Cambodia and Laos would offer another picture where the incidence of landless peasant cultivators was not as critical as in the more densely settled parts of Vietnam. But the overall success of French agrarian policies also called down a pact with the peasantry who quite obviously had the wherewithal to derail the best-intended projects should they withhold their consent (as demonstrated in the events of 1930–31). While natural population increase, along with increased parcelization of land and low crop yields, suggested a looming Malthusian situation in the northern delta and south-central provinces, many other elements imposed on subsistence levels as well.

More generally, though, the French adopted a strict managerial approach to food sufficiency across Indochina, backed by the regular collation of province-level statistics. The French not only kept and calculated rice reserves, but they also established a finely detailed picture of food needs across vast territory. As discussed in chapter 4, timely food relief and work-for-pay schemes were features of colonial policy under the Popular Front government.

Vulnerable in the extreme to externalities or international factors, the French also vainly sought to micromanage the macroeconomy. As the rice report also pointed out with respect to the Mekong delta, the fundamental principle determining the types of rice fields was the hydraulic regime and the way that water was used. As with the precolonial state, the French simply could not ignore the hydraulic regime if it wished to keep its pact with the millions of peasant producers of the two delta regions as well as the even more vulnerable central region.

NOTE

1. Although the frequency of typhoons in southern Vietnam is less than in the center and north, they can also be devastating. Visiting a rubber plantation zone in Dong Nai Province, some thirty kilometers northeast of Saigon at midday on April 1, 2012, I experienced what the Vietnamese National Center for Hydro-Meteorological Forecasting termed an *abnormal* storm, the first to appear in April in forty years. Making landfall in central Binh Tuan and Ba Ria–Vung Thau Provinces, tropical depression Pakhar downed some 5 percent of trees in Saigon District 1 alone and caused widespread flooding in a swathe of coastal Vietnam with thousands of hectares of rice fields damaged in Binh Dinh, Phu Yen, and Kien Giang Provinces. Fortunately, around seventy-one thousand hectares, or 40 percent of the winter-spring rice crop, had already been harvested. On the upside, the heavy rain helped to reduce the risk of forest fire in southern Kien Giang Province. It also provided freshwater to check the intrusion of saltwater to rice fields in Chau Thanh District in Ben Tri Province and Gong Rieng in Kien Giang Province (*Viet Nam News*, April 2, 2012, 3).

Chapter 2

Anticolonial Resistance

Not of a piece, resistance to French colonial rule in Vietnam took a panoply of forms, from traditionalist invocations around the monarchy, to religious revivalism, to peasant revolts tinged with messianism, to the entreaties of liberal reformers, and to the sometimes violent actions of radical political elements and parties. A single essay can hardly do justice if we bring into play a range of subaltern and wayward groups, including bandit and smuggler gangs, new religions, labor strikers, and anarchists along with alienated princes, mandarins, notables, and intellectuals. For Vietnamese, patriotism was a rallying call, just as those with which the symbols of the imperial past in the form of the emperor, literature, history, and memory were replete. In Indochina, the most fully worked out and coherent claims on national awakening or identity were played out by Vietnamese to whom, paradoxically, the French looked up to as superior collaborator-administrators. One thing is sure, namely, that change was of the essence. Just as the modern world of science and technology arrived, so the Vietnamese educated classes came to outwit their *colon* counterparts in playing the French game through literature, journalism, and city hall politics. Even if the Vietnamese were not quite yet ahead in engineering, military skills, and armed combat, the gap was also closing by the end of the colonial period.

While necessarily select, given the volume of writings on this broad subject, not to mention widely conflicting narratives, this chapter seeks first to set down the origins of noncommunist nationalism as it emerged out of the first encounters with the French, in turn setting the scene for a subsequent phase, largely led by Moscow-trained professional revolutionaries. As discussed, while one group of young Vietnamese would be attracted to Japan, larger numbers came to experience France, as soldiers, workers, or students. Essentially, this chapter looks to the intellectual and cultural roots of

Vietnamese nationalism, reserving the details of organization and struggle to subsequent chapters. Yet another trap remains in reconstructing Vietnamese national history, namely, what Christoph Giebel (2004) terms in his dedicated study of one such anointed hero of the revolution, future DRV president, Ton Duc Thang, "imagined ancestries," or the proclivity of official historians to massage the story line to fit shifting and current orthodoxies.

This chapter divides into six sections, in part chronological, in part thematic. A first deals with local resistance to the French invasion and presence, certain resistance neotraditionalist in style and certain other with overtones of the Black Flag–Taiping rebellion remnant activities. A second section turns to elite challenges, as with the figures of Phan Boi Chau, Prince Cuong De, and the Gilbert Chieu episodes. A third traces the activities of the educated elite-turned-revolutionaries attracted to France, of which Nguyen Ai Quoc/ Ho Chi Minh is the most celebrated and central to our narrative. A fourth section discusses the activities of the student-returnees from France in tandem with the burgeoning "print revolution" in Saigon, the issue of collaboration. A fifth section explains the game-changing event of the Yen Bai mutiny in 1930. A final section examines the appeal held out by Moscow to young Vietnamese and the setting down of Vietnamese revolutionary networks in neighboring countries.

RESISTANCE TO FOREIGN OCCUPATION

With good reason, Vietnamese historians of all persuasions take the first French naval attacks on imperial defenses as the opening shots of the war of national resistance. This was the action of French warships in sinking five armored Vietnamese junks in Danang port on April 15, 1847, with a French squadron returning to attack Danang the following August. From 1858 to 1884, annexation took many stages. Fatefully, it was under the Treaty of Hue or Protectorate Treaty, concluded on June 6, 1884, between France and the Vietnamese court, that France moved to garrison troops in Hanoi and Haiphong, thus securing the Red River for trade and the piecemeal annexation of Indochina.

In the words of Vietnamese historian Nguyen Khac Vien (1975, 12–17), the Nguyen court, internally weak, was both cowed and seduced by French bluster, just as it was duped into thinking that the French wished only for commercial privileges. But a number of mandarins and the majority of scholars and people stood for resistance. The defection of the monarchy undermined the efforts of the Vietnamese patriots. Efforts by the Nguyen court with its capital in Hue to seek Chinese support at a time when China itself was under attack failed. But the loss of Cochinchina, as southern Vietnam was known, caused great concern among patriots, and many petitioned emperor Tu Duc (r. 1848–83) to advocate reforms to strengthen the defenses of the country. Stuck in conservatism, the "feudal reactionary" court—as described by Nguyen Khac Vien—refused to consider these recommendations, just as the Nguyen faced down internal rebellions.

Having seized the imperial capital in June–July 1885 after a protracted fight, the boy emperor, Ham Nghi (r. 1884–85), was spirited out of the Forbidden City by the regent to a base in the mountainous part of Quang Tri and Quang Binh. From there, backed by a resistance group, he issued a proclamation calling on the entire population to support the monarchy in its struggle. But on November 1, 1888, pushed deeper into the mountains, Ham Nghi was captured and subsequently exiled to Algeria. Adherents of the royalist Can Vuong or "save the king" movement, as it was known, eventually settled in northeastern Thailand, many becoming the nuclei of future anticolonial struggles. Meantime, the defeatist faction of the court went over to the French, leading to the enthronement of a new king in Hue on September 19, 1885. Still, the capture of the young king did not put an end to popular resistance, many uprisings breaking out until 1897.

As Nguyen The Anh (1998b) explains, "The *Can Vuong* movement, for all that, had no real concept yet of Vietnam as a nation-state in competition with other nation-states." As Woodside (1987, 312) elaborates, the actions of Vietnamese literati against French intervention in the latter half of the nineteenth century were not yet nationalistic but merely "a compound of xenophobia and Confucian loyalism." Nevertheless, in modern Vietnamese historiography, such as that reflected in Nguyen Khac Vien's writings, the popular uprisings are viewed as nationwide, protracted, and heroic, contrary to the actions of the royal army, which collapsed under French attacks. However, lacking a central united monarchical resistance, foreign aggression could not be countered.

Although the French would manipulate the dynastic line in Hue in the interest of pliant, royal leadership, one emperor in particular stands out in modern Vietnamese history for his patriotism, namely the boy-king Duy Tan, born on August 14, 1899, to Emperor Thanh Thai (r. 1889–1907) as Prince Nguyen Vinh San. With his father removed from office ostensibly for insanity, the prince took his place on the Golden Dragon Throne in 1907 at the age of seven, assuming the reign name Duy Tan, or "friend of reforms." However, contrary to French expectations, Duy Tan (r. 1907–16) proved to be as obstinate as his father before him. Opposing the excessive aspects of French rule, Duy Tan called for a revision of the 1884 Protectorate Treaty. Against the background of local indignation at conscription for France's wars in Europe and acting on the counsel of "patriot mandarins," Duy Tan organized a revolt on behalf of troops about to be sent to France. Timed for May 3, 1916, the plot was foiled and Duy Tan detained, dethroned, and exiled, joining his father, "the mad king," in the remote French Indian Ocean colony of La Réunion. Two of the mandarin conspirators were executed amid a wave of repression (Nguyen Khac Vien 1975, 12–17, 22–25).

In turn, it was Nguyen Phuc Tuan who, taking the reign name of Khai Dinh (r. 1916–25), served as emperor of Annam until his death. His replacement, Bao Dai (r. 1926–45), born Nguyen Phuc Vinh Thuy, was not only the emperor who, as discussed in chapter 3, petitioned the French to unify Vietnam but the one who also delivered up the empire to the Viet Minh, although he had second thoughts as well. Vinh San would resurface in the throes of World War II in support of the Free French Forces, although tragically dying in a plane crash in central Africa, putting an end to any lingering dynastic ambitions.

Reprise of the Black Flags: The De Tham Rebellion (1884–1911)

Meantime, as events in Hue played out, Taiping rebellion remnant groups known as, respectively, the White, Yellow, and Black Flags started to carve out fiefdoms in the northern part of the country (see McAleavy 1968). These incidents are too numerous to mention and range from activities of opium smugglers in northern Laos, to maritime incursions in the Gulf of Tonkin, to the more enduring legacies of Black Flag invasions, though assuming a more modern form. Running the gamut from the piratical to the political, these incursions sometimes operated with the apparent complicity of provincial Chinese authorities.

Undoubtedly, the most damaging of the rebellions following on chronologically from the Black Flag incursions, if not a spin-off, was that of the De Tham rebellion in the frontier province of Yen The, a traditional redoubt of antigovernment rebels. A twenty-seven-year rebellion engaging a succession of governor generals, it not only consumed large military and civilian resources but inflicted serious French and civilian casualties. Confined to Yen The, a remote mountainous border area some one hundred kilometers to the northeast of Hanoi and inhabited by a mix of tribal groups who had ready access to Chinese territory, it would also reemerge forty years later as an anti-French guerrilla base. As Claude Gendre (2009, 202) observes in a dedicated study of this revolt, not only was it the same peasantry who would rally to the Viet Minh, but the combat techniques and camouflage adopted by De Tham would also be taken up by the Viet Minh. Such may be an exaggeration, but plausibly, as De Tham demonstrated and as the Viet Minh understood, by controlling Yen The, the group could also threaten the lowland delta region.

THE *DONG DU* OR "LOOK EAST" MOVEMENT

As intimated, the French faced down organized opposition from Nguyen dynasty forces the moment they set foot in Vietnam. While Vietnamese Catholic converts would tend to emerge as collaborators with the French, a long line of traditionalists associated with the court in Hue would spearhead the resistance. With time, "nationalist" opposition came to be expressed through the writings and actions of an educated elite, in part bridging the world of the traditional literati with that of the modern world, of which Japan was an important lodestar after its naval victories against Russia in 1904–5. The actions of Chinese revolutionaries around Sun Yat-sen were also an inspiration. More broadly, we can term the responses of this eclectic group of mandarins, royals, and followers as neotraditional in their challenge to French power, although they were also part of a modern Asian age, as symbolized by the rise of Japan.

The impact of the Russo-Japanese War on the Vietnamese was described by a senior colonial official shortly after the event as leaving the mass of the population "indifferent." However, elite responses *were* awakened. For instance, certain Hong Kong newspapers circulating in Tonkin broadcast the message that the Vietnamese people were living in "slavery" under the French. As the official conceded, by early 1905, a certain "nervousness" could be discerned among the population with regard to external affairs, just as some sections of the population may have actually believed that such a chain of events could lead to the ouster of the French. As also conceded, it was incontestable that Japan's victory in the war revealed to intelligent Vietnamese just how modern science was capable of augmenting their intellectual and social values. Accordingly, some turned to Japan for inspiration, although the majority still looked to France (Beau 1908).

The official was basically correct as, alongside France, Japan would emerge as a lodestar for Vietnamese nationalists, especially the monarchist and monarchy restoration group. This has been dubbed the Dong Du, or "look east" movement. Spearheaded by Prince Cuong De (1882–1951), scion of the Nguyen dynasty emperor Gia Long, followed by leading Confucian literati-monarchist Phan Boi Chau, and joined by some dozens of young Vietnamese students who would enroll in Japanese schools and universities, the movement would also suffer various setbacks, not only at the hands of the French but by the Japanese authorities as well. As with youth of their generation, so youth would be standing at the vanguard of change though crucial stages of modern Vietnamese history.

As assiduously researched by Tran My-Van (2005, 25), Phan Boi Chau and associates banked their hopes on Prince Cuong De. As a symbol of the imperial restorationist cause, Cuong De was an attractive figure, but, turning to Japan, he also linked his destiny to that country's fortunes as well as to Japanese benefactors and others who flocked to his cause in Tokyo. Among them was General Iwane Matsui, of the Koakai or Raising Asia association, along with Toyama Mitsuro (1855–1944) and Inukai Tsuyoshi (1853–1932), also linked with the New Asia or Japanese-sponsored pan-Asianist movement. Notably, both Phan Boi Chau and Cuong De initially looked to Japan, not China, with their "travel east" vision. In fact, Japan had already been selected as a base for Chinese revolutionaries around Sun Yat-sen, and it was in Tokyo in 1905 that he established the protorevolutionary Tongmenghui association. Even so, the first generation of Vietnamese nationalists to set up in Japan also underestimated the Machiavellian diplomatic moves between France and Japan that would see the Vietnamese nationalist cause sacrificed.

Phan Boi Chau

Founder in 1903 of the Reformation Society, Phan Boi Chau undoubtedly represented the first generation of anti-French nationalists. Visiting Japan in February 1905, prior to Japanese victory in the Russo-Japanese War, Chau was obviously impressed with that country's modernization. There, he took in hand young Vietnamese student acolytes, extended his contacts with better-funded Chinese contacts, made strategic contact with Japanese sympathizers, and set up a meeting with Sun Yat-sen, who, unsuccessfully at this stage, sought him to relinquish the monarchist cause and to embrace the newly founded Tongmenghui (Marr 1971, 126). Until forced out of Japan on March 8, 1909, he also turned to penning anti-French tracts calling for independence. Moving on to Hong Kong, he linked up with Chinese revolutionaries, further continuing his literary and political activities in Thailand in early 1911, although by now also somewhat adrift.

But news of the Wuchang uprising in China on October 10, 1911, leading to the collapse of the Qing and the advent of the Chinese Republic, prompted Phan and many Vietnamese admirers of Sun Yat-sen to converge in Guangzhou. Arriving in the southern Chinese city in January 1912, as historian David Marr (1971, 216) explains, he now sought to launch the Viet-Nam Quang Phuc Hoi (Restoration League) "unabashedly and to the smallest detail patterned after China's republican Tongmenghui." Phan Boi Chau's Restoration League (with Cuong De as president and Chau as vice president) also became the rallying point for a unified nationalist leadership. Although obtaining a brief audience with Sun Yat-sen in Nanjing in April 1912, he achieved little more than an offer to train Vietnamese in Chinese military academies (Marr 1971, 217–18). By this point, according to Féray (1979, 131), the monarchist Phan Boi Chau had become a republican revolutionary.

Nevertheless, various insurrectionist attempts by the league during World War I were easily suppressed by the French military.

Even prior to leaving Vietnam, Phan Boi Chau had been accused of committing acts of violence, as with the bomb thrown on April 12, 1913, that killed the native governor of Thai Binh and, four days later, the bomb thrown at the Hanoi Hotel in the capital that killed the *chef de battalion* of the colonial infantry and wounded several Europeans and Vietnamese. Under suspicion of complicity in these events, Chau escaped to China. Condemned to death by a French court *pen contumace*, he continued his activities from exile (AOM Indo NF/327/2640 "Note au Sujèt de Phan Boi Châu," ca. 1932).[1]

In midlife, Chau entered into a dalliance with Soviet Russia and renewed contact with Nguyen Ai Quoc/Ho Chi Minh, whom he had known as a young man (Tran My-Van 2005, 14–15). In 1924, from his base in Guangzhou, Chau and other Vietnamese exiles also made contact with Chiang Kai-shek and Li Jishen, the vice-president of the newly opened Whampoa (Huangpu) Military Academy, with a view to admitting Vietnamese (Hue-Tam Ho Tai 2010, 42). By this juncture, the Kuomintang (KMT) had also entered into a united front with the Chinese Communist Party (CCP) and accepted Soviet advisers. In short time the KMT would establish branches in Cambodia and southern Vietnam, wherever Chinese communities congregated (Gunn 1985, 31–34).

Arrested by the French in Shanghai in 1925, the veteran Vietnamese nationalist leader was transported to Hanoi. After facing trial, he was sentenced on November 25, 1925, to forced labor in perpetuity, confirmed on December 9 by the Council of the Tonkin Protectorate. However, on December 23, 1925, Governor General Alexandre Varenne prudently granted him a total remission (AOM Indo NF/327/2640 "Note au Sujèt de Phan Boi Châu," ca. 1932). Imprisoned and subsequently placed under house arrest back in Hue, the now-aging revolutionary remained out of the picture for the rest of his life. Even though separated by generation, Chau would have influence on a future group of Vietnamese nationalists, as with Nguyen Ai Quoc/Ho Chi Minh, who, as intimated, learned directly of the Dong Du movement (Marr 1971, 209, 260).

France, Japan, and Prince Cuong De

Having fled Hue for China in January 1906, Prince Cuong De arrived in Tokyo in March the same year. Representing himself as a Chinese of the Dobun Kai society, he enrolled in an Imperial Japanese Army preparatory school for Chinese students. In early 1908, the prince made the first of several trips to Thailand before returning to Tokyo in February 1909. However, at French prodding, he was forced out of Japan for "abusing its hospitality," arriving in Shanghai on October 30. After a six-year period of wandering, including visits to Hong Kong (arrested in July 1913 but released), repeat visits to

Thailand, and a long sojourn in Europe, including stays in Berlin and London, he returned to Japan on January 1, 1916 (see Tran My-Van 2005, chaps. 3, 4). Taking up residence in Omete-cho in Tokyo, and assuming the Japanese name Hayashi Juntoku (or Takamatsu), he again sought to link up with his compatriots, making short visits to Guangzhou and Hangzhou. Thereafter, however, his activities took a more discrete turn, as with sending coded messages in mixed Chinese characters and roman letters to his agents in Vietnam and China (JACAR BO2032273800 1919.05.05–1925.06.24, Nadaud Report, nd).

The role of Prince Cuong De alongside the Japan- and China-based dissidents cannot be underestimated, especially as he was a nationalist figure or card that Japan kept at close quarters until the 1940s, ready to deal if their objectives were not met by the likes of Emperor Bao Dai (such as profiled in chapter 5). Over many years, France sought Japanese cooperation in neutralizing Cuong De's activities in Japan, just as they linked the prince to a range of anti-French terrorist activities. A letter of December 20, 1924, addressed by the French Embassy in Tokyo to Baron Shidehara Kijiro, Japanese imperial minister of foreign affairs, explicitly linked the prince with individuals who narrowly failed to assassinate French Governor General Martial Merlin in Guangzhou on June 19, 1924, on his return journey from Japan. French ambassador Paul Claudel sought the prince's place of abode, his means of support, and his local and international contacts. He also sought clarification on an upcoming conference in Tokyo on "la Grand Asie" where it was expected that Cuong De and other Vietnamese revolutionaries would attend. Notably, Claudel pledged to share information gathered by French intelligence on Korean revolutionaries in Shanghai and Guangzhou, if Japan would cooperate. As asserted, "This reciprocal surveillance can only be of profit to our two countries." While offering the prince's Tokyo address, as the Japanese authorities replied with understatement and possibly subterfuge, "he receives few visitors" (JACAR, BO2030763700).

Besides the Merlin assassination attempt in 1924, the French authorities were adamant that Cuong De had never renounced the goal of overthrowing the French administration and that "terror" was his weapon, as with two bomb incidents in 1913, including one directed against Governor General Sarraut. The turn to terror on the part of Vietnamese perpetrators, the French argued, was also linked by association with the actions of Korean revolutionaries in exile in China, as with the assassination of the Japanese governor of Korea, Prince Ito Hirobumi, in Harbin in 1909. The French also linked Cuong De with Bolshevik circles in China, observing that in January 1922 one of his confidants had used a revolver to assassinate a pro-French Vietnamese in Hangzhou (JACAR BO2032273800 1919.05.05–1925.06.24, Nadaud Report, nd).

According to Tran My-Van (2005, 110–11), it was only in 1925 that Cuong De stepped out of the shadow of Phan Boi Chau with the latter's arrest. His failures in the 1920s had only given cause to the Thanh Nien group of radicals, as profiled below. However, as discussed in chapter 6, even the hopes he placed on Japan during its wartime occupation of Indochina backfired as Japan's agenda did not include true independence outside of the Greater East Asia Co-Prosperity Sphere. Finally, his efforts to return to Vietnam to work alongside ex-emperor Bao Dai also failed in the face of the ability of the communists to rally nationalism to their anticolonial cause.

Rebellion in the South

Especially in the frontier zone of the southern delta, an extraordinary range of heterodox religious challenges to colonial order would emerge, certain of them linked to secret society activities, and others Buddhist-millennial, as with the case of the "revolutionary monk" who led an attack on the central prison in Saigon in February 1916 (Coulet 1928, 11). Still other militant, territorially organized sects promised religious redemption, as with the Cao Dai, founded in 1926 with its base in Tay Ninh, and Hoa Hao, emerging in the western delta in 1939. Harnessed to Japanese designs during the Second World War, the sects with their armies would also come to the heart of the struggle over land, rice, and population in the early postwar period.

L'Affaire Gilbert Chieu

A no less dangerous, albeit intellectual threat to the French status quo in the early decades was the case of Gilbert Chieu (1867–1919), also known as Tran Chanh Chieu. French intervention favored a French-educated class of collaborators over and above the old mandarin class. Chieu, a southern landlord, was one such individual to suffer the loss of status of his own class—Chinese and mandarin—at the expense of the French education system. A confidant of Phan Boi Chau, newspaper editor, writer, and activist on behalf of Vietnamese students in Japan, he also ran foul of the French in what became known as "L'Affaire Gilbert Chieu." Although proceedings against him were quashed, as disclosed at his trial (1908–9), he upheld links with Chinese secret societies and Japanese agents, the upshot of which was the expulsion of Vietnamese students from Japan in 1909 under French pressure and their rallying in southern China. In part inspired by the Japanese Meiji Restoration and Chinese reformers, Chieu sought to modernize Vietnam. He and his followers also wished to be treated as equal by the French. As Brocheux (1995, 141) embroiders, the "syndrome de Gilbert Chieu" endured and continued to influence the Vietnamese elite of the twentieth century. As intimated below, such efforts by conservative mandarin-royalist groups were soon eclipsed by other groups during the interwar period (see Marr 1971, 145–46).

THE ROAD TO FRANCE: THE MANDARIN PROLETARIANS

The dangers posed to French hegemony in Indochina by exposure of the local population to the external environment was not unanticipated by the French, and the first generation to be afforded the privilege to live and study in France were drawn from the aristocracies or the various countries that constituted French Indochina. Vietnamese volunteers and conscripts into the French army and navy during World War I, reaching ninety-nine thousand at peak, also experienced Europe firsthand, certain ones of them absorbing Marxist ideas (see Hill 2006, 274–75).

The role of Ton Duc Thang (1888–1980), studied by Giebel (2004), is illustrative. Succeeding Ho Chi Minh in the presidency (1969–80), the "celebratory" status of this individual in Vietnamese communist history flowed from his putative role in the 1919 Black Sea mutiny by the French navy, thereby ending Allied interference in the Russian civil war following the October Revolution of 1917. While evidence supports Ton Duc Thang's role in Toulon, France, in joining mass demonstrations in the aftermath of the mutiny, his alleged core role in the actual mutiny suffers much examination in this account. In any case, with some eighty thousand Indochinese then resident in France, the authorities were hard pressed to track and neutralize political activism among this group.

Nguyen Ai Quoc/Ho Chi Minh

Entering the early biography of Ho Chi Minh into this narrative also illustrates the act of political awakening of young educated Vietnamese as to the cocoon imposed on their lives and nation by colonialism. Heeding Sophia Quinn-Judge (2003, 6), the role of the future president should not be exaggerated in the pre-1945 period, especially as he spent a long period of time in the 1930s "in the political wilderness," at a juncture when other Moscow-trained agents stepped into the arena. Neither, however, can we dismiss an individual whose life and times also connected Vietnam with the Comintern, especially in Guangzhou, prior to his arrest in Hong Kong in June 1931.

Hailing from rustic Nghe An, the life of the young Ho Chi Minh exemplifies the transitional age from mandarinate to modernity. Born Nguyen That Thanh (ca. 1890) in the village of Kim-Lien Lam Tinh in the subprefecture of Nam Dan, astride the Ca River some thirteen kilometers west of Vinh, the scene was one of flat rice lands, just as the region had long produced rebels against both mandarin and colonial authority (see Duiker 2000, 33–37). As explained in chapter 3, his natal province and even district would also be the arena of major clashes between rebels and French power in the 1930–31 Nghe-Tinh rebellion. Nam Dan would also see many victims to famine in

1944–45. Ho Chi Minh's father, Nguyen Sinh Sac, had studied the Confucian classics and moved with his family to the imperial capital in 1895 before taking up a minor official position. As intimated, he was also a confidant of Phan Boi Chau. By autumn 1907 Ho Chi Minh, along with a brother, was enrolled in the Quoc Hoc academy, the highest-level Franco-Vietnamese school in Hue and a training ground for aspiring bureaucrats. According to Duiker (2000, 33–37), when Emperor Thanh Thai (enthroned in 1889) was forced to abdicate on suspicion of involvement in rebel activities, the young Ho Chi Minh appeared to take the side of peasant protestors seeking a remission of onerous taxes only to be expelled. Arguably, he also dishonored his father, who suffered a retrogradation of rank and, shadowed by imperial and French authorities, fatally entered a clandestine life. Politically, the events in Hue were a prelude to a failed political play by Phan Boi Chau in Hanoi, leading to a wave of French police repression that swept Annam.

There is no question that the French tax regime, including opium and alcohol along with individual abuses meted out by capricious French officials in his province, provided part of the lore informing Ho Chi Minh's future publications on colonial iniquities. But the fate of his father, a virtual déclassé mandarin following the revocation of his position in 1910 for siding with the reformists, and that of his siblings, a sister implicated in the theft of a gun in 1918 and a brother likewise indicted for offering shelter to a rebel chief, was undoubtedly a major influence. Failing grades, in the French version, or expelled, he was obliged to leave the Quoc Hoc college, also known for such alumni as Ngo Dinh Diem and Vo Nguyen Giap. As with many Vietnamese before him, a life in exile may have been an obvious choice.

By all accounts, working aboard the Messageries Maritimes line *SS d'Artagnan*, bound for France via a number of African ports, exposed the young Ho Chi Minh to the darker side of colonial life. Arriving in Marseilles in July 1911, he then shipped aboard the Chargeurs réunis line, an experience which also took him to the Americas. He also saved money for himself and his father. These voyages included a single return trip to Saigon. Washing up in London in 1914, the least documented period of his life, the young Vietnamese evidently labored, studied English, fraternized with progressive Chinese, kept abreast of developments in his homeland, and awaited the end of the Great War. Arriving in Paris in December 1917 (although not apparently entering French police logs until late 1919), the future leader of his country changed address a number of times before lodging at no. 9 Impasse Compoint (Seventeenth District). Police logs of his activities also recorded daily visits to Parisian libraries, including the landmark Bibliothèque Nationale, as well as frequent meetings with compatriots (Borton 2010, 37). Looking back in later life, as he recounted, "After World War I, I made my living in Paris, now as a retoucher at a photographer's, now as painter of 'Chinese antiquities' (made in France!). I would distribute leaflets denouncing the crimes committed by the French colonialists in Viet-Nam" (Fall 1967b, 23).

The young Vietnamese also began to blossom intellectually, launching his career as trenchant anticolonial writer and political activist. Famously, under the name Nguyen Ai Quoc (Nguyen the Patriot), he petitioned for recognition of civil rights for the Vietnamese people at the 1919 Peace Conference at Versailles. Assiduously tracked by the French police, on November 23, 1920, he joined the Seine branch of the Fédération Socialiste Révolutionaire, coming under the Section Française de l'Internationale Ouvrière (SFIO), the Parti Socialiste Français (PSF), or French Socialist Party, section of the Second International (Ho Chi Minh Museum). Having launched his writing career in the PSF newspaper *L'Humanité* on November 4, 1920, in April 1922 he also helped to found and produce the broadsheet *Le Paria*, to which he contributed. The story has been told many times and indeed celebrated in print and in museums in Vietnam today, but from his base in Paris, Nguyen Ai Quoc also attended the Tours Congress of the PSF on December 26, 1920, siding with the left wing to approve the resolution to found the Parti Communiste Français (PCF) and to join the Third International (Comintern). In the spring of 1921, he also participated with Nguyen The Truyen in setting up the Union Intercoloniale (Intercolonial Union), a PCF project to promote Marxism in the colonies. He also attended the First PCF Congress at Marseilles in December 1921 and, notably, on October 10, 1923, visited Moscow to attend an International Peasant Conference. Although under intense police scrutiny, in June 1924 he again departed Paris for Moscow to address the Fifth Comintern Congress, returning to his theme of colonial exploitation of the peasantry. Among his lesser-known writings of the time was the political satire "Le Dragon de Bambou" (ca. 1922), first performed on the occasion of the visit to France of Emperor Khai Dinh. From France, in 1925, he also published *Le Procès de la Colonization Française*, a trenchant Marxist critique of French colonialism including Indochina (MAE AOI 162 "Biographie d'Ho Chi Minh établi par F.O.M. c. 1/9/49"; Duiker 2000, 54–86; Brocheux 2007, 19–20).

As Féray (1979, 138) points out, it is also true that, contrary to his ambitions and background, the young Vietnamese "outcast" or, in modern parlance, migrant worker, also underwent a kind of proletarianization. Insofar as his life in London and Paris straddled the period between the demise of the Second International (1889–1916) and the rise of the Third International founded in Moscow on March 4, 1919, we may also surmise that the young Ho Chi Minh was not naïve as to the debates surrounding this transition, just as he would embrace the latter. Still, it is impressive that, contrary to PSF priorities on class struggle and worker interests, Ho Chi Minh stood out for his concern for the colonial question. Besides close contact with leading French communists, the young Vietnamese also bonded closely with a circle of fellow colonials from Madagascar, Guadeloupe, Martinique, and elsewhere (Brocheux 2007, 18–19). Notwithstanding this range of experiences, further embroidered below, it was Paris that offered the future president of his nation, as with many other compatriots, a full suite of political experiences along with a taste of equality, liberty, and freedom.

Phan Chau Trinh

Another Vietnamese who made the voyage to France was Phan Chu Trinh (1872–1926), also known as Phan Chau Trinh, a pioneer figure alongside Phan Boi Chau in seeking an end to France's occupation. Born in central Vietnam in 1872, the son of a rich landowner and scholar, he graduated in 1901 with the highest mandarin degree, entering the bureaucracy only to resign in 1905. Calling for the abolition of the monarchy and its replacement with a democratic republic, he then went to Japan with Phan Boi Chau as part of the Dong Du movement. Back in Vietnam in 1907, he opened a patriotic modern school in Hanoi, inter alia using Phan Boi Chau's writings, important in Christine White's (1974, 82) opinion, for its use of *quoc ngu*, or Vietnamese romanized script, as a vehicle for popularizing modern ideas and techniques. After peasant tax revolts erupted in 1908, Trin was arrested, and his school was closed. Sentenced to death but commuted to life imprisonment, he was sent to the remote and ever-serviceable Poulo Condore island penitentiary. Pardoned in 1911 and sentenced to house arrest, he was deported to France. Refusing to be conscripted for French military service, he was incarcerated for another ten months (September 1914–July 1915). Once out of prison, he sought to win the support of progressive French politicians and Vietnamese exiles. Hosting the "Club de Faubourg" in the middle-class Gobelins precinct in Paris, his circle included such compatriots as Nguyen Ai Quoc (who had been in letter contact since London days), lawyer Phan Van Truong, Nguyen The Truyen, and the future radical nationalist intellectual Nguyen An Ninh (as profiled below).

However, it is also true, as Duiker (2000, 86) points out, that in departing Paris for Soviet Russia, Ho Chi Minh made a "symbolic break" with Phan Chau Trinh's reformist path. As Vinh Sinh (2009, 1, 8, 18) embellishes, in contrast to Phan Boi Chau and many other political activists, Phan Chau Trinh eschewed violence against colonial rule, counseled against accepting foreign support, and argued that true independence could be achieved only through effecting change within Vietnam's political culture, as with antifeudal/antimonarchical reforms. His experience in Japan also taught him that Vietnam's modernization was imperative if independence was to be won.

Woodside (1976, 234–5) has gone further in introducing the concept of "mandarin proletarians," offering a number of examples of future Communist

Party figures with their roots in long-established mandarin families in Annam. The first secretary general of the Indochinese Communist Party (ICP), Tran Phu, for example, was the son of a district magistrate in Quang Ngai in the early 1900s; revolutionary heroine and martyr Nguyen Thi Minh Khai (now celebrated in a street name replacing Barbier Street in Saigon), was the daughter of a classical scholar, and her grandfather was a provincial governor; future DRV premier Pham Van Dong was a son of the *chef de cabinet* of Emperor Duy Tan. Woodside—who neglects to mention Ho Chi Minh or at least his father—allows that such examples could be multiplied. Sharing a background of "loss of nation" and the humiliation of the scholar mandarin class, obviously such individuals went through a shift of (class) affiliation. This is true, and it was an attitude shared by such noncommunist literati as Phan Boi Chau as well as members of the Annam royal family, notably Prince Cuong De.

The Interwar Period

The interwar period saw the Vietnamese nationalist movement begin to redirect itself toward the need to establish a modern state along Western lines and with leadership increasingly drawn from French-trained intellectuals rather than from the traditional literati. Direct experience in France by soldier-conscripts during World War I along with the impact of the Russian October Revolution and acquaintance of some with socialism and communism all played their part. The upsurge of democratic ideas in Vietnam following the war, receptivity to concepts of press freedom, assembly and association, and local social and political reforms were further carried through under the governor generalships of Albert Sarraut (1917–20) and Maurice Long (1920–22) (US Govt. *Political Alignments of the Vietnamese Nationalists*, 1949). Outside of southern Vietnam, however, no political parties were formed. Notably, the burgeoning French colonial surveillance system saw to it that the development of political consciousness was arrested.

As French Vietnam specialist Pierre Rousset (1978, 94) confirms, through the 1920s the tendency of the nationalist movement, especially among Vietnamese immigrants in France, was toward communism. This led the *Courier de Saigon* to state in 1930 that "the road to France is the road to anti-France." The seriousness of the situation for the French authorities was carried in a French police report of January 1927. At that time, the "Indochinese" colony in Paris alone numbered some three thousand, of whom seven to eight hundred were students or intellectuals, cooks, domestics, or workers employed in the lacquer industry. As conceded, if a certain number of them displayed proof of loyalty toward France, many were also suspected of being in sympathy with "xenophobic doctrines" and secretly wishing to be free of French tutelage. The most threatening of these groups were identified as those which had rallied to the PCF (AOM NF Paris F713408, Prefecture Police à Intérieur, Jan. 1927).

By 1932, the total number of Vietnamese residing in France (including troops and workers) had diminished to below ten thousand. Meantime, however, the universities emerged as the leading centers of anti-French political organization. During the 1920s and 1930s, most French universities hosted Vietnamese students just as they increasingly took advantage of the opportunity of a foreign education. They were also well organized. As tracked by the authorities, all across the university cities and towns in France, they set up discussion groups, cultural associations, and welfare organizations, many suspected to be of political orientation (Dion, n.d., 3). Certain graduate-returnees, as with Tran Van Giau, a future ICP apparatchik in Cochinchina, along with many young Vietnamese intellectuals attracted to Trotskyist ideas, would take up the mantle of struggle back in Saigon.

For many young Vietnamese born in the first decade of the new century, the metropolitan experience was a transformative one. Entering and graduating from French colleges and universities during the interwar period, they were a vanguard generation. As an educated and bilingual group they were perfectly poised to serve as political-cultural brokers for their compatriots back in Vietnam, just as they were looked up to by their less educated fellows as providers of solutions. The 1920s saw a new wave of political activism led by young middle-class beneficiaries of the French school system. Reading *quoc ngu* and French, they found elements of the French colonial system both attractive and repugnant to Vietnamese sensibility. Needless to say, with its large French and Chinese population, including its prosperous elements, Saigon was the crucible of this movement. But with its large working class and underclass, Saigon also revealed stark contrasts between rich and poor.

Collaboration

The other side to anticolonial resistance was the co-optation or winning of collaborators, a complex process of negotiation that also involved concessions, liberalizations, and a more participatory colonization. At least the most controversial individual giving voice to middle-class Vietnamese resentment to colonial discrimination was the wealthy agronomist Bui Quang Chieu (1872–1945). Yet he was also a key collaborator. Launching *La Tribune Indigène* in 1917 with secret subsidies from the administration, along with *L'Echo Annamite*, created in 1919 by Nguyen Phan Long, Chui was also a founder of the Constitutionalist Party, the first formal political party in Indochina. Two themes emerged in Constitutionalist goals: one was expanded opportunities for Vietnamese in the colonial system, and the other was reducing the influence of the large and economically influential Chinese minority with its control over rice exports. In 1926, Chui had traveled to Paris to press the authorities for political and economic reforms. He also held talks in Paris with radicals among the Vietnamese community, but, in the end, he refused to cooperate and, on returning to Saigon, disappointed his fans. By coming out for Franco-Vietnamese cooperation, he also earned the scorn of the communists, Ho Chi Minh included (R. B. Smith 1969; Cook 1977; Duiker 2000, 111–49; Brocheux and Hémery 2009, 304).

THE PRINT REVOLUTION IN COLONIAL SAIGON

The virtual revolution in journalism and publishing taking place in Saigon between 1917 and 1928 cannot be seen outside of a general print revolution touching Asia, including the European colonies. Writing in both French and *quoc ngu*, the new intelligentsia launched, in the words of Brocheux and Hémery (2009, 306), "a constant campaign for a radical cultural and social modernization, even as they positioned themselves consistently in opposition to the colonial administration." Although restricted to only a few thousand educated youth, unquestionably the constitution of youth as a political force was singular in Vietnamese history and for a Confucian society. Notably, sons and daughters began to distance themselves from family backgrounds, including many future leaders alongside the revolution. By the 1920s, the old literati-influenced activists were surpassed by the youthful "revolutionary intelligentsia." Subject to multiple influences, whether from Europe, Soviet Russia, or India, feminism also made its appearance in the publications of the time.

Even prior to the establishment of the Thanh Nien and the formal Communist Party, Saigon produced its share of radical intellectuals. One of the better-known activists of the 1920s was Nguyen An Ninh (1900–1943). Having studied in a French *lycée* in Saigon, he won a scholarship to France. There he was accused of joining the PCF. Back in Saigon he published the *La Cloche Fêlée* (1923–26). For his efforts, he was imprisoned several times, including a three-year spell from 1928 for establishing an anti-French society and an army of sorts. Arrested one last time in October 1939, he died in a French prison (Truong Buu Lam 1967). Arriving back in Saigon in June 1925 after a decade abroad, Phan Chau Trinh contributed to *La Cloche Fêlée* as well as to the Paul Monin-André Malraux paper, *L'Indochine*, "not without courage," as Féray (1979, 133) allows, assailing the colonial regime in the name of democratic principles such as he knew from France. A popular figure, Phan Chau Trinh's funeral in Saigon in April 1926 attracted a patriotic rally of twenty-five thousand. Nevertheless, as Duiker (2000, 68–69) points out, that is not to say that Nguyen Ai Quoc agreed with the latter's tactics of using France to modernize the country.

The Varenne Interlude

Departing Vietnam in April 1925, Merlin was replaced as governor general by Alexandre Varenne. Vietnamese nationalists and members of the intelligentsia held high expectations for Varenne, the first and only socialist to hold this position. Yet they were disappointed by his refusal to implement sweeping reforms, making him the butt of the progressive French-language press, as with Malraux's *L'Indochine* (1925) (see Marr 1971, 272). Relaunched between November 4, 1925, and February 24, 1926, as *L'Indochine Enchainée*, the paper included twenty-five articles or editorials penned by Malraux. Varenne also aroused the ire of the *colons* as with his amnesty of December 24, 1925, for Phan Boi Chau, who had earlier been arrested in Shanghai, repatriated, and tried. Responding to huge popular protests calling for clemency, Varenne consigned the veteran revolutionary to house arrest in Hue.

Other papers also weighed into this battle, notably, *L'Impartial*, owned by grand colonial figure Ernest Outrey. Edited by the pro-French Eurasian and future president of the Colonial Council of Indochina, Henry Chavigny de Lachevrotière, *L'Impartial* railed against both Paul Monin and Governor General Varenne, labeling the former a Bolshevik and claiming a KMT-inspired rebellion. *L'Impartial* also heralded the launching of a defense committee for French colonial interests (Tedral 1926; Marr 1971, 268). Departing *L'Impartial* in 1926, Chavigny de Lachevrotière established his own paper, *La Depêche*. *La Presse Indochinoise*, founded in May 1924, was another publication virtually calling for a recall of Varenne with such articles as "La collusion est enfin prouvé entre les communistes de Paris et le Parti Républicain Progressiste annamite fondé ici par M. Varenne" (*M. Varenne et la presse indochinoise* 1926).

Reaching back to October 1926 but becoming prominent in November, the French-language press in Saigon launched a campaign in support of a systematic boycott of foreign goods as well as determined noncooperation with the French administration. Notable, in this respect, was *Le Tribune Indochinoise* (Nov. 29, 1926), the mouthpiece of the Constitutionalists, literally announcing the campaign under the heading of "Politique abstentioniste." According to a French analyst, the major goal of the campaign, such as taken up by *L'Echo Annamite* under Nguyen Phan Long, along with *Era Nouvelle*, was to push for the development of indigenous industry. Radical as it may have sounded, this was still a policy from within a collaborative framework. Undoubtedly, *L'Echo Annamite* (Nov. 15, 1926) also challenged official tolerance by printing the provocative byline: "Compatriots, when you have a cup of coffee or a liqueur, it is the blood of the country that you are drinking" (AOM SLOTFOM III 40, "Note sur le Politique Abstentioniste").

While all political tendencies in this debate saw the overall benefits of colonialism—Malraux included—they only disagreed as to its administration. In the short term, Malraux attracted some solid support from the local bourgeoisie, although not the die-hard *colon*. Notably, a statement attributed to Malraux, whose fame grew with his literary name, "Il est difficile de concevoir qu'un annamite est autre chose que révolutionairre," would resurface on the masthead of the communist paper *Le Travail* a decade later.

Within the year, however, Nguyen An Ninh would be imprisoned and *La Cloche Fêlée* closed down. Varenne would be recalled to France. As an official French observer wrote, "In all spheres of social life, whether religious, social, educational, sporting, philanthropic and business, we more or less witness an underground opposition whose activities extend across the three components of Indochina seeking to unite the efforts of the nationalist groups." Veritably, France now confronted in its eastern colony "*une conscience nationale annamite*" (AOM Indo NF/2681568, "Note sur l'activité des partis d'opposition anti-Français en Indochine," 1st tri 1926), although the terms *Vietnam* and *Vietnamese* would enter French vocabulary only after 1945. In any case, as discussed in chapter 4, the journalism or print revolution in Vietnam would enter an even more radical phase during the Popular Front years (1936–39).

"To Ignite a Wildfire:" The Power of Ideas

Reaching back long before the advent of international communism, anti-French nationalism obviously had deep roots in Vietnamese society. However, by the late 1920s, the anti-French current was also fed by activists and propagandists arriving from Guangzhou in China. As a Sûreté analyst wrote in 1928, especially in northern Annam and particularly in the provinces of Vinh and Thanh Hoa, "the *lettrés* of the old mandarinal school are still our adversaries." Arriving from southern China, among other places, during the winter of 1926 and again in 1927, their propagandists began to make contact with local secret societies. Nothing was written—all messages were conveyed orally and committed to heart ("in the method of Moscow"). They then set about creating specialized cells by class, as with cells for *lettrés*, officials, workers, peasants, and merchants. Some used commercial premises as fronts. "They don't preach revolts, they don't announce specific events," the analyst continued, "they merely create favorable dispositions to ignite a wildfire in the event of a movement being launched." As recorded with some derision, even their children recited poetry with militant proletarian themes

(Indo NF/208/1562 "Note sur l'Activité des partis d'opposition anti-français en Indochine," Sûreté Générale, premier semestre de 1928).

With reference to individuals, as the Sûreté analyst commented, "It is incontestable that Phan Boi Chau is one of the secret animators of the anti-French movement in north Annam. The personal actions and prestige of the old revolutionary remains considerable. Not a single agitator, *chef de groupe*, or journalist will pass Hue without paying him a visit." The most notable among these visitors included Nguyen The Truyen,[2] Nguyen The Nghiep,[3] Nguyen Van Ngoc,[4] Nguyen The Phu,[5] Vu Dinh Dy,[6] and Dao Thao Con (unidentified). Meetings were on "very secret terms," often held on Phan Boi Chau's sampan on the Huong Giang (Perfumed River) in Hue. But of these names, the analyst concluded, "It is certain that Phan Boi Chau and Huynh Thuc Khang are the chief animators and advisers of the anti-French movement in Annam" (Indo NF/208/1562 "Note sur l'Activité des partis d'opposition anti-français en Indochine," Sûreté Générale, premier semestre de 1928).[7]

THE FAILED VNQDD OR YEN BAI UPRISING

The communists, however, had no monopoly over Vietnamese nationalism. Pike (1978, 25) describes a "vast and bewildering welter" of nationalist organizations that emerged in the late 1920s and 1930s, many of them small, informal groupings, morphing into larger groups or dissolving in the face of police investigation or repression. Certain so-called nationalist organizations were even created by the Sûreté to entrap the unwary. The oldest and most prominent of the secular nationalist organizations was the Viet Nam Quoc Dan Dang (VNQDD), modeled after or supported by the Chinese nationalists (KMT). Founded in 1927 by Nguyen Thai Hoc, in turn the VNQDD was beholden to the pioneering actions of Phan Boi Chau (Hoang Van Dao 2008, 12–23).

While the VNQDD included civil servants and members of the military, as Pike (1978, 26–27) declares, its membership was actually more proletarian than that of the communists. With its base in Tonkin, much of its language was Marxist, and its organizational methods mirrored those of the communists or KMT. Its methods were also bloody-handed, such as an assassination attempt against a governor general. Although the VNQDD would be revived during the wartime struggle against the Japanese under Chinese nationalist auspices, it met its apotheosis following a bungled mutiny by Vietnamese soldiers serving in the French army. Repression was swift, including execution of the leadership and flight to China by survivors.

A minor administrative center astride the railroad clinging to the east bank of the Red River and some 150 kilometers northwest of Hanoi, Yen Bai seems an unlikely site for the first major armed challenge by an organized Vietnamese group against French military power. It was also a minority zone, with Tho (Tay), Man, Meo (Hmong), Muong, and Nung outnumbering Vietnamese. In the event, as Paris learned via a cable sent by Governor General Pasquier on February 10, 1930, two companies of Vietnamese riflemen at Yen Bai barracks staged a rebellion at 2:00 a.m. Some five French military personnel were killed, with an equal number of Vietnamese on the side of the defenders. The assailants were repulsed. Armed units fanned out in pursuit of the rebels, with aerial surveillance also undertaken. But Hanoi was also the scene of a number of bomb attacks and incidents, notably at the prison and the police commissariat (AOM 3 SLOTFOM/129 code tél., Hanoi, à Colonies, Paris, Feb. 10, 1930). Although Pasquier remarked on a red flag left behind by the rebels at Yen Bai, he did not identify the attackers or their party or cause.

The red flag with white star surrounded by a blue circle was, in fact, that of the KMT-modeled VNQDD. As Duiker (2000, 172) elaborates, crucial to VNQDD plans for an uprising was the subversion of Vietnamese troops in the military. Eschewing the patience required by the Leninist strategy of building up a mass base in the country, the VNQDD impulsively decided on overthrowing the French establishment via a military putsch. An attempt to stockpile arms in 1929 had been discovered, and a crackdown commenced, pushing the VNQDD into planning a major attempt targeted for February 10, 1930, not only at the Yen Bai base but also at a number of locales in the highlands.

Repression in the wake of Yen Bai was wide sweeping, with thirteen of the ringleaders executed in June–July 1930, including the top VNQDD leaders, Hoc and Pho Duc Chinh. Besides executions, a range of prison sentences were passed down in a major judicial crackdown. The event was not passed over by the local and metropolitan media. For example, *La Tribune Indochinoise* (March 28, 1930) declaimed that "entire villages were bombed and shot up" (Co Am village of seven thousand inhabitants was completely destroyed by five airplanes flying at low altitude, dropping twelve-kilogram bombs). Highlighting the keywords *hunger*, *misery*, and *death*, on May 1, 1930, a Toulouse-based group signing itself "Les émigrés Indochinois en France" called for the release of fifty-six individuals condemned to death for Yen Bai. The PCF also took up the cause, leading directly to protests outside the Elysée Palace in Paris, an act which subsequently resulted in the repatriation to Vietnam of pioneer members of the fledgling but influential Trotskyist movement in the French colony.

A number of administrative recriminations followed the Yen Bai mutiny, for example, the exposure of administrative and military weaknesses leading to a reshuffling of concerned personnel. But as more than one historian of Vietnam has pointed out, the near destruction of VNQDD cadre through executions, imprisonment, and other measures, along with the flight of surviving leaders to Yunnan, left the field clear to the communists, just as the crushing of the Yen Bai rebellion offered a salutary lesson to would-be revolutionaries tempted to mount a premature putsch against superior colonial power. Following Pasquier's prescription, military security, political intelligence, and surveillance of anticolonial activities across Indochina was vastly enhanced. For the colonial authorities two processes were at work, namely, nationalist tendencies as manifested by secret societies and, from 1924 onward, communist-inspired activities, drawing on and exploiting the former. More generally, the colonial response during this period was to nip this festering activity in the bud, whether by administrative fiat, by deportation of foreign agitators, by arrests of subversives, or by other control measures. Ironically, however, the colonial authorities still believed that they were acting in the French tradition of liberalism, a Gallic version of manifest destiny which became increasingly untenable as crisis beset the colonial order by the turn of the decade.

MOSCOW AND THE GUANGZHOU CONNECTION

Having attended Comintern conferences in Moscow, the now-seasoned orator-activist Nguyen Ai Quoc/Ho Chi Minh literally announced himself to the French as a dedicated and dangerous anticolonial revolutionary (in fact, the Comintern theorist on Asia). From the time of his visit to Moscow in June 1923, the Soviet Union had been an important lodestar for Asian nationalists attracted to Lenin's doctrine with its anticolonial clarion call. In December 1923, along with numerous other students from Asia (future People's Republic of China [PRC] premier Zhou Enlai was one), Nguyen Ai Quoc (going by another alias) enrolled in the University of the Toilers of the East [Workers of the Orient] (also dubbed the Stalin School) (Duiker 2000, 92–93). Even so, as discussed below, his return to Vietnam would be long postponed.

As indicated, the Comintern or Third International emerged in January 1919, in large part under the impetus of Lenin, out of a reunion of eight parties and communist groups. Until it was dissolved in May 1943, the Comintern served as the center of the Moscow-inspired "international worker movement." According to Trager (1959, 249), the developments initiated at the Second Comintern Congress in 1920 were steadily carried forward by the third, fourth, and fifth congresses (1921, 1922, and 1924, respectively) even though the debates between Lenin and the Indian delegate to the Comintern, M. N. Roy, initiated at the 1920 meeting, had not actually been resolved.

Over the opposition of Roy, who favored a strict class approach to the anticolonial question, Nguyen Ai Quoc leaned toward the original Comintern thesis with respect to the anticolonial project, that is, seeking out alliances with the indigenous bourgeoisie.[8]

As mentioned, a delegate to the Fifth Comintern Congress, Nguyen Ai Quoc gave vent to his disenchantment with the metropolitan communist parties, inter alia, pointing out that Lenin had broken with the erroneous line of the Second International, which did not put people of different races on the same footing. In line with Lenin's belief, he argued that the success of the revolution in western Europe was bound up with movements of national liberation and anti-imperialism in the colonies (Ho Chi Minh 1979, 25). The practical implications of the Fifth Congress for Indochina were also not lost on the French security services. In their estimations, its most important decisions concerned, first, the reorganization of parties by means of the cell system; second, the "Bolshevization" of the parties; and, third, the launching of propaganda. In Indochina, where formal communist parties did not yet exist, the authorities surmised that the Comintern would launch an initiative. They were correct, and they were also correct in predicting that the mission would fall to Nguyen Ai Quoc (AOM Paris SLOTFOM III, 48, "Les associations anti-français en Indochine et la propagande communiste," Oct. 23, 1929). As shown below, other "internationalist" figures were also delegated by the Comintern to Indochina.

As Trager (1959, 249) points out, in a departure from the working principle set down at the Fifth Comintern Congress, Lenin's relatively flexible approach to the anticolonial question was abandoned at the Sixth Congress (September 1928) in favor of an ultraleft phase (identified with the Indian communist Roy) until, in turn, replaced by the "right-wing" phase ushered in by the Seventh Congress in 1935. A consequence of the shift to an ultraleft position, however, was the increasing isolation of the communist movement from the ongoing nationalist struggle, which largely derived its impetus from the anticolonial antinationalist movement.

Thanh Nien and the Guangzhou Connection

Departing Moscow for Guangzhou, where he arrived in January 1925, and with Soviet or Comintern backing, Nguyen Ai Quoc set up alongside Mikhail Borodin, political adviser to Sun Yat-sen. As a gathering place for many Vietnamese political exiles, the southern Chinese city also emerged as headquarters of the protocommunist Thanh Nien, or Revolutionary Youth League, established in June that year. From Guangzhou, while running a political training academy in Guangzhou, Nguyen Ai Quoc also helped to bring into the fold such future communist leaders as Tran Phu and Pham Van Dong.

Setting aside Moscow's role alongside the CCP, launched with Comintern assistance in the French concession in Shanghai in July 1921, and the KMT Left, Guangzhou remained a *terre santé* or "holy place" for the Vietnamese revolutionaries, at least as observed by the French authorities. For one thing, it counted such heroes of the revolution as Phan Hong Thai, the individual who died during the failed bomb attempt against Governor Merlin in Shamien and whose grave marker became a place of pilgrimage for Vietnamese visitors, "whether nationalist or communist." Another pole of attraction was the nearby Whampoa Military Academy with Chiang Kai-shek as superintendent. Through this period, the French authorities detained numerous Vietnamese youth attempting to visit Guangdong province with this purpose. As a concerned French authority remarked, "But just as these young Vietnamese idealists leave clandestinely for China, so they secretly return in equal numbers" (AOM Indo NF/2681568, "Note sur l'activité des partis d'opposition anti-Français en Indochine," 1st tri 1926).

From his new base in Guangzhou and operating under various aliases, Nguyen Ai Quoc spent a period of time writing and translating, including contributions to Soviet journals (letter of November 12, 1924), while also engaging in the training of Vietnamese youth, certain of them going on to study at Whampoa. Then serving as Comintern representative on peasant questions, in early May 1925 he joined Chinese communists in organizing a conference on this issue. The following month, as alluded, he established the Thanh Nien with its special attention to the younger generation, including young women. Phan Boi Chau also weighed in, nominating core candidates for the newly founded underground association (Tran My-Van 2005, 115). In turn, Thanh Nien drew on an even earlier society called the Tam Tam Xa, or Like Hearts Society. According to Hue-Tam Ho Tai (2010, 29), Thanh Nien also received assistance from the CCP, then in an alliance with the KMT.

Certain Vietnamese youth, such as Thi Nguyet (Bao Luong), a young woman of barely nineteen years of age, joined the Thanh Nien school in Guangzhou, where Nguyen Ai Quoc's Chinese wife was part of the circle. The school also struck copies of a newspaper (*Thanh Nien*), eventually entering distribution in Vietnam, Thailand, and elsewhere. Returning to Saigon, Thi Nguyet focused on women's issues and, prior to her arrest in mid-1929, had set up nineteen women's cells in Saigon, My Tho, and Can Tho, with about one hundred members and double that number of sympathizers (Hue-Tam Ho Tai 2010, chaps. 2–4). According to French intelligence also active in Guangzhou, as of October 1929, some six thousand individual members of anti-French revolutionary groups inside Indochina were "touched" by Nguyen Ai Quoc's propaganda, including one thousand at Thanh Nien (SLOTFOM III 48, "Les associations anti-française en Indochine et la propaganda communiste," Oct. 23, 1929).

But following the dramatic crackdown and purge of the Left in Guangzhou at the hands of Chiang Kai-shek, Thanh Nien was dissolved in May 1929, eventually making way for the full-blown communist party. Nguyen Ai Quoc himself made a quick exit to the Soviet Union, returning to Asia only the following year. The order to dissolve the painstakingly constructed Thanh Nien groups was not well received back in Saigon, where leading members were implicated in the murder of a comrade. Dubbed the "Affaire Rue Barbier," the three alleged perpetrators of the crime committed in the Saigon street of the same name were arrested along with a wider circle of Thanh Nien members (forty-four in all). Among them was Thi Nguyet/Bao Luong, convicted, inter alia, for conspiring against the security of the state. Thi Nguyet was spared the guillotine. Dubbed "feminist and communist" in one official report, she was sentenced to five years in prison with another three years added for haranguing the judges, albeit gaining her freedom in July 1937 under the Popular Front (Hue-Tam 2010, chaps. 6–11; AOM 3 SLOTFOM/129 "Affaire Barbier: Crime de la rue Barbier à Saigon," Dec. 9, 1928).

Gaining major press publicity at the time by an audience piqued by stories of jealousy and rivalry over a female comrade, the Affaire Rue Barbier was also a small victory for the colonial authorities. As *L'Indochine* (Oct. 5, 1930) summarized, the guilty were very young; the three assassins were aged, respectively twenty-six, twenty-one, and twenty-three. Thi Nguyet was twenty-one. Many of the conspirators were schoolteachers, over half originating from Vinh, while the three assassins along with Thi Nguyet had spent time in Guangzhou. Importantly, as Hue-Tam Ho Tai (2010) makes clear in a book-length study of this affair, this was a transitional period between the preparty and largely patriotic Thanh Nien and the surfacing of a full-blown Marxist-Leninist communist party.

The Bangkok Networks

Well known to the French authorities, the Sino-Thai populated city of Bangkok was both a refuge and a gathering place for Vietnamese exiles and activist elements, some moving on to Hong Kong and Guangzhou, others clandestinely entering Vietnam via the arduous land route across Laos. As discussed below, the Vietnamese exiles in Thailand were not a homogenous group; certain of them were Buddhist, certain Catholic, and not all entered the anticolonial struggle. The reasons for Thailand, especially the remote northeast, emerging as a revolutionary rear base for the Vietnamese revolution are complex but also followed a certain logic (Gunn 1998, 27–42). First, the French could not control or monitor immigration easily across the long boundary between Laos and Cambodia and Thailand. Second, the Bangkok authorities were not entirely hostile to tolerating anti-French Vietnamese exiles. Even when it was proven that certain of the refugees had made common cause with communism, the Thai were not easily persuaded (AOM Indo NF/2681568, "Note sur l'activité des partis d'opposition anti-Français en Indochine," 1st tri 1926).

In 1929, the French legation in Bangkok sought to take stock of the Vietnamese diaspora in Thailand, estimated at between six and seven thousand and divided among "immigrants" and "refugees." Generally, the Vietnamese were deemed to be well informed as to political trends, whether by newly arriving refugees or by political tracts arriving from Guangzhou, including the *Thanh Nien* newspaper. Some of them entertained relations with local Thai nationalists, as with those who, in 1927, published articles on Phan Boi Chau. The "refugee" group, responding to contemporaneous political events in Annam, did not exceed three hundred. But alongside the newer arrivals were also a number of older dissident mandarins from the Court of Hue, veterans of a forty-year Cam Vuong struggle against the French. Many remained fixed in Thailand with no ambition to return. They worked the land and practiced their trades. Residing in scattered communities across the rural northeast, they were also separated by place of origin, with those from Annam and Cochinchina residing at separate locations. Although claiming the cooperation of the Thai authorities in keeping these groups under surveillance, the French also admitted that it was a matter of nuance as to whether the radicals among them were "nationalists" as opposed to "communists." Additionally, the French registered concern over the increasing number of elite Vietnamese figures visiting Bangkok, as with a minister of the Court of Hue and with newspaper editor and member of the Colonial Council Buy Can Chau (SHAT, Rapport Annuel, Siam 1928, Annam, Legation de France au Siam, Bangkok, Jan. 1, 1929). Although not corroborated, a French account of 1926 reveals that Ho Chi Minh's father, Nguyen Sinh Sac, also went into exile in Thailand, having earlier sheltered in a Buddhist temple in Phnom Penh.

Doubtless fearful of the French police surveillance, Nguyen Ai Quoc staged his return to Asia from the Soviet Union and Europe aboard a Japanese ship, arriving in Bangkok in autumn 1928. As told by Le Manh Trinh (2008, 58–76), he then embarked upon a clandestine tour of northeastern Thailand, meeting up with compatriots in exile, reportedly once slipping across the Mekong into Laos. Going by the name Thau Chin, he taught, translated, launched the *Thanh Ai* newspaper, and propagated his cause before exiting the northeast in June 1929 for Bangkok. It is pure speculation, but he could also have been seeking information about the fate of his father. Nguyen Ai Quoc made a final appearance in Thailand in March 1930, following the foundation of the ICP, as part of an international mission at the bequest of the Comintern, which included visits to Malaya and Singapore (May 1, 1930) (Goscha 1999, 82). Although little was immediately achieved by the

Southeast Asian venture, in the early postwar period the Vietnamese colonies in eastern and northeastern Thailand would rally in favor of the Viet Minh, a thorn in the side of the returning French administration and an ally alongside anti-French Lao and Cambodian nationalist groups.

In a word, Vietnamese were going out to China, Japan, Thailand, and France as sailors, students, and refugees. With a remarkable degree of solidarity, they also reconstituted themselves into communities in exile. While certain of them achieved a greater degree of assimilation in their new homelands, others formed discrete, isolated "colonies," also reproducing the politics of homeland. They also served as frontline soldiers for France's wars, labored in metropolitan factories, or worked as contract labor in France's distant Pacific island colonies. Colonialism had virtually created this vast diaspora with its metropolitan and regional Asian links. Without question, France had brought Vietnam into the modern world in myriad ways.

The Birth of the Indochinese Communist Party

With the foundering of the protocommunist Thanh Nien over the issue of turning it into a communist party, a group of former members returned to Cochinchina and, in 1929, founded the Annam Communist Party (Annam Cong San Dang). Another faction returned to Tonkin and there organized the Dong Duong Cong San Dang. At the same time, the communist-leaning New Annam party (Tan Viet) changed its name to the Communist Federation (Cong San Lien Doan) (SLOTFOM III, 52 1st tri 1933).

From June 19, 1925, the date that Nguyen Ai Quoc set up a branch of the Thanh Nien in Hong Kong, until his arrest in the British colony on June 6, 1931, the port city would become the major external base of the Vietnamese revolution (SLOTFOM III 54, NP, no.35, 2nd tri 1935). At a meeting in Hong Kong on February 3–7, 1930, two rival communist factions amalgamated into an organization called the Vietnamese Communist Party (Dang Cong San Viet Nam). Now called the Unification Conference, this meeting was convoked by Nguyen Ai Quoc in the name of the Comintern, and the date is commemorated as the birthday of the Vietnamese Communist Party (Huynh Kim Khanh 1982, 125). At an October meeting in Hong Kong and in Nguyen Ai Quoc's absence, the name of the organization was changed to the Indochinese Communist Party (ICP), with Tran Phu serving as is first secretary general. The Lao and Cambodian communist parties would also look to this date as their point of origin, although the change in name to the Indochina Communist Party (Dang Cong San Dong Duong) has been subject to much conjecture.

As Huynh Kim Khanh (1982, 128) explains, the appellation "Vietnamese Communist Party" was considered a dangerous ideological deviation in the way it suggested national chauvinism while downplaying the importance of proletarian internationalism. Party documents reveal that it was thought necessary to include comrades from Laos and Cambodia, even though of different ethnic and linguistic background. Duiker (1976b, 19), for example, contends that the change in name was a response to a Comintern directive that support for regional parties was more effective than support for parties representing a single area in the enterprise of linking of embryonic cells in Laos and Cambodia. Hodgkin (1981, 243), in turn, is less positive that the Comintern was behind the change in name. The reported presence of ethnic Lao and Khmer delegates (as well as those from the three regions of Vietnam and Thailand) at the founding conference would not only have impelled the committee to favor the Indochina appellation but would suggested that the Comintern actually dispatched the delegates from the various regions.

The Comintern connection also deeply concerned the colonial authorities. As French sources reveal, from 1925 to 1932, thirty-four Vietnamese had been admitted to the University of the Toilers in Moscow. In the first trimester of 1933, an additional ten had departed for Russia with the same goal. Meantime, fourteen graduates of the school had returned to Indochina and were actively involved in underground communist activity. Although thousands of militants had either been arrested or condemned following the events of 1930–31 (a reference to the Nghe-Tinh rebellion, as discussed in chapter 3), many had also served out their sentences or been beneficiaries of an amnesty on the occasion of the return from France to Vietnam of Emperor Bao Dai. Once liberated, the young revolutionaries worked to rebuild their old communist networks on a new basis, successfully in central and southern Vietnam. In the words of Governor General Pierre Pasquier, "they have no less ardor, certitude, much less *savoir-faire*, maturity, or prudence, than they had at the time of their original actions even if, as the Comintern judged, these rebellions were premature, poorly prepared, and led by *des étourdis* (the blinded)" (AOM Indo NF 55/594–640, "Notes Situation Politique de l'Indochine," Pasquier, March 22, 1933).

Arrest and Trial of Ho Chi Minh/Nguyen Ai Quoc

Back in Hong Kong on June 6, 1931, and at that time going by the name Sung Man Cho, Ho Chi Minh was apprehended and incarcerated by the British authorities. The previous week, events had taken a major turn with the arrest of Comintern agent Joseph Ducroix (Lefranc) in Singapore along with Comintern agents Noulens/Ruegg in Shanghai and the seizure of letters compromising the Hong Kong–based revolutionary. Inside Indochina, ICP Secretary General Tran Phu was arrested and "terminated," along with other Moscow returnees, one by one. The story of the arrest of Sung Man Cho along with a female Vietnamese companion at his Tam Kung Road address in Kowloon, his rearrest on June 12, and his subsequent incarceration and trial was widely reported in the Hong Kong press of the time. This was all the more newsworthy as it coincided with the "White Terror" mounted by Chiang Kai-shek against the communists in Guangzhou in tandem with the British authorities in the colony (Duncanson 1974; Chan 1999, 189). The events were also recalled by Ho Chi Minh in later life (Lan 2009, 74–98).

It also infuriated the French authorities that, having been condemned to death by a Vietnamese court (Vinh city court minute of October 10, 1926), the anti-French revolutionary was also a beneficiary of British justice (Ho Chi Minh Museum). Following his eventual release from prison in January 1933 and a thwarted bid to proceed to Europe via Singapore, Nguyen Ai Quoc/Ho Chi Minh eventually made his exit from Hong Kong to Xiamen, in part with the support of the deputy British governor's wife. As Brocheux (2007, 54–58) confirms, the newborn ICP was in dire straits by 1933.

The British also threw the French off Nguyen Ai Quoc's trail by issuing a false report of his death from tuberculosis. Writing in 1934, the communist organ *Bolchevik Revue* also reported on his death in a British prison. Even at the moment of the Viet Minh takeover in Hanoi in August 1945, the French foreign ministry had to double-check to ensure whether Ho Chi Minh was the same person as Nguyen Ai Quoc and/or Bui-Ai, another pseudonym adopted during his Moscow days. According to an official French interlocutor, "I can signal that the British authorities in Hong Kong advised the Gouvernement Général in 1934 that Nguyen Ai Quoc died of tuberculosis in prison in Hong Kong." Because he was known to suffer from TB, this declaration rang true. As the report continued, "In fact the dossier in place in the archives of the Service, otherwise very complete until 1935, ends abruptly at that date" (MAE AOI 138 E165 Secrétaire d'Etat aux Colonies, Direction des Affaires Politiques, "Note," no. 11848, Sept. 18, 1945). This is important, as it reveals the successful subterfuge of Ho Chi Minh vis-à-vis the French over a period of fifteen years, at least until he made contact with the American OSS in early 1945.

CONCLUSION

The lesson emerging from this chapter is that opposition to French colonialism across Indochina was multivariant, touching virtually all levels of Vietnamese society. There was nothing particularly subtle about late nineteenth-century European colonialism, a virulent form of imperialism that masked gunboat diplomacy with pacts and treaties. It should not be lost that the French invasion and occupation of Indochina also coincided with the virtual submission of Qing China to a range of depredations at the hands of Western nations, headed by Great Britain. It is true that the monarchs of Laos especially and Cambodia found signal advantage in submitting to French "protection," but the French defeat of the Court of Hue, including both its southern and northern satraps, was tantamount to an assault on Vietnam's tradition and history. All but a privileged, albeit motley cast of collaborators fell in with the new colonial status quo. The "save the king" movement and the early dissent on the part of the scholar-mandarins spanning most of the French period was eloquent testimony of this demonstration effect.

Simply, armed French pacification along with divide-and-rule tactics were resented by a myriad local communities, especially as the French compromise involved submission to highly resented *corvées* and tax collections alongside a trove of new and onerous duties outside of traditional bonds. Although space precludes analysis, the reverse side of French military pacification was also defense of ancestral lands and forest on the part of the ethnic minorities, notably the southern *montagnards*. Certain other minority groups, as with the Meo/Hmong of northern Laos and Tonkin, turned to desperate millenarian struggles (still ongoing). From another quarter, namely the sprawling Mekong delta region, a range of Mahayana Buddhist and other heterodox sects morphed into virtual feudal satraps hosting their own military formations up to the early postwar period. Other dissident elements turned to social banditry, a time-honored profession in times of crisis.

But just as French colonial capitalism spawned a working class alongside a new, modern urban culture, so it generated malcontents. Undoubtedly, the *paix français* conferred educational benefits on a minority, but education was also a two-edged sword. It was precisely from the ranks of the educated that a new dissident class arose in the 1920s and 1930s, what we have termed mandarin-proletarians swayed by Marxist-Leninist doctrines, which they grafted to local conditions, albeit variously, according to personality, political faction, and circumstance. As taken up in a following chapter, communist agitators soon found a ready mass following in the poverty-stricken regions of central Vietnam and, consistent with our overarching thesis, would find fertile ground in 1944–45 as the means of subsistence collapsed in the face of the scourge of famine and disease.

As it happened, however, the *paix français* offered both space and pause for a more considered evaluation of French power by members of the mandarin, or rather *declassé* mandarin, classes. As an educated avant-garde rightly indignant at the erosion of traditional values, they looked outside Vietnam for models. The major pole of attraction for the likes of Phan Boi Chau, followed by Prince Cuong De and many cohorts of Vietnamese students, was Japan. But China was closer to home, and progressive Vietnamese nationalists could hardly ignore either the methods of example of Chinese nationalists, as with Sun Yat-sen. As it transpired, by the 1920s and 1930s, both sympathetic

Japanese and Chinese nationalists would actively engage anti-French elements within Vietnamese society, although few could have guessed the kind of cataclysm that would emerge with Japan's actual invasion of Indochina.

France was another pole of attraction for Vietnamese, especially students entering metropolitan universities and schools. Other Vietnamese entered Europe as seamen, or laborers, or soldiers. Such exchanges obviously invoked complex responses, just as French officialdom worked hard to cultivate a Francophone *collaborateur* class. But for many of the thousands of Vietnamese returnees from France, the experience had awakened a sense of injustice which easily translated into political thinking around colonialism, around capitalism, around racial equality, and around nation. Revolutionary journalism, as indicated, would also become a vocation for many, further blossoming in the late 1930s under the Popular Front government when the lid was lifted on press freedom.

Most rebellions and anticolonial outbursts failed or were quickly neutralized by fierce French repression. Certain rebellions even gained metropolitan sympathy, but none would have succeeded within their generation were it not for the rise of a militarist Japan. Japan both swept French military power and exposed its sense of invincibility to aspiring Vietnamese nationalists. The vacuum created by the Japanese surrender also opened the way for the Machiavellian actions of armed groups and gangs, certain of them linked with China, alongside the victor anointed by the Americans as the best bet to lead the struggle to defeat Japanese expansionism and fascism, namely, the newly anointed political-military entity dubbed the Viet Minh.

At the end of the day, it was not the triumph of political ideas and intellectual arguments, such as those touted with such great elegance and force by urban intellectuals in Saigon and Hanoi, but the force of modern arms turned back on the French invaders. But not all Vietnamese were ingrates, either, and defense of a multiparty noncommunist ideal would eventually pit Vietnamese, Cambodians, and Lao against each other in a thirty-year fratricidal war—so unnecessary in retrospect, as we contemplate the present-day triumph of promarket capitalism across Indochina, if only compromises could have been made.

NOTES

1. *Pen contumace* (in the absence of the accused) is a legal process repealed in French-administered territories only in 2004.

2. Nguyen The Truyen, as mentioned, was a former associate of Ho Chi Minh in Paris, a radical nationalist but not a communist.

3. Born in Thai Binh, Nguyen The Nghiep was a cofounder of the Viet Nam Nationalist Party (VNQDD) who led a breakaway faction in 1929. Arrested by the French but released, he then moved to Yunnan, continuing his activities. Arrested again in Shanghai in 1934, he gained his release during the Popular Front period, continuing his activities.

4. A ranking VNQDD member in Haiphong turned French informer in 1927, Nguyen Van Ngoc was assassinated on May 12, 1930, by VNQDD agents.

5. Nguyen The Phu was a member of the *Viêt-nam Hon* group set up by Nguyen The Truyen in Paris.

6. Vu Dinh Dy, a native of Tonkin, became one of the most prominent pro-Japanese leaders.

7. An associate of Phan Chau Trinh, Huynh Thuc Khang (1876–1948) spent thirteen years in Poulo Condore prison on account of his participation in antitax demonstrations in Quang Nam in 1908. Having gained his freedom, he went on to found the *quoc ngu* newspaper *Tiang Dan*, published in Hue for over sixteen years from 1927. In late 1945, he joined the provisional government of the DRV with the position of the minister of the interior and became acting president of the DRV from June to September 1946, during Ho Chi Minh' s stay in France.

8. Rousset (1978, 52) styles Roy's interpretation as "Stalinist," a designation generally employed here to symbolize the ultra-left Comintern line but not to be confused with the Trotskyist position outside of the Comintern.

Chapter 3

The Rice Rebellions, 1930–31

A mere three months after the Yen Bai uprising of January 1930 and its repression, widespread peasant rebellion broke out in troubled Nghe An and Ha Tinh (or Nghe-Tinh) Provinces of north-central Vietnam (Annam), sending ripples throughout Indochina and bringing down another wave of repression and arrests. Dubbed "rice" or sometimes "depression year" rebellions, at their apogee between September 1930 and February 1931 the rebels set up rural "soviets" in the name of the infant Indochina Communist Party (ICP), although not necessarily under its leadership. In northern Annam, their major locus, French colonial structures overlaid but did not completely supplant an ancient imperial system. There were also deeply rooted Catholic villages dating back to the seventeenth century and the age of early-arriving Jesuit missionaries. Host to a long history of rural rebellion, Nghe An and Ha Tinh were also ecologically marginal provinces subject to climatic vagaries as much as economic deprivation at the hands of local authorities and colonial tax collectors.

While not ignoring the importance of French neotraditionalism and elite politics such as played out in the court of Annam, this chapter is primarily concerned with examining the economic and social conditions under colonialism that pushed large numbers of mostly rural people in this part of central Vietnam to desperate actions. Such a perspective approaches state-society relations from the viewpoint of the ruled majority, the mostly indigent rural peasant masses, and not only the French authorities. Ranging back to colonial times, the Nghe-Tinh rebellions have been the subject of significant research, not only through official inquiries but also through modern scholarship (Brocheux 1977; Duiker 1973, 1976b; Ngo Vinh Long 1978; Bernal 1981; Hue-Tam Ho Tai 1983, 1996; Luong 1986). Certain authors have also used the rebellions to test peasant responses to market intrusions, as with

James Scott (1976) writing on the "subsistence ethic" and Samuel Popkin (1979) examining the nexus between social differentiation and market activity. Without ignoring this literature, the approach adopted here is, first, to establish peasant vulnerabilities to market intrusions under colonial capitalism; second, to elaborate on political responses; and third, to examine state responses to the crisis, both repressive and ameliorative if that was the case. More generally, I seek in this chapter to set the scene for the agrarian crisis of 1944–45.

It is not without hyperbole, as Hy Van Luong (1986, 156) contends, that "in many respects, the Nghe-Tinh social movement epitomizes the dynamics of the Vietnamese revolution at large." In endorsing this statement, we can point to a number of shared features, namely agrarian crisis, the specter of famine, the role of the Communist Party, and the agency of peasant victims in taking matters into their own hands, whether or not targeting traditional authorities or railing against colonial iniquities.

This chapter is structured as follows. First, the events of the Nghe-Tinh rebellions are described. Second, the analysis turns to economic grievances underpinning the rebellions. Third, the focus shifts to French responses to the rebellions, taking the form of a committee of inquiry, as well as suppression. Finally, the chapter turns to intra-elite challenges arising from the figure of Emperor Bao Dai whose vision of a united Vietnam came to parallel by that of the Viet Minh.

THE NGHE-TINH REBELLIONS (1930–31)

Setting aside the question of origins of the Vietnamese Communist Party (VCP), the French authorities were rudely awakened to its potency or at least its potential for mischief in the weeks running up to May Day 1930, "the first and fiercest stage" of the Nghe-Tinh rebellion (Ngo Vinh Long 1978, 17). It was also not lost on the French authorities that major organizational changes in the communist underground had recently taken place. As mentioned in chapter 2, leading members of the diverse communist organizations then existing in Vietnam convened in Hong Kong on February 3–7, 1930, with the purpose of unifying and with the change of name to ICP formalized at a subsequent meeting in Hong Kong in October 1930. The timing of this event is important as it goes to the heart of the discussion about the role of the ICP in orchestrating events in Annam.

First Stage: The May Day Events of 1930 to September 1930

In the event, from May to September 1930, there would be sixty-six large demonstrations across Indochina, Annam especially, certain of which I selectively profile. Commencing on April 22, 1930, communist pamphlets and tracts were distributed across a large number of centers in northern Vietnam, including Hanoi and Haiphong. Some of them in the French language addressed French soldiers, marines, and legionnaires. Others, written in *quoc ngu*, were for local consumption. Practically all provinces of Annam were targeted on May 1, along with a showing of red flags, although preventive measures restricted the distribution of revolutionary tracts in Tonkin to the streets of Hanoi. In Saigon and Cholon, pamphlets were thrown from a moving car. Phnom Penh, Kampot, and Kampong Trach in Cambodia were likewise targeted (AOM Indo NF/327/2644 "Note de la Sûreté,"May 1930).

Events in Nghe An took a confrontational style, leading the authorities to believe that a demonstration at Vinh and nearby Ben Thuy, a trading port at the mouth of the Ca River, was the work of ex–Thanh Nien elements drawn into the VCP. The presence of Communist Party members, although not actively participating, suggested to the authorities a unity of purpose. As the Sûreté determined, as of April 22, the VCP and the ICP had become fused (AOM Indo NF/327/2643, "Note sur les incidents de 1e Mai au Nghe-Tinh," May 8, 1930).

Anticipating trouble surrounding the symbolism of May 1, Governor General Pierre Pasquier informed Paris beforehand that the Communist Party had launched open propaganda in favor of a general strike along with a distribution of pamphlets, red flags, and revolutionary insignia. Somewhat erroneously, given the rural dimension of the future rebellions, he believed that revolutionary agitation would be particularly violent in the worker cities of Haiphong and Nam Dinh. In the event, he gave strict instructions that no demonstrations would be tolerated and that precautions would be taken to prevent the least agitation (AOM 3 SLOTFOM/42 "Rebellions dans le Nghe Tinh, nord Annam," Pasquier à Colonies, April 24, 1930). To restate, the urban centers and industrial and mining sites were not the locus of the rebellion but, rather, the backwater rural districts of central Vietnam.

According to the police report, preparations for May Day demonstrations in the Vinh area were in place from April 20–30, 1930. On the night of April 29–30, numerous peasant groups crossed the river at Nghi Xuan, a rural district in Ha Tinh Province, to meet in the village of Yen Dung, an important commercial center near Vinh, also hosting workshops at Trung Thi. As a preventative measure, *garde indigène*, or French-officered local militia, were placed around the Trung Thi ateliers as well as at the forestry works at Ben Thuy. Although no abnormal activity was observed, the demonstration began at 7:00 a.m. All workers were present at the atelier on the morning of May 1 when a group of some eight hundred demonstrators massed outside the premises. With the military opening fire, one group of demonstrators surged back along the main road toward Vinh while another headed toward the Ben Thuy quay. Although this demonstration was neutralized, secret meetings continued to be held in the villages around Vinh (AOM Indo NF/327/2643, "Note sur les incidents de 1e Mai au Nghe-Tinh," May 8, 1930).

A separate incident concerned the attack and looting on the afternoon of May 1 at a concession owned by a "Tonkinese" in the villages of Yen Lac and Hanh Lam in the canton of Cat Ngan (Thanh Chuong), an impoverished mountainous rural area northwest of Vinh. As this affair is relatively well documented, suffice it to add that, as with many other confrontations of the time, a rally of hundreds met with deadly military repression, in this case twenty dead and twenty wounded. Its mission accomplished, the military column withdrew, attempting to take the wounded over the determined resistance of the villagers. Among the red flags flying over Hanh Lam village was one displaying the inscription *Dang-Cong-San* (Communist Party) and, in four characters, "*Malheure à qui l'enlevera*" (woe to those who remove this) (AOM Indo NF/327/2643, "Note sur les incidents de 1e Mai au Nghe-Tinh," May 8, 1930). As Duiker (1976b, 37) points out, in general the land was poor and overcrowded and with substantial tenancy around Thanh Chuong. Even where private ownership existed, the plots were minuscule. By all accounts, Thanh Chuong was one of the more immiserated and famine-stricken places in rural Annam.

Although significant urban worker strikes in Cochinchina preceded the Nghe-Tinh events, overall it was the actions of peasants that dominated the Nghe-Tinh rebellion, just as more peasants were swept up in arrests than were striking urban workers. It is significant as well that Nghe-Tinh then hosted a disproportionate number of Communist Party members, some three hundred in 1930. According to a document attributed to Ho Chi Minh, who closely monitored the rebellion from Hong Kong prior to his arrest on June 6, 1931, of the 226 demonstrations that occurred between May and December 1930, rallying 255,000 participants, three were to get released political prisoners held in district jails, forty-five were purely economic, either to reclaim land for poor peasants or in refusal to pay taxes, five were to celebrate May Day, five were timed for August 1, five were organized to celebrate the October Revolution, four were to commemorate the Guangzhou insurrection, and seven were against the "gentry." The remaining 141 were dubbed "anti-imperialist" demonstrations, such as those showing solidarity with villages destroyed by the police or victims killed by the French (Ho Chi Minh Museum, "Revolutionary Movement in Indochina," Jan. 24, 1931).

On September 12, 1930, a date that later came to symbolize the anniversary of the soviet movement in Nghe-Tinh, the largest and most violent confrontation of the period ensued. On that day, twenty thousand peasant demonstrators marched from Hung Nguyen District toward Vinh in support of striking workers and to press their demands. Summoned by the resident superior of Annam, A. E. Le Fol, the French deployed troops, including legionnaires, alongside aerial bombing raids to break up the demonstration, leading to hundreds of casualties on the side of the unarmed peasant demonstrators (Viollis 1935, 144–47; Ngo Vinh Long 1978, 22; Bernal 1981, 152; Harrison 1989, 77). The mortality figures to which we allude above are staggering and undoubtedly fueled resentment across the decades.

Second Stage (October 1930–January 1931): Launching the Soviets

Following Ngo Vinh Long's (1978, 17) enumeration, the rebellion entered a second stage from October 1930 until January 1931, with demonstrations diminishing in number and intensity. As Scott (1976, 127) explains, by the end of September 1930, the peasant rebels succeeded in taking over power in the most populated parts of Nghe An and neighboring districts in Ha Tinh, setting up autonomous village republics (or "soviets"), some of them holding on for up to nine months before being overcome. However, as Ngo Vinh Long (1978, 22–25) argues, the creation of soviets was not just a result of local Communist Party planning but also a result of the disintegration of colonial administrative structures. But in Saigon, where the Communist Party center was meeting, the creation of "red villages" in Nghe-Tinh came as a fait accompli and accordingly were deemed premature. Meeting again in October, the party (now under the name of the ICP) called for a national defense of the struggle, though it also sought to rein in excesses of both the Left and the Right. As discussed below, while the creation of "soviets" became a signature element of the Nghe-Tinh rebellions, it was a short-lived phase as well, alongside rallies, marches, demonstrations, land seizures, assassinations, and repressions.

Revolutionary activity during this phase, however, did not completely abate. Notably, on January 2, 1931, the *tri huyen* (subprefect) of Nghi Loc was assassinated by communist "bandits" who overwhelmed a government force, killed the party, and dumped the bodies in a river. Having arrested the perpetrators, an inquiry established that the majority of the population reproved the attack undertaken by the lowest class (*pègre*) of vagabonds and terrorists. In writing of this affair, the resident superior of Tonkin, René Robin, allowed that a "great communist movement" had washed over Vinh/Ha Tinh in the previous months but, owing to various measures taken, the administration was back in control of Vinh (AOM 3 SLOTFOM/42 "Rebellions dans le Nghe Tinh," Robin, Hanoi, Jan. 29, 1931). This, as with other colonial reporting on the rebellion, is obviously top down and totally ignores the effects of the tenth-month 1930 drought and harvest failure that drove the starving peasant population to the brink. In reality, agricultural conditions were worsening as there would be no relief from the drought, just as the upcoming fifth-month harvest would also fail.

Third Stage: Solidarity with Cochinchina (February–May 1931)

According to Ngo Vinh Long (1978, 17), a third stage lasted from February to May 1931 with demonstrations in the central provinces of Cochinchina staged in solidarity with the Nghe-Tinh rebels. Mainly conducted at nighttime, they did not bother the authorities, who kept their focus on Nghe-Tinh. Additionally, in March, the entire ICP central committee was seized in Saigon by the French police. From the beginning of March, famine conditions were also reported in the southern districts of Ha Tinh. The famine then hit Nghe An the hardest, with rice stocks depleted and people obliged to eat secondary or even forest foods. The spring crop in Ha Tinh was better, but the season also coincided with tax collection. French repression was unrelenting as well. Only in mid-July would the administration attempt to offer any kind of food relief such as "*soupe populaire*"; otherwise, it was a carrot-and-stick response by the colonial authorities.

Further, on April 12, 1931, four *garde indigène* posts in the Do Luong region of Nghe An, near Vinh, were confronted by demonstrators carrying red flags. In this unequal confrontation, as Robin laconically reported to Paris, standing down one thousand demonstrators, the Cho On detachment gunned down twenty-one; facing down two hundred rebels, the Nhao Bo post wounded one; pitted against five hundred rebels, the Yen Linh detachment killed three; while the Trile post squared off against two hundred rebels and shot nine dead. Meantime, in Ha Tinh Province, the authorities both confronted and dispersed groups of rebels numbering in the thousands. On April 14, a considerable number of rallies were reported at the Lai Tech and Lac Thien posts, some forty-five kilometers northeast of Vinh and with Lac Thien deemed the most "contaminated" zone. In the official version, a rifle detachment encountered "tenacious resistance" by organized bands maneuvering over several hours. Ostensibly to avoid encirclement, *tirailleurs* (rifle company men) led a bayonet charge leaving eighty rebels dead. In typical divide-and-rule tactics, as Robin remarked, "this affair allows us to remark upon the excellent attitude of the Tonkinese *tirailleurs*" (AOM 3 SLOTFOM/42 Robin, code tel, Hanoi à Colonies, April 18, 1931). On April 20, in the Phu Phong region of Ha Tinh, the Chu Lé post turned their arms on a crowd of 1,500 demonstrators, killing thirty and wounding thirty. In the affray, a *chef de poste* and a *linh* were lightly wounded (AOM 3 SLOTFOM/42 Robin, code tel, Hanoi à Colonies, April 22, 1931).

Rebels still not deterred, the occasion of May Day 1931 saw a major rekindling of rebellious activity, especially in Ha Tinh. No incidents were reported in Quang Ngai, and the situation was deemed improved in Vinh. Incidents took quite violent form in Ha Tinh with the May 3 assassination of a Catholic priest and his followers in a village northeast of Can Loc *huyen*. A spate of incidents saw massed groups in their hundreds, some numbering up to a thousand, confronting military or administrative posts and, characteristically, with the *garde indigène* answering with fire. On May 3–4 in the Catholic village, fifty were killed; on May 6 in the same *huyen*, ten were killed; on May 9 in the same region, there were twenty-five dead; on May 12 at the administrative center of Huong Khe, a mountainous area in southwest Ha Tinh, several dead; against a band of one thousand at the Thanh Son customs post (Cau Giet region), two dead; on May 9 in the region of My Nguc, a group of one hundred were dispersed by aerial actions. Continuing through the month, a series of selective assassinations of *chefs de village* and head watchmen were conducted by the rebels. On May 22, eight were killed following an antitax demonstration in the Phu Dien region, with a *bang te* (indigenous notable) decapitated in the *huyen* of Nghi Loc. On May 29, the authorities recorded the assassination of a mayor and the kidnapping and assassination of a French soldier, with his body dismembered (AOM 3 SLOTFOM/72 GG to Colonies, NP 1929, June 1, 1931).

Writing on May 12, 1931, as Governor General Pasquier explained, the rebellions were highly localized across three out of fifteen provinces of Annam and restricted to certain regions of the provinces. Propaganda launched on May Day included demands against taxation, the nationalization of industry, redress for the unemployed, and opposition to the dispatch of Vietnamese soldiers to unhealthful regions, along with diatribes against imperialist war and repression of local villages by Vietnamese troops. Key propaganda words included *imperialism*, *feudalism*, *bourgeoisie*, "*mandarinalism*," and *capitalism*, along with demands for the eight-hour working day, equal wages for men, women, and children, work equality, rice for the indigent, redistribution of rice lands, salary increase for the military, freedom of speech, freedom of movement, release of detainees, and the complete independence of Indochina. As Pasquier summarized of this heterogeneous list, "it shows that we are in the presence of a fantasizing crowd ready for any excess beyond good sense and reason" ("Rebellion dans le Nghe Tinh," op. cit., tél. Colonies, Hanoi, May 12, 1931). Obviously, then, there was a wide breach between official and peasant expectations.

The Politics of Assassination and the Denouement of August–September 1931

As Brocheux and Hémery (2009, 318–19) point out, already weakened in January–February 1931, the peasant movement took a turn to food riots with the confiscation of paddy from better-off peasants, the theft of rice between villages, and spiraling violence turning in on itself as the authorities launched their plan of "resistance and combat." Although solidarity actions by peasants and workers kicked off in Cochinchina, the movement in Annam never regained its dynamism and, by July, was defeated in northern Annam. Even so, sporadic outbursts of anger and violence in the countryside continued.

For example, on June 25, 1931, in the region west of Vinh, communist agitation was again detected. With demonstrators massing at the Du Loung and Thanh Chuong posts, at Myngoo, a rifle company patrol shot twenty dead. Throughout the month of June, a spate of assassinations of subprefectual and hamlet officials was reported across Vinh and Ha Tinh provinces. In one case (June 24), the victim was a journalist working for *France Indochine*, and in another case, the victim was a recalcitrant communist assassinated in Haiphong (AOM 3 SLOTFOM/42 tél., Saigon, Pasquier, July 9, 1931).

Peasant rallies also continued, as with actions on August 1, 1931, by a band of three hundred individuals in an isolated mountain region on the road connecting a village in Nghe An with Ha Tinh Province. However, no rallies were recorded at Thanh Chuong and Anh Son, places which had earlier served as the center of revolutionary activities. Continuing through August, however, a number of *bang ta* in Vinh and Ha Tinh Provinces fell victim to assassination, acts to avenge the arrests of comrades, according to the resident officer of Annam. But order was restored. This was also the case for Quang Ngai and Binh Dinh Provinces. Meantime, the Bong Son region in Binh Dinh, the center of revolutionary activity in July, also returned to calm. Overall, numerous arrests were effected in Nghe An, Ha Tinh, and Quang Ngai, including the arrest of one Coc Cach, deemed an important leader (AOM Indo NF/329/2650 RS, Annam, Bulletin Politique, August, Hue, Oct. 15, 1931).

In any case, the movement had ebbed by the summer of 1931, with the last soviet (Anh Son) forced to surrender in August (Luong 1986, 156) but not the domestic repression, which continued with some ferocity. Externally, the communist infrastructure linking with Vietnam would also be gravely weakened within the year. In April 1931, two months prior to the arrest of Nguyen Ai Quoc in Hong Kong, the entire ICP central committee in Saigon had been arrested as well as most members of regional committees, along with the capture of key Comintern personnel in Shanghai and Singapore. The colonial authorities could congratulate themselves on having made a *tabula rasa* of communist activities in Cambodia, whether from the Chinese or Vietnamese quarter. No distribution of pamphlets of revolutionary activities was recorded by the Sûreté between June 1931 and June 1932. As in other parts of Indochina, the Sûreté cultivated informers, established dossiers, and monitored anti-French activities in general.

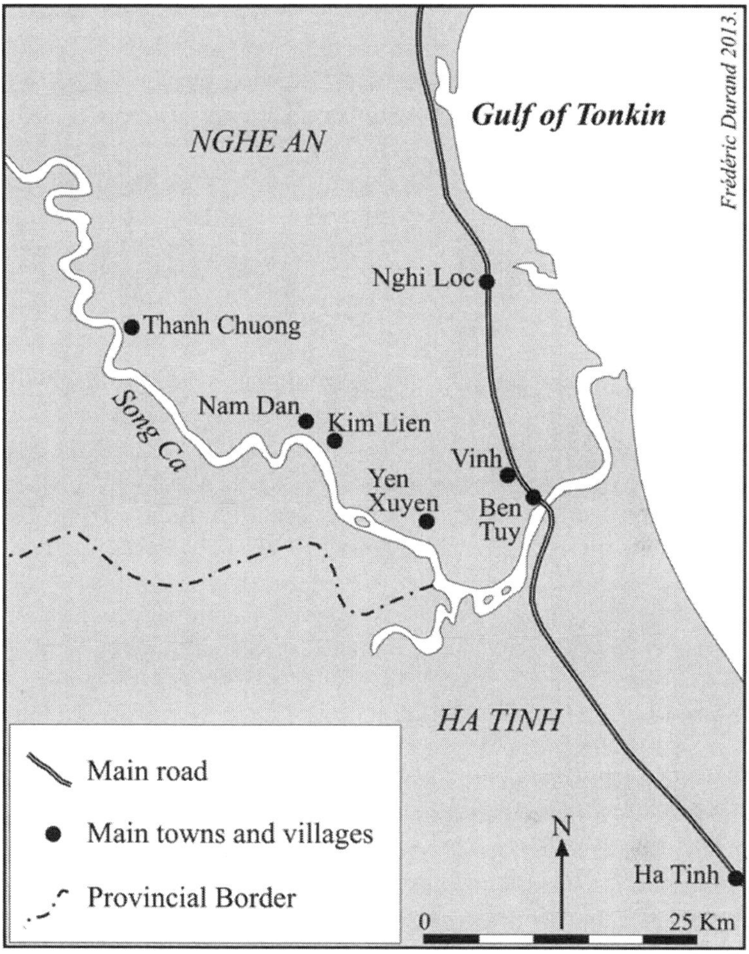

Locus of the Nghe-Tinh Rebellion, 1930–31

THE ECONOMIC CONTEXT OF THE REBELLIONS

Having surveyed the political context of the Nghe-Tinh uprising and the general narrative of their development, this section turns to the economic context, inter alia testing arguments alternatively suggesting a linkage between deteriorating economic conditions and agrarian unrest (Scott); or more agnostic (Brocheux); or dismissive claims (Luong) and also setting the scene for subsequent political actions.

In the event, most writers agree that the economic crisis of 1930–33 assumed an exceptionally grave character in Indochina. As viewed by

Vietnamese historian Ngủyen Khac Vien (1975, 69), the drop in world prices for Indochina's key exports of rice, rubber, and coal deeply affected the local economy. Exports fell from 228 million piasters in 1929 to 102 million in 1932, with a corresponding falling away in imports. The labor force employed in mines likewise fell away. Even lower French functionaries went through hard times. The segment of unemployed workers and employees hit one third. As this writer reflected, it might appear that the fall in rice exports would lead to a lessening of hunger in the countryside. Not at all, he asserted. In order to pay their taxes, the peasant-farmers had to sell three or four times more rice to raise money to pay their taxes. Before 1930, fifteen work days were necessary to get enough money to pay the head taxes; two to three months' work would not suffice during the crisis years. Alongside famine in northern Annam, food shortages appeared even in the richest provinces of Cochinchina, as with with Bac Lieu. The price of land dropped, with indebted farmers selling to big landowners. Land concentration increased. Likewise, currency circulation dropped significantly, 35 percent down on the 1920s (Nguyen Khac Vien 1975, 71–72). Footloose and desperate migrants, including scavengers from the troubled Nghe-Tinh region, also began crossing into Laos across difficult mountain passes and trails, some entering Cambodia as well, all in search of livelihoods (Gunn 1988, 44–45).

As Harrison (1989, 54) adds, in contrast to the south, where the problem was one of tenancy and landlordism, in Nghe-Tinh, overpopulation deprived the masses of land. Landholding in northern Annam was small (about 0.2 ha), but many peasants (up to 90 percent in some areas) had no land at all. Besides vulnerability to falling rice prices, natural and man-made disasters hit the region after 1929, with disastrous floods in 1930 followed by drought. Conditions were abysmal in both country and town in the early 1930s. Even the poor were taxed 20 to 35 percent of their meager incomes.

We may well ask what specific economic pressures were faced by the rebellious peasant farmers of Annam in 1930–31. As confirmed by a colonial report of late 1930, the rice harvest in Nghe-Tinh was bad, "almost all mediocre." Rice, it was reported, suffered from "meteorological irregularities" for the duration of the trimester. The drought of October had already impacted negatively on the preceding trimester. The harvest was particularly deficient in the northern part of the province as well as rice culture on *rays*. The harvest was acceptable only on the very low-lying rice fields situated proximate to sources of water for irrigation. But, the report continued, despite the bad harvest, the price of rice (in the marketplace) remained low because of imports by rail and sea (presumably arriving from Cochinchina).[1]

Falling Rice Price

More often than not, famines are foreshadowed by a rise in grain prices, forcing consumption downward to more market levels and obliging consumers to save, forgo, or starve (see Jordan 1996, 49). This, we will see, was the case with the Great Famine of 1944–45. But economic depressions, as with the Great Depression, are also accompanied by falling commodity prices as global markets slump. This was the pattern in Cochinchina, most closely linked with regional and global markets, although peasant farmers in Annam would also experience a less steep decline in prices. While, as mentioned, local famine did occur in the context of the Nghe-Tinh rebellions, it was not apparently the general condition; neither was it generalized. It would appear that distribution networks held up in all but the most isolated areas, just as the ability of the state to intervene in the market with imported supplies created a new safety equilibrium.

In Cochinchina, as studied by Brocheux (1995, 153–58), the depression lasted from 1931 to 1934, beginning to impact rice growers around May or June of 1931. As reflected by paddy prices on the Cholon market, prices fell from $7.15 per quintal in 1928, to $5.54 per quintal in 1930, to $3.79 per quintal in 1932, to $2.30 per quintal in 1933, and to $1.99 per quintal in 1934, the bottom, before beginning a slow recovery. In the western Mekong delta, the price of land also quickly fell. But the administration did not relent in its collection of taxes (poll tax, land tax, etc.). Meantime, the chetty, sometimes in alliance with Chinese wholesalers, put heavy pressure on rural debtors. The more callous landowners, also hard pressed, then placed pressure on the *ta dien* or "tenant farmers," thus breaking down the moral bonds linking landlord and tenant. For many, reversion to a subsistence economy was the only option, though rural banditry was another.

But is it correct to draw a direct causal link between the 1930–31 rebellions and the economic crisis? Luong (1986, 159–60), for one, has sought to deny the assumption of a strong correlation between agrarian unrest and a fall in the price of rice. Brocheux (1995, 152, 176) is actually agnostic on this count. While he allows that events leading up to the rebellion were definitely linked with the Great Depression, namely the fall of rubber prices in 1928 and mass bankruptcies on the part of Chinese rice traders in 1928–29, "the great wave of peasant unrest that erupted in 1930 does not appear to have been related to that economic crisis." He does allow, however, that the bond that connected the rice grower to the mill and finally the market and the weakening of the commercial link could cause a chain reaction. He also allows that four years of political unrest, including labor strikes and communist preparation following Phan Chau Trinh's death in 1926, preceded the 1930–31 events. Elsewhere, Brocheux and Hémery (2009, 318–19) point to the loss of two harvests (owing to the drought of the tenth month of 1930 and the drought of the fifth month of 1931), with famine breaking out in northern Annam in the early weeks of May as provoking the Communist Party to call for a "fight for rice" and turning the movement into a food riot. Even so, given the demonstrated role of the Communist Party, can we go as far as to acknowledge that in the countryside, the rebellion "obeyed a logic of its own" or, rather, that linked with the Communist Party and an obvious subsistence crisis, it obeyed a time-honored peasant logic of revolt?

Turning to Annam, as revealed in table 3.1, the price of rice at Vinh fell through October–November 1930 by 10–15 percent. The picture for nonrice crops was quite mixed. Actually, the maize harvest in December was deemed satisfactory, although potatoes—another standby—yielded a harvest of "little importance." Sericulture, coffee, and sticklac collection in the highlands all suffered because of the drought. Fruits were good (AOM Indo NF 104/999–1004 "Rapport Economique, Province de Nghe-An," 4th tri 1930). My data thus contradicts Luong (1986, 160), who asserts that in spring 1930 the price of rice in Nghe-Tinh actually rose by 15 percent, in part owing to inadequate supply. But, all in all, with rice arriving in Annam by rail and sea, and with maize as a backup, the food sufficiency problem appeared to be manageable, but only for those with money, a steeply diminishing category in a situation of accentuating social differentiation between haves and have-nots, elite and masses, landed and tenant farmers, owners and debtors. As mentioned, famine would also stalk parts of Nghe-Tinh.

But the picture was no better for the indigent peasant producers in the first trimester of 1931. Thanh Chuong, one of the rebel centers, may have been spared the drought in 1930 (Luong 1986, 161), but bad meteorological conditions continued in Annam in January. Because of the drought of October 1930, the rice fields had not been completely prepared, and rice transplanting was delayed with less planted than usual. Only after Tet, thanks to drizzling rain, transplanting work was accomplished in a number of rice fields. However, because of a recurrence of drought in March combined with weak returns stemming from delayed transplanting, the rice perished in the rice fields. Even though some rice fields with access to water fared better, only "weak production" was forecast. Meantime (to the obvious disadvantage of

Table 3.1. Price of Rice (in Piasters) at Vinh, October–December 1930

Quality of Rice	*October*	*November*	*December*
First grade	$13.80	$10.00	$9.50
Second grade	$12.50	$9.70	$8.50
Third grade	$11.00	$8.80	$8.00

Source: AOM Indo NF 104/999-1004 "Rapport Economique, Province de Nghe-An," 4th tri 1930.

Table 3.2. Price of Rice (in Piasters) at Vinh, January–March 1931

Quality of Rice	*January*	*February*	*March*
First grade	$11.00	$11.50	$9.10
Second grade	$9.50	$10.50	$8.50
Third grade	$9.50	$9.70	$8.50
Paddy	$6.50	$6.50	$6.00

Source: AOM Indo NF/334/2689 "Province de Nghe-An, Rapport Economique de premier," 4th tri, 1931.

local producers and sellers), the market price of paddy remained very low owing to the continual arrival of rice from Tonkin and Cochinchina. The stabilizing effect of rice imports in the Vinh market (at least for the monied classes) is revealed in table 3.2. As customary, rice witnessed a small price increase during Tet. But whereas Nghe An had produced a surplus of three thousand tonnes of paddy and rice in the previous year, in the year under review, thirteen thousand tonnes of rice had to be imported. Since March 1931, following the fall in the price of rice, and acting upon a mistaken assumption that the next harvest would be good, the peasant producers liquidated all their stock from the previous harvest, in turn further depressing the selling price of paddy.

While the market price for rice at Vinh suffered a 10 percent decline between January and March 1931, the statistics are also revealing of the macromanagement of the rice price through dumping imports into the marketplace (AOM Indo NF 104/999–1004 "Rapport Economique, Province de Nghe-An," 1st tri 1931). In fact, as discussed below, the percentage fall in the price of rice in the 1932–34 period was far more dramatic, even though the rebellion had largely run its course. Nevertheless, I cannot agree with Luong (1986, 160) in entirely refuting a link between agrarian unrest in Nghe-Tinh and a downward movement in the price of rice, although to be sure other factors were at play as well. Weather events, drought especially, may also have contributed more than Luong allows.

The Antitax Movement

In his study of the peasantry in southern Vietnam, Samuel Popkin (1979, 148–49, 170) sought to investigate how colonialism increased village stratification and therefore added to peasant discontent and even led villagers to overthrow the notables, reorganize their villages, and join revolutionary movements. As Popkin determined, colonialism added to the comparative political advantage of the notables. At the heart of his analysis is the colonial tax system, by 1901 already more deeply implanted than in other colonial regimes in Southeast Asia and, with the shift in paying taxes in kind to taxes in money, creating ripple effects across Indochina. Even in the backwater of Laos, tax and *corvée* demands notably triggered intergenerational *montagnard* or ethnic minority revolts (Gunn 1990). But in Annam, as Popkin explains, the immediate effects (of the switch to tax in money) was a glut of grain on the market and a dramatic fall in grain prices as desperate peasants sought the necessary cash. The grain glut may have been a boost for exporters and the better-off villagers who already had a cushion with which to pay the tax and who could use their reserves to profit from their cash-needy fellow villagers. However, the new tax system fell most heavily on subsistence-level peasants, who lacked cash reserves. Popkin allows other reasons for stratification in the countryside, namely seasonal vagaries, floods, locusts, and so on, but during the depression years peasants also had to face the vagaries of the international market. He also demonstrates that, in fact, there were no major discontinuities in village procedures for tax collection (although the French did introduce the tax card system) but that decisions on the way taxes were to be distributed and the choice of tax options were still made within the village and that no changes in the organization of the village government were made until 1942.

In 1934, the French detected a recrudescence of the movement to resist paying taxes. This information was confirmed on February 1 with the discovery of a communist cell in the troubled Thanh Chuong region. Following the arrest of several concerned individuals, it was learned that this movement had been stimulated by émigré activists arriving from Thailand (via Laos) seeking to link up with former political detainees and other comrades with a view to reestablishing the broken cells. Especially as the circulation of propaganda tracts was now outlawed, their actions were very discreet. As observed, peasants and workers were specifically targeted, activists broadly urging them to refuse to acquit their taxes. The intellectual milieu was ignored. The activists also offered specific advice on how to dissimulate in the face of tax collection operations, such as by pleading lack of money, by suggesting to acquit *en nature*, by temporizing, or by claiming to have already paid it to the notables (AOM NF/329/2650 Protectorate de Annam, BP, "Activité Révolutionnaires et Situation Politique," Feb. 1934).

Elements of the Crisis in Annam

Undoubtedly a variety of elements contributed to the crisis in Annam, not all of them strictly economic. As described, in succession, these elements included Annam's isolated and compartmentalized geography, the technical lack of monetization in the countryside, the rice procurement system, the land system, tenancy, the role of notables, and the tax burden, with special attention to the alcohol monopoly.

The complexity of the situation is brought into relief in a report by Resident Superior Léon Thibaudeau, looking back at the 1932–34 period and reflecting on the impact of the world economic recession on the local economy. Alongside Cochinchina and Tonkin, Thibaudeau described Annam as a virtual "closed economy." By this he meant that Annam stood out for its weak exports of rice in particular in a situation where production almost equaled consumption, otherwise just about precluding any exports and therefore external trade. Geography was also important, as described below. Otherwise, commodity prices were higher in Annam than in Tonkin or Cochinchina. Favorable conditions for rice cultivation were at an end. As local rice lost its premium, (cheaper) Cochinchina rice was sought out. Not only rice but other products were subject to depreciation and difficulties. Annam, Thibaudeau argued, fitted the status of other producer countries facing down the global economic crisis (AOM Indo/NF/ 2664 "Compte-Rendu de la gestion du RS Thibaudeau," July 1934).

It is certainly important to acknowledge, as Thibaudeau pointed out, that Annam is a long and narrow band of territory (wedged between the sea and the mountains) extending 1,500 kilometers from north to south and therefore supporting a range of climates and productions. Accordingly, Annam was not a homogenous economic unit but, according to region, was divided into veritable *casiers* (units), each of them hosting numerous centers of imports and exports. In normal times, he pointed out, Annam was known as a producer of a wide range of commodities, including cinnamon, coffee, tea, vegetable oils, fibers, corn, tobacco, domestic animals, forestry products, albumin, dried fish, *nuoc mam*, cotton, and silk (AOM Indo/NF/ 2664 "Compte-Rendu de la gestion du RS Thibaudeau," July 1934).

With specific reference to local rice cultivators and market transactions, Thibaudeau continued, they preferred to stockpile their rice rather than to sell for a price deemed insufficient. To him, this suggested such an aggravation of the crisis in Annam that it produced an abnormal effect, all things being equal, even exceeding that of other countries also facing down the world economic crisis. A number of consequences stemmed from this condition. First, a diminution of exports. Second, difficulty in reimbursing consensual loans to banks and agricultural credit organizations. Third, a great difficulty in collecting taxes. Fourth, subversion of the *régie* by illicit manufacture of rice wine. Fifth, the collapse in value of nonlegal money in circulation, a reference to the particular coinage used in lieu of legal money in short supply (AOM Indo/NF/ 2664 "Compte-Rendu de la gestion du RS Thibaudeau," July 1934).

Monetization

Allowing that a rigorous analysis of social differentiation in colonial Annam would necessarily examine a range of variables, one test must be the ability of the peasant producers to pay taxes in cash as required by the colonial state. Such also relates to the degree of monetization attained under colonial capitalism as much as to the ability of the taxpayers to acquit their obligations in cash as opposed to kind, or payment in paddy. Obviously, without the wherewithal to acquit tax, the peasant producer-taxpayer would come under severe strain, especially as other claims on scarce income pinched at the means of livelihood.

According to an official memorandum of 1934, at various times the administration had drawn attention to the difficulty of rural dwellers in acquitting their fiscal payments to the administration owing to the shortage of cash. The money universally used in the countryside was the *sapeque*, albeit long superseded by a silver standard coinage. First issued between 1879 and 1905, the *sapeque* was a traditional-style copper coin embossed with Chinese characters on one side and Latin script on the other, with a characteristic square hole in the middle. From 1905, Tonkin also struck *sapeque* coins in zinc. Unfortunately for these desperate taxpayers, the *sapeque* was not publicly accepted by the government cashier. It meant that to acquit their taxes the people had to change their *sapeque* at the time of tax collection and, in the transaction, suffered an abnormal elevation in the rate of exchange. (Presumably, money changers imposed themselves on the population at this time of the year.) The conversion translated into a supplementary charge imposed on the taxpayer, and many complaints were received on this subject. To remedy this matter, as one official suggested, it would appear efficacious, although arbitrary, to regulate the exchange rate for the *sapeque*. This measure would allow the taxpayers the possibility of changing the *sapeque* at a fixed rate (AOM NF/329/2650 "Activité Révolutionnaires et Situation Politique," BP, Feb. 1934).

It was only in late 1940 that the administration really moved on the *sapeque* question. In part, this owed to a complaint voiced by the *Tuan vu* (mandarin) of Quang Binh to the authorities in Hue that scarcely any metallic coins, *sapeque* included, were in circulation in the province, just as speculation on existing coins increased. As he explained, not a "sous" remained for small merchants to transact business, to the great inconvenience of the population. As pointed out, paper money was disfavored as it was difficult to preserve over time. Rather, the peasants preferred to save their money in *sapeques*, even though this currency had no legal tender. The administrative solution was seen as striking new metallic coins of, respectively, a one-cent, a half-cent, and a quarter-cent denomination. But banning the *sapeque* was viewed as a "delicate situation," and it remained to be seen whether or not the new coins would gain real currency and acceptance (AOM Indo NF 127/1143 "Conseil des Ministres (Annam)," Dec. 7, 1940).

Rice Procurement

We also wonder about the rice procurement in Nghe-Tinh, especially as it affected peasant livelihoods. Who controlled rice procurement and distribution? How did the markets work? Who were the buyers? What reciprocal relationships existed? And what were the key distribution links connecting Nghe-Tinh with other rice importing–rice exporting provinces? According to a colonial report of ca.1931–32, rice export commerce was practically nonexistent in Nghe An in 1931. On the contrary, rice imports were more active in late 1930 and early 1931. Nevertheless, a certain export activity by coffee plantations continued on the northern fringes of the province in very productive regions toward Phu Quy. Some exports (of rice) were made in the sixth and eleventh months after taxes were collected or in the run-up to Tet. However, richer peasants who had the luxury of waiting held onto their paddy stocks until the second or third month, when the prices were better. In bad years—the majority of years—rice was sourced from Thanh Hoa, occasionally from Cochinchina, and especially from Tonkin. Upon harvest in the fifth, eighth, and tenth months, rice was valued between $0.13 and $4.40 per quintal (or one hundred kilograms), with the price of rice rising in the second, third, and seventh months to $5.50, $6.00, or even $7.00 per quintal. The usual method of procurement of paddy was by direct purchase effected by a vendor who bought by the kilogram. Typically, the peasant-farmer brought the paddy rice to the market, where he directly engaged the buyers and agents of the big Chinese and Vietnamese merchants. The latter would remit fifteen to twenty piasters to their clients, who pledged to redeem this sum in paddy. The same practice held at Thanh Hoa, where the vendor also bought paddy by *prêt sur recolte* (commodity loan). The loan was tendered only by Vietnamese (agents), along with one Chinese merchant from Phu Dien. Fifteen days before the transplanting, the peasant received the loan advanced for the paddy and, following the harvest, was obliged to reimburse with paddy exclusively. The Phu Dien market was located four kilometers from the railway station of the same name. It received less than half the harvest from Dien Chau and more than half the harvest from Yen Thanh, a partly mountainous zone. The rice was exported to Vinh, mainly in the form of paddy. The rice from Yen Thanh was descended downriver by junks of thirty to forty tonnes capacity to Phu Dien. The Cao Si market received a small quantity of rice from Yen Thanh and much more for Dien Chau, exclusively in the form of paddy. Rice flowed toward Vinh and Phu Cui by way of Yen Ly station, while Cao Gia market exported (half rice–half paddy) to Quynh Luu. Yen Ly market was only a transit market for rice coming from Phu Cui. Po Luoy market was also a transit market for rice coming from Phu Dien station. By far the most important market, however, was Vinh/Ben Thuy (both seaports), from where rice sourced from Nghe An and Ha Tinh was exported and from where rice destined for the two provinces was also imported, whether by rail link or by way of the Ca River (Castagnol 1930, 10).

Fall in the Price of Rice (1932–34)

According to Scott (1976, 120), the link between the price of rice and expressions of peasant resistance was strikingly illustrated in April–May 1930 when the price of rice (paddy) began to plunge and an unexpected rash of protests and violence occurred in Cochinchina and Annam. Continuing through July 1931, demonstrations, tax protests, and seizures of rice occurred throughout Cochinchina at Long Xuyen, Can Tho, Dadec, My Tho, and other centers. As we have seen, events in Nghe An and Ha Tinh differed to the degree that beginning in September 1930, the rebels seized power and installed village republics or soviets.

The general economic condition in Annam is also reflected in statistics tracking the percentage fall in the price of rice between 1932 and 1934. Price fluctuation varied across regions but also fell into a pattern. In Vinh, in 1932–33, rice fell by 30.26 percent (paddy, 33.07); in Hue (rice, 29.06; paddy, 35.23); and in Quin Ham (rice, 36.32; paddy, 29.32). In 1934, the percentage fall in the price of paddy was particularly noted in Thanh Hoa, Vinh, Ha Tinh, Hue, and Binh Dinh. As Thibaudeau recorded, "Le mal est a peu près sans remède" (The evil is practically without remedy). The fate of the cultivators in Annam appeared highly constricted alongside those of other regions of Indochina (AOM Indo/NF/ 2664 "Compte-Rendu de la gestion du RS Thibaudeau," July 1934).

The Anti–Alcohol Monopoly Movement

Under the colonial regime, alcohol, like salt and opium, was constituted as a government monopoly (*régie*). Strictly regulated with sanctions against infractions, the alcohol *régie* was also widely resented by the rice farmers. After Scott (1976, 110–12), the wide-scale defiance of the alcohol monopoly in colonial Vietnam should be viewed in its historical and social context. However, defiance on the part of the population also took on the form of a canny survival or coping strategy for indigent rice farmers caught up in the "scissors" of falling rice procurement prices and rising poverty. The colonial dilemma, or the travails of the "state as claimant" in Scott's language, and the needs of ordinary people staring down famine is starkly illustrated by the peasant recourse to an illegal or parallel economy around bootleg rice wine, subversive of state revenues but offering a narrow opening for cash-starved producers.

Details of the tax evasion were spelled out by the resident in an official report, deploring the fact that, compared to Tonkin, the population of Annam did not in general contribute to the alcohol regime. Rather, they sold their rice to local organizations for the production and refining of local rice wine, notwithstanding the dangers implied in the use of distilled alcohol for private use. Obviously, such subversion of the *régie* led to a diminution of returns to the state. To the contrary, it imposed a burden on the state to repress the contraband trade in illicit alcohol, not to mention the burden on the court system and the penitentiaries, especially involving an increasing number of violators. In attempting to turn the situation around, special measures were implemented, including the hosting of a conference at the end of 1933 involving the administration and local authorities, including the notables (Scott 1976, 10–12).

Even allowing for the use of rice wine in religious and social ceremonies such as backgrounded by Scott, we doubt that the shift from rice sales for export to rice for illicit alcohol production was just a protest against the iniquitous *régie*, nor was it a case of peasant cultivators drinking away their sorrows with home brew. Far from it, as the consumers of the home brew were undoubtedly from the more monied classes. Reading between the lines and taking into account the dramatic fall in the local market price of paddy and milled rice in this period and the recourse to stockpiling (a risk in itself owing to wastage to rodents, etc.), selling rice to local alcohol distillers was not only a risk-averse strategy on the part of the indigent peasant rice cultivator in the face of the vagaries of the international marketplace but a clever gambit that realized instant and usable cash in a dire situation (albeit illegal and running the risk of incarceration in a colonial prison). But for the authorities as much as the actors, it was also an act of protest fitting the tumultuous times, even if spontaneous and outside any kind of communist agitation, but we cannot be sure of that as well.

Taking stock of circumstances and conditions, these were desperate actions by a desperate and starving people. As Scott (1976, 137) observes, the dominating fact of the famine was, for many observers, the "key to the revolt." All the "outriders" of famine were there, as with an "evolutionary retreat" back through the stages of production to scavenging, resorting to slash and burn, and retreating to the forest to collect edible wild roots. Although the detailed documentation on famine mortality is lacking, alongside hunger, malnutrition, and the occurrence of famine in at least five of Nghe An's districts, unlike the events that would unfold in the crowded northern delta some fifteen years later, this was not cataclysmic famine on a mass scale, possibly because of the agency of the victims in seeking relief. Yet it is also true, as Scott says (1976, 191–92), that the hunger experienced by the Nghe-Tinh peasants translated into a collective "rage," especially as the elites had failed them. In Nghe-Tinh, that included the colonial state, which had so gravely compromised its "hydraulic bargain" with the rural-dwelling peasantry, such as described in chapter 1, and through the unrelenting imposition of imposts and other burdens at a time of natural adversity in the form of drought and unfavorable conditions.

OFFICIAL RESPONSES TO THE REBELLION

Repression preceded inquiry into the rebellions, but metropolitan French opinion also demanded an investigation into these alarming events. Meeting in Hue in July 1931, the French authorities launched a wide-sweeping investigation of the damaging Nghe-Tinh rebellions. Not only did they interrogate prisoners swept up in the repression, but they also sought answers from the notables and other local mandarin officials. This was dubbed the French Commission of Inquiry. In fact, as certain of the interrogations reveal, the French were looking only for answers that fitted French colonial logic, totally ignoring the iniquities of the tax system and other burdens imposed on the mass of cultivators that obviously provoked the discontent, whether or not exploited by outside agitators.

The French Commission of Inquiry (July 1931)

As archival sources reveal, the official commission of inquiry collected a large number of depositions or, basically, confessions from suspects, certain of which I have chosen to replay here as representative. Although the commission was dismissed by critics as a "whitewash," the individual depositions do offer rare insights into local mentalities.

Taking the declaration of one peasant-cultivator, a soldier returnee from France, Bui Hat, as emblematic, the judicial official asked, "Why did you join the communist party?" To which Bui answered, "It took me by surprise. It happened that I was forced to join the communist party." "What is communism?," he was asked, to which he replied, "I deny having been a communist. I spent several years in the military infirmary. I spent three years at Fréjus after the war" (AOM Indo NF/334/2689 "Commission d'enquête sur les evénéments du Nord Annam," July 9, 1931).[2]

Tran Van Lien, a peasant cultivator from the *huyen* of Hing Khe, was asked, "Why did you join the communists?" to which he replied, "I was forced to join." "What is communism,?" he was asked, and he replied, "I don't know."

Bui Han, a peasant-farmer from Phu Viet in Ha Tinh, was asked, "Why are you a communist?" to which he answered, "At first I was a nationalist because I am rich but in the 10th month of last year I became a communist." "Why?" he was asked, to which he replied, "Because all the people in my village being communists, I did not wish to be isolated." "What is communism?" he was then asked, and he replied, "I don't know, my affiliation is very recent." "What were you told to entice you to join the communists?" he was asked, to which he replied, "That the nationalists, being isolated, would draw a blank while the communists were bound with the assistance of Russia to chase the French out of Annam and restore the dynasty."

Bui Dieu, a peasant-farmer from Nghi Xuan, was asked, "Were you a communist?" to which he replied, "I was forced to join the communists. I carried a flag in the demonstration." Questioned as to the goal of the demonstration, he replied, "To destroy the *huyen*." "Why would you want to destroy the *huyen*?" he was asked. "I don't know," he replied, "I was told to go to the *huyen*, I obeyed." "What is communism?" "I don't know anything. They haven't explained. They just told me to obey orders."

Changing tack, the declaration of retired mandarin Le Van Luyen was also considered. He was asked: "To what causes do you attribute the revolutionary movement?" to which he replied, "To communist doctrines which over the past seven or eight years have been propagated in the country by émigrés arriving from Russia." "How come neither the notables nor the administration knew about these activities?" he was asked. "The communists know how to hide and escape the vigilance of the authorities," he replied. Asked about the motives for discontent, he replied, "The population complains of taxes on salt, alcohol, forestry taxes, franchise taxes, and abuses by the mandarins and the notables." "Do they know what is communism?" he was asked. He replied, "The goal of communism is the expulsion of the French. Peace can hardly be re-established in the provinces."

Nguyen Van Tinh, another retired mandarin, was asked, "What are the causes of the revolutionary movement at the present?" to which he answered at length:

> The principal cause of the trouble is the propaganda made by such émigrés as Phan Boi Chau, Phan Chu Trinh, Nguyen Ai Quoc, Ngo Duc Tri among others, whether settled in Japan or Siam, China or Russia. All of these people are natives of Nghe An and Ha Tinh. They are all graduates of the schools without any special situation or future, including even students from exclusive colleges. These young men have powerful impact upon the population bringing both social promise and communism, imposing their own brand of authority and terror. The spread of revolutionary propaganda has been favored by the present teaching regime and by the deplorable economic situation of the province. Education reform has been marked by the abandonment of the study of Chinese characters. This measure has involved forgetting traditional morals. The people no longer respect the king of Annam and, with stronger reason, the French protectorate. On the other hand, the limited number of vacancies does not permit the administration to create a situation to [employ] all graduates leaving school. Those not

> finding [work] are embittered and are ripe for revolutionary ideas. The soil is poor, the villages have few communal goods. The poor people are at the mercy of the big landowners who exploit them without pity. The food shortage adds to the misery of the masses.

Asked as to what remedies to recommend, he replied, "The recourse to armed force to reestablish order, the creation of new *garde indigène* posts to maintain order in the countryside, a return to the study of Chinese characters and, finally the maintenance of the French protectorate and the Annam monarchy" (AOM Indo NF/334/2689 "Commission d'enquête sur les evénéments du Nord Annam," July 9, 1931).

From the neotraditionalist utterances of the mandarins to the in-your-face declarations of the peasant rebels, the French were goaded into action. While repression was uppermost, a sheet of reforms was also on the agenda in Annam. Specific measures taken following the 1930 May Day events included reviews of the roles of mandarins, judicial reorganization, reform of the criminal commission, review of French personnel, new efforts to master local languages, reduction in the number of officials, promotion of locals in administrative circles reserved for the French, new disciplinary measures, clemency for young students, and new empowerment for the governor general relating to press and expulsions, along with a number of economic reforms, including new work legislation and social assistance plus educational reforms (AOM Indo NF/334/2689, "Note, 1 Mai incidents nord Annam").

Red Terror/White Terror in Rural Annam

The events in Annam were also the object of a lengthy study by André Louis Marty, French director of political affairs in Hanoi and former police commissioner in Vinh from May 1930 to May 1931. As Marty wrote in his evocatively titled *La Terreur Rouge en Annam, 1930–1931* (1933), some speak of "White Terror," but such an accusation is Bolshevik propaganda. As Marty explained, leaders of the communist movement succeeded in creating peasant collectivities (soviets) and in attacking administrative posts. Using Bolshevik methods, they transformed peaceful crowds into veritable *jacqueries*, or open rebellions against local authority. Excited by alcohol and chanting slogans, they launched themselves against police and military. Self-defense groups armed themselves with bamboo staves of three to four meters in length, albeit no match for police bayonets (and bullets). This is true, although French police and judicial practices then included the capricious use of torture, forced confessions, imprisonment, deportation, assassinations, and so on, not to mention the guillotine (see Zinoman 2001), just as both the communists and the French would trade propaganda insults as to which side was perpetrating the violence.

What are the facts? Marty assembled scores of *procès-verbal* (statements) and signed depositions. He admits to being selective, and we do not know whether he deliberately chose the worst cases in order to underscore the terror dimension, as opposed to other undercurrents of peasant dissatisfaction, namely hunger, dislike of the French, antitax sentiment, or whatever. But a pattern does emerge across these scores of depositions. The perpetrators were all male, all rural dwellers, and mostly peasants. The scene of the conflict was also rural, just as actions were more than often local, perhaps with certain of the victims known. Some of the perpetrators were in their forties, with the youngest aged just seventeen. All admitted to being members or recent adherents of the Communist Party, although some claimed to be members of syndicates. All appeared to be following orders and were not the leaders of the movement. Many had already adopted aliases. Another pattern is the degree of violence used (Zinoman 2001).

Generally, what emerges from this dossier and what obviously concerned mandarin as much as French authorities was that the Communist Party had set up and socialized its raison d'être among a very large cohort of individuals as a third moral force, with life-and-death power over enemies, however construed. Nationalism was not ostensibly an issue, at least not grasped, although resistance to paying tax would emerge as a theme. Rather, the cases add up to a picture of class struggle or warfare, with the mandarins and notables as the most proximate targets and with the French as the ultimate enforcer of colonial law and order (Zinoman 2001).

Colonial Repression

Known as the "White Terror" in communist history, some 10,000 Vietnamese died in the repression that included land and air attacks, 100,000 were jailed, and 50,000 were exiled. Communists and VNQDD members alike faced the guillotine. In 1932, an estimated 10,000 political prisoners still languished in French jails in Indochina or outside. According to Pike (1978, 21), a figure with little sympathy for French or American antagonists in Vietnam, the noncommunist nationalist movement suffered disproportionate losses, even compared to the communists, and would never again recoup its strength. By mid-1932, the party would be at low ebb, apparently moribund but lying low, having learned the lessons of premature action but alert at the same time to the uses of revolutionary violence.

Writing in 1933, Governor General Pierre Pasquier advised the French ministry of colonies that the events of 1930–31 were defeated only by mass arrests. He doubted whether preventive repression would be possible owing to negative sentiment in France, the role of the media, and reactions of the Indochinese. Given these restraints, he petitioned the minister of colonies to offer the kind of legislation necessary to prevent a recurrence of such outrages against public order, namely by outlawing the activities of the Third International in Indochina, proscribing membership in communist organizations, and dissociating the Moscow School returnees from illegal associations. Even so, as the minister replied to Pasquier, "I am in agreement with your goals, but I differ somewhat as to your opinion as to means." The minister was likewise concerned at external sensitivities and instructed Pasquier to make the best use of existing legislation, including the power to deport foreign agitators and, moreover, to uphold the humanitarian ideals befitting France and its legitimacy (AOM Indo NF 55/594–640 "Notes Situation Politique de l'Indochine," Pasquier, March 22, 1933). Undoubtedly, this rejoinder was a blow to Pasquier, who was demonstrably more inclined to repression than to the niceties of humanitarianism.

For good reason, the years 1932–35 are described in Vietnamese communist histories as a "low ebb," just as attempts made to resurrect the party were interrupted by the colonial authorities. In any case, as discussed below, new direction would be given to the communist underground with the return to Vietnam from Moscow by the future ICP supremo in the south, Tran Van Giau. The energetic repression of 1931–32 that had disorganized the communist political movement also left it bereft of local leadership. Between July 1931 and March 1933, 6,661 conditional releases were effected, with 665 reductions in sentences. But the revolutionary movement again showed signs of renewal. For example, in Vinh Province on March 29, 1934, individuals recently arrived from China sought to reorganize cells and to organize the revolutionary party. Certain agricultural societies were set up in the province with newly liberated prisoners participating in these activities. For the first time it was acknowledged that the revolutionary movement had turned to theatrical performances to get across its message. Its tactics had changed as well, targeting the notables and committing acts of vandalism against religious places and pagodas. In Ha Tinh, one Phan Can had "terrorized" the entire region and in April 1933 established an agricultural society, gaining attention all over the province. In Quang Ngai, worker and peasant syndicates had been operational for over a year, discouraging the notables, who also became objects of attack (AOM Indo/NF/ 2664 "Compte-Rendu de la gestion du RS Thibaudeau," July 1934).

THE BAO DAI/NGO DINH DIEM CHALLENGE

From the outset, the French achieved their protectorate over Annam by *force majeure*. The establishment of the resident system backed by French military power sat uncomfortably with an ancient dynastic system modeled along the lines of the Ming court of China. Undoubtedly, the French modernized a creaking Asian feudal system, but they also alienated the court, such as evinced by the "save the king" movement. In their manipulation of the royal line along with the mandarinate in favor of pliant clientele, the French walked a tightrope. Bao Dai was only the last of a line of carefully vetted monarchs installed by the French, though far less tractable than certain of his predecessors. Privileging Catholics within the mandarin system (the Diem family, as mentioned below) was only one of many shocks to traditionalism, but the sacrifice of court protocol and even Chinese language (in its written form) were no less body blows, just as the French invented their own version of a neotraditionalist court.

As Luong (1986, 165) confirms, it was true that most of the ICP leadership of the period originated from Nghe-Tinh, as with Ho Chi Minh, Le Hong Son, and Tran Phu, and they also came primarily from the local Confucian elite. For them, Luong contends, violation of local "normative conceptions" by the colonial state, such as manipulation of traditional hierarchies and so on, was the last straw. This is an important observation and fits his understanding of a "cognitive crisis" besetting many members of the elite while also transforming (certain of) them into anticolonial revolutionary leaders. While Emperor Bao Dai hardly fits this pattern, can it be said that he also experienced a shift in attitude toward the colonial state? And what of such lesser mandarins and men of destiny as Ngo Dinh Diem?

Just prior to his return to Vietnam in 1939 after an extended stay in France, Emperor Bao Dai composed a letter bearing his elaborate royal chop or seal to Minister of Colonies Georges Mandel, pledging his loyalty to France in difficult times but also candid in seeking to strengthen the role of the court within the French protectorate system—"to galvanize the energy of [his] subjects to place them entirely in the service of France," as he expressed the matter. There was much irony in this pledge given the way events turned out, but the mere suggestion of the potential disloyalty of his subjects was also a lever to gain concessions from France. As the letter alluded, Bao Dai had already taken part in a number of inconclusive discussions with Mandel as to future administrative reforms in Annam and, pointedly, Tonkin, although he also claimed that time prevented him from elaborating on the actual modalities. The basis of discussions to which Bao Dai constantly referred was the Treaty of Protectorate of 1884. First, he sought an expanded local representation in the National Assembly. He also sought to place a senior mandarin alongside the resident superior who would serve as a direct collaborator in charge of local administration. He was not about to restore the title of *kinh luoc* but sought a rank commensurate with inspector or controller of the mandarin administration. The authority of the resident superior would remain intact, but liaison with the court and the Vietnamese mandarins would be smoother. On the other hand, the Privy Council in Tonkin, created by his own ordinance of October 24, 1933, was too limited to bring any efficacious collaboration with the resident superior. He wished this council to be enlarged with an extended mandate. Presided over by the resident superior as with the Council of Ministers in Hue, the Privy Council, he recommended, should host the proposed inspector general of the mandarin administration as its vice president. A third measure concerned the court budget, which in fact was annexed to the Annam budget. He wished that this budget be given a different form. Fourth, he observed, although coming under the disposition of protectorates, neither Annam nor Tonkin was represented at the Council Supérieur des Colonies. A permanent representative of the court to the Ministry of Colonies would ease communication and help solve problems relating to both Annam and Tonkin. Usefully, this individual could also represent the diverse Vietnamese communities residing in France, including workers, students, and soldiers (AOM Indo NF/1197 Bao Dai à Georges Mandel, Ministre des Colonies, Paris, Aug. 27, 1939).

The following month, duly installed in Hue, Bao Dai pursued his reform agenda with incoming Governor General Georges Catroux in polite but far more direct language. In this missive, signed but embossed with the dragon seal of the court, Bao Dai directly questioned the validity of French control over Tonkin, noting that this part of the empire of Annam had virtually escaped his authority. The resident superior in Tonkin, he continued, was both *chef de protectorate* and Bao Dai's representative in Tonkin. This double quality, he asserted, had created an equivocal situation that was not without serious inconveniences. Taking aim at the incumbent resident superior, he also asserted that this individual had taken sides with certain local opinion in a way that was prejudicial to the prestige of the court. As alluded, the minister of colonies was well aware of these facts. To remedy this situation, Bao Dai asserted, certain institutional changes would be necessary, even within the framework of existing institutions. First, the Privy Council, which performed but a "derisory role," should be reorganized to admit greater indigenous participation. As noted, only the most insignificant matters even appeared on its agenda. Not even the question of personal tax was entertained by this council. He repeated his wish to appoint a high mandarin alongside the resident superior to improve liaison between the court and Tonkin. This measure, he suggested, would put an end to "the equivocation that allows the Resident Superior to be both the representative of France and the representative of the Emperor in Tonkin." Bao Dai sought discussion on this overriding issue at the highest level, naming such distinguished French colonial administrators as Desalle, Marty, and Grandjon, alongside his own choice of "moral representative" in Tonkin representing the view of the mandarinate and the court, Hoing-Trong-Phu (AOM Indo NF/1197 Bao Dai, à Catroux, Sept. 13, 1939).

As reported in early 1940, news spread with persistence in northern Vietnam that the administration envisaged the reattachment of Tonkin to Annam. The resident superior of Tonkin was obliged to publish a communiqué designed to quash these rumors. On May 12, the editors of *L'Effort*, *L'Annam Nouveau*, *Tien Tuyet-Thu-Man*, *Demain*, and *Dong Phap* all protested the rumored measure, deemed a "veritable political and social regression." A unanimous motion was adopted to request the government to renounce all decisions relating to the extension of powers of the court of Hue and requesting the French president to grant the Vietnamese people a clearly defined liberal political statute (AOM Indo NF/330 2664–2667 Catroux, à Colonies, Feb. 3, 1940). Although not mentioned in this list of newspapers, back in the Popular Front days, the communist press in Tonkin regularly lambasted the feudal regime in Annam.

Ngo Dinh Diem Confronts the French

At this juncture, local Annam court official and future South Vietnam strongman Ngo Dinh Diem (1901–63) also showed his hand prior to dismissal from service, marking him out as a maverick for his anti-French posturings. According to an official version, Diem, then serving as minister of interior, had first come under investigation in July 1933. Identified as the younger brother of the *tong doc* of Quang Nam, Ngo Dinh Khai, in turn the son-in-law of the former Prime Minister Nguyen Huu Bai, Diem had advanced rapidly in a mandarin career. His ability and honesty was noted but, as the beneficiary of a deeply impressionable Catholic religious education, he was also marked down as having a "tendency towards mysticism." Early on, Diem was convinced by Ngo Dinh Khai and, especially, his father-in-law, Nguyen Huu Bai, as well as his other brother, Abbé Ngo Dinh Thuc, along with certain other ministers to protest the application of the Treaty of 1884 (AOM Indo/NF/2664 "Compte-Rendu de la gestion du RS Thibaudeau," July 1934).

Vexed that his brother had been passed over as minister, Diem began to distance himself from close collaboration, leading him to pen a letter of resignation on June 12, 1933. Addressed to the resident superior and to Emperor Bao Dai, his resignation was rejected, obliging him to withdraw it. Upon an intervention of the resident superior, he was advised to avoid all political activities. But, on July 17, Bao Dai issued a *du* (proclamation) accepting Diem's resignation. Meantime, further sanctions were imposed on Diem as well as on fellow "conspirators," namely, Nguyen De, Bao Dai's secretary, along with Nguyen Thanh Hung, former *bang ta*, entrepreneur, and member of the Chamber of the Representatives of the People (AOM Indo/NF/2664 "Compte-Rendu de la gestion du RS Thibaudeau," July 1934). At the same time, the Saigon press, as with *La Dépêche*, and André Malraux's *Tribune*

Indochinoise, made great play of events in Annam, including an upcoming election for the chamber, with the latter newspaper even suggesting that Hue was on the point of internal revolt. Allegedly, the Diem group sought to make common cause with the communists on tax issues to advance their goals. As the official report recorded, propaganda in favor of a tax strike was not the first attempt at collusion between the communists and the Diem/Nguyen De Party (AOM Indo/NF/ 2664 "Compte-Rendu de la gestion du RS Thibaudeau," July 1934).

Notably, in February 1934, a delegation of the Secours Rouge International (International Red Aid) arrived in Indochina. An international social service organization established by the Comintern in 1922, this was led by French communist deputy Gabriel Pèri (1902–41). Pèri's intention was to second the intentions of the PCF in discrediting the official inquiry into the 1931–32 rebellion and its suppression. The Diem group calculated that Annam would under no circumstances prevent the entry of a commission led by a French deputy and, accordingly, prepared a reception along with a specially prepared dossier to be distributed to communist newspapers in metropolitan France. However, under a decree of February 13, 1934, the Secours Rouge commission was forbidden to enter Annam. An attempt to use the Diem-inspired dossier by local newspapers was made, but had only limited effect (AOM Indo/NF/ 2664 "Compte-Rendu de la gestion du RS Thibaudeau," July 1934). Gravely compromised, as Jacobs (2006, 30) recounts, the French stripped Diem of decorations and kept him under surveillance and even threatened him with arrest. Diem then withdrew to his family house in Hue, biding his time, although making occasional contact with Phan Boi Chau in Saigon or by letter with Prince Cuong De in Japan. Though banned from government service, he was not indicted for any crime. Though sidelined by the colonial regime, Diem would resurface in the wake of the Japanese military occupation of Indochina and again following the Viet Minh takeover in Hanoi.

CONCLUSION

Without question, the signature event of the Nghe-Tinh rebellions was the act of locking out of mandarin and colonial authority in a number of rural locales by mass peasant actions and the creation through August–September 1930 of agricultural communes or soviets along the communist model. All sources agree that the astonishing culmination of the rebellion was the creation of soviets or village republics, certain of them managing to hold on for up to nine months before being overcome (Vietnam 1978, 19). It is not quite the same as saying that Nghe-Tinh was a rehearsal for the 1945 August Revolution, but the slogans of abolition of colonial taxes, "land to the tillers," seizure of rice to feed the famine victims, sacrifices, loss of family members, heroic struggles against all odds, and so on, undoubtedly had major resonance among the peasant cultivators of Vietnam and also became part of local peasant (and communist) lore (See Rousset 1978, 114). However, as official history allows, conditions were not yet ripe for an insurrection, although the Nghe-Tinh soviets constituted an important landmark in the development of the revolution (Nguyen Khac Vien 1975, 74–75).

Possibly at the time, the Communist Party backed away from endorsing a rebellion deemed premature and adventurous or, possibly as well, the rebellion had a spontaneity of its own only belatedly recognized by an opportunist party (see Scott 1976, 148). But ownership by the party has also been claimed.[3] On the other hand, if we accept that the newly founded ICP was actively involved, then, as in China, the Comintern led the communists into an adventurist trap. Even coming out of the depression years in Indochina, a worker-peasant alliance led by metropolitan, educated men was not a formula that could have produced a revolutionary situation even approximating Lenin's two-stage democratic revolution. The Nghe-Tinh rebellion was a mixed success for the ICP, especially as the French reaction fell heavily on the participants, while wave upon wave of arrests in Saigon and elsewhere crippled the communist movement for years to come. Even so, local communist agents demonstrated a high level of agency and organizational skills, as in adopting standard Leninist practices of secrecy linked to a cell structure or organization. We may only surmise, but such methods were well attuned to the more familiar Vietnamese secret-society type of behavior.

Yet there was a logic behind the 1930–31 rice rebellions. The coincidence of the Great Depression impacting the general economy, including the all-important rice export economy, has been widely noted and debated in the literature. While certain strata and certain zones may have been cushioned from the most deleterious effects of the global economic crisis, those on the margins of subsistence expanded significantly in the countryside. As also widely identified in the literature, Nghe-Tinh was one such ecologically marginal zone. On the one hand, the procurement price for rice slid to the point where diverting paddy rice to bootleg rice wine manufacture became a more attractive option. On the other hand, government-supplied rice reaching the Vinh marketplace was priced out of reach for all except the monied classes. Meantime, the unrelenting weight of regressive taxes and other imposts on an indigent peasantry, some of them staring down famine, contrived to ignite a spark, pushing them into desperate collective actions—violent, highly creative, and founded on new forms of solidarity—yet fatally vulnerable to the colonial repression which followed. Peasant revolt was not unknown in Annam and especially Nghe-Tinh, but the 1931–32 conjuncture also coincided with the weakening hold of the traditional elites over the rural masses.

Here, as elsewhere in the two deltas of Vietnam, the dissolution effects of colonial capital sharply conflicted with the traditional socioeconomic order represented by the notables and landlords, not to mention the dislocative effects of the colonial state. The taxation system, the systems of *régies*, the *prestation* and *corvée* obligations, the need to acquit taxes and imposts in cash rather than kind, and the rise of rural indebtedness all threw up new categories of poor, not only in the urban areas but for the first time on a mass basis in rural Vietnam, at least in a situation where traditional relief had also broken down.

Concluding from the above, just as the Nghe-Tinh rebellion of 1930–31 took an extremely violent and unprecedented form, so social stratification among the rural population increased as capitalist relations of production became primary into the furthest reaches of the countryside. Such would appear to endorse the Popkin thesis, namely how colonialism increased village stratification and therefore added to peasant discontent, but we are alluding to Annam in 1930–31, not the hypermarketized economy of southern Vietnam in 1960, which offered new empowerments to the peasantry. It is also true, as Scott avers, that the peasantry of the ecologically more vulnerable central Vietnam was essentially conservative and defensive. But not in 1930–31, when they went over to direct action, albeit stimulated by outside agitators. These are two different yet complementary perspectives on state-society relations. In the introduction we wondered whether these posturings are two separate problematics or just two sides of the same coin, and we are obliged to conclude, somewhat ambiguously, that both conservation and dissolution effects of capital came into simultaneous play in that conjuncture in central Vietnam, albeit remade again and again down through the colonial and postcolonial era. Hunger, deprivation, and exploitation by the notables as well as the colonial state were all undeniable themes in the Nghe-Tinh rebellions, but they were still localized, just as their claims appeared to be local. As terrible as the conditions were, they were still not of the nature of desperate mass famine rebellions such as would galvanize Viet Minh propagandists on the cusp of the Great Famine of 1944–45. In any case, it remains to test this assertion against the evidence as demonstrated in chapters 7 and 8.

NOTES

1. Writing on February 19, 1931, from his base in Hong Kong, Ho Chi Minh also penned a descriptive sketch of Nghe-Tinh, highlighting the lack of industry (no more than four thousand workers alongside a poor and middle peasant population of over one million). He also drew attention to this mountainous land where it is "lean and scarce, irrigation is lacking, flood and typhoon are often . . . with peasants underfed

and badly housed" ("The 'Red' Nge-Tinh," typewritten letter in English discovered by British police in Ho Chi Minh's lodgings, reproduced in Borton 2010, 58).

2. Fréjus, a town of medieval origin in Provence, had been the site of a military camp for forces leaving for Indochina. A pagoda, an Indochina war memorial, and a marine museum recall this link with the past. The signing of the Franco-Vietnamese protocol of 1986 necessitated a search for a site in France for the placement of a cemetery. http://www.war-memorial.net/The-Memorial-to-the-Wars-in-Indochina-in-Frejus-1.157.

3. According to documents attributed to Ho Chi Minh, namely "Revolutionary Movement in Indochina" dated January 24, 1931, he took careful stock of the number of conflicts and the number of persons involved in the events of 1930–31, while a second document issued on the occasion of the fourth anniversary of the birth of the ICP (February 3, 1934) asserted that it was the ICP "that led worker strikes, peasant demonstrations against landlords and installed Soviets in north Annam" (Ho Chi Minh Museum).

Chapter 4

The Popular Front Years, 1936–39

Having examined the agro-economy and "rice rebellions" of the early 1930s in the abstract, we should not neglect to observe that the political milieu was quickly maturing. Forming the government of France between 1936 and 1937, the Popular Front combined three of the main leftist metropolitan parties. In Indochina, and especially in Saigon, the Popular Front period saw an unprecedented flourishing of political activity on the part of the legal opposition, communists included. These years also saw the emergence of what today we would term a lively urban civil society, a generation which had been the beneficiary of a mixed Vietnamese-French education, albeit clouded by the rise of fascism and militarism in both its European and Asian variants. Alongside the rise of mass politics, a major feature of the communist opposition was the strength and dynamism of the minority Trotskyist factions in a rare cooperation with the "legal" communists, especially in city hall politics. Although Indochina had recovered from the worst of the economic depression by the mid-1930s, even during the prosperity years the drought and flood cycle continued, presenting the local Popular Front administration with a major agricultural-humanitarian crisis in 1936–37.

This chapter divides into six sections. A first describes the advent of the Popular Front and its political ramifications for Indochina. The chapter then traces the Trotskyist-Stalinist collaboration as it panned out, especially in Saigon. An additional section is devoted to the Luttiste contest over the Saigon Municipal Council and the campaign for an Indochinese congress. The chapter then tracks the labor arena under the Popular Front, including visits by French socialist deputies. Yet another section turns to the agrarian crisis of 1936–37, a combined drought and flood event, while a final section deals with the trials and tribulations of the communists in 1938–39, at least before war sets in.

THE ADVENT OF THE POPULAR FRONT IN INDOCHINA

Headed by socialist Léon Blum, the Popular Front government (Front populaire) brought together an alliance of left-wing groups, including the PCF, the SFIO, and the Parti Radical. While Blum lost power in June 1937, the Popular Front was dissolved only in autumn 1938. As literary critics Andrew and Ungar (2005, 1) point out, the Popular Front was not only a dramatic political period during the final years of the French Third Republic, it also connoted "social solidarity and the possibility of the democratic attainment of humane values." By this, they mean that not only did the Popular Front deliver such gains as the forty-hour work week and paid vacations but also offered a vision of "an authentic culture of and for the people." Such utopianism not only touched the literary and political world of Paris but also the colonies.

The effect of Blum's electoral victory in the French general election of May 3, 1936, on Indochina was immediate. In substance, the liberal policies of the Popular Front translated into reforms which permitted legal political activity. Notably, a large numbers of communists who had been arrested following the events of 1930–31 won their freedom, including future ICP strongman in the south, Tran Van Giau. Alongside the lively Vietnamese-language press in Saigon, such as signaled in chapter 1, a range of communist publications also saw the light of day, as with the journal *La Lutte*, mouthpiece of the Struggle faction. The period also witnessed a rise in demonstrations and strikes by workers and peasants pushing their demands. As in metropolitan France, communism progressed by both legal and illegal means (Hémery 1975, 281; Rice-Maxim 1986).

During this period a number of official emissaries were dispatched from France to Indochina to investigate grievances. National Assembly deputies and progressive labor organizations joined suit, further raising the expectations of the Vietnamese people for better working conditions and other concessions. The political landscape in colonial Indochina did not exclude participation by metropolitans, whether or not as activists or members of metropolitan political parties, just as the full spectrum of political ideas was represented in Indochina. This we saw in the actions of André Malraux and his circle in Saigon in the late 1920s.

The Special Place of Saigon in Popular Front Politics

In chapter 2 we discussed the print revolution as it developed in Saigon under difficult conditions in the late 1920s. Setting aside the press in Hanoi, Haiphong, Hue, and other localities, the French-language and vernacular press of Saigon continued to develop with the advent of the Popular Front. As analyzed by Philippe Peycam (2012), such papers ranged from pro-establishment, to independent, to anti-French and pro-communist, just as literacy in both *quoc ngu* and French expanded, especially among the urban classes. Taking the index of print media as a standard, by 1937 the government tallied a total of 110 dailies and 159 magazines and bulletins published in Indochina, overwhelmingly in Saigon. In 1939, this figure rose to 128 dailies and 176 magazines. As Brocheux and Hémery (2009, 235) remark, even though the illiteracy rate remained high outside the urban middle classes, one should not underestimate oral transmission of the new and potentially revolutionary messages implied by both literature and popular and practical science.

THE TROTSKYIST-STALINIST UNITED FRONT IN SAIGON

From its origins in January 1933, a "united front" entered into between Trotskyists, pro-Moscow "Stalinists," and other anticolonial elements, lasted until 1937–39, when ideological dissension led to its disintegration. Spanning the years of the Popular Front government in France, it also coincided with cooperation on the part of the communist opposition in Saigon to convene an Indochinese congress or a proposed forum of discussion between the colonial authorities and representatives of the Indochinese peoples as to the future status of Vietnam.

To explain this unusual collaboration leading to the joint publication and editorship of a newspaper (*La Lutte*), we should also be mindful of, first, personal contacts between the militants (undoubtedly shared schooling experience, perhaps even in France); second, an apparent lack of international organizational pressure against its formation; and third, the specific historical circumstances and colonial setting in Indochina, including the advent of the Popular Front government. According to Brocheux (2007, 76), the ICP-Trotskyist collaboration around *La Lutte* was considered so unorthodox that the PCF sent deputy Maurice Homel to Indochina to "advise" on a rupture.

Among those deported from France on May 30, 1930, following mass demonstrations in front of the Elysée in support of the Yen Bai rebels were Ta Thu Thau, Phan Van Chanh, and Huynh Van. All had been students in France. All had drifted into the communist milieu but from 1929 had also been exposed to the arguments and debates over the split between the Fourth International (the Trotskyists) and the Third International (the Stalinists). Back in Saigon in the summer of 1930, the Paris returnees looked to the creation of a Trotskyist party eventually taking shape in the winter of 1931–32. But around mid-1932, divergences emerged between Ta Thu Thau and Phan Van Chanh, leading to a splintering of the Trotskyist factions. With Ta Thu Thau heading up the Dong Duong Cong Son (Communism International), in late 1931 Pham Van Chanh set up the Left Opposition (Ta Dui Lap), also known as the October Group, under the leadership of Dao Hung Long and Ho Hau Tuong. Personalities aside, differences between the groups focused on attitudes to be taken toward the ICP. In 1932, the Left Opposition and the October Group were joined by communist militants who had split with the ICP leadership in Cochinchina (Hémery 1975, 41–42). From February to May 1935, as discussed below, Saigon became the focus of an extended electoral campaign for the Saigon Municipal Council. *La Lutte* candidates came close to success in the first round and were victorious in the second, with the election in 1937 of Ta Thu Thau.

Born in Long Xuyen in 1906, Ta Thu Thau had been an activist in Young Annam and other nationalist groups prior to leaving for France in 1927, where he studied science at the University of Paris. As key player in the Luttiste or Struggle narrative, Ta Thu Thau has been compared by Daniel Hémery (1981, 193) to the Indonesian Trotskyist Tan Malaka as a figure standing outside of grand communist and nationalist narratives, although both of them served as vanguard figures in the independence histories of their respective countries, and both of them were dispensed with by the revolution they helped to foment.

The Trotskyist Position in Indochina

In this light, it is important to understand just what the Vietnamese Trotskyists stood for. As Hémery (1975, 47) explains, in distinguishing themselves from the communist mainstream, the Vietnamese communists generally applied in Indochina the notion of "retarded capitalist development" to describe the impact of imperialism on the country. But given that French monopoly capitalism had achieved only an "artificial economic revolution," the Vietnamese bourgeoisie was unable to advance beyond agrarian and usurious forms of development. Even so, in this argument, the capitalist mode of production had become predominant in Indochina. "The working masses are exploited not by the feudal nationalists but by a very modern imperialism and by capitalist means of exploitation."

One of the key texts from which Hémery (1975, 46) distills this understanding is Huynh Van Phuong's "La mise en valeur de l'Indochine et la bourgeoisie Annamite" (Indochina development and the Vietnamese bourgeoisie). Trotsky had previously arrived at this conclusion with reference to China and had propounded the thesis most forcefully in his critique of the Third International resolutions pertaining to the problem of prosecution of the proletariat revolution in countries with immature economic bases. Trotsky argued that feudal systems simply could not have survived the onslaught of mercantile and bank capital, the subordination of the Chinese village to the city, the dependence of important agrarian districts on this market, and the ever-growing role of foreign trade (Trotsky 1970, 209).

The problems of revolutionary practice were conceded by Trotsky in the form of an admonishment delivered to his local followers in Indochina. Writing in September 1931, Trotsky admitted lack of local knowledge and, as such, sought "ideological clarity," especially concerning developments surrounding the establishment of the ICP. While national independence was a necessary element of the Indochinese revolution, the struggle, he argued, should be directed against the "national" agents of foreign imperialism, that is, the Indochinese bourgeoisie. Nevertheless, some degree of collaboration was required between the proletariat, the poor peasantry, and the most exploited and oppressed lower urban petty bourgeoisie. Class collaboration, he agreed, was mostly camouflage for the rule of the capitalist class. Trotsky recognized that nationalism interpreted as the hatred by the masses of imperialism could not be ignored but, doubting that the Indochinese proletariat was sufficiently advanced to have grasped the necessity of "simultaneous" struggle of national independence, democracy, and socialist revolution, as argued by local militants, he counseled for the prosecution of "democratic" struggle as a precondition for socialist revolution in tandem with the world revolution (Trotsky 1973).

To summarize, the fundamental ideological divergence between the Stalinists and the Trotskyists in Indochina turned on whether to target as the primary enemy the capitalists (foreign imperialists), the Trotskyist position, or the feudalists (big landowners), the ICP line. Even so, compromises were allowed, as with the surprising united front entered into between the two communist protagonists. But as the Stalinists moved from a basically left position in the early 1930s to a right position under the Popular Front years, the Trotskyist position, by contrast, remained fairly fluid with respect to the national and social questions, especially when confronted with practical considerations (Duncanson 1968, 394).

The Macau Conference of the ICP (1934)

While the discussion so far has focused on the activities of the "legal communists," it should be recalled that the ICP remained outlawed and continued its clandestine existence both inside Indochina and in various external bases. With the arrest of Nguyen Ai Quoc in Hong Kong in June 1931 and his eventual release in January 1933 and journey to the Soviet Union, local initiative passed into the hands of a small group of Stalin School graduates who, under the noses of the authorities, began to assemble in the Portuguese colony of Macau. Coming to the attention of the French secret police, the Macau Conference of the ICP, bringing together top-ranking members of the newly created ICP, was convened June 14–26, 1934.

A preliminary to the landmark First National Congress of the ICP held nine months later in Macau, four figures in particular stand out at the Macau

Conference: roving China-based Comintern apparatchik Le Hong Phong, a future ICP secretary general, Ha Huy Tap, another future secretary, Thailand-based Tran Van Chan, and undoubtedly the most tenacious Stalinist of them all, Tran Van Giau (1910–2010), the individual who briefly seized power in Saigon in August 1945 on behalf of the Viet Minh in the wake of the Japanese capitulation. Also joining this circle was Nguyen Thi Minh Khai, confidant of both Nguyen Ai Quoc and Le Hong Phong and, ambiguously, wife and/or *maitresse* of one of them (AOM SLOTFOM/54 NP 34, 2nd tri 1938).

The Macau or First National Congress of the ICP

Convened March 27–31, 1935, the Macau or First National Congress of the ICP brought together fifteen delegates, albeit in the absence of the two most important members, Nguyen Ai Quoc, then in Moscow, and Le Hong Phong, then attending the Seventh Comintern Congress. The Macau Congress also coincided with an extreme-leftist period in the history of both the Vietnamese and Chinese communist movements. Notably, the congress manifesto placed great stress on "armed struggle" (Harrison 1989, 66). Nevertheless, as mentioned, the fundamental decisions of the Macau Conference were overridden by the Comintern (the Eighth Congress of the Third International). In 1935, as alluded, with the European situation in mind, Moscow sought to create a broad anti-imperialist front drawing on all the nationalist parties and linking up with the extreme-left French groups. Still, the Macau Congress offered the first major discussion on ethnic minority issues, an awareness that would serve the future Viet Minh well in ethnic minority zones contiguous with Guangxi Province of China. For the first time, the delegates from northern to southern Vietnam, not excluding the ethnic minorities' representatives, bonded in Macau as "Vietnamese," although, ambiguously, they also embraced "French Indochina" as the arena of their struggle.

With his return from the ICP conference in Macau, Tran Van Giau also confronted the problem of bringing isolated and renegade communist opposition forces in Cambodia and southern Vietnam into closer liaison with the regional bureau of the ICP in Saigon under his leadership. While other Moscow-trained returnees such as Le Hong Phong served the Comintern in northern Indochina, Tran Van Giau performed a similar task as head of the five-member Federal Committee of South Indochina brought into being in March 1935. Centered on Saigon/Cholon, the committee linked east, west, and central Cochinchina along with Quang Tri, an emerging guerrilla zone in 1945. A committee in Cambodia was also brought under the control of west Cochinchina (AOM SLOTFOM III, 54, NP 35, 2nd tri 1935; Hémery 1975, 435).

Still, another element was at play. Virtually countermanding the ultraleftist resolutions of the Macau Congress of 1935, ruled on the exploitation of liberal legislation to create an anti-imperialist front. According to a French police analyst, the tactics were first adopted in 1936 by *La Lutte* in Cochinchina, *Le Travail* in Tonkin, and the Nguyen Khoa Van (L'Epi de Riz) group in Annam. Success soon followed, especially in winning a mass following for their anticolonial cause. The revolutionaries gained a reserve of experienced cadres following the releases of political prisoners such as those facilitated by Governor Robin and the French minister of colonies from 1934 (AOM SLOTFOM III, 59 NM, April 1937).

THE SAIGON MUNICIPAL COUNCIL ELECTIONS AND THE INDOCHINA CONGRESS MOVEMENT

The year 1935 witnessed three elections in Cochinchina: that of the colonial council, the chamber of commerce, and the municipal council, respectively. Held May 5–13, the Saigon Municipal Council elections led to the unprecedented electoral gain by the Luttiste-backed Nguyen Van Tao group, winning four out of six of the places reserved for Vietnamese (alongside the twelve places reserved for French). Nevertheless, in a second round and in a system of restricted franchise, conservative French and pro-French Vietnamese support prevailed, with the Constitutionalists winning the two seats reserved for the Vietnamese. As Governor Maurice Pagès railed, in this "*infantine*" campaign, the Luttistes successfully exploited discontent among chauffeurs over parking issues, they stood behind the staff of the Continental Hotel over salary increases, they identified with working conditions of the Tramway Company employees, they championed dispossessed squatters, and they backed strike actions (AOM NF/329/2686–2659 Gouverneur, Cochinchine à GG, "Situation Indochine au mois de Mai 1935," Saigon, June 12, 1935). Undoubtedly this was correct, but as a Vietnamese source points out, notwithstanding the overall victory by pro-French interests, "The Municipal Council became a tribune for the propagation of progressive ideas" (Nguyen Ngoc Thi 1973, 69–70).

Control of the Saigon Municipal Council in October 1936

As Governor Pagès commented on a session of the Saigon Municipal Council in October 1936, the four legal communist councilors once again demonstrated their influence over the French majority. Such was their "lively and acerbic critiques" as much demagoguery that no single French member could respond with such authority or vigor. Increasingly, Pagès lamented, in all the elected assemblies the Vietnamese representatives had become "masters of the game." This situation held true for the chamber of agriculture, where the president was "prisoner" of the Vietnamese. By accepting Bui Quang Chieu's motion, the newly elected French representative to the colonial council revealed himself "as lethargic as his predecessors." The same tendency appeared with the chamber of commerce, which hitherto upheld 100 percent French representation. Whereas in the past the Vietnamese had been a minority in influence and numbers, now, for the first time, a local vice president took his place. As Pagès commented on this state of affairs—which he obviously deemed deplorable and demeaning to French status and privilege—the rise of a new Vietnamese elite matched by an awakening Vietnamese public opinion meant that defense of the "imperial idea" required verbal talent and "undisputed superiority." In a less-than-veiled reference to the French *colon*, he argued, many of them had put down roots, overstayed in the colony, and were out of touch with metropolitan developments. To the advantage of the locals, even the climate sapped away at their "intelligence and energy" (AOM Indo NF/329/2656 Gouverneur, Cochinchine à GG, Directeur des Affairs Politiques, Hanoi, Oct. 1936).

Once again, the partial elections of April 25, 1937, to the city hall revealed to the French authorities the triumph of the Luttiste group. The Luttiste slate of Ta Thu Thao, Duong Bach Mai, and Nguyen Van Tao collectively outvoted the moderates and conservatives by an excess of 100 votes each over their adversaries, or a total of 2,213 versus 1,905 votes. The Luttistes were now confirmed as municipal councilors with a term of office lasting until spring 1939. As Governor Pagès conceded in a letter to Paris, and perhaps seeking to shift the blame, the prestige of the Luttistes had now grown, thanks to the neutrality exercised by the administration in line with instructions cabled by Paris. But in trying to explain away the Luttiste success, Pagès conceded excellent electoral preparation. Backhandedly, he acknowledged, the work they had put in over the previous two years in the commission had not been forgotten. On the one hand, the repeal of their positions by the council of state had been presented as a triumph of colonialism, turning the recent elections into a political protest. On the other hand, the "innate prudence" of the Vietnamese held them back from standing up to the Luttistes. Added to that was the low voting rate and the large number of abstentions. Whereas in 1935 the Luttistes had gained an average of 365 votes from a total of 5,689 registered voters, in the 1937 elections they attained the same average with a total of 2,402 registered voters (AOM Indo NF/330–2296 Gouverneur, Cochinchine à GG, April 27, 1937).

The Indochinese Congress Movement (July 1936 and March 1937)

As alluded to, between July 1936 and March 1937 the major anti-French protagonists in Saigon, namely, the "legal" communists" and the Trotskyists, jointly attempted to form an Indochinese congress as a prelude to a "people's assembly" in which the Vietnamese would be able to negotiate colonial reforms with the French authorities. In so doing, the communists came into conflict with the colonial administrative goals, which insisted on the arrival of a parliamentary committee of inquiry. Eventually, the congress movement was suppressed, no colonial commission was ever sent (only a minister of labor, Justin Godard), and no serious or genuine colonial reforms were undertaken.

According to Sud Chonchirdsin (1999, 338–46), the ICP was the only party which actually managed to exploit this short-lived period of relaxed colonial policy to its own benefit by expanding its membership to the masses in rural areas of Cochinchina. Even so, as explained, the Trotskyists also managed to show their hand and sow their influence, actively pushing for the preparation of an Indochinese congress, as with the formation of "action committees" or virtual communist cells across wide swathes of rural Vietnam, especially in the southern delta (see map in Hémery 1975, 304–5).

Described as the organ of the legal faction of the ICP, *La Lutte* was actively tasked with organizing the campaign for the congress. Notably, on July 29, 1936, *La Lutte* published an appeal under the name of crusading anticolonial journalist Nguyen An Ninh, headed "People of All Tendencies for the Convocation of an Indochinese Congress," to present a petition to the metropolitan government. With Nguyen An Ninh's call, revolutionaries across Vietnam kicked off their work. With the first action committees set up in Cochinchina in August, they were followed in Tonkin the following month, where the action was led by Tran Huy Lieu of *Travail*, leading to the establishment of a Section Tonkinois du Congress. In Annam, a group of freed political prisoners led by Nguyen Khoa Van organized a Comité de Congress. Within 2 months, the *La Lutte* group managed to set up 600 action committees with 25 percent of members either condemned political prisoners or common-law cases besides hosting some 200 public meetings or gatherings and distributing 450,000 copies of some 200 different pamphlets (AOM SLOTFOM III, 59 NM, April 1937). Besides recourse to print media, the Luttistes also broadcast their message by oral means, as with the staging of theatrical plays.

La Lutte also managed external affairs alternatively with the French Left in Paris, in Saigon, and with the Vietnamese-language press in the rest of Indochina. In September 1936, it assisted with the foundation in Hanoi of the legal communist group and newspaper *Travail*, resulting in a northerly extension of Luttiste formula and of the Congress movement (albeit engaging different personalities and politics). Flag carrier of the movement in Annam was the communist paper *L'Epi de Riz*. *Le Militant*, the legal paper of the Trotskyists, warned against holding any illusions as to the politics of the southern bourgeoisie.

According to an official Vietnamese source, the movement attracted wide support with the formation of a provisional national committee. Composed of delegates of workers, laborers, even reformist members of the bourgeoisie, former political prisoners, and progressive members of the French community alongside, committee activities, including public meetings, climaxed in August 1936. By the end of 1936, the colonial administration became alarmed at the inroads of the movement against the traditional authorities, pro-French mandarins, and other collaborators from within the Constitutionalist Party. It then began to close down progressive newspapers and eventually forced the closure of the broad-based provisional national committee (Nguyen Ngoc Thi 1973, 71–72).

As a Sûreté report interpreted, while the action committees as represented by *La Lutte* were temporary and solely charged with collecting the sentiments of the people and preparing the work of the congress, the reality was different. In reality, these organizations were "veritable communist cells" under the authority of province or town committees, answering to a central committee and seeking to sap away at the authority of the government and indigenous representatives (AOM SLOTFOM III, 59 NM, April 1937).

Still, as the Sûreté acknowledged, the movement was genuinely popular and had high-caliber leadership. Notably, *La Lutte*, *Travail*, and the *L'Epi de Riz* group had attracted "immense sympathy among the masses," who admired them for their daring to attack the government. Ta Thu Thau, Nguyen Ai Minh, and Nguyen Van Tao, who had all been subject to lengthy trials and prison terms, had become "heroes of legend" for their hunger strikes while incarcerated. Accordingly, it was not surprising that sympathizers followed their orders and that the ICP increased its membership even beyond its own expectations (AOM SLOTFOM III, 59 NM, April 1937).

This was undoubtedly a backhanded compliment for the leaders of the legal communist movement. But in an era before the name of Ho Chi Minh and other clandestine figures of the left became known, Vietnam, or at least the urban dwellers, already had its leaders. As skilled self-propagandists through the use of print media, they had earned their esteem through their extraordinary energy and intelligence. But separated from the masses by their metropolitan education and elitism, they also fell into the mold of mandarin-proletarians following Alexander Woodside's depiction.

The 1939 Municipal Council Elections

In February 1939, the Trotskyists again stood for the Saigon Municipal Council elections with a list of candidates headed by former Trotskyist municipal councilor Ta Thu Thau, released from prison on February 10, along with the Stalinist Van Tau. Front candidates may have failed to win (a majority) in the elections owing to disagreement over choice of candidates (Nguyen Ngoc Thi 1973, 79), but individual candidates were successful. Incoming Vichyite governor René Veber attributes this success to "irregular inscription" of candidates, excessive government benevolence, and communist command over the media. Following on from communist victories in the municipal council, elections for the colonial council taking place in May 1940 led to the victory of several communists, including leaders of the party. Only Bui Quang Chieu's Constitutionalists opposed them. As Veber bewailed, these were the same individuals who, in 1936–38, created a veritable peasant *jacquerie* in the Transbassac and instigated worker strikes in the plantations (AOM Indo NF/330/2664 "Rapport des Colonies," Veber à Colonies, April 19, 1941).

THE LABOR ARENA, 1936–37

With the sponsorship of Minister Maurice Moutet, a new labor code was brought out on December 30, 1936. Its impact would be far ranging and unprecedented in Indochina. As Moutet informed the French president, the time had arrived to extend to Indochina, as far as practicable, "all the benefits already enjoyed by workers and employees in France." Wide in scope, the new measures were—predictably—not well received by employers of labor in Indochina. The new code abolished fines, provided for minimum-wage scales, protected women and children, reduced working hours from ten to nine and then to eight over a period of three years, offered a weekly day of rest, paid annual holidays, and compensation in case of accident, and provided a government inspector of labor to look after workers' interests in time of dispute (PRO CO 273 267 Consul Hogg, Feb. 4, 1937). The right to demonstrate was also seized on by the communist opposition. But whereas the colonial authorities sought to stymie protest through ameliorative measures or through official investigations, the ICP sought to capitalize especially on peasant grievances at the hands of native landlords and colonial capital together.

As a British consular report of late 1936 observed, "Cochinchina has now become the center of interest, the petty strikes in progress being completely overshadowed by the new strikes among the tramway workers and among the laborers of the naval arsenal." In these and other strikes, workers now began to agitate for the application of the new "social laws." When, for instance, tramway drivers and conductors refused to work, the tramway company responded by recruiting new staff. Aside from the larger enterprises, many small strikes continued taking up the catchword "immediate and integral application of the social laws" (PRO CO 273 267, Vice Consul L. A. Scopes, Saigon, Dec. 16, 1936). Worse was to come, however, such as the strike of April 1937 in the Saigon arsenal involving some nine hundred workers believed to have been agitated by a communist cell. At the time, this was described as one of the "worst strike centers in the country" (PRO CO 273 267 Consul Hogg, April 23, 1937).

But rural unrest also broke out at this juncture. On April 13, 1937, one thousand demonstrators paraded in the villages of Tan Hiap, a rural district of present-day Kien Giang Province, with banners demanding the abolition of head tax and a new tax on tobacco. Meantime, a "considerable" number of women and young men were involved in protests over tax in the Ba Diem-Hoc Mon area, then in the rural outskirts of Saigon. Concern was also expressed by the authorities over the nature of school protests. As a measure to neutralize school activities, political meetings near schools were forbidden, as were displays of banners, processions, slogans, strikes, and similar manifestations by schools. The plight of pardoned political prisoners was also raised by one petitioner, especially as hundreds were unemployed and in distress (PRO CO 273 267 Consul Hogg, May 5, 1937).

In August of the same year, "pandemonium" broke out in the Saigon prison. Fire brigades were called out. The British report attributed blame for the affray to the "hard-handed" methods of the Corsican jailer. Prisoners also demanded a new prison regime and better conditions (PRO CO 273 267 Consul Hogg, Sept. 4, 1937). Not only were French colonial prison abuses registered by foreign consular reports, they were actively taken up by prisoner's families, the left-wing parties, international humanitarian organizations, and Christian groups, although without apparent effect during the colonial period.

As the British consulate minuted, after a lull of some two months, strikes again broke out in various parts of the country, appearing, however, "to be devoid of any political character" and to be provoked mainly by a recent rapid rise in the price of rice. As the consulate reported, the strikes for the main part involved the lowest-paid coolie clans, for whom rice was the staple diet (and doubtless consuming a large quotient of their income). Coolies also struck at Texas Oil Company and Stanford Oil Company near Saigon to demand a wage increase and better conditions, with Texas Oil granting increased wages. Chinese brick works and sawmills were also affected by strikes for increased wages. Strikes also immobilized four passenger and cargo vessels in the port of Saigon (PRO CO 273 267 Consul Hogg, "Indo-China," 1937). In mid-1937, the governor general's hint of the possibility of legalizing Vietnamese trade unions resulted in the creation in Saigon of a committee to consider ways and means in anticipation (PRO CO 273 267 Consul Hogg, "Indo-China," July 5, 1937).

Vietnamese sources confirm that numerous workers' demonstrations occurred in Saigon in 1936–37, especially as laws restricting demonstrations were lifted. During this period, struggle activities touched almost all industries in Saigon, also spreading to cabdrivers, railwaymen, stevedores, and mill workers in Cholon (Nguyen Ngoc Thi 1973: 74–5). Still, such activities are not even surprising by the yardstick of other European colonies and hardly bothered the authorities.

French Emissaries to Saigon

Seeking to mollify the working population, in January 1937 Paris dispatched to Indochina a labor ambassador, Justin Godard, a radical. The arrival of Godard sparked a mass mobilization that led to the French emissary being mobbed by a crowd of twenty thousand Saigon workers. Godard was also greeted by crowds in rural My Tho (D. Elliot 2006, 27). Both Godard and Governor General Joseph Jules Brévié, a socialist, were obliged to offer concessions to the trade unions. On the other hand, Vietnamese emissaries also traveled to Paris to demand the legalization of the Indochina congress. Accordingly, Minister Moutet promised a special commission to examine people's claims (Nguyen Ngoc Thi 1973, 73). Evidently impressed with the restraint shown by the masses of people greeting Godard and Brévié, as a Sûreté analyst declaimed, this "offered proof of discipline otherwise lacking among Vietnamese mobs" (AOM SLOTFOM III, 59 NM, April 1937).

The arrival in September 1936 of incoming Governor General Brévié was ominous. As Brévié was being received with full ceremony at the landing stage in Saigon, nearby the colonial police were engaged in a "violent struggle" with several thousand communists from Saigon and surrounding districts, including a thousand-strong contingent of workers from the Naval Arsenal and sundry "malcontents," along with more than one thousand rice-mill coolies from Cholon who had gone on strike. Many were injured in the confrontation. Local opinion held that the demonstration was organized by *La Lutte*. In Hanoi, it was found prudent to prohibit processions and banners on the day of Brévié's arrival. As the British consul remarked, operations of this nature had not been seen in Saigon since the attack on the prison in 1914 (PRO CO 273 267 Consul Hogg, Jan. 13, 1937), a reference to the actions of a southern rural-based politico-religious cult, shocking nevertheless for the audacity of its members.

The visit to Indochina in 1937 by Z. M. Hamel, the communist deputy for Clichy, produced a range of reactions by local sections of the population besides becoming a source of great embarrassment to the authorities. In Saigon-Cholon, as the British consul recorded, Hamel received a petition from municipal workers. Among their demands was a general amnesty for political offenders then undergoing punishment, press freedom, freedom of speech, the right to associate, the right to hold meetings, and the right to travel. They also demanded the constitution of an Indochinese parliament elected by universal suffrage, the suppression of the poll tax, and financial assistance for impoverished laborers. They called on Hamel to rally the workers of France to the cause of their comrades in Indochina and to take up their cause in the French Chamber of Deputies. As Hamel acknowledged in a public address, the Popular Front government had not greatly altered the state of affairs in Indochina, and such social laws as had been applied in theory seemed in many cases to be evaded in practice, especially with regard to the weekly day of rest and paid annual holidays. Specifically, he referred to certain French officials, police officers, and magistrates in Indochina who did all in their power to neutralize the good intentions of the government. However, he expressed approval of an attempt by the governor to impose a tax on income for the relief of poorer classes (PRO CO 273 267 Consul Hogg, Sept 14, 1937).

Hamel's visit in particular and the space opened up by the Popular Front government put the local authorities on the defensive. For example, during a visit by the governor general to Can Giuoc, south of Saigon, 1,500 peasants staged a demonstration and acclaimed the Popular Front with fists clenched. Among their demands were suppression of the poll tax, amnesty for political offenders, and freedom for the formation of workers' associations. No less, as Minister Moutet declared in Paris in reply to queries, only six hundred political prisoners remained in prison (mainly those arrested in 1930–31), and their cases would be examined. He also made it known that he would permit liberalization only when calm was restored and when he had confidence in local officials. As a vernacular newspaper commented on this statement, nothing could be expected from France unless it was forced from her. It suggested the formation of an Indochina Popular Front allied to the Popular Front in France but under the aegis of the ICP (PRO CO 273 267 Consul Hogg, "Indo-China," Aug. 1937).

In October 1937, Governor Pagès complained to Moutet that the ICP and the Trotskyist Party were together mounting a systematic press propaganda campaign to disrupt public order. Notably, *La Lutte* and *Avant Garde* ran an antiauthority campaign in the wake of Hamel's visit. Pagès also sought to put an end to certain activities of the metropolitan press "prejudicial to the French oeuvre in Cochinchina." This was a specific reference to critical articles appearing in *L'Humanité*, actually naming French officials in Indochina accused of committing abuses (AOM Indo NF Pages à Colonies, Oct. 18, 1937).

MANAGING THE AGRARIAN CRISIS OF 1936–37

Recovering from a low of 960,000 tonnes of rice, including unhusked paddy and rice derivatives exported from the port of Saigon during 1931 at the height of the depression, the figure for 1934 rose to 1,505,493 tonnes. Major export markets were, in rank order, metropolitan France, other French colonies, Hong Kong, and China-Shanghai. A certain quantity of rice was also reaching Japan (sixty thousand tonnes in 1931–32), although still a new and irregular market. Cochinchina and Cambodia combined provided the overwhelming bulk of rice exports from Indochina, just as rice represented 27 percent of the total tonnage exported, contributing up to 36 percent of the total value of exports (AOM Indo/NF/104/1004 Gouverneur, Cochinchine à GG, no.734, Dec. 25, 1934; BEI, Dec. 1938).

Writing in early 1935, governor of Cochinchina (1934–39) Pierre Pagès, the leading official voice pronouncing on social, economic, and political life during the Popular Front years in the south, observed that the economic life of the colony had rebounded. Among the positive indices he recorded were an increase in taxes recovered for the local budget; an increase in the quantity of rice exported; an increase in the consumption of electricity; a spike in the number of cars sold; and an expansion of currency in circulation. All in all, he signaled a picture of an export-oriented colony in full spate. As discussed above, he was also perplexed to report the "paradox" of good economic numbers and "the growing influence of left-wing" politics, such as reflected in the Saigon electoral arena (AOM NF/329/2686–2659 Gouverneur, Cochinchine à GG, June 12, 1935). Although adverse seasonal conditions and bad harvests would conspire to drive large numbers of the peasantry to the brink by 1937, urban dwellers nevertheless gained a lease on life offered by the temporary recovery, at least prior to the tragic war years fast closing in.

Drought

Owing to a delay in the arrival of the monsoon rains, large areas of Indochina were subject to an abnormal drought in the winter of 1936–37, affecting a swathe of territory from southern Tonkin to northern Annam, north and central Laos, and even the northeast of Thailand. Because of the prolonged drought, the spring harvest was found to be deficient, and in some provinces, the populations were threatened with famine. Needless to say, rice exports from Indochina also fell away. As a remedial measure, the Popular Front government imposed a total ban on the export of rice from Laos (including rice surplus in Bassac in the south) while seeking to reserve all quantities of rice for local consumption. With northern Annam suffering a marked lack of precipitation, especially in Vinh and Thanh Hoa Provinces, fifty thousand piasters was earmarked for distribution of rice to victims. In order to prevent speculation on existing stocks of rice, the administration opened a forty thousand piaster line of credit with the official small loan institution, Credit Agricole Mutual, a measure seen as helping to regulate the price of rice. Answering back to the minister of colonies, the Indochina government claimed to be monitoring the situation with "extreme caution," and this is borne out by the facts (AOM Indo/NF/48/578–583, GG à Colonies, Paris).

A colonial report on the agricultural scene in Nghe An in late 1936 deemed all the harvests mediocre and the rice harvest particularly bad. Rice suffered irregular meteorological conditions. The drought of October compounded the bad effect of the previous trimester. Notably, the harvest recorded a deficit in the northern part of the province both for rice fields and for *rais*, or dry-field cultivation. Only rice fields located near sources of water used for irrigation achieved "acceptable" harvests. Despite the poor harvest, the market price of rice still remained low owing to imports by rail and by sea (AOM Indo NF/334/2689 "Province de Nghe-An, Rapport Economique de quatrième tri," Vinh, 1936).

Meantime, the resident superior in Hanoi scrambled to take stock of food reserves in Tonkin by conducting a province-level investigation. As he concluded, the *soudure* or gap between the intervening harvests was not then at a critical level in Tonkin. From his investigation, 566,217 tonnes of rice were held in reserve (stockpiled), amounting to some 56,000 tonnes in excess of (annual) consumption needs of 510,310 tonnes. To this was added stocks of maize then amounting to approximately 22,500 tonnes, along with a reserve or basket of secondary items of everyday consumption, including potatoes, soybeans, manioc, and taro, "which also makes up an appreciable part of the diet of the indigenous population," albeit an amount difficult to accurately calculate owing to the small-scale or household character of its production (AOM RST GG, Hanoi, April 10, 1937; BEI, Dec. 1938).

Floods

As alluded to in chapter 1, both the northern and southern regions of Vietnam were struck by floods in the summer of 1937. In early August 1937 a series of typhoons, also ravaging Hong Kong, provoked abnormal rains in the Thai Binh and the Red River basin. The provinces of Bac Ninh, Hai Duong, Hung Yen, and Phu Lang Thuong (Bac Giang) were all affected by an almost unprecedented rupture of the dikes of the Canal des Rapides, the Canal du Song Cai, and the Thong Ba Canal and with the floods covering half of Phu Lan Thuong, three quarters of Bac Giang province, three-quarters of Bac Ninh, and a part of Haiphong. In the meantime, incessant rains submerged almost all the low-lying rice fields in Tonkin. Material losses were evaluated at 160 million francs. The disaster affected 732,000 people, of whom 300,000 required total assistance (AOM Indo NF 227/1858 "Note des inondations en Indochine"). In six districts of Bac Ninh Province (northeast of Hanoi), about fifteen thousand famished peasants were reduced to begging (Nguyen The Anh 1998a, 214).

In the southern delta, where the Mekong River was fully swollen by rains in the superior basin, the equinox tide constrained the river's natural flow, leading to massive saturation of the lower basin. Between September 1 and

14, 1937, the flood submerged all the "floating rice" across several provinces of Cambodia and Cochinchina. In central Vietnam, a late typhoon toward the middle of October struck Thanh Hoa Province. The deluge which accompanied the typhoon destroyed large parts of the cultivations along the coastline (AOM Indo NF 227/1858 "Note des inondations en Indochine").

In late 1937, Governor Pagès again referred to the economic recovery in the colony, instancing a favorable trade balance, good note circulation, and a diminution in the number of bankruptcies, along with an active flow of labor. However, in late August 1937, the rice harvest, then representing 60 percent of total exports by value, was ruined by floods. The hardest-hit areas in Cochinchina were Chau Doc, Long Xuyen, Ha Tien, Sa Dec, Rach Gia, and Can Tho, along with Prey Veng in Cambodia, with seventy-five thousand hectares of rice fields underwater and where, for the most part, the rice crop was ruined. Although the government stepped in with assistance for shelter as well as rice seed, reportedly its efforts were neutralized by profiteers and rumormongers (PRO CO 273 267 Acting Consul General, Saigon, Nov. 7, 1937).

Assistance

As a way of assisting the various regions of Indochina to cope with the floods, special funds were allocated from the general budget to all parts of Indochina (188,000 francs for Laos; 335,000 for Cambodia; 3,200,000 for Annam; 1,055,000 for Tonkin; and 500,000 for Cochinchina). Additionally, five hundred thousand francs from Credit Agricole was awarded peasant victims of the drought. Meantime, public works projects were initiated to absorb unemployed labor (AOM Indo NF 227/1858 "Note des inondations en Indochine"). China, in the name of Chiang Kai-shek, was also moved to contribute fifty thousand Shanghai dollars to assist with the 1937 flood disaster, an act which Governor General Jules Brévié termed "a gesture of great humanity" (AOM Indo NF 227/1858 tél., Brévié à Colonies, Nov. 22, 1937).

Within three days of the rupture of the Canal des Rapides dike, rice supplies were in place. Some 2000 tonnes of rice especially procured from Cochinchina were directed toward Tonkin, with another purchase of 5000 tonnes of rice at a price of 2,800,000 francs in the course of realization. Meantime, the administration multiplied public works projects, supplied rice for transplanting, and built up seed stocks, among other measures. The cost to the 1937 general budget was 12,460,000 francs plus the cost of the rice procurement, not taking into account special assistance. Metropolitan France was not indifferent to the human tragedy. Tellingly, as an official notice remarked, discontent at inaction could also be exploited by "extremists" at a time when Japan was also threatening the Far East (AOM Indo NF 227/1858 "Note des inondations en Indochine").

In early 1937, a number of locales in Thanh Hoa Province were drastically affected by poor harvests, leading to a certain "malaise" (read: major discontent) on the part of the affected population. No doubt with memories of 1931–32 in mind, the authorities did not stand idly by. A series of public works projects, roads especially, were created, offering indigent peasant farmers a stipend to cover their needs. This was not a small investment but translated into 192,000 paid workdays. Roads and bridges in the view of the authorities would open new markets, thus satisfying a long-held demand on the part of the population. More than that, the extra income earned would enable the peasant-farmers to purchase rice seed ready for planting in the next season. In the words of an official rapporteur, "Misery was banished owing to the generous support of the government and the agricultural rhythm reestablished in the best conditions while allowing even the most disinherited to receive support" (AOM Indo/NF/104/1004 Indochine et Pacifique, p. 7, May 17, 1937).

In justifying his response to the flood crisis of 1937 in Tonkin, the key concerned official, Resident Superior Yves C. Chatel, asserted that "quick response was vital in the circumstances." To that end, he claimed to have delivered the necessary assistance efficiently and with dispatch. As he reported, the majority of the victims had already suffered from the flood of a year earlier and the spring drought and, with the 1937 flood crisis upon them, were "lacking everything." As he rationalized, "It was a problem of immediate and total assistance that had to be resolved." Once the fields had dried out, the devastated land had to be recovered, or at least the cultivator had to be offered the means to regain his economic sustenance. Special solutions were required. Notably, it was found necessary to limit the amplitude of price variations of rice and to "strangle" the numerous speculators who sought to take advantage of the crisis. Linked with this was the need to act on the local market in a way that would permit the entire population to obtain its basic needs at a normal price without having to pay a premium to speculators. Although no special budget existed for dike repair, the resident superior nevertheless drew on special funds for immediate rice relief (Bac Giang, Bac Ninh, Hai Duong, and Hung Yen) and to cover the costs of dike repair. In view of the scarcity of rice, the drawdown on stocks, and the rise in price, he sought to regularize the market price, such as by commanding additional rice from Cochinchina (two thousand tonnes). Chatel asserted, "On every count I sought to avoid famine. To this effect, I began to distribute rice as it arrived from the south, either free or at a modest price." Some 1,567 tonnes were distributed in this fashion. To allay the effect of speculation and to reduce the market price of rice, Chatel placed one hundred tonnes of rice on the market throughout Tonkin at a price of $0.05–$0.10 per kilogram. With justification, as he claimed, the experience proved that even a small quantity of rice entering the domestic market in Tonkin could make its impact felt on price. He also instructed residents to set up shelters at the village level "to provide for the most disinherited; children, women, elderly and infirm, food and care required to fulfill their physiological needs." Meantime, public charity money collected from Cochinchina and elsewhere was used to provide *nuoc mam*, dried fish, clothing, and so on. Certain of these shelters held more than two thousand persons (Bac Ninh; Bac Giang). Food aid and financial assistance were also distributed. Coolies recruited *en place* to repair the dikes were paid $0.05 with rations. Tobacco and alcohol were distributed courtesy of Distilleries de l'Indochine and tobacco factories (AOM Indo NF 222/1858 "Aprovisionnement en riz du Tonkin," RS Chatel à GG, Oct. 22, 1937).

Emergency measures aside, as Resident Superior Chatel pointed out, the interests of the collectivity had not been neglected, and, accordingly, the largest allocation of all went to "giving life and renewal of production." By this he meant that encouragement was given to the production of such secondary food crops as potatoes where suitable, thus allowing food for the fifth month, while also offering rice seed for the fifth month. Agricultural banks at Bac Giang facilitated loans for growers. Chatel also claimed to have instructed agricultural banks to grant a one-year moratorium to debtors and/or victims of the floods. Residents of flooded provinces were instructed to keep him informed as to local needs right up until the fifth month on the basis of regular rice requirements deemed indispensable to preventing famine. The total demand for rice to be procured from Cochinchina was set at 5,300 tonnes, with 2,800 allocated for Bac Ninh, 1,300 for Bac Giang, and 1,200 for Hai Duong. Even so, Chatel calculated, at the time of writing, Tonkin had sufficient stocks of rice to tide over the *soudure*. Harvests in the provinces not affected by the floods were otherwise good (AOM Indo NF 222/1858 "Aprovisionnement en riz du Tonkin," RS Chatel à GG, Oct. 22, 1937).

The 1935–37 Rice Crisis in Laos

To wit, as signaled in a November 1935 report, the northern provinces of Laos, Hua Phan (Sam Neua) and Tranh Ninh were identified as suffering a food shortage. Measures were taken to establish rice stocks, and pecuniary assistance of 1,300 piasters was offered to rice farmers. As a conservation measure, an order went out to forbid rice exports from these two provinces (AOM Indo NF 329/2657 RS Laos à GG, Affaires Politique, Nov. 14, 1935). With its population of just one million during late colonial times, food deficits in Laos, such as encountered in the more vulnerable northern provinces, could be made up from surpluses produced in the better-endowed southern provinces, although logistics was always a problem in remote areas of this landlocked country, then as now.

The year 1936 was also a year of bad harvests in Laos, and the colonial authorities sought to take stock of a threatening situation. In any case, in line with official decrees, the export of rice and rice derivatives was prohibited from the southern provinces of Bassac (July 1936) and Khammouan (November 1936). That meant a total prohibition on rice export from Laos to Thailand or other parts of Indochina. All rice in Laos was reserved for local consumption. At this point, the minister of colonies intervened, instructing the governor general to assist people in Laos suffering from the *dissette* (a loaded term connoting shortage, dearth, drought, or even famine) (AOM Indo NF 48/583–758 GG á Colonies, 1937).

But an agricultural crisis also meant a fiscal crisis for the Laos administration, and this was undoubtedly uppermost in official thinking. Without a rice surplus, the Lao peasants lacked the means to acquit their taxes and *prestations* for 1936, leading to a massive shortfall in budget support. Such a situation meant drawing down even further subventions from the federal Indochina budget, invariably attracting censure from Hanoi in line with the logic that colonies were meant to pay for themselves. Moreover, the rice crisis coincided with the devaluation of the franc and the special need in import-dependent Laos to control prices and prevent speculation (AOM Indo NF 48/583–758 GG á Colonies, 1937).

As the resident superior of Laos revealed, to meet the anticipated food crisis, especially as it threatened the large concentration of immigrant Vietnamese workers in the Phontieu and Boneng tin mines in the remote mountainous border region with Annam, urgent measures were required. This was no ordinary cohort, as suggested, since they also formed the vanguard of the ICP in Laos and were under constant surveillance by the authorities for the slightest sign of political agitation such as had broken out in this milieu in 1931–32 (Gunn 1988, 44–45). To this end, the resident superior sought concessionary freight rates for a special consignment of rice from Tonkin and Annam (November 16) "at the moment that the Resident of Thakek signals that supplies of rice (at the mines) threaten to become deficient" (Gunn 1988, 44–45).

While one might be skeptical at Chatel's report written to ingratiate himself to distant superiors, it is nevertheless an important account written during the Popular Front period when a metropolitan audience was also watching and, of course, at a time when France could hardly afford to inflame rural rebellion. Colonial paternalism, expediency, and humanitarianism all came into play. International relief agencies, such as present-day FAO (Food and Agriculture Organization), IOM (International Organization for Migration), and UNHCR (United Nations High Commissioner for Refugees), would not have been disappointed with this general approach to disaster management. My contention is that the relief offered by Chatel and others was not just a Band-Aid or charity, such as argued by Nguyen-Marshall (2008), but substantive and far reaching in its impact on village society. For the sake of this book as well, we can say that colonial responses to the 1937 floods arguably served as a dress rehearsal for management of future tragedies, as with the Great Famine of 1944–45, to the extent, of course, that the French were still in the driving seat. Unquestionably, by this juncture, the colonial administration had acquired ample experience in the crisis management of both natural disasters and food supply shortages.

Postcrisis

From October 1938, the price of rice began to fall. Between September and December 1938, the price of rice on the Saigon market fell 30 percent, with paddy diminishing 40 percent in value. Although the fall in price was less accentuated in the Haiphong marketplace, it still declined 15 percent. The reasons given for this state of affairs was the arrival in Saigon-Cholon of an abundant new harvest at a time when France and the major global cereal producers were also experiencing a good harvest, combined with a fall in demand in China owing to the war. Simultaneously, the cost of living index continued to increase in the fourth quarter of 1938, affecting Europeans and middle-class locals alike, and with an even deeper impact on the ability of those in the working class to manage their budgets. Linked with a major devaluation of the piaster in September 1936, the average cost of living in Hanoi during this period increased a steep 44 percent, with an even more alarming 60 percent increase for the working class (AOM Indo NF/330/2664, "Rapport Gouverneur Veber," Vichy, April 22, 1941). Undoubtedly, the price of rice was not the only factor affecting affordability and livelihood in urban areas alongside rent, fuel, and other costs, but it would have been an important component of the household budget on the part of the more indigent classes.

But with the worst of the 1937 crisis behind it, total rice production in Indochina (including exports, reserves, and rice for local consumption) rose to 1,650,000 tonnes in 1939, declining to 1,500,000 tonnes in 1940. The year 1940 also marked a shift away from traditional markets. Owing to the war, the China-Shanghai and Hong Kong market was lost. Shipping linking France and its colonies to Indochina simply disappeared. In 1940, Japan stepped into this market in a big way, shipping five hundred thousand tonnes of rice on its own vessels to homeland or Japanese-controlled territories (AOM Indo NF/330/2664, "Rapport Gouverneur Veber," Vichy, April 22, 1941). Hitherto, rice exports to Japan from Indochina were never important and were shrinking, with Korea, Taiwan, and Manchuria, as Japan's most important prewar external suppliers (Robequain 1944, 329). Averaging 109,000 tonnes annually in 1913–28, Japanese rice imports from Indochina dropped to thirty-six tonnes in 1929–32 and barely two tonnes in 1933–37.

Subsequently, however, Japan would also benefit from the March 1941 annexation by its wartime ally, Thailand, of the rich rice-producing province of Battambang in Cambodia, otherwise depriving Indochina of around five hundred thousand tonnes of paddy between 1941 and 1946, not to mention, as discussed in chapter 5, rice consumed or requisitioned by arriving Japanese occupation forces (Brocheux and Hémery 2009, 439n33).

TRIALS OF THE COMMUNISTS (1938–39)

Triumphantly, as the Sûreté summarized, by late 1935 the liaison apparatus of the ICP had been almost completely destroyed. This was achieved by a succession of arrests conducted in Tonkin, leaving the party bereft of communications with other groups locally as well as with Longzhou across the Indochina border in Guangxi and the Comintern Orient Bureau in Shanghai. Likewise, arrests conducted in Annam interrupted links between Nghe An and the ICP in Thailand (via Laos). Similarly, arrests conducted in Cochinchina (Tran Van Giau's among them) interrupted links with France and the PCF (AOM SLOTFOM III, 59 NM, Dec. 1936). Even so, while the ICP was undoubtedly set back in the south by wave upon wave of arrests, detentions, and even executions, it also began the patient task of rebuilding itself as a clandestine organization. As detailed below, while the ICP lay low in the south it steadily rebuilt in the north, the future zone of recruitment for the Viet Minh and, as developed in subsequent chapters in much detail, the site of the human tragedy of 1944–45.

The ICP in the North

As described in an official French report of July 1935, although northern Vietnam was ostensibly "calm," the ICP went about its activities with "prudence" but also with a "tenacity of method," especially in targeting the coal-mining region of Hong Gai-Cam Pha. The ICP was also seen to be active in Haiphong and surrounding areas, targeting such urban elements as soup vendors, hairdresser assistants, and chauffeurs, with a view to setting up syndicates. They also sought to orient the press to their cause. In Nam Dinh, youth came together with the pretext of studying Chinese boxing while, in Thai Binh, secret mutual help associations were set up. Taken together, such sporting and mutual aid groups tended to take their orders from the ICP (AOM Indo NF/329/2659).

By November 1936, major strike actions occurred in the French-owned Hong Gai and Cam Pha coal mines. At Cam Pha, some six thousand coolies ceased work in protest for higher wages. Eventually, a total of fifteen thousand workers were involved as strikes spread to all the workings in the district, with the military called out to restore order when small-scale rioting broke out. Smaller-scale strikes broke out among sawyers, carpenters, and bricklayers. By September 1937, as the British consul signaled, for the first time in the history of French occupation of Indochina, strike actions in the Tonkin coalfields were accompanied by acts of violence committed against private property. Massing an astonishing thirty thousand striking coolies, the mob attacked the dwellings of unpopular supervisors along with the establishments of "extortionist" shopkeepers. Order was restored by the military and work resumed only after arrears were paid (PRO CO 273 267 Consul Hogg, Nov. 27, 1936; Jan. 13, 1937).

Meantime, in the later part of January 1937, strikes broke out in the three major urban areas of northern Vietnam, namely Hanoi, Haiphong, and Nam Dinh, involving such tradespeople as tailors (numbering 1,500), hatters, cobblers, hairdressers, embroiderers, joiners, and joss-stick makers, along with vegetable sellers in the city markets, altogether involving 4,500 persons. Most of these conflicts were resolved amicably between labor and employers through administrative intervention, notwithstanding the apparent efforts by *Le Travail* to torpedo such efforts (AOM SLOTFOM III, 59 NM, April 1937).

The ICP also looked to a rear base in China and, to a lesser extent, Thailand. In February 1939, the Sûreté recorded an intensive propaganda activity emanating from across the border in Yunnan. As identified, on January 27, 1939, a nine-member leadership committee of the ICP had been established in Kunming. While seeking to link up with comrades in Tonkin, the Kunming-based committee was also in communication with the external leadership committee in Guangzhou and the CCP. With China coming under the shadow of Japanese military invasion, as discussed in chapter 6, the southern Chinese city became a pole of attraction for numerous Vietnamese émigrés, a future nucleus of support for the Viet Minh. Links between Thailand and the Tonkin-based ICP were revived on December 25, 1939 (AOM SLOTFOM III, 39 "Note sur la Propagande Révolutionnaire," Feb. 1939).

Significantly, for future revolutionary outcomes, by late 1938 progress realized by clandestine organizations was reportedly very strong in the lower Red River delta, on the north-central coast in Thua Thien, and in Quang Tri. In Tonkin, the ICP country committee had set up a leadership association for all legal and semilegal organizations. These included political affairs, club affairs, agricultural cooperatives, tourism, education, theater, an anti-illiteracy campaign, a democratic front, the newspapers, *Tin Tuc* (News) and *Tin Giau* (Universe), and the so-called Anh Sang League against Slums. The ICP in Tonkin had also created a shelter for women and families living around the military barracks along with "*entreaide*," or agricultural exchange associations. More generally, legal associations of the ICP across the five countries of Indochina were then well advanced. Such associations ranged from clubs to professional associations, sports, youth groups, mutual help groups, popular help groups, popular instruction, including *quoc ngu* and Esperanto, librarian training courses, cooperatives, and ex–political prisoner associations (AOM Indo NF/330 2664–2667 NP 63 Directeur de la Sûreté Général Indochinois, Oct. 1938).

According to a document issued by the ICP's Tonkin (Bac Ky) Committee, dated May 9, 1939, the most urgent task facing the party was to create bases in localities where a "popular current" already existed. As stated, *dong chi* (comrades) were required to direct all their attention to areas with a high concentration of workers, as with the mining regions of Hong Gai and Dong Trieu. The resolutions also called on ICP members to expand and consolidate existing bases and to rally "the most conscious and ardent party agents." Candidature for membership was to be based exclusively on spirit for struggle and activity as well as acceptance of the party's program and status. Knowledge of Marxist or Leninist doctrine was not compulsory, which, in any case, could be acquired later on. *Dang Bo* (local party committee members) in each location were advised to teach the party policies, "secrets of the Indochinese revolution," modes of organization, mass support in the struggle, and the "destructive maneuvers" of the Trotskyists (AOM Indo NF/366/2905–2908 Annex à la lettre No.42 SG, Aug. 11, 1939). Still, this was a fairly doctrinaire approach on the part of the ICP, both vis-à-vis the Trotskyists and the French, especially with its focus on the still-restricted working-class nuclei and hardly touching the masses of peasant cultivators or minority peoples.

The 1938–39 Stalinist-Trotskyist Divorce

Notwithstanding the marriage of convenience between the Third and Fourth Internationals during the Popular Front period, the knives were soon out, at least when the political conjuncture had shifted. As late as February 1939, the Stalinists and Trotskyists still upheld certain tactical alliances. Notably, as the Sûreté recorded, three of the newspapers aligned with the Third International, namely *Dan Chung*, *Dan Nuit*, and *Tan Tien*, fell in line with the Trotskyist mouthpiece *Tia Siang* on the issue calling for unity around claims for universal suffrage (AOM SLOTFOM III, 39 "Note sur la Propagande Révolutionnaire," Feb. 1939).

The tension between the two rivals is captured in an ICP document issuing from Tonkin in August 1939. As stated, the victory of the Trotskyists in the Cochinchina colonial council elections "leads us to recall one more time the need to be vigilant and to guard against the Trotskyists who resemble a dangerous germ in the popular current." Their victory can be explained variously. First, the peasant working masses did not have the right to vote (all the colonial oppression was borne by the communists). On the other hand, the document continued, the antagonistic colonial policy helped the Trotskyists in propagating their "demagoguery." To the extent that the Trotskyists gained influence over the petit bourgeoisie, the intellectuals, and the workers, it owed to *La Lutte*, which, "owing to an error on our part, we also supported several years ago." Until today, the report continued, "this error persists among a number of our *dong chi* who believe that the Trotskyists in Indochina relate to the situation in which they find themselves by keeping up an anti-imperialist spirit." Furthermore, "This spirit has greatly weakened the struggle against the Trotskyists. The Trotskyists use all their means to deceive the population despite their small number. Sometimes they pass themselves off as communists in order to better dupe the masses. Vis-à-vis the capitalists and big landowners, they invest all means to oppose communism and worker strikes," and "because the Trotskyists are a very dangerous germ, we have to make war against them." In Tonkin, the Trotskyists are still in an embryonic state: "we must kill them now while it is still an egg." Already the Trotskyists make their propaganda among students and workers through offering free anticommunist newspapers (AOM Indo NF/366/2905–2908 Annex à la lettre No.42, SG, Aug. 11, 1939).

While the author of this document is unknown, according to Brocheux (2007, 76), in his report to the Comintern on July 12, 1940, Nguyen Ai Quoc forbade any collusion between the ICP and the Trotskyists, taking specific aim at the "hypocrite and pseudo-savant" Ta Thu Thau. Brocheux, in fact, directly attributes responsibility for the physical elimination of the Vietnamese Trotskyists to Nguyen Ai Quoc. Whatever the veracity, at a time when he was Comintern envoy in China, Nguyen Ai Quoc/Ho Chi Minh published articles in the ICP newspaper *Our Voices* (May–August 1931) condemning the betrayal of the Chinese Trotskyists.

Dissolution of the Communist Party and Repression

In a turn of the wheel, incoming Vichy governor Veber, successor of Pagès, took up office in Cochinchina on July 14, 1939. By his own admission, from practically the day of his arrival he sought the dissolution of the Communist Party. As he vowed, "The benevolent measures in favor of the communists will be rejected." This he achieved through a decree of September 26, 1939, invoking articles 90 and 91 of the modified penal code and allowing him to issue an order of a police warrant against the Communist Party headquarters and associated organizations and groups in Saigon-Cholon. The first wave of suppression netted ninety under police warrants along with one hundred arrests, the proscription of fourteen periodicals, two Vietnamese-language dailies, and two French-language periodicals, all deemed to be pro-communist in orientation. The dissolution of Communist Party organizations was also achieved. Another ordinance of October 11 led to police actions against all the party printing presses along with bookstores across Cochinchina, leading to the seizure or removal of all pro-communist publications. Altogether, this first sweep netted 323 persons under police warrants and the seizure of 26,000 newspapers and 2,333 brochures. All the security services were mobilized for this operation. The ordinance was drawn so broadly that even the presumption of breaking the law could be acted on. From September 1, 1939, to October 1, 1940, 389 individuals were sentenced to a total of 770 years in prison (the comparative figures for the liberal year, 1937, was fourteen individuals for seventeen years, for 1938, forty-two individuals for eleven years, and for January–October 1939, fifty individuals for seventy-eight years). These figures do not include those arrested for membership in illegal associations (law of September 26, 1939), which were far more numerous although involving lesser sentences (AOM Indo NF/330/2664 "Rapport des Colonies," Veber à Colonies, April 19, 1941).

The months of September–November 1939 were marked by particularly important operations mounted in Saigon and in the provinces of Gia Dinh and Thu Dau Mot. Beginning in October, a major operation was mounted in the Plaine des Joncs, described as an immense swamp extending from Vaico Oriental to the Mekong with difficult access and long a refuge of wrongdoers and individuals escaping the security services. This operation netted one hundred individuals while roundups in Saigon swept up some one hundred individuals. Despite the opening of an annex for female prisoners at Phu My and the constant dispatch of the condemned to provincial prisons or to Poulo Condore penitentiary, the Maison Centrale in Saigon was bursting at the seams. The Sûreté premises were also crammed with individuals undergoing interrogations. Taken together, 1,200 individuals were "neutralized" by various means. The arrests were given maximum publicity in the official media as a warning (AOM Indo NF/330/2664 "Rapport des Colonies," Veber à Colonies, April 19, 1941).

Among the more important Communist Party members swept up by this wave of arrests were Thi-Kay (Nguyen Thi Minh Khai), as mentioned, the female delegate to the Macau Congress and assistant to Ho Chi Minh at the time of his arrest in Hong Kong, along with three or four central committee members all committed to prison in Saigon. Arrested on July 30, 1940, and executed by the French on August 26, 1941, Nguyen Thi Minh Khai remains a heroine of the revolution (Hong Chuong 1965, 70), with a prominent street in Saigon as well as a school both named after her. Not only did the ICP come under heavy repression, but many of Ho Chi Minh's collaborators, such as Le Duan, Duong Bach Mai, and Tran Huy Lieu, were arrested before the party went underground in 1939.

With much of the ICP network repressed in the south, a new leadership was constituted in the Hanoi region around Truong Chinh (Dang Xuan Khu), released from prison under the Popular Front government. Having evaded arrest during the entire wartime period, Truong Chinh would emerge as a leading figure in the Viet Minh camp alongside Ho Chi Minh, first as editor of the party's regional newspaper and then as propagandist-ideologue. Although it would be the northern party personalities, Vo Nguyen Giap, Pham Van Dong, and Ho Chi Minh, who would eventually lever themselves to power in Hanoi, it was not without trying on the part of the southerners around Tran Van Giau who would eventually gain his release from prison by the Japanese.

CONCLUSION

As we underscored, the formation of the French Popular Front government in June 1936 not only facilitated the legalization of the various communist parties for the first and only time in the colonies, Vietnam included, but dramatically changed the domestic political situation. In Indochina, it also led to a unique cohabitation between adherents of the Third and Fourth Internationals in standing up to French colonialism. Unique in the history of international communism, the *lutteurs* could count on the hidden support of the underground militants of the Communist Party. In contrast to the period following the establishment of the ICP in 1930, the Popular Front years were marked by lively press freedom and the flourishing of journals of the left. As I have discussed at some length, it was the Saigon-based journal *La Lutte* which best exemplified the politics of the age.

As expressed through their writings, the Trotskyists distinguished themselves by their intellectual approach to the social problems of the day as much tactical considerations in opposing French colonialism. As urban, educated intellectuals, the Trotskyists also worked to build a base among the majority peasantry, a feature setting them apart from their European counterparts. The Indochina Trotskyists also distinguished themselves from global counterparts, not only through their enthusiastic embrace of legal political activity but by their willingness to enter into a temporary alliance with their would-be ideological rivals among the ICP. As such, they were bilingual, worldly, and modern in their outlook, and this was expressed in their prolific publications. While the Trotskyists shared with the communist mainstream the full brunt of French police repression, their urban identities would leave them vulnerable to repression at the hands of their ideological antagonists in the wake of the Japanese surrender in August–September 1945.

As Osborne (1969, 281) comments, participation by Vietnamese in the Saigon Municipal Council had its limits. After all, the Vietnamese delegates were always outvoted, just as the power structure remained firmly in colonial hands. Although a tiny minority of Vietnamese did achieve important positions in the colonial administration, and while a class of *collaborateurs* did emerge from among a group of "naturalized" Francophile Vietnamese, the major feature of the French rule in Vietnam in general during the nineteenth and early twentieth century was the reluctance of the French administration to allocate any real responsibility to Vietnamese.

But still in the saddle through the Popular Front years, the French also became increasingly aware of the fragility of the agrarian-hydraulic pact into which they had entered with both the Vietnamese elite as well as the masses. Stepping into the shoes of the imperial state, the colonial state not only had to manage agrarian crises, such as demonstrated with the floods and drought of 1937 in central Vietnam and Laos, but had to react proactively if they were to redeem their honor as administrators of merit or as just legatees of the "mandate of heaven." Less than a decade remained to test these assumptions, and the challenges ahead were more dire than even the most pessimistic French administrators could have envisaged.

Chapter 5

Vichy and the Japanese Occupation, 1940–45

Following the German invasion and occupation of France in May–June 1940, Japan sought in the Vichy French administration of Admiral Jean Decoux to advance its interests in Indochina. These were both political-military and economic, especially as Japan sought to capture Indochina's rich supplies of rice, rubber, and minerals. Under the double yoke of Vichy and the Japanese military, Indochina was also warped into Tokyo's Greater East Asia Co-prosperity Zone concept with all its attendant economic and ideological features. Coming at a period when Allied forces were rolling back Japanese advances in the Pacific, the Japanese military coup of March 9, 1945, against the Vichy French administration of Indochina presented the Vietnamese nationalists with new opportunities. Seeking to set the scene for both the devastating famine that broke in early 1945 as well as the Viet Minh ascendancy, this chapter divides into four sections. A first section exposes the political pressure imposed by Japan on the French administration in both the political-military and economic domains. A following section expands on the Vichy economic etatism as it panned out in wartime Indochina. The analysis then turns to an evaluation of armed insurgency threats to Vichy control in northern and southern Vietnam, actually premonitions of the revolution to come. Finally, the significance of the armed Japanese takeover of March 9, 1945, is canvassed with respect to its immediate political and military consequences.

JAPANESE PRESSURES ON VICHY FRANCE

With the June 1940 surrender of France to Hitler's army and the establishment of the Vichy regime under Marshal Philippe Pétain, Governor General Georges Catroux became increasingly vulnerable and, on July 20, 1940, was replaced by Admiral Jean Decoux, then heading up French naval forces in the Pacific. Initially, however, Vichy France aspired to protect French interests from Germany and treaty partners. Fearing Tokyo's designs to turn Indochina into a "new Manchuria" and following his predecessor's lead, Decoux kept up trade with Britain and its colonies (Devillers 1952, 70). Contrariwise, taking advantage of the German victory over France, Japan began to ramp up its pressure, not only on Indochina but also on French concessions in Shanghai, Hankou, and Tianjin. As discussed below, Japanese wartime pressures on the French in Indochina took both economic and political form and progressed through a number of discrete stages.

There was obviously much subterfuge involved in Japan's pressures imposed on French Indochina, especially in the way of keeping Great Britain and the powers offside, but it was also clear that Nazi Germany gave Tokyo the green light or was even complicit. In something of an intelligence coup, in early August 1941, Free French forces discovered secret Nazi documents relating to Indochina in the archives of the French high commissioner in Beirut created by the secretariat of the Vichy Ministry of War. As these documents starkly revealed, the Germans were "the true masters of Vichy foreign policy." Notably, "the German (Armistice) Commission upholds its refusal to reinforce personnel and matériel in the defense of Indochina." On February 15, 1941, the tenor of this instruction was repeated, disallowing any reinforcement of Indochina in personnel or matériel, whether arriving from metropolitan France or Madagascar. The same restriction applied to American-type aircraft otherwise stranded on a vessel in French Martinique. As the Free French analyst offered, no other proof could so ably testify to the "flagrant collusion between Germany and Japan over Indochina" (AOM Indo NF/134/1307 "Documents découvert à Beyrouth," Aug. 1, 1941).

In the words of the Free French analyst, the acceptance by Vichy in the complete seizure by Japan of Indochina marked a new stage in the policy of erosion of the national patrimony advanced since June 1940 by the complicity (*fauteur*) of capitulation. The principle stages were identified as, first, the September 22, 1940, accord under which Japan was granted the rights to establish air bases in Tonkin to facilitate passage of troops toward China and to occupy military barracks in Haiphong; and second, the March 4, 1941, accord that ceded the western provinces of Laos and Cambodia, including rice surplus Battambang Province, to Thailand. German infiltration into North Africa, beginning in January 1941, then continued to aggravate. At the same time, the disposition given to the Luftwaffe to establish air bases in the French mandate of Syria rendered necessary actions by Allied forces to preempt a scenario such as the one that unfolded in Indochina. As the analyst continued, it was clear that Decoux had placed Vichy in a bind. The verbal assurances of Marshal Pétain were contradicted by the facts, which only underlined the tragic character of the situation. The Vichy attitude was rendered more odious by the pretexts invoked. By accusing Britain and the United States of aggressive intentions and invoking the protection of Japan, as with the dismemberment of Indochina, Vichy imposed a gratuitous humiliation on France (AOM Indo NF/134/1217, tél., Affaires Politiques à de Gaulle, July 25, 1941).

As the report continued, by placing Indochina under Japanese military control, Vichy lent weight to the military interests of the Anglo-Saxon powers, whose victory represented the only possibility for the liberation of France. "Renouncing even the pretext of neutrality, it is ostensibly placed in the camp of the aggressors of the country at the moment when the Russian resistance has probably changed the map of the war in favor of the Allies." The major points emerging from this discussion were that Vichy had no right to speak in the name of France; that France suffered the double oppression of the Vichy police and the Gestapo; and that Vichy rule would not last one day longer than the German domination. In this scenario, Free France represented the only possibility to rescue the material patrimony of the country. Such was the "sacred" character of de Gaulle's mission (AOM Indo NF/134/1217, tél., Affaires Politiques à de Gaulle, July 25, 1941). At this point we should recall that the United States did not enter the war until after the Japanese attack on Pearl Harbor on December 6, 1941. On the other hand, the United States granted Vichy full diplomatic recognition, seeking by diplomacy to turn elements within Vichy away from German allegiance.

Indochina was not, of course, the only French colony where Vichyite administrations were challenged either by Gaullists Allies, or a combination of both. Events in New Caledonia were a case in point. In the French Pacific colony, the Vichy-appointed interim governor, Colonel Maurice Denis, was removed in a bloodless coup staged by Gaullists. Deported to Saigon in September 1940 with de Gaulle's approval, he was joined by more than two hundred officials, including bureaucrats and gendarmes (Munholland 2005, 55). As the former Vichy governor general of Cochinchina recorded, those French chased out of New Caledonia, namely Colonel Denis and his group, were given a high official welcome in Saigon (AOM Indo NF/330/2664–67 Veber à Colonies, Vichy, April 19, 1941).

The December 8, 1941, Ultimatum in Hanoi

On December 8, 1941, in the immediate aftermath of the attack on Pearl Harbor, Tokyo signed an agreement for closer military cooperation with Decoux. Under this arrangement, the Japanese moved thirty-five thousand troops into Indochina, set up military, air, and naval bases, assembled its military assets, and harassed Allied shipping. Less than two hours after the attack on Pearl Harbor, Japanese forces began landing in Thailand, with the bulk of the guards force entering via Cambodia (Hasemen 1978, 1). Saigon became a launching pad for the destruction of the Singapore-based British fleet (December 10) and invasion of Malaya.

Simultaneously, Japanese troops infiltrated Hanoi and were posted at government buildings, major intersections, and so on while tanks advanced on French general military headquarters. With a great display of pomp, Japanese military officials then arrived, informing Decoux that Japan was at war and that French Indochina had better accede or else (Gaudal 1947, 125–26). Temporizing, Decoux soon fell in line with this subterfuge, allowing autonomy for its military and administration while delivering Indochina carte blanche to the Japanese military. In this bizarre cohabitation, the tricolor kept flying and stayed there until March 9, 1945.

The Yunnan Railroad Question

As French intelligence summarized, even prior to September 1939, Japan had made numerous representations concerning the transit from Haiphong of American-supplied war matériel destined for China. The Japanese answered by bombing the Yunnan-Vietnam Railway's line in Chinese territory, though not entirely putting it out of action. Even so, quantities of war matériel began to accumulate in Haiphong. Managed by Chinese business groups, more than one hundred depots in Haiphong and Hanoi were stocked with considerable caches of weapons, munitions, war materials, metals, lorries, medicines, clothing, and so on. Though slowed down by various acts of destruction effected by the Japanese on the rail line, nevertheless, during September 1939–June 1940 the transit of war matériel to the Nationalists continued as usual (MAE AOI 28 E 167 3 "Arrêt du Transit de Material du Guerre," Paris, June 10, 1946).

But on June 19, 1940, or three days before the fall of France, the Japanese demanded that Catroux sever all supply routes to Nationalist China and permit Japan to set up a military mission in Hanoi. As the Americans and, in turn, the Free French learned from an intercepted Nazi German telephone conversation, this took the form of an ultimatum, reserving other measures if rejected. As the French government replied, such measures would be a breach of sovereignty, although it had already stopped the passage of arms some eight or nine months earlier. Still, it insisted, such terms could be negotiated only by a free agreement. Berlin was also duly apprised of these arrangements (MAE AOI 27 tél., IPS doc. 3360). Although Catroux demurred, Vichy accepted the demand, and the last munitions train bound for Kunming crossed the border at the end of June 1940. On June 22, Tokyo further demanded the installation of a Japanese naval presence in

Guangzhouwan and the complete closure of the Chinese border by July 7. Arriving in Hanoi on June 29, General Nishihara Issaku, the top concerned Japanese military official, then demanded French agreement as to the passage of Japanese troops and the use of airports in Indochina (Le Manh Hung 2004, 252).

The Matsuoka-Henry Pact of August 30, 1940

With the forced resignation of the Tokyo government on July 16, 1940, the new Konoye cabinet appointed Matsuoka Yosuke as minister of foreign affairs (1940–41) and General Tojo Hideki as minister of war. On August 1, the cabinet presented Matsuoka's concept of the Greater East Asia Co-prosperity Sphere. On August 30, 1940, Vichy ambassador Charles Arsène Henry entered into an exchange of notes with Foreign Minister Matsuoka regarding an understanding that Japan would recognize the sovereignty and territorial integrity of France in French Indochina and France, on her part, would undertake to offer special facilities for the stationing of Japanese troops in specified zones while also recognizing Japan's dominant position in the Far East (Devillers 1952, 77–78).

On September 4, 1940, this pact was duly complemented by a Franco-Japanese military accord, ostensibly restricting total Japanese troop strength in Indochina to twenty-five thousand, with access to Hanoi rigorously controlled and with strict restrictions on the use of Haiphong port and airports. Still, the French hesitated with Decoux and his military commander, General Maurice Martin, seeking to prolong negotiations over a confidential military protocol attached to the agreement. The pact was ratified only on September 23, the day before the bombardment of Haiphong and battle of Lang Son (an event whereby a Japanese force overwhelmed a French military position on September 22–26, 1940), in order to intimidate both the French administration and the Thai government (AOM SLOTFOM 1129–45 "Texte de l'Accord Militaire," Sept. 4, 1940).

As replayed by General Tojo Hideki at the Tokyo War Crimes Tribunal, the Lang Son action was actually attributed by the Japanese high command (the emperor included) to an error or to insubordination. In the event, Japan also began to ratchet up its demands, leaving Decoux with little choice but to accept them, as with the order to deliver up the port of Haiphong and territories in the region of Lang Son as well as free use of Indochina airspace. As Le Manh Hung (2004, 254–55) observes, the Nishihara-Martin Agreement marked the end of the first phase of the Japanese advance into Indochina, but it still did not give the Japanese any special access to Indochina's resources. That would be a second stage, but it would take until May 1941 to be accomplished.

The Vichy-Japan "Rice Accord" of 1941

Notwithstanding France's protectionist bias, such reservations would be swept aside as Tokyo launched a series of démarches and measures seeking not only access to French Indochina markets but a virtual grip on Indochina's rich rice reserves. The culmination of this policy, dating back to December 10, 1940, was the interim Vichy-Japan agreement of January 20, 1941, leading to the "Accord Commercial Franco-Japonaise" or "Rice Accord," signed in Tokyo on May 6, 1941.

Brokered by Matsumiya Jun for Japan and former Indochina Governor General René Robin for Vichy France, negotiations on the rice agreement were long and disputed, with Vichy highly cautious over any attempt by Japan to dilute its political or economic sovereignty in Indochina, although that is precisely what happened. Represented by its ambassador to Vichy, Tokyo obviously played on its freshly concluded Tripartite Pact with Italy and Germany of September 8, 1940, in negotiating from a position of strength. In that regard, negotiations on the accord were conducted as much in the Vichy capital in France as in Tokyo.

Imposed under duress, even the Vichy regime entertained grave reservations as to entering this accord. As the Japanese chargé d'affaires to Vichy made it known to his French interlocutors, the question of supplying rice to Japan overrode all other economic issues engaging Japan and France. Answering back to Japanese insistence on locking France into a contractual obligation for a three-year term, the French held to an agreement of one year maximum, the conventional period entered into by France on commercial issues. Moreover, France reserved the right to sell Indochina rice as well as nonrice commodities in traditional markets besides Japan. Vichy demanded that Japan pay one tranche of payments in American dollars at the end of each year and the balance in yen for the "*compte special riz*" (special rice account). As the archival record makes clear, the bottom line for Vichy in these negotiations turned on the concept of "unimpeachable" French sovereignty over Indochina (AOM Indo NF 127/1143 "Accord Franco-Japonaise sur le riz," n.d.).

As Le Manh Hung (2004, 105–9) explains, under an interim agreement of January 20, 1941, Indochina would export to Japan within the year seven hundred thousand tonnes of milled white rice (as opposed to the Japanese demand of one million tonnes) along with seventeen thousand tonnes of rubber (as opposed to the demand of sixty thousand tonnes), pending ongoing negotiations over payment. France duly maintained its quota for traditional markets, as with the French concession in Shanghai. Meanwhile, Decoux entered into "secret" discussions with the British on economic issues, further encouraging the Japanese to up the ante. All up, the accord was premised on

Cochinchina's supplying an annual exportable quantity of rice reaching two million tonnes, achievable only under optimum conditions (BEI 1944, 165, 187).[1]

With the exchange of ratifications taking place in Tokyo on July 5, 1941, the "Rice Accord" took the form of a thirty-one-article treaty, replacing an earlier commercial agreement of May 13, 1932. Initially valid until December 31, 1943, there was provision for an extension. Guangzhouwan was not included in this accord. Article 1 offered a most-favored nation clause vis-à-vis each nation's tax regime. An annex listed the minimum tariffs on Japanese imports into Indochina, while a separate annex indicated a long list of products that would enjoy tariff exemptions with Japan, notably maize, castor, salt, iron ore, manganese, tungsten, zinc, antimony, and teakwood. Setting aside the considerable commercial advantages provided for by such tariff exemption, Article 21 set down the terms under which the Banque de l'Indochine would place at the disposal of the Yokohama Specie Bank a counterpart of the equivalent yen in Indochinese piasters necessary for payments, at rates which would be determined. Under Article 22, yen acquired by the Banque de l'Indochine would be paid into two "special yen" accounts opened in the banks (MAE AOI 254).

As Le Manh Hung (2004, 111) explains, these piasters would then be used by Japan to buy goods from Indochina. The Yokohama Specie Bank would similarly provide the Banque de l'Indochine with yen for the payment of Japanese goods. Both yen and piasters would be converted into gold-convertible foreign currencies (mainly US dollars) when the accounts were settled at the end of each month. A complicated formula of three separate accounts was established. Payment for rice was in yen and deposited in the special account "B," which would be available to Indochina only a year after the purchase date. "Designed to satisfy Japan's raw material needs, rather than to promote special benefits between Japan and Indochina, the Franco-Japanese economic agreement effectively tied Indochina's economy to Japan and severed nearly all commercial relations between Indochina and other countries."

The Rice Committee

To better facilitate the accord, to control the market, and to liaise with Chinese and French rice exporters, on February 2, 1941, the administration created the so-named Comité de direction pour le commerce et l'exportation des paddy, riz et dérivé, or "Rice Committee." Besides fixing prices to eliminate rice stocks and a fluctuating market, as had been the norm, crucially the committee determined the monthly rice purchase-delivery quota. On the Japanese side, the rice monopoly was given to Mitsui Bussan Kaisha, with responsibility for maize given to the Fodder Distribution Company. Additionally, the Japanese Ministry of Commerce and Industry designated the South Seas Trade Association as the "principal organization to carry out any commercial relations with Indochina." It should be noted, however, that the Rice Committee held jurisdiction only for rice exported from Saigon, whereas rice exported from Tonkin (Haiphong) came under the control of the Hanoi-based Directions des Services Economiques, an administrative anomaly besetting the two regions that was also exploited by profiteers (BEI 1944, 166–70; 189).

Needless to say, the leverage exerted on the French by Japan was also viewed with grave concern in Washington. This is reflected in a memorandum by the acting secretary of state (Welles) regarding a conversation with the Japanese ambassador (Nomura) on July 23, 1941, who stated that Japan was now importing a million tons of rice a year from Indochina and that it sought an uninterrupted supply of rice and other raw materials from Indochina. As Nomura defended, Gaullist French agents and Chinese "agitators" were sowing trouble. Additionally, Japan had to look to its security. As Wells replied (and the evidence supplied above confirms), "any agreement which Japan might have reached with the Vichy Government could only have been reached as a result of pressure brought to bear upon the Vichy Government by Berlin" otherwise offering assistance to Hitler in his quest for world domination (US Government 1943, 692–96).

The Japanese Survey Mission of 1941–42

As provided for in an annex to the accord, between September 1940 and April 1942, Japan launched a major economic mission ostensibly to study Indochina's total economic patrimony, even including hydroelectricity potential, albeit clearly designed for the Japanese exploitation of Indochina's riches. Surveying Indochina's total resource patrimony from coal, iron ore, salt, rice, maize, rice, fisheries, and forest resources, the mission was not short on expertise. Dubbed the Mission Economique du Japon en Indochina, it comprised 151 officials and technical officials sponsored and financed by the Ministry of Foreign Affairs and Ministry of Colonies. The head of the mission was Yokoyama Masayuki, a veteran diplomat who joined the Japanese diplomatic mission in Indochina as economic counselor in October 1942 and future postcoup supremo at the Court of Annam.

In his analysis of the mission report, Le Manh Hung (2004, 148–52)[2] signals the low opinion the Japanese held of Indochinese agriculture and French efforts to develop it. Reporting on rice, the report indicated that modern methods in general were not used. Fertilizer and insecticide were not employed. And by emphasizing industrial crops, France looked with contempt at native crops such as maize, sugarcane, peanuts, and others. Even the personnel of the Rice Office were criticized for lacking the requisite skills. The survey also found that rice yield per hectare in Indochina was quite low, with the highest yields in Tonkin at 1.47 tonnes per hectare and Annam and Cochinchina with 1.37 and 1.34 tonnes per hectare, respectively. Even seeding and replanting techniques were criticized, as with the local practice of using too many seeds when sowing and replanting the seedlings too densely. The idea was to bring in Japanese and Taiwanese experts to instruct the Indochinese on soil working and seeding techniques. Formosan rice, which had been given a trial on Hainan, was recommended for introduction into Tonkin. The Japanese also recommended extending and improving the irrigation network. To get the rice out to Japan, the mission recommended a shake-up of the rice export trade, basically by replacing French companies that were using Chinese middlemen with Japanese. The cultivation of maize, cotton, and a range of other items was similarly examined and critiqued. The target for export of maize to Japan in 1942 was also set at four hundred thousand tonnes to replace lost supplies in Manchuria and India. The mission proposed an additional five hundred thousand hectares be given over to maize cultivation in Cambodia to be grown in fields which produced only a single rice crop.

As much a prescriptive as descriptive report, it was clear the mission knew who was taking control of the economy. There is no doubt that Japan had successively modernized rice cultivation at home as well as in its colonies and the yields it achieved were far ahead of those of Indochina. Nevertheless, the mission took little heed of local or traditional practices or the vast diversity of local conditions such as the various climatic regimes differentiating north, central, and southern Vietnam, just as Indochina's overall agricultural production was to be subordinated to Japan's needs whatever the local consequences.

The Franco-Japanese Accords of 1942, 1943, and 1944

Yet another Franco-Japanese accord on rice export from Saigon was signed on July 18, 1942. As tracked by Free French military intelligence, following initial discussions between Decoux and Japanese Minister Kuriyama Shigeru on January 11, 1942, an agreement was arrived at whereby Indochina would export rice and maize to Japan. Kuriyama declined to reveal the quantities or price but touted the deal as a major contribution to the Greater East Asia Co-prosperity Sphere (AOM NF Indo/134/1275 Tutenges, BR, no. 116, Chungking, Feb. 15, 1942). He was right. Under the accord, Japan contracted deliveries of over one million tonnes of Indochinese rice a year (1,050,000 tonnes of rice and 45,000 tonnes of white flour), alongside maize. It also determined the quality of rice exported. Under this dispensation, the details of deliveries were examined by a committee including the Japanese consul general in Saigon, a representative of Mitsui Busan, the director of the government Rice and Maize Agency (Comptoir du riz et mais), and a government commissioner. True to the agreement, the grand total of rice deliveries collected by the Agency for delivery in 1942 totaled 1,043,700 tonnes (BEI 1944, 213–14, 218).

As discussed below, this figure would increase as the war progressed (Franco-Japanese Accord of January 25, 1943 and the accord of January 5, 1944), just as rice came to be extracted under increasing duress, including forced or compulsory deliveries outside of any market conditions or consideration for local needs. In this regard we might single out the special pressure applied by Mitsui Bussan Kaisha, such as in September 1943, through squeezing the *prime de rendement*, or "yield premium system," in order to command even greater rice deliveries. Mitsui alone commanded rice warehouses in Saigon capable of stockpiling fifty thousand tonnes of rice (BEI 1944, 242, 285).

Financial Pressures

Under a series of devices, Japan progressively moved large tranches of counterpart funds out of French Indochina, offering the counterpart of "special yen" parked in the Yokohama Specie Bank in Tokyo by the Banque de l'Indochine. Pejoratively dubbed "yen rice," it was obvious to both the French and the peasant producers that this was a system under which Japan nakedly plundered Indochina's cereal resources. The parallel, as far as French opinion was concerned, and as reclaimed by France of Japan in the postwar period, was the "clearing system" imposed by Nazi Germany over occupied France.

Japanese pressure on Vichy to make piasters available to its forces through an exchange of currency between the two banks was also tracked by American intelligence "Magic" intercepts. As revealed, dispatches flowed between Vichy and Tokyo and between Hanoi and Tokyo. Notably, on August 18, 1941, Japan claimed 4,500,000 yen, although a month later France had still not delivered. By September 16, 1941, these interbank arrangements were transferred to the diplomatic conference table, with Japan essentially gaining its demands as the tranches of money were delivered (US Government 1978, 3:318, 530). Even so, throughout the occupation, it is clear that Vichy strongly objected to this pressure and repeatedly stonewalled, especially as the measure was wildly inflationary. It is clear in this and other capitulations that Vichy acquiesced only out of duress imposed by its German patrons.

For example, on March 18, 1944, at a conference held at Vichy at the request of the "head of government," the following individuals came together: Pierre Cathala, minister of national economy and finances, Admiral Henri Blehaut, secretary of state for marine and colonies, Charles Rochat, secretary

Table 5.1. Monthly Payments (in Piasters) from Vichy to Japan, 1940–45

Year	*Amount*	*January–March*
1940	6,000,000	2,000,000
1941	51,000,000	4,000,000
1942	86,000,000	7,000,000
1943	111,000,000	9,000,000
1944	363,000,000	30,000,000
1945	90,000,000	30,000,000*

Source: Decoux 1949, 446; Vietnam 1979, 41.
*Not including 780,000,000 piasters paid by the Banque de l'Indochine to Japan March–August 1945.

of state for foreign affairs, and Mitani Takanobu, the Japanese ambassador to France. As Ambassador Mitani indicated, he had "invited" Decoux to pay a debenture of 246 million piasters for the cost of the Japanese occupation. The governor general, in turn, submitted the question to the Vichy government. In the course of the meeting, the Vichy minister of finance made it known that the requested payment by Japan represented a sum equal to two-thirds of the *fiduciare* (financial assets) in circulation in Indochina. As he remonstrated, the inflation thus provoked would have severe consequences and would quickly translate into a rapid inflation of prices and salaries. The operation would backfire in its effect when Japanese troops found themselves holding a large quantity of money of which the value tended to zero, not to mention the social troubles that it would undoubtedly provoke. As he argued, the phenomenon so provoked would even have repercussions on the Japanese yen and the Far East. As the minister clarified, on his advice, Indochina would be able to deliver only up 123 million piasters taking into account the 58 million already paid. In any case, the French government could not accept a payment for Indochina in excess of that amount. However, the French treasury could offer French francs under a form to be determined (MAE AOI 27, "Note . . . des frais d'occupation de l'Indochine," Vichy, March 21, 1944). As presented in table 5.1, Vichy nevertheless fell in line with Japanese demands, with a steady increase in payments until the end of the Japanese-Vichy collaboration.

THE VICHY FRENCH *ECONOMIE DIRIGÉ*

Setting aside a range of imposingly fascist doctrines and gestures adopted by Decoux, as with purges of Jews and Masons, Indochina nevertheless stood out by remaining "remarkably autonomous" alongside other French colonies under Vichy (Jennings 2004, 140). Under conditions of extreme isolation from the global economy, among other constraints, Indochina under Decoux came under the strict diktat of the Vichy state, whereby all sectors of the economy—industry, transport, agricultural production, local production, import and export—entered an *économie dirigé* subject to strict administration intervention and controls, not excluding the all-important Cochinchina rice market (BEI 1944, 148). Pandering to big French business and mining interests through the creation of state-run economic agencies (*comptoirs*) and, to a limited extent, developing producer cooperatives, Decoux's new corporatism would also mesh with a system of Japanese procurements such as handled by specially created military-linked companies.

On the eve of war, according to an internal Vichy report deemed credible but "unduly optimistic" by Gaullist French intelligence, 45 percent of exports and 56 percent of imports from Indochina were destined for or procured from France or French colonies. However, with the outbreak of hostilities in Europe, the signing of the "Franco-German armistice" of June 1940, and the outbreak of war in the Far East, economic links between Indochina and France slowly unraveled, obliging an economic reorientation in line with the new situation. Up until December 8, 1941, Indochina had benefited from some imports from Australia and the United States but too little in volume to build up stocks, resulting in a breach between the peacetime and the "wartime economy." With the total rupture in communications with France, the signing of the "Rice Accord" of May 6, 1941, and the charter of economic relations with Japan governing the exports of rice, maize, coal, and minerals, Japan became the "exclusive client and provider" of Indochina, otherwise isolated from the external world (AOM SLOTFOM 1129–1145 127/1135 BR no. 238, SREO, Chungking, May 10, 1944).

As the Vichy-sourced report acknowledged, the accord of May 6, 1941, awarded Japan the total expendable surplus of rice and corn production, "base elements of the Indochina economy." Rubber and minerals followed. Although Japan pledged to supply a "large quantity" of manufactured goods, it never met its promise, in any case tapering off owing to shipping difficulties. On the other hand, Decoux's *économie dirigé* was strictly geared to production destined for Japan. It entailed progressive restraints on production of items lacking foreign markets and deprived of imported producer goods. The new orientation also accorded high priority to agricultural and industrial activity with a view to achieving immediate import substitution. In theory, but hardly in practice, the system was supposed to deliver an "equitable and judicious distribution" of imported goods to the population with a view to maintaining ordinary economic activity as long as possible (AOM SLOTFOM 1129–1145 127/1135 BR no. 238, SREO, Chungking, May 10, 1944).

As indicated in table 5.2, the actual quantities of rice and maize delivered to Japan reveal rice exports in particular recording a steady increase between 1941 and 1943 and with total rice and maize exports exceeding one million tonnes per annum by 1942. The 1943–44 harvest was the worst

Table 5.2. Rice and Corn Exports from Indochina to Japan

Year	*Rice Exports (tonnes)*	*Corn Exports (tonnes)*
1940	468,280	177,023
1941	583,323	119,252
1942	961,941	123,980
1943	978,699*	100,763
1944	600,000**	—

Source: Annuaire Statistique de l'Indochine; Ministre de l'Information.
*Nguyen The Anh (1998a, 210).
**BEI 1944, *265*.

in Cochinchina (and Cambodia) since 1938, realizing a yield of 2,600,000 tonnes, or 19 percent less than average. This resulted from a diminution of area cultivated, a prolonged drought in July–August 1943, and "labor problems." With local consumption further reducing the exportable surplus, total rice exports from Cochinchina for 1944 (six hundred thousand tonnes) was actually the worst result since 1912 (BEI 1944, 271–72).

The *Comptoirs*

But how did Governor General Decoux and collaborators realize their program of mitigated autarky, the report queried? First, Decoux gained extraordinary administrative powers vis-à-vis metropolitan France, including control over the Indochinese economy. Rather than strictly *étatique* considerations, local directions came into line with the corporatist principles of New France adapted to the particular conditions of the colonies. Accordingly, the new economic and social rules established by Vichy were implemented in Indochina. Second, as examined below, the Decoux administration then acted through the creation of intermediary group corporations or agencies (*comptoirs*) to connect with the Indochina war economy.

Tightly controlled by the government, the *comptoirs* were entrusted with collecting, transporting, and processing raw materials (Nguyen The Anh 1998a, 210). In 1941–42, two special *comptoirs*, for paddy and for rice and maize, were also established, initially limited to keeping statistics on stocks and so on, but coming to complement and overlap with the function of the Rice Committee in overseeing the production, transport, domestic trade, and export of cereals. From inception in May 1942, however, the Rice and Maize Agency was vested with absolute control of the market, with total monopoly purchase of all rice, paddy, and derivatives earmarked for export, thereby delimiting the role hitherto played by French and especially Chinese buyers (BEI 1944, 199).

In the event, the modus operandi of the Rice and Maize Agency did not meet with official approval and on December 1, 1942, was replaced by a new body called the Comité des Céréales (Grain Board). Coming under the control of economic services and incorporating the Rice and Maize Agency as well as the professional rice producer associations, the new committee was likewise vested with a monopoly over rice procurement, smoothing the delivery of cereals to meet international obligations. Significantly, it was also brought into closer liaison with Mitsui Bussan. No less significantly, it also brought Tonkin, Annam, and Cambodia into its compass with branch offices set up in Haiphong and Phnom Penh (BEI 1944, 223–24).

As the Vichy French report further observed, while the "public powers" (the Vichy state) remained "masters of all decisions," it also worked in strict collaboration with representatives of the private economy (French and native). In a speech delivered to the opening session of the inaugural meeting of the Conseil de l'Economie Indochinoise, Decoux underscored the corporatist and anti-*étatique* character of governmental planning. He also declaimed that, as proven by experience, the administration lacked aptitude in economic organization. As such, he made appeal to corporative groups comprising "moral persons with true public service." But as the principle engagement of Indochina with Japan concerned rice and corn exports, he found it indispensable to prevent speculation and fraudulent activities in the circulation of rice and paddy. The single most difficult task, he contended, was to decontrol the operations of the ubiquitous Chinese intermediaries standing between producers of paddy and the great rice mills. Vested with the question, the Comité des Céréales acquitted itself "honorably" (a subject revisited in the context of a discussion on the Great Famine). The quantities demanded by Japan were largely provided, and the margin of profit of the rice farmer and the various intermediaries was maintained, he announced with evident pride (but not without hyperbole). Notably, the capital branch of the Indochina economy, that which supported the entire edifice of the colony, maintained its activity and prosperity (AOM SLOTFOM 1129–1145 127/1135 BR no. 238, SREO, Chungking, May 10, 1944).

The Rice Procurement or Requisition System

Undoubtedly, the most controversial and troubled plan in the Japanese-Vichy economic order was the issue of forced requisition of food crops. It was also the most fateful, becoming, as discussed in chapter 8, a leading factor in peasant immiseration and eventual famine. At the heart of the Japanese rice requisition system stood the levy under which the Vichy administration was obliged to lean on the peasant producer to offer up a prescribed number of kilograms of rice per *mau* in addition to a slate of federal, protectorate, and local taxes. According to an official account, the conclusion of the 1941 economic agreement with Japan necessitated a major governmental intervention in the cycle of rice export operations to ensure conformity, notably by fixing the purchase price of rice at the expense of the (Chinese-dominated) market. In a second stage, again at the expense of Chinese and other brokers, the state assumed monopoly control over the purchase, transport, milling, and sale of paddy, rice, and derivatives in all Cochinchina and Cambodia (BEI 1944, 160).

As Nguyen The Anh (1998a, 211–12) explains, the purpose of compulsory requisitioning was to constitute safety stocks and to fulfill the covenant of August 19, 1942, under which Japan was to receive the entire exportable surplus of rice during the 1942–43 harvest at a minimum of 1,050,000 tonnes of the highest-quality white rice. In 1942, the resident of Tonkin imposed a system of paddy reserves on villagers "proportional to the production, available on request and payable on delivery." In practice, the administration forced each farmer to deliver a part of his harvest in proportion to the surface he cultivated. Under this formula, owners of five *mau* of rice land or less were obliged to sell to the government twenty kilograms per *mau*, farmers who owned five to ten *mau*, eighty kilograms per *mau*, and those who owned over fifteen *mau*, their entire surplus. The rates were further ratcheted up in 1944. On this basis, Tonkin had to supply by way of compulsory deliveries 130,205 tonnes of rice in 1943 and 186,130 tonnes in 1944. In Cochinchina from late 1943, as Le Manh Hung (2004, 253) explains, the French fixed the rate at fifty kilograms of paddy per *mau* for those who owned five *mau*, rising to two hundred kilograms for those who owned more than twenty *mau*. Progressively, through 1944, the rate was increased.

However, in addition to the accustomed taxes and levies such as set down by colonial France over the preceding decades, under Vichy an additional *prélèvement*, or levy, was imposed on the peasant farmer. Such would be collected in kind by a local agent, a trusted mandarin or provincial or communal leader, and delivered to an agent of the Grain Board. One part of the paddy levy could be held in storage—such as was the case in Tonkin during the Great Famine—or it could be diverted to fulfill the Japanese quota. Obviously, the greater the rice surplus every harvest time, the greater the levy. The reverse also held, at which time the rice deficit became the object of intense bargaining, vastly complicated by local hoarding, speculation, and leakage.

But the official rice price was far below the free-market level. Neither did the rate differentiate between cultivated area and yield, meaning that the burden fell most heavily on middle landowners with poor-quality land. Neither did the official requisitioning of rice at a fixed price take into account rising production costs relative to the trebling of the cost of living index between 1940 and 1943. Many peasant cultivators unable to meet the quota were forced to purchase rice on the free market, while many were ruined, the landless and poor sinking further into poverty. As Nguyen The Anh (1998a, 212) summarizes, "Requisitions thus constituted a crushing burden for the population who, having made the compulsory deliveries, would be obliged to buy rice at a much higher free market price in the event of a bad harvest." Yet the authorities remained oblivious to the downside of this system. Obviously, the system required a well-oiled inspectorate to collect the levy, to report on nondeclared stock, and to punish defaulters. The rice levy collection was duly delegated to officials of the Grain Board, including its inspectorate.

The system obviously required careful management and administration, including the rigorous collection of data. Many variables were obviously at play, depending on region and on seasonal vagaries, as well as on major weather events and such. The case from Cao Bang, an isolated highland province, is illustrative. As the resident superior of Tonkin, Jean Haelewyn, elaborated in a missive directed at provincial-level officials in February 1943, the "optimum" solution as to administering the rice levy in Cao Bang would be, first, to determine exactly the number of persons who were required to furnish the rice obligation, the quantities of rice required each month, and the zones in Cao Bang which produced a surplus of rice and the quantities. Second would be to make a census of rice merchants in the main towns in Cao Bang and to ascertain their status, as with the Chinese congregation, and determine where (locally or externally) and in what quantities they procured rice. Third would be to oblige the merchants to keep a stock of rice proportional to their permitted amounts. For the recalcitrant merchants, strip them of their permit, and absolutely forbid them to operate locally or in neighboring provinces. Fourth would be to ascertain the demand for silver in Cao Bang and calculate the exchange rate for rice against a kilogram of silver. Fifth would be to ensure that merchants or distributors dealing with local rice or rice sourced from the delta (as well as consumers?) were provided with vouchers or cards (AOM RST *1B/379 Haelewyn, "riz de Cao Bang," Hanoi, Feb. 12, 1943). As suggested, variations on this kind of census operation played out all across Indochina. But, as revealed in chapter 8, lack of an efficient and standardized information collection regime severely handicapped the central authorities from making quick and informed decisions in the face of the looming food crisis of late 1944 and onward.

The Black Economy and Ration System

Alongside the state-private economy, a parallel black or underground economy also thrived. According to an Allied intelligence report of mid-1943, items smuggled into northern Indochina included tung oil, coins, gallnuts, hemp, quicksilver, wolfram, and copper, in turn exchanged at the border for piece goods, medicines (quinine), coffee, pepper, foreign-made goods, and clothing. The transport of these goods was conducted by smuggler networks, certain of them fully armed, on behalf of merchant clients mostly based in Nanning in Guangxi (PRO HK KWIZ/09d/14/8/43 Report 106 Source FA/1).

More generally, as shortages in the supply of consumer goods along with food started to bite, a central supply committee was created and entrusted with setting quotas for different regions and services. In turn, local committees allocated the quota for each region among its provinces and main urban centers. Their activity covered just about every possible consumer need, as with textiles, soap, matches, and sugar (Nguyen The Anh 1998a, 210). Rationing also held for daily or monthly quotas for rice. Urban dwellers, civil servants, and certain other categories were issued with ration cards. Generally, daily rations of rice decreased as the war years progressed. In May 1941 the authorities restricted the daily ration of paddy to 750 grams. Already inadequate, this amount was reduced to 500 grams in 1943. But these figures were only notional in a situation where major disruptions occurred to transportation and distribution networks such as discussed. Alongside rationing came price inflation. As revealed in chapter 8, price inflation accelerated even faster and higher during the famine crisis of early 1945.

Labor Recruitment under Vichy

Japanese labor recruitment under Vichy is an understudied area but encompasses a variety of methods and ruses used to mobilize labor either for economic projects or for military *corvée* details, as in the more remote parts of Indochina including Laos, or as an adjunct to French *corvée* obligations. Willy-nilly, the Vichy French administration accommodated labor recruitment by Japanese outfits. As recorded in early 1945 by Haelewyn's successor, Resident Superior Paul Chauvet, the Japanese company Showa Tsusho was actively engaged in the recruitment of labor for the collection of ash material used in the manufacture of gunpowder, in turn used in the mining industry. Reportedly, through 1943–44, two Japanese individuals had made private profit from this recruitment activity. However, abuses in this recruitment also led to a refusal on the part of the local French administration to cooperate with Showa Tsusho (AOM RST *1B/93 RS à GG, Jan. 23, 1945).

In any case, Japanese military-linked recruitment, such as in the mining and extractive sector, should not be confused with French or private recruitment of labor for plantations in Cochinchina, which was ongoing during the Vichy period. But this was a highly regulated labor exercise and governed by strict labor regulations (regulation of June 2, 1944) formulated as a result of exposure of major exploitation in the late 1930s. For example, in June 1944, a private "emigration agent" was authorized by Chauvet to recruit 1,800 plantation workers (at least 10 percent female, as required) from Bac Ninh, Ha Duong, Nam Dinh, Nam Binh, and Thai Binh to be employed in determined plantations in Cochinchina (e.g., Long Thanh) according to a specified salary

($0.35 a day for males; $0.28 for women), clothing, and benefits (AOM RST *1B/83, RS à "emigration agent," Jan. 30, 1945). In January 1945, 645 workers were recruited for the cinchona plantations of Annam, Laos, and Cochinchina. Used as the raw ingredient for the production of quinine, cinchona grew at high altitudes. Observing that Vietnamese were "reticent" to sojourning in highland zones, the resident superior directed that their health conditions first be satisfied, alongside other benefits (AOM RST *1B/93, RS Chauvet à GG, Jan. 4, 1945). Such examples could be multiplied, but almost invariably, recruitment of labor was sourced in the delta provinces of Tonkin.

Penal labor was another category. For example, in February 1943, the French authorities dispatched a group of fifty "healthy" prisoners from the Maison Centrale in Hanoi to replace or fortify the notorious and insalubrious Son Tay prison population, described as being in "deplorable condition." As implied, the Son Tay prison veterans were in no condition to accomplish certain important local work projects. This was no humanitarian gesture, but the prison authorities were also advised to seek out alternative prison sites in the delta (AOM RST *1B/379, Haelewyn, Jan. 19, 1943). In another instance, in January 1945, the resident of Bac Giang requested penal labor to repair a local road. Accordingly, fifty prisoners were dispatched from Hanoi under the watch of "forest guards" (AOM RST *1B/93, RS à Resident, Bac Giang," Jan. 24, 1945). Such prisoners may have been criminal cases, but there was also a category of "special work gangs" comprising political prisoners.

The Industrial Sector and Import Substitution

One of the first actions taken by the Vichy administration at the outset of the war was to downplay those sectors of the economy of marginal interest to Japan. Certain agricultural products such as rubber and especially tea were reduced or stockpiled. The plantations were not greatly impacted. On the other hand, coal mining in Tonkin was deeply affected. Prewar China and Japan absorbed 80 percent of Indochinese exports of coal, reaching 1,750,000 tonnes in 1939. Circumstances of war did not allow China and Japan to maintain the level, and other markets failed completely. Production was 2,800,000 tonnes in 1939, falling to 950,000 in 1942. But under the control of big companies, the report allowed, they could afford to wait out the war. If mines and agriculture were subject to external demand, other industries were suffering from an insufficiency of imported goods. Notably, the railways were obliged to reduce their traffic. Other industries, especially the cotton industry of Tonkin, were even harder hit and forced to rely on meager local sources of cotton, leading to a reduction in activity of 75 percent. But because Indochina was not highly industrialized, the report continued, all these constraints did not imperil the economic equilibrium. The problem was not to limit production. To the contrary, the most difficult problem was to stimulate import substitution. As the report estimated, considerable autarky had already been accomplished, both in the industrial and agricultural domains, a trend that would change the economic orientation of Indochina until the end of the conflict (AOM SLOTFOM 1129–1145 127/1135 BR no. 238, SREO, Chungking, May 10, 1944).

In the meantime, Indochina experienced a surge in local manufacture of such import substitution items as alcoholic drinks, rice wines, jams, biscuits, and so on. Another consequence of Indochina's isolation was to stimulate the local production of artisanal goods, metalwork, woodwork, cotton work, and so on. Equally, the isolation led to a boom in the use of local medicines, especially in Saigon. As alluded to with reference to the cinchona plantation workers, one example was a turn to the production of quinine-based drugs. As the report underscored, what transpired in Indochina was an industrialization push, part ephemeral, part durable. Undoubtedly, the report predicted, certain of the new productions would survive the end of conflict (AOM SLOTFOM 1129–1145 127/1135 BR no. 238, SREO, Chungking, May 10, 1944).

Japanese Economic Control and the Looming Disaster

As time wore on, it became apparent to French observers that the Japanese regime was determined to impose an increasingly *dirigiste* economic system on Indochina. As Indochina increasingly came to serve Japan's Greater East Asia economic bloc, so Japanese military-business interests would wrest commanding control over banking, mining, plantations, and the all-important rice commerce trade. As the DGER (Direction générale des études et recherches) reported in January 1945, Japan sought to impose a *plan de partage*, or plan to place all economic activity under its control, a veritable "directed economy." By sector, the Japanese-directed economy embraced banking (the Yokohama Specie Bank); the grain trade ([Mitsui] Bussan Kaisha, Mitsubishi Shoji Kaisha); the minerals industry, with the exception of coal (Compagnie Indochinoise de Commerce et Industrie, an affiliate of the Bank of Taiwan); and transport (Osaka Shosen Kaisha). The army and navy also upheld their own business interests, especially in Saigon, through the creation of a *dainan koshi* purchasing office (MAE AOI 26, DGER, "Annex sur la Situation Budgetaire en Indochine," March 6, 1945). According to Patti (1980, 303), this was headed by the "notorious" Matsushita Mitsuhiro. This list is hardly exhaustive, as in chapter 8 we also learn of other Japanese companies engaged in the jute business (Marr 1980, 133).

Industrial Crops

The first and undoubtedly most important result of the isolation of Indochina was the obligation to make up for lost gas and lubricants for its industry.

Gasoline was replaced with local oil, namely, that manufactured from oil-bearing plants or fish oil. To this end, an intensive agricultural campaign was launched with the extension of cultivation of oil-producing plants. Notably, between 1940 and 1942, the area planted with peanuts increased from twenty-three thousand hectares to forty-five thousand hectares, whereas the cultivation of castor increased in the same period from six thousand hectares to ten thousand hectares. Coconut plantations in the south were likewise harnessed for copra-oil production. Centers of extraction refining increased little by little. Notably, a fish factory was established in Cambodia for oil replacement. In the first trimester of 1942, the average monthly production of vegetable and animal oil reached 640 tonnes versus 12 tonnes only in the second trimester of 1941, basically sufficient to satisfy the existing number of gas-production machines. The production of fish oil was sufficient to power several electricity generators, lacking coal. A setback was experienced in July 1942 with the failure of the castor crop. In summing up, the report concluded that in spite of numerous difficulties, Indochina had won the battle of hydrocarbons. Although the stoppage of jute imports from India impacted heavily on local users of jute sacks for bagging rice, Indochina had stepped up its local production of jute and manufacture of jute sacks accordingly (AOM SLOTFOM 1129–1145 127/1135 BR no. 238, SREO, Chungking, May 10, 1944).

According to Nguyen The Anh (1998a, 211), in the span of three years, the area occupied by industrial crops nearly doubled, reaching 42,586 hectares in 1944. Tonkin hosted some two-thirds of the total Indochinese production of jute and castor oil production and half the sesame production. Needless to say, as this writer observes, the rural population found it difficult to cope with this forced conversion, necessitating certain food plants being driven off fertile lands in preference to growing castor oil and textile plants. But neither did the administration even care as to the production of subsidiary crops that could have supplemented meager incomes and diet.

The scale of industrial crop substitution is illustrated in table 5.3, but, as Resident Superior Chauvet asserted, these were official statistics masking a wide discrepancy with the real output, especially as commune-level officials hesitated to declare higher-level statistics, strongly suggesting that a large volume escaped the official procurement monopoly. The tightly controlled jute industry might have been an exception, but the real figures for oil-producing crops as with castor, he contended, was more likely five thousand tonnes and with peanuts and sesame exceeding two thousand tonnes and five hundred tonnes, respectively (AOM RST *1B 18/425, RS Chauvet à Services Economiques, Feb. 12, 1945).

Table 5.3. Japanese Industrial Crop Production in Tonkin, 1943–45

Commodity	*Year*	*Tonnage Harvested*
Castor	1943	3,084
Castor	1944	3,332
Peanuts	1944	902
Peanuts	up to January 15, 1945	1,390
Sesame	1944	252
Sesame	up to January 15, 1945	259
Jute	1944	2,643
Cotton*	1944	127 (minus Yen Bai)

Source: AOM RS Tonkin *1B 18/425, RS Chauvet à Services Economiques, Hanoi, Feb. 12, 1945.
*1,704 ha on higher ground.

Crop Diversion

We have noted that Vichy itself ordered a shift toward industrial crops in the interest of biofuel production, so it is difficult to precisely determine the extent to which Japan pushed this measure. Nevertheless, certain details emerge from the "Tonkin Residence archives." For example, in mid-March 1943, an indigenous official, the *tri phu* of Lang Giang (a *huyen*, or district, of Bac Giang, fifty kilometers east of Hanoi) made it known that the Japanese had hired coolies and rented buffaloes and oxen for the purposes of jute cultivation at Ben Tram, notably in the canton of Tin Liet. The coolies were paid $1.20 a day (AOM RST *1B 94/95/96, March 15, 1943). This matter-of-fact statement reveals little in itself but does tell that arable land was diverted to nonfood production in a traditionally food-producing area.

Another report from the same region (Bac Giang), however, reveals that the Japanese army had also organized peanut cultivation. Peanut growers were required to deliver their crop to the Office Indochinois du Crédit Agricole Mutual monopoly for the profit of the Japanese army. However, this "act of good faith" brokered by (or required of) Vichy in its dealings with the Japanese army was subverted by Vietnamese middlemen "who engage in trade of an illicit kind" for personal profit. The authorities—either French or Japanese—then conducted seizures of this contraband, netting seven hundred kilograms from one individual. An investigation determined that a large portion of the 1942 peanut harvest in this area was diverted to the illegal vegetable oil trade, evidently diverted to Sept Pagodes in the Hai Hung region, suggesting an external market. Highly embarrassed by this wanton commercial sabotage, the French made contact with the Hanoi office of the Japanese Syogaibu (public relations section) to intervene in the matter. In the meantime, it was felt prudent to step up collection of castor oil production

(AOM RST *1B 94/95/96, Commissaire Général aux Relations Franco-Japonais, Hanoi, March 19, 1943).

In a follow-up report from early 1943 we learn that, under a governmental decree, the Phu Lang Thuong cooperative in Bac Giang in the delta had been nominated as the sole organization vested with the authority to purchase peanuts from the producers at a fixed price. But owing to the illegal trade (evidently undiminished), the top French official (in the absence of the resident superior) wrote, "I estimate that it would be preferable in these conditions that the organization be centralized and the production be directly turned over to the Japanese" (AOM RST *1B/379, RS Brand [acting], Jan. 22, 1943). From these reports we learn not only of early Japanese military-business activities but also of the shadowy Bureau des Affaires Japonais and the Commissaire Général aux Relations Franco-Japonais, the liaison offices through which Japanese kept watch over Vichy administrative practices or exercised control through them. We also learn of a general Vichy acquiescence or desire to please the Japanese authorities, although it is also hard to measure the kind of duress involved for noncompliance.

PREMONITIONS OF REVOLUTION UNDER JAPAN

Japanese support for nationalist groups inside Indochina cannot be reduced to a single factor, especially as they succored a range of parties and religious sects, as with Cao Dai and Hoa Hoa in the south, alongside strategic collaborators including pro-Wang Jing-wei Chinese. Nevertheless, Japanese support for Cuong De's Guangxi-based Phuoc Quoc, or Restorationist Society, bears examination, especially as its armed actions in the rugged northeast of Vietnam against French garrison forces served as a precursor to a range of anti-French actions on the part of armed groups in this sector. In retrospect, these actions were even premonitions of the revolution to come.

Japan and the Phuoc Quoc Army

As Harrison (1989, 77) explains, taking their cue from the Japanese attack on the French garrison at Lang Son on September 22–26, 1940, the Phuoc Quoc army also staged a rebellion. With an army of forty thousand to fifty thousand locally recruited men instructed by Japanese cadres, they achieved successes, albeit also abandoned by the Japanese high command, virtually sinking the carefully planned enterprise with huge losses (Tran My-Van 2005, 144–46). Nevertheless, as Tran My-Van (2005, 155) estimates, it is difficult to ascertain the level of official Japanese support for the Phuoc Quoc rebels at this stage, especially as their goals seemed to be somewhat at variance, and with the Phuoc Quoc placing priority on taking control of a provisional government in Hanoi.

Revolt of the Tho/Tay in Bac Son

Though the Phuoc Quoc failed in both its political and military objectives, its legacy was nevertheless important in consideration of the locus of the rebellion in the northern mountains of Vietnam bordering on Guangxi. In turn, these destabilizing events set off an uprising by six hundred members of the Thi-ti (Tho) and Nung minorities, who seized several districts of Bac Son, southwest of Lang Son in Thai Nguyen Province. By September 27, 1940, local communists of both minority and Vietnamese origin took the head of the Bac Son uprising, "But they did so without the knowledge of higher Party authorities." The scene of resistance to the French in the 1890s, Bac Son also experienced an antitax-antirailway conscription revolt by the Tho (Tay) minority in the 1920s. Importantly, as well, from 1925 to 1926, the first Vietnamese communist elements had begun to infiltrate into the high country of Tonkin, creating cells and recruiting members of the Tho (Tay) and other minorities (M. Elliott 1974, 15).

According to Mai Elliott (1974, 12), although the insurrection failed, it provided the ICP with the nucleus of an army and a base on the fringe of the Red River delta. In February 1941, under the command of Chu Van Tan, a future minister of national defense in the provisional revolutionary government, the Bac Son guerrilla unit would be reconstituted as the Army for National Salvation. Born in Thai Nguyen from the Nung minority, Chu Van Tan joined the ICP in 1934 and was given the task of organizing communist activity in the Vu Ngai area of Thai Nguyen. During a subsequent Bac Son uprising of October 1941, he became commander of the Army for National Liberation, setting up a war zone in Vu Ngai.

According to Gaudal (1947, 48–49), a close French observer then in Hanoi, it was not until December 1941 that the French authorities were able to push these bands back into China. Lasting from October 1940 until January 1942, military actions immobilized three French-mixed battalions precisely at the time when the French required these forces on the frontier with Thailand. Remnants from these bands would be welcomed by the Chinese authorities in Guangxi with certain of them subsequently rallying to the Viet Minh. Lang Son was not truly pacified until June 1941, and it took a year to ameliorate the social damage sowed by the Japanese and their bands. Meanwhile, the French executed the key Phuoc Quoc military leader.

As a French intelligence report reflected on these events, military repression of the Tho revolt, consecutive with the events of 1940 (an allusion to the Lang Son attack), was regrettable because the oppression only deepened the spirit of rebellion on the part of the Tho. As it transpired, the French military column was commanded by the same officer who, a few weeks prior, had turned Tho rebels over to the Japanese. In other words, those who had initially taken up arms against Japan were in turn punished by French force of arms, leaving an indelible (negative) impression (of the French) on the population (MAE AOI 29 "Note Interpretative . . . Decoux," 30/5/1044).

The Mekong Delta Uprising of October–November 1940

Seeking to take advantage of the new political conjuncture, elements around Tran Van Giau launched what was obviously a doomed and premature rebellion in southern Indochina that was crushed with blood. By 1939, according to McAlister (1969, 132), Tran Van Giau (released from imprisonment during the Popular Front period) had formed his first rural-based paramilitary units in then distant and inhospitable Plaine des Joncs, southwest of Saigon. In terms of manpower, the southern ICP mustered some eight hundred cadres, seven hundred well-indoctrinated members and one hundred more persons in associated groups. Giau was thus well placed at the outset of the Japanese occupation in late 1940 and, during the period when the French sought to bolster their defenses against irridentist Thai claims on Cambodian territory, to capitalize on local discontent to launch an insurrection. As official Vietnamese historian Hong Chuong (1965, 71) adds, the French mobilization of Vietnamese auxiliaries for service on the western frontier with Thailand also gave way to an antiwar movement.

Falsely, the communist underground in southern Vietnam arrived at an understanding that the Vichy French could be overthrown by a popular rebellion. Known variously as the Mekong delta or Nam Ky uprising of October–November 1940, it represented to degrees the opening shots of the First Indochina War. Acting on the resolution of the sixth meeting of the ICP central committee held in November 1939, the southern networks of the ICP set about mobilizing some fifteen thousand militia members, of which five thousand were armed. In July 1940, the party conducted a special regional meeting at My Tho in the delta to discuss the plan for armed insurrection. Preparations were laid with the red flag with the golden star, Vietnam's future national flag, chosen as the emblem. However, the seventh meeting of the ICP central committee, held at Bac Minh in the north, did not approve the insurrection and Phan Dang Luu, the southern emissary who attended the meeting, was arrested back in Saigon before being able to convey the message.

As Vichy governor Veber recounts of this little-documented affair, on the morning of November 22, the Sûreté gained crucial information that the central committee had instructed members to steal munitions from the forts surrounding Saigon and to attack the Maison Centrale prison and the arsenal. Forewarned, Veber alerted his security forces. On the side of the rebels, simultaneous with rural actions, a number of forts on the periphery of Saigon were attacked, leading to casualties. The rebels also attacked a government position in Hoc Mon. Under pursuit by the military, the rebels fled toward the inaccessible Plaine des Joncs wetland, in turn occupied by army mobile groups and patrols armed with automatic weapons. At least six military companies were deployed in the zone surrounding Chau Doc, Long Xuyen, Sa Dec, Bac Lieu, and Can Tho, including one European company and one dispatched from Cambodia. At least until the final bloody denouement, incidents continued for several days in Can Tho, Soc Trang, My Tho, and Vinh Long. As Veber recorded, "Cochinchina under the communists had become a veritable '*travail de taupinière*' (work of derangement) . . . everywhere our energetic action led to many of the rebels being killed" (AOM Indo NF/330/2664–67 Veber à Colonies, Vichy, April 19, 1941).

At this juncture, Tran Van Giau was also arrested. By exposing the southern branch of the party to further repression, however, Giau again incurred censure from the ICP center. As Hong Chuong (1965, 76) states, this was not a spontaneous revolt; it was mistakenly ordered by the party. Even so, he allows, oppressive conditions of the time were ripe for rebellion. In quickly gathering momentum among the landless tenant farmers of the southern delta, the rebellion also appears to have elements of a peasant *jacquerie*, as instanced by attempts to seize land.

Recovery (1943–44)

As Brocheux (1995, 193–94) explains, through 1943–44, ICP militants patiently rebuilt their cells in the central and western delta, including Saigon-Cholon. By mid-1943, the reorganization was a "matter of fact." By August 1942, the ICP had launched its *Giai Phong* (Liberation) newspaper in the south. Captured documents revealed provisional committees and local cells established in Saigon-Cholon, Gia Dinh, and Thu Dau Mot. By July 1943, the ICP listed 104 militants. By August 1944, the French had evidence of a linkup between communists in the south and the central committee. From September 1944, the term *Viet Minh* commenced to enter police reports in the south. Yet there were setbacks, as with the arrest of Vo Van Kiet. Meanwhile, the leaders of the 1940 uprising were executed, six on October 1943, two in June 1943, four in February 1944, and two in July 1944.

Very little intelligence appears in the French record on communist activities during this period. In April 1941, however, according to a Japanese source, members of the Vietnam Anti-French Movement for the Independence of Annam (a reference to the Viet Minh) sought unsuccessfully to derail the eastbound train taken by Decoux as it passed near Vinh. By error, the westbound train was derailed instead (AOM Indo NF 127/1145 (2) Domei, April 12, 1941). In any case, the Viet Minh took no credit for this action. This episodic and a somewhat desultory catalog of strikes and labor actions in the south strongly suggest that the war years were not considered by the communists as a propitious time to show their hand, and it would appear that the lessons of the premature and adventurous Mekong delta uprising had been learned.

THE JAPANESE *COUP DE FORCE* OF MARCH 9, 1945

Although Japanese Foreign Minister Shigimetsu Mamoru had apparently voiced the need for Japan to offer "independence" to Vietnam, the question was vetoed by the military. Reaching back to January 1944, the military hatched a plan to disestablish French authority. To this end, a Yasu Butai or Annam Unit intelligence agency was set up and placed under the southern army at its headquarters in Saigon. Meanwhile, in November 1944, Japanese military headquarters in Manila was moved to Saigon and the Japanese army in Vietnam reorganized as the Thirty-Eighth Army. In a devastating action, and a setback to Allied theater planning in the war against Japan, on March 9, 1945, the Japanese high command set in action Operation Meigo Sakusen, leading to the military usurpation of the French Indochina administration. The Japanese military *coup de force* saw the complete eclipse of the Vichy order by the Japanese authorities. This was accomplished with considerable violence, leading to a series of massacres.

According to American intelligence, the Japanese action was prompted by two interrelated concerns. First, despite a relationship of convenience with Admiral Decoux, the Japanese sensed a "fluctuating" attitude on the part of elements from within the French administration, as an increasing number of individuals came to identify with the Free French cause. The second fact of life for the Japanese in stimulating the Meigo action was the deteriorating military situation for Japan and the Axis alike in both the "eastern and western hemispheres." Of no less consequence was the fact that Allied bombing of Indochina proper commenced when the Americans wrested back control of the Philippines (Detwiler and Burdock 1980, 1–36).

History records that on March 9, 1945, at 18:00 hours, Ambassador Matsumoto Shin'ichi, for the Japanese side, visited Governor General Decoux at French government headquarters in Saigon and delivered an ultimatum demanding the subordination of all French forces to Japanese command. As elaborated by Ellen Hammer (1954, 38), Decoux temporized as he had previously done when receiving Japanese ultimatums, but this time he was arrested just as Japanese troops seized administrative buildings and public utilities, took over radio stations, telegraph centers, banks, and industries, attacked military and police positions, and interned French civilians and military authorities. On March 11, the Japanese high command released the names of those arrested. They included, besides Decoux, General Aymé (Resistance code name Pierre) and General Mordant (Resistance code name Narcisse), along with Sûreté chief Louis Arnoux, known to have been tracking Ho Chi Minh since 1919 (Patti 1980, 74).

Where they did not resist, French military and civilians were interred along with Decoux and senior administrators. Vichy's Marine Indochine fleet ships were either sunk by artillery fire or scuttled by their crews with their personnel made prisoner. In northern Vietnam, a major incident occurring at Lang Son resulted in the massacre by Japanese military of hundreds of imprisoned French military personnel (Koburger 1997, 15). In central Vietnam, the resident superior and his deputy were assassinated. In Phnom Penh the *chef de cabinet* was shot, while the resident of Stung Treng (Cambodia) was killed. In Laos, the resident and other French officials or military and civilians were massacred at a dinner party hosted by the Japanese military in what became known as the Thakek massacre. In central Vietnam (Annam) and southern Vietnam (Cochinchina), Japanese military and police committed a series of abuses against the French military and civilian population. Meanwhile, Japanese troops in Shanghai took parallel actions (NAA A1838 3103/11/62 Part I, March 11, 1945).

As Yoshikawa Kenkichi, the long-serving Japanese ambassador in Indochina, declared at a press conference shortly after the Japanese coup, it was the incitement of the French population by Anglo-Americans that led to a rupture of Franco-Japanese relations. Decoux, he pointed out, had fulfilled most of his obligations in line with treaties, although he also "lacked obedience" on certain matters as well. Nevertheless, the ambassador declared, he departed his post in November 1944 following a three-year term in Indochina "without reproach." But in "strongly collaborating" with Japan, Decoux also followed the orders of the "legitimate" (Vichy) French government. However, with the exit of the "legitimate government of Marshal Pétain" from Vichy on August 20, 1944, the French population and authorities had succumbed to Anglo-American propaganda. With more than a little inside knowledge, Yoshikawa declared that it was this last fact that led to a rupture in relations between Japan and French Indochina (AOM Indo NF/337/271 Yoshikawa, March 16, 1945).

More generally, sources such as Archimedes Patti of the American OSS attributed the French debacle to poor planning on the part of the Mordant resistance organization, disregard for secrecy, and lack of coordination between military and civilian elements. Only Generals Sabattier and Alessandri took civilian warnings of a Japanese coup seriously and managed rearguard actions before evacuating their five thousand troops to China and Laos. This was out of a total of ninety-nine thousand French Indochinese forces. Nevertheless, Patti (1980, 74–75) allows for great French heroism at Lang Son and Dang Don, another border town north of Lang Son, along with resistance at Hue and Hanoi. But otherwise, he rationalizes, the French capitulations can be explained only by lack of central organization coupled with lack of will on the part of Vietnamese troops. Even the troop evacuations by Sabattier and Alessandri would come under criticism from Gaullist elements among the French, especially for virtually retreating from Indochinese soil. Obviously, Patti (1980, 100) continues, from an American and Chinese perspective, the French debacle in March 1945 leaving Japan in undisputed control of Southeast Asia and exposing Yunnan to infiltration was a great disappointment and strategic setback in war planning.

According to a postwar investigation, the number of French prisoners of Japan held in Indochina after the coup totaled twelve thousand military and nineteen thousand civilians. Conditions of internment or concentration differed, however. Of the military, seven thousand were interned or consigned to barracks (as with the Hanoi citadel group); five thousand were placed in work camps or held under special confinement as disciplinary measures. Of the civilians, one thousand were incarcerated in prison cells under *kempeitai* control; two thousand were interned along with the military, including a large number of officials. That added up to a grand total of nine thousand civilian and military personnel interned in close confinement for Resistance activities (AOM Indo NF 181/1001–1101, d'Argenlieu, Saigon, Jan 1, 1947). Rounded off in thousands, it is clear that the French had no independent means of knowing the exact number of internees.

With little success alongside the Viet Minh, Japan also sought to take in hand a range of nationalist groups, and certain of them saw short-term advantage in this arrangement. As Lebra (1977, 135–40) explains, in unfolding Operation Meigo, Emperor Bao Dai came under particular surveillance by the Yasu Butai group, just as Japan looked for future puppet leaders of the disparate entities that made up Indochina. Allowing for fundamental differences between the early postwar scene in north, central, and south Vietnam, we shall return to the Vietnamese independence narrative in a following chapter.

CONCLUSION

Setting set the scene for the devastating famine that broke in March 1945, this chapter has detailed Japan's progressive control over the vital levers of the rice economy. Even so, it is hard to offer a snapshot of the economy of the vast and heterogeneous Indochinese region before and after the Japanese takeover, especially as rural and urban dwellers were affected differentially. Obviously, the prewar economy privileging French colonial interests virtually collapsed, just as Indochina came to be segregated from its European umbilical cord. The *dirigiste* economic order ushered in by Vichy was also an economy of extreme austerity, no matter the valiant attempts at import substitution. In reality, a black economy emerged parallel to an officialized economy, privileging a selective group of Japanese and French business-corporatist entities imposed on the wreckage of the colonial economy. But even prior to the Japanese armed takeover in March 1945, a large share of the agricultural economy, including food production, had been engineered for export. In forcing the pace of rice requisitions to serve both local military needs as well as Japan's empire, there was little planning or consideration for local vulnerabilities or margins to serve as cushions in times of adversity. In modern language, there was little transparency in the procurement system on the part of the paternalist Vichy regime, and as part and parcel of a ruthless military procurement system under Japanese auspices, there was no accountability to local consumers, who bore the brunt of spiraling prices, much less the peasant producers.

Japan's humiliating defeat of France and occupation of Indochina obviously created opportunities for organized Vietnamese, Lao, and Cambodians to respond. For Pétain and his Vichyite supporters, survival of a French Indochina was at stake, but for the Gaullists within the French community, collaboration with fascist Japan was too odious to endure. Although space precludes analysis, the Japanese also entered into complex opportunistic alliances, few of them binding, as with the religious sects, Wangist Chinese, and those Vietnamese and Cambodians drawn into pro-Japanese front organizations. Certain elites, as with Bao Dai, played opportunistic collaborationist roles. Others, such as the king of Cambodia, played dutiful roles, waiting for future outcomes. The Japanese also played wildcards, such as Son Ngoc Thanh in Cambodia, and at the hour of defeat in Cochinchina even sanctioned an improbable alliance of Trotskyists, religious sect leaders, and nationalists, tenuously including the southern Viet Minh. But more than anything, the power vacuum created by the Japanese surrender provided a window for Ho Chi Minh's advance into Hanoi and declaration of independence.

To say the least, the Japanese occupation of Indochina commencing in 1940–41, climaxing with the *coup de force* against the Vichy French administration in March 1945, was epochal. Not only did it effectively draw a curtain over French colonial administration in Vietnam, Cambodia, and Laos, but the power vacuum created by the eventual Japanese surrender offered a historical moment unlike any since the French invasion of Indochina. For those Vietnamese looking to tradition as a guide, they might have concluded that the "mandate of heaven" had fallen for the French. How the Viet Minh responded to the Japanese coup is reserved for a separate chapter.

NOTES

1. For details of the January 1941 rice agreement between the Vichy authorities with Japan, see Andrus and Greene (1944, 367–78).

2. Le Manh Hung (2004, 171) gives the source of this report as "Mission to Investigate Natural Resources of French Indochina Sept 1940–April 1942" (untranslated) to a Japanese Ministry of Foreign Affairs archive source, in turn accessed via a Library of Congress, Washington, microfilm.

Chapter 6

Allied Power Plays over Indochina

With France occupied by the Nazis and the Vichy French-Japanese cohabitation a reality, Free French planners on the outside, joined by a growing resistance movement on the inside, prepared for the eventuality of a Japanese defeat. The notion that the Indochina theater would come under two commands, the British South-East Asia Command (SEAC), south of the sixteenth parallel, and a possible Sino-American collaboration north of the parallel both angered and perplexed Gaullist French planners. Clarity on the division of spheres taken at the Potsdam Conference on July 6, 1945, was slow in coming, just as the Chinese entertained their own vision of northern Indochina, especially working through proxy parties. The Japanese *coup de force* of March 9, 1945, however, gravely compromised Allied plans, especially as the French capitulation galvanized the activities of the Viet Minh and a small number of anti-French nationalist competitor parties, certain of them backed by China. The Americans also emerged as actors in the field alongside the Viet Minh, perceived as the best anti-Japanese allies on the ground, just as a range of Vietnamese nationalists came to envisage an Indochina without France.

Seeking to unpack the events surrounding these fault lines, this chapter divides into five sections. A first outlines the evolution of Gaullist policy on Indochina in the face of Japan. This is followed by an examination of the strategically located French mission in China. A third section examines the roots of American entanglement in Indochina from Rooseveltean idealism to Truman pragmatism. Then follows a discussion on the deadly effect of wartime American bombing on infrastructure and inadvertently on civilian victims. A final section offers a reflection upon the challenge posed by Vietnamese nationalism and the evident loss of the French "mandate of heaven" to the Japanese by a leading Gaullist French thinker, Vietnam specialist, and official.

EVOLUTION OF GAULLIST POLICY ON INDOCHINA

For Charles de Gaulle, heading up the London-based French National Committee, the liberation of French colonies still under Vichy control (New Caledonia, Madagascar, Syria, and Indochina) was integral with France's own liberation. Not only was the United States tardy in offering its full support to the Free France movement, still in full diplomatic relations with Vichy, but de Gaulle was also mistrustful of US intentions toward France's former colonial empire. De Gaulle's Indochinese strategy was long in the making but, as explained, took more concrete shape following the establishment of his Resistance government headquarters in the French colony of Algeria in 1942–43.[1] As Thomas (1997, 148) relates, the creation in Algiers on June 3, 1943, of the Comité Français de la Libération Nationale (French Committee of National Liberation), or FCNL, rekindled Gaullist interest in Indochina. From long distance (and notwithstanding the importance of New Caledonia), Algiers constituted the major Gaullist base for the reoccupation of Indochina.

The principles of de Gaulle's strategy were expressed in a formal declaration to the peoples of Indochina delivered in the Free French–ruled West African colony of Congo on December 8, 1943, effectively declaring a state of war with Japan. Reaffirming the principle of French sovereignty in Indochina, the Brazzaville Declaration looked to collective development in the form of a "free and close association between France and the Indo-Chinese peoples" (d'Argenlieu 1985, annex I). It also came to be taken as an article of faith by postwar French military and civilian planners.

The Collapse of Vichy, the Japanese Coup, and de Gaulle's Declaration of March 24, 1945

The liberation of Paris and the installation on August 31, 1944, of the Provisional Government of the French Republic obviously deprived the Vichy Etat Français of any legitimacy. The new circumstances also impacted Decoux and, in turn, the Resistance. Press reports indicate that on August 20, 1944, Vichy vested Decoux with absolute powers to pursue full autonomy in his collaboration with Tokyo and with Tokyo declaring on August 25 that Indochina was an "autonomous province of the Japanese empire." This led the FCNL to issue a declaration that Vichy ceased to exist and that its competence to engage Decoux was void (MAE AOI 29, Cominfor, Alger, tél., Aug. 31, 1944). Even so, the Japanese did not take this diplomatic route but opted for military action.

In the event, France's wartime resistance leader reacted swiftly to the Japanese coup of March 9, 1945, by issuing a statement of condemnation dubbed the Declaration of March 24, 1945 (Marr 1997, 329; Thomas 1997, 151).

As declared, "The Indochina Federation will form—with France—and other parts of the community, a French Union whose external interests will be represented by France. Indochina will uphold within the Union its own liberty." The declaration also claimed to grant citizenship on the basis of both membership of the Indochina Federation and the French Union, an association of French colonies bound to Paris. It claimed eligibility to government office on the basis of merit, irrespective of race, religion, or origin. It pledged press freedom and association through democracy within the five countries of the federation. The union would guarantee defense of the federation (d'Argenlieu 1985, 412).

Correctly, as David Marr (1997, 328) has explained, de Gaulle's March 24 declaration continued to be cited for several years, notwithstanding radical changes in circumstances. It could be further argued that constant official reiteration of the declaration placed a brake on diplomatic compromise and policy evolution. The image conjured by the declaration was of French and local people struggling for a common goal of an Indochina federation within the French union. Vietnamese unity—the *non plus ultra* of Viet Minh and other nationalist claims—was preempted by the tripartite division into Tonkin, Annam, and Cochinchina with no opt-out clauses countenanced. Notwithstanding professions of progress and liberties and so on, France would control foreign affairs and defense. Even so, the Declaration of March 24 has to be seen against the background of earlier policy statements and conferences relating to the question of postwar French colonial administration, reform, and devolution of authority (Thomas 1997, 141; Dommen 2001, 131–32; Tønnesson 2010, 39).

DEALING WITH CHINA: THE FRENCH MISSION IN CHONGQING

Joining other Allied representatives engaged in the war against Japan, the French mission in China was set up in the Nationalist Chinese capital at Chongqing, hosting both military and diplomatic missions. Inter alia, watching the rising Viet Minh and American cohabitation, France with its representative in Kunming was also concerned with the political allegiance of large numbers of Vietnamese who had fled Japanese-occupied territory for sanctuary in Yunnan. The Chinese wartime capital would also emerge as the major venue for future power plays between the French and the Americans on the one hand and the Chinese on the other.

Undoubtedly, the most important of France's diplomatic representatives during this period was Zinovi Pechkoff (b. 1895), a Russian émigré World War I veteran on the side of France turned legionnaire. Appointed by de Gaulle in 1943 to head the French military mission in Chongqing, on January 25, 1944, Pechkoff was named FCNL representative in China, a fairly anomalous status in the eyes of some, the Americans included, especially as this role would increasingly devolve to Blaizot and de Crévecoeur at SEAC headquarters in Kandy. On November 22, 1944, however, Pechkoff was specifically designated by the incoming French provisional government Foreign Minister Georges Bidault as ambassador extraordinary and plenipotentiary for China. Under the new dispensation, Pechkoff was charged with a double brief. One related to China and the other related to Indochina, making him the key French actor on the spot (MAE AOI 29, Bidault à Pechkoff, Chungking, Nov. 22, 1944).

With respect to China, Pechkoff was briefed to enhance Franco-Chinese relations and to defend French economic, cultural, and political interests in China. He was also obliged to develop relations between the two countries at the state-to-state level. Pechkoff was also vested with another weighty duty, namely, to negotiate the abolition of French extraterritorial privileges in China. Necessarily, the negotiations would involve a complete inventory of all treaties entered into between France and China ranging back to the late nineteenth century as well as boundary conventions between China and Indochina. The quid pro quo would be a consular convention on the basis of reciprocity between France and Indochina on the one hand and China and Indochina on the other. Pechkoff was also instructed to seek economic collaboration on the basis of equality and reciprocity. As Bidault noted in an aside, because postwar China will need to avoid the consequences of "American quasi-monopoly," France can fit the bill in the industrial as well as financial areas. France was also ready to renegotiate some of the conditions relating to the Yunnan railroad. In particular, Pechkoff was briefed to play up the already good rapport established with Chiang Kai-shek and Nationalist Foreign Minister T. V. Soong (MAE AOI 29, Bidault à Pechkoff, Chungking, Nov. 22, 1944). Even so, as Bidault underscored, the supreme goal of French policy in the Far East was the liberation of Indochina.

Notably, as Pechkoff signaled Algiers on August 29, 1944, while the disappearance of Vichy deprived Decoux of all legitimacy as well as legal cover for his actions, de facto, the administration and army remained in place. As he also signaled, the collapse of Vichy dealt a psychological shock to the population. Pechkoff duly instructed the Chinese Nationalist government to direct all official communications relating to Indochina through his mission in Chongqing and not via the Vichy rump in Hanoi. As he also made clear, "We will do nothing to hinder Decoux as long as he uses his resources to defend against the power and prerogatives remaining in Japanese hands" (MAE AOI 29, Pechkoff, Chungking, tél. Diplofrance, Aug. 29, 1944). Clearly, Pechkoff was walking a diplomatic tightrope.

As Algiers responded, it was imperative not to risk conflict between the French mission in Chongqing and Decoux on the one hand or the Committee of Action and the Resistance on the other. Pechkoff was instructed to step in with Hanoi in the contingency that the secretly anointed head of Resistance, General Eugene Mordant, was unable to convey instructions from the provisional government when requested. Above all, as Pechkoff was instructed, "avoid all written communications with the Chinese government" (MAE AOI 29, tél. Diplofrance à Chungking, Sept. 5, 1944). Obviously, Pechkoff's superiors in Algiers wanted to maintain flexibility in the face of an ambiguous situation.

In what was viewed in Paris as something of a breakthrough, on October 11, 1944, Pechkoff achieved an interview with Chiang Kai-shek. Reportedly, the generalissimo offered a strong endorsement of Chinese-French relations. Looking ahead to future economic relations, he appreciated that the French were closer to the "Chinese mentality" than the British or Americans. Breathlessly, he asserted, "We have no designs" on Indochina. Moreover, should French forces be driven into China by the Japanese, they were not only welcome but would receive full Chinese assistance in their military efforts (MAE AOI 29, tél., Chungking, Oct. 11, 1944). Unfortunately, as it panned out, some of this was wishful thinking, especially as the Nationalists also saw their future role in northern Vietnam as paramount.

Giraudist-Gaullist Tensions

In part reflecting the tension in Algiers between de Gaulle and Henri Giraud, his American-backed commander in chief, different French personalities lined up according to loyalty. Intra-French tensions also spilled over into the Indochina resistance. With Gaullists and French officials arriving in Kunming from Kandy and Calcutta, as represented by Pechkoff and his delegation, the Giraudists gravitated to Commander Robert Meynier (and his influential aristocratic Vietnamese wife) (see Bartholomew-Feis 2006, chap. 3). Archimedes Patti also describes bickering between members of the Gaullist intelligence agency, the Direction Général des Etudes et Recherches (DGER), or General Directorate for Studies and Research, and the French general staff in Chongqing. He also became aware of personality clashes between Generals Sabattier, Alessandri, and Pechkoff (Patti 1980, 100). In any case, according to Brocheux (2007, 88), both Gaullists and Giraudists were condescending and even dismissive of the Viet Minh.

Writing in February 1945, Pechkoff warned de Gaulle that the rivalry question simply had to be addressed. As he stated, the presence in the resistance of a duality or rivalry between two distinct groups risked to sap away at the effectiveness of the resistance. In effect, as he explained, the military resistance worked with a French organization attached to Mountbatten's India-based command, while the civil resistance collaborated with the Americans in China. As Pechkoff argued, only a single political leadership could address this state of affairs. He also advised that it was "dangerous" to confide exclusively in the military (a reference to General Mordant) (MAE AOI 29 1944–1945 tél., Pechkoff, Chungking à Paris, Feb. 27. 1945). Eventually, with the retreat of Meynier and the Giraudists from the Indochinese theater, Pechkoff himself would emerge victorious in this turf war.

Anti-French Vietnamese Revolutionaries in China (1940–45)

With their consular office in Kunming, the French authorities registered with alarm the activities of large numbers of Vietnamese exiles spread throughout Yunnan, especially in the border regions as well as in the city. While certain were deemed loyalist, the majority were organized into anti-French nationalist groups. As of 1944, French intelligence reckoned that some four thousand to five thousand Vietnamese revolutionaries were based in Yunnan in zones proximate to the Vietnamese border. The most important were identified as the rump of the old VNQDD and the Nationalist Chinese–backed Vietnam Revolutionary League (Viet-Nam Cach Menh-Dong-Minh-Hoi), Dong Minh Hoi, or DMH, along with underground elements of the Communist Party, including the newly formed Viet Minh. On its part, the VNQDD had two thousand men trained in guerrilla warfare in place in Yunnan and had set up a number of posts in the mountainous regions of Tonkin ready to guide the Chinese army (AOM Indo NF 134/1217 "Agissements Chinois contre le réablissement de la gouvernment Français en Indochine").

As mentioned below, the American intelligence agencies would also become engaged alongside the Viet Minh in the mutual struggle against the common enemy, Japan. Notably, from October 1943, the Americans played the DMH card, providing funds and arms to fight the Japanese. However, owing to complaints from other nationalist groups that the DMH was squandering this assistance, between February and May 1944 the subsidy was suspended (Dommen 2001, 74). As explained below, none other than Ho Chi Minh would play a role alongside the DMH, albeit under rather mysterious circumstances, at least until he reentered the Viet Minh fold.

The Chinese Double Game

As far as the French were concerned, it was always difficult to gauge true Chinese intentions with respect to a postwar Indochina. Undoubtedly the Chongqing authorities played a double game with the French. On the one hand, they evinced correct relations as allies in the common struggle against

Japan and, sharing a border with Indochina, also dealt with the Vichy regime in Hanoi. For example, as Ambassador Pechkoff reported in April 1944, Yunnan governor Long Yune along with the provincial administration was viewed as upholding good relations with France (AOM Indo NF/209/1574, Pechkoff à Affaires Etrangères, Algers, April 17, 1944). Yet what most vexed the French was the tolerance or even active support by local Chinese authorities to Vietnamese nationalist groups in southern Yunnan and western Guangxi for more than just humanitarian reasons (See Dommen 2001, 73).

As profiled in a Free French report of October 15, 1944, many of the Vietnamese revolutionaries in China were actually in the pay of the Chinese government, frequently participating in official events attended by senior Chinese officials. Occasionally, as well, they received assistance from provincial governments and officials. Notably, in Guangxi Province, General Zhang Fakui and his entourage of warlords afforded them protection, besides training and arming them with a view to the liberation of Indochina. Obviously, the central government could not have been oblivious of such actions at the behest of provincial officials in Guangxi. Official French protests, however, were invariably deflected, whether by Vice Minister Victor Huu, Lone Liang of the Europe bureau, or K. C. Wu and T. V. Soong of the foreign office, otherwise terming these actions as mere "information collection" activities (MAE AOI 29 "Note: Situation en Extrême-Orient," Oct. 15, 1944).

In reality, Chinese policy with regard to Indochina was described by a French intelligence report as "fluid and elusive" and difficult to discern. Notably, with its "characteristic realism," the Chinese government had not completely broken with Decoux. As an example of this "double game," the French consul at Longzhou, Joseph Siguret, served both Governor General Decoux and the Free French while also cooperating with the Chinese. Acting as an intermediary between Decoux and Chiang Kai-shek, Siguret also adjudicated a number of boundary questions. Known to be privy to the terms of a secret military agreement between Decoux and the Chinese, Siguret was also in liaison with Nationalist Chinese intelligence chief Tai Li (Dai Li), as indeed were the Americans. Inter alia, as the report rationalized, the Chinese sought through relations with Indochina to prevent frontier tension spilling over into Guangxi (MAE AOI 29 "Note: Situation en Extrême-Orient," Oct. 15, 1944).

As the French consul in Kunming, Jean Royère, observed in February 1945, American successes in the Pacific along with Japanese setbacks on the battlefield gave reason to believe that an American invasion of the coast of China to the north of Guangzhou was likely. Given this scenario, he believed it highly credible that the Chinese and Americans would launch a joint operation on Indochina, especially taking advantage of the growing activities of the Vietnamese revolutionaries in northern Tonkin. In this scenario, he pointed out, owing to the series of uprisings in conjunction with the famine in the Red River delta as well as in south Annam, the revolutionaries could even force the hand of the Americans to intervene. Moreover, the Chinese could exploit the present "crisis" in Franco-American relations. Chinese ambitions in Indochina, he summarized, went back as far as Pearl Harbor, with many trial balloons floated since then. More concretely, he also found increasing evidence of impending Chinese terrestrial action in Tonkin, as with the assembly in Kunming or further south at Mongtzeu of Chinese army reinforcements. He also remarked on an active Chinese liaison with American agents and the expanded recruitment of Vietnamese from among Yunnan railroad employees. In the absence of rice in Tonkin, he noted, the Chinese were assembling large stockpiles of cereals. Competition within the Vietnamese camp, namely, between the VNQDD and Viet Minh, was also observed (AOM NF 209/1571, Royère, Consulate de France à Kunming à Pechkoff, Chungking, Feb. 23, 1945).

Portentously, as well, Consul Royère also announced to Pechkoff the arrival on the scene of a "new communist leader," one "Ho Ching-ming" (Ho Chi Minh), an individual believed to be active in seeking cooperation among the Vietnamese factions (AOM NF 209/1571, Royère, Consulate de France à Kunming à Pechkoff, Chungking, Feb. 23, 1945). He was correct and far ahead of French intelligence assessments who had hopelessly lost the trail. More or less simultaneously (February 1945), Decoux's police ascertained that the man going by the name Ho Chi Minh was the same person as Nguyen Ai Quoc, long believed dead, an individual who had dropped off their records over ten years prior (Dommen 2001, 74).

THE ROOTS OF AMERICAN INVOLVEMENT IN INDOCHINA

The direct American role in Indochina was not determinant at this stage of the story, at least alongside the French and the Nationalist Chinese, yet it was never out of the background either. In the larger scheme, the US role in Indochina preceding and following the Japanese surrender flowed out of its commitments in support of Chiang Kai-shek and the Chinese Nationalists in the China theater, which included those parts of Thailand and Indochina then occupied by the Allies. Importantly as well, at the Quebec Conference in August 1943, US president Franklin D. Roosevelt and British Prime Minister Winston Churchill agreed on the creation of SEAC, although coming under British control.

As the Pentagon Papers (1971, 1–52) reveal, US policy toward France and repossession of its colonial territories was ambivalent. On the one hand, the United States supported Free French claims to all overseas possessions.

On the other hand, in the Atlantic Charter (the joint US-UK declaration of August 14, 1941) and in other pronouncements, the United States proclaimed support for national self-determination and independence. As alluded to, US support for the Free French was also qualified. President Roosevelt continued to uphold relations with Vichy on a "day to day" basis. And it was only on October 23, 1944, that the United States even recognized the Provisional Government of the French Republic, much earlier established in Algiers.

The Potsdam Conference and Allied Spheres of Influence in Indochina

Eventually, the die was set for the future of postsurrender Indochina by the terms of the Potsdam Conference of July–August 1945, but not before elaborate conversations among the Allies and serious remonstrations between Paris and Washington. The Potsdam Declaration, or the Proclamation Defining Terms for Japanese Surrender, of July 26, 1945, was a statement calling for the surrender of Japan issued by Truman, Churchill, and Chiang Kai-shek. Issued as an ultimatum, the declaration also stated that if Japan did not surrender, it would face "prompt and utter destruction." At Potsdam, it was also decided to temporarily partition Indochina at the sixteenth parallel. Under this arrangement, Allied chiefs of staff assigned British forces to take the Japanese surrender in Saigon and in Cambodia, while Japanese troops were to surrender to Nationalist Chinese forces of Chiang Kai-shek north of the sixteenth parallel, a zone that included northern Laos.

No question vexed the French as much as future spheres of influence in Indochina following the defeat of Japan, whether it would fall under SEAC exclusively or whether the Chinese would also push for a role. Much confusion remained in the minds of French planners as to how the Allied spheres of influence in Indochina would play out. France understood that it lacked the resources in the Asia Pacific to perform the role of taking the Japanese surrender and that it would be dependent on the Allies. But the details long remained vague or veiled by secrecy in intra-Allied war councils. While Chiang Kai-shek exercised preeminence over the Allies in the China theater, at a meeting at his wartime headquarters in Chongqing on October 16, 1943, SEAC commander Admiral Louis Mountbatten gained the generalissimo's approval for the British to operate inside these boundaries.

The Roosevelt Vision

Known for his anticolonial views, US president Roosevelt went further with respect to French Indochina and made it known that he favored a kind of trusteeship to be imposed over the territory. He also proscribed direct US support for French resistance groups inside Indochina and on several occasions prohibited joint intelligence collection and resistance planning with the French (Thomas 2000, 950–51). Roosevelt's anticolonial views were elaborated at the Tehran Conference of November 28, 1943, where he concurred with Stalin that Indochina should not be returned to the French and reiterated in January the following year over the opposition of the British "who fear the effect [trusteeship] would have on their own possessions and those of the Dutch" (Paterson and Merrill 1995, 189–90).

However, as Tønnesson (2007, 65–72) contends, contrary to the view that Roosevelt changed his thinking on colonialism toward the end of his life, the reverse was the case. Even after the Japanese coup, Roosevelt did not yield on opposition to French colonialism. Only after his death on April 12, 1945, did top Washington officials work to revise policy in a pro-French direction, although still giving lip service to the old policy. Tønnesson singles out June 7, 1945, as the turning point, though he admits that the shift had been long germinating with respect to the increasing importance of de Gaulle's France in international affairs and the reevaluation of China in Allied strategy in pressing toward an invasion of Japan.

By January 1945, US concerns had shifted decisively to the Japanese archipelago and the prospect of US force commitments to Southeast Asia was nixed, leaving this sphere to British forces. Following the Yalta Conference (February 4–11, 1945), US planners declined to offer logistical support to Free French forces in Indochina. But the American position came under French criticism in the wake of the Japanese armed takeover in Indochina of March 9, 1945. The American decision to forgo commitment to operations in Southeast Asia prompted India-based SEAC commander Mountbatten to liberate Malaya and Singapore without US assistance. At the time of Roosevelt's death on April 12, 1945, US policy toward the colonial possessions of Allies was in "disarray."

There may have been other reasons for Roosevelt's hesitation on the trusteeship issue as well. As Gibbons (1986, 5) elaborates in a detailed study of the issue, beginning in 1944, Secretary of War Henry L. Stimson, among other service secretaries, particularly the navy, strongly opposed State Department plans for an international trusteeship system, fearing that this could prevent the United States from obtaining control and future base rights in the Pacific islands captured from Japan during the Pacific War. While for many members of the US Congress India was the colony that symbolized colonialism, American suggestions that it be granted independence after the war ran into strident opposition from the British (Prime Minister Churchill included). Neither were the British suggestive to loosening controls over other colonies as well. While ultimately the American trusteeship plan prevailed at the newly born United Nations (chapter XIV), French Foreign Minister Georges Bidault had already made it clear on May 2, 1945, that France did not intend to place Indochina under a trusteeship system (Gibbons 1986, 14).

The Truman Approach

The advent of the Truman administration (January 20, 1945–April 12, 1945) represented a turning point in Washington's thinking on the larger questions of colonialism and independence. The New Deal idealism of Roosevelt and his circle, which viewed the struggle against Western colonialism as part of the struggle against tyranny, came under intense scrutiny in the light of a reappraisal of the Soviet Union and changing conceptions of the US global role in general and its position in the Asia-Pacific in particular. The building of an American alliance with France under the Truman administration also came to be based on a broad Atlanticist reading of the relationship.

The change of direction in the Truman administration was also matched by a more assertive approach by the State Department, especially the European section. In April 1945, French diplomats in Washington "skillfully" applied pressure to gain official recognition of French sovereignty in Indochina. Notably, at the United Nations Conference at San Francisco in May–June 1945, James Dunn, undersecretary of state, together with Secretary of State Edward Stettinius assured the French about the unchanged colonial status of Indochina, asserting that Washington had never "officially" questioned French sovereignty. As revealed below, the French operatives in Indochina still harbored doubts as to American intentions. At this stage, however, as Richard J. Aldrich (2000, 305, 343–45) points out, Americans in the field were obviously "out of step with metropolitan policy-makers," especially as to the larger issues of colonialism and communism.

The OSS Mission in China

Feeling the need to revamp US intelligence collection alongside wartime theater engagements in Europe and Asia, in July 1941 Roosevelt launched the predecessor of the Central Intelligence Agency (CIA), the Office of Strategic Services (OSS), itself a split off from the wartime Office of the Coordination of Information. Enjoying close ties to Roosevelt, the OSS was headed—and dominated—by successful businessman-lawyer William Donovan (see Richard Smith 1972, 1–2). Nevertheless, the newly founded intelligence organization had to strive to gain Allied acceptance, not only from the French and Chinese but also from the British. With respect to Asia—China in particular—Donovan was instructed to provide cover to support national liberation movements to resist the Japanese. Whereas in France the OSS worked alongside the Free French to resist the Nazi occupation, in Asia the situation differed.

In July 1942, with Japanese occupation of Southeast Asia a reality, the OSS set up a guerrilla base in India for operations in Southeast Asia and China and, from 1943 to 1945, played a major role in training KMT troops in China and Burma (Patti 1980, 52). Even so, as Richard Smith (1972, 243–44) explains, the OSS met with resistance from "Vinegar" Joe Stilwell, the commander of American forces in China, India, and Burma. The OSS also had to win the support of Claire Chennault, heading the Fourteenth US Air Force or "Flying Tiger" air group, also known as the American Volunteer Group (AVG). Complicating this picture, in early 1943 and with Roosevelt's verbal agreement, Donovan entered into a pact with Chiang Kai-shek to create a joint secret service, the Sino-American Cooperative Organization (SACO), under the leadership of Chinese intelligence chief Dai Li and with US naval officer Milton Miles serving as deputy head. Eventually, in October 1944 the OSS set up staff headquarters in Kunming under Col. Richard Heppner, strengthened with the arrival of new recruits from the European theater (Richard Smith 1972, 259; Miles 1967). In his new command, Albert Wedemeyer was also named chief of staff to Generalissimo Chiang Kai-shek (see Richard Smith 1972, chap. 8).

Although the Free French and the American OSS entered into a fruitful cooperation in the liberation of France, matters were otherwise in the Indochina theater, where, as mentioned, from as early as 1942–43 clandestine American parties were operating inside China, and by 1944 the OSS was actively seeking the support of the Viet Minh in the anti-Japanese cause (Patti 1980, 52). From a French perspective, OSS-Viet Minh cooperation via the agency of "Deer Team," as discussed in chapter 7, was the single most damaging factor in their reoccupation plans, just as it sullied on-the-ground relations with the Americans in Kunming and Chongqing.

As Thomas (2000, 956) interprets, by the end of 1944, OSS planning for Indochina was impeded by the uncertainty as to whether the French garrison forces or the Vietnamese nationalists would be more likely to take up the resistance baton against the Japanese. Still they hedged, understanding that "only if Japanese economic exactions increased significantly might spontaneous resistance develop" on the part of the locals. In fact, that is what transpired, but it was not yet a certainty. In 1945, the OSS was reorganized with the tacit agreement of SEAC and China, setting up staff headquarters in strategically located Kunming. The Japanese *coup de force* of March 1945 also galvanized the OSS into action in the north at the critical juncture, as described, when Free French guerrillas took to the mountains in northern Vietnam and Laos to prepare for an eventual colonial restoration.

Also as explained in chapter 7, the Viet Minh were also not backward in seeking out American support. Ho Chi Minh in particular sought Allied recognition of the Viet Minh and their cause. As Thomas (2000, 962) points out, the foremost example of such agency was Ho Chi Minh's personal contact with China command, notably Chennault of the US Fourteenth Air Force, immediately following Ho's release from thirteen months of imprisonment by the Chinese Nationalists. In turn, Chennault's reception stimulated Viet Minh cooperation with US Ground Aid Service Air (AGAS in the French acronym) in assisting the evacuation of downed US fliers.

THE AMERICAN BOMBING OF FRENCH INDOCHINA

The arrival of the OSS team in southern China was not the United States' first involvement in Vietnam. For three years American air and naval forces had been harassing Japanese positions in and around Vietnam. The success of these bombing raids depended on accurate weather reports from within Indochina as well as up-to-date intelligence on Japanese troop movements. In addition, a network of agents within Indochina was necessary to rescue shot-down or crashed US pilots, to hide them from the Japanese, and, if possible, to smuggle them out of Indochina back to Kunming (Patti 1980, chap. 11; Bartholomew-Feis 2006, chap. 3). As viewed below, such activities would draw the Americans into contact with the Viet Minh.

Although the bombing of strategic Japanese targets in northern Vietnam had started in August 1942 with the Flying Tigers, the tempo increased under the Kunming-based China Air Task Force of the Tenth Air Force and later by the Fourteenth Air Force, as with the bombing of Haiphong as early as October 1, 1943, and the Hanoi-Haiphong area in April 1944. Haiphong was repeatedly targeted until, by late 1944, Japanese ships appeared to be avoiding the port entirely, just as coastal shipping remained a US priority (Koburger 1997, 14). Additional attacks were made by B-29s of the Twentieth Bomb Group flying out of India and by Liberators, Mitchells, and Lightnings belonging to the Fifth and Thirteenth Air Forces operating from bases in the Philippines. Beginning in December 1944, attacks on Japanese targets in southern Vietnam were made by the US Navy Seventh Fleet's Catalinas, B-24s, and Privateers as well as by carrier aircraft from Admiral William Halsey's Third Fleet (Mickelsen 2008).

Still, raids made over northern Vietnam by China-based Curtiss P-40 (Warhawk) fighter-bombers should not be ignored, especially as they explicitly targeted communication infrastructure. Notably, on March 20, 1943, a train carrying coolies toward Lao Kay was bombed, leaving eighteen wounded. The same day, P-42s bombed a Japanese camp and the railway station at Pho Ly on the Ninh Binh to Son Tay route, inflicting "heavy losses," both material and human, besides leaving a one hundred-meter gap in the rail line. The following day it was the turn of Lao Cao, bombed by three American Curtiss planes hitting the Cam Duong mines and stations at Lang Giang and Thi Nien, among other targets. The first air attacks on Yen Bai station occurred on March 23, 1943. Simultaneously, Ha Giang was subject to an air raid aimed at cutting river and terrestrial communications along the Clear River (Song Lo) (AOM RST NF 1B92, RS, Hanoi, March 1943). For the victims, including the hapless mine coolies, America's global war against fascism might have appeared as a somewhat remote consideration.

Beginning in April 1944, US India-based B-29s targeted the Saigon Naval Yard and Arsenal. Japanese shipping at Cape St. Jacques (Vung Tau) and terrestrial transport between Tuyen Quang and Ha Giang also became targets with five to seven ships sunk in a raid of April 15, 1944. Meanwhile, American submarines began to take their toll on both Japanese and French shipping (delivered up by Decoux to the Japanese, notwithstanding the resistance of French crews). Notably, on April 29, 1944, two French ships heading north were sunk by submarines off the coast of Vietnam, one a French destroyer lost with all hands, the other a merchant vessel which, according to Allied intelligence, was "carrying badly needed rice to Tonkin and Annam" (NAA A3269 G5/4 [South China Sea, South China, French Indochina and North] SHARK).

This is actually an important revelation—or admission—as the Allies would have known something of the human consequences of their actions beyond the mere sinking of ships In this operation, Vice Admiral John S. McCain, operating in the South China Sea, hit Japanese shipping, airfields, and other shore installations in southeastern French Indochina.[2] More generally, alongside the Japanese record of deliberately shelling and bombing Chinese cities, the American wartime bombing of ostensibly military targets in Vietnam was also part of an extended Allied wartime bombing campaign that would inflict widespread "collateral" damage on civilian populations (see Tanaka and Young 2009).

Transport, Distribution, and Logistics Issues

We detour somewhat to explain Japanese distribution and logistics issues guiding the American bombing of a variety of targets in Indochina. Dating back to the construction of the Trans-Indochinois rail line, transport logistics were viewed by the French as the key to managing rice deficit situations with rapid resupply from rice surplus in Cochinchina. Before the war, coastal navigation hauled the bulk of north-south traffic, especially rice from the south returning with coal from the north. But as American submarine raids began to impact Japanese and coastal shipping, boats were few in number, and the rail line experienced difficulties in ensuring essential traffic, notably a lack of spare parts for rolling stock.

But while north-south traffic was slowing down owing to the American destruction of infrastructure, the traffic between Bangkok and Saigon was also observed by Allied intelligence as extremely heavy. Besides rice shipped to Bangkok via Battambang in western Cambodia, rice from Phnom Penh was also freighted to Saigon for shipment in larger vessels. The Bangkok-Battambang rail connection was understood to be extremely important to the Japanese and was being taxed to the limit (PRO HK KWIZ /04d/27/6/43 Report no.87).

The above leads to the question: What kind of shipping was entering French Indochinese ports, for what purpose, and toward what destination? Saigon and its oceangoing port of Vung Tau were the most important for Japanese shipping between Taiwan and Singapore, with shipping movements in 1943–44 averaging between five (Saigon) and thirteen (Vung Tau) ship visits a day. As the assembly point for Japanese ship convoys plying between the South Seas and Japan, during the same approximate period, up to thirty-three ships a day sometimes anchored off Vung Tau. Allied intelligence offers highly detailed weekly summaries of shipping movements into and out of these ports. In April–June 1944, a large number of Japanese troop-carrying vessels reportedly arrived in the Saigon River and immediately reloaded with rice directly from barges floated down from the Mekong delta rice fields. Summarizing from a single day's maritime activity out of Saigon in early August 1944, Allied intelligence stated that the Japanese were shipping considerable rice from Saigon to occupied Java, Singapore, Hong Kong, and Shanghai, as well as Japan.

But with the US interdiction of Japanese shipping taking its toll, the deployment of available shipping also added to the problem of servicing the coastal trade. Dated July 19 (1944), an Allied intelligence source stated that at Saigon, "there are 300,000 tons of rice awaiting shipment, part of which is rotting on the quays." Even if the figure covers all Japanese-held rice in Saigon, including quantities earmarked for local Japanese consumption and production of alcohol, the account confirmed that "the accumulation during the first six months of 1944 amounts to over a quarter of the total tonnage scheduled for shipping this year" (NAA A3269 G5/4 [South China Sea, South China, French Indochina and North] SHARK). With a superabundance of rice rotting in the harbor, we may ask, why wasn't even a proportion of this food surplus freighted north to cover the then-apparent rice deficit in north-central Vietnam and the lower Red River delta?

Another measure undertaken to alleviate the lack of shipping was a concerted attempt by the Japanese authorities in Saigon to construct some two hundred wooden ships of five-hundred-tonne capacity, an industry involving more than one thousand local Chinese and Vietnamese craftsmen. An engine plant was supplied by Mitsubishi, with other engines arriving by freighter from Hong Kong. But rather than deploy these vessels in the coastal trade, the first four were dispatched to Singapore, carrying a total of nine hundred tonnes of rice. One foundered, and two others returned to port badly leaking. Other motor-driven wooden ships were directed toward Thailand and the Khra Isthmus. On September 2, 1944, the Japanese commanded four Chinese-owned steamships to carry military personnel and supplies between Phnom Penh and Saigon. Although we lack parallel data for Haiphong port, the point is that almost all of this maritime activity was geared to meet Japan's greater strategic needs, while coastal navigation connecting up the south, center, and north of Vietnam was either disrupted or neglected, fatally as it turned out (NAA A3269 G5/4 [South China Sea, South China, French Indochina and North] SHARK; Andrus and Greene 1944, 385).

Besides intense Japanese naval activity in and around Saigon port, the picture that emerges in 1944–early 1945 is one of near total command of rice produced in rice-surplus southern delta and Cambodia and its export under Japanese military auspices to virtually all parts of the Japanese empire wherever this was feasible (NAA A 3269 G5/4 [South China Sea, South China, French Indochina and North] SHARK). As explained below, the transport grid and Japanese shipping would become the target of repeated American bombing and submarine attacks.

Even so, as mentioned, the main transport conduit for the domestic movement of rice was the rail system. Rail transport was, of course, the more reliable north-south communication link, especially during the typhoon season (July–October), when any kind of maritime activity was hazardous. The Saigon-Hanoi Trans-Indochinois line was single track, meter-gauge line with double track at all stations. The steepest gradient was 1:100. Normally—or before the bombing started to interrupt the timetable—a journey from Saigon to Hanoi took forty-two hours, at an average of forty-two kilometers per hour, with a somewhat reduced speed on newly opened track between Nha Trang and Quang Ngai. The capacity of the line was six trains in each direction every twenty-four hours. According to an Allied intelligence report of 1944, express trains ran daily between the two centers. This was not a disinterested report but offered four optimum target sites for submarine-based landing parties where the line was at its closest point to the sea, from Thanh Hoa in the north to Quang Nam-Danang in the south (NAA A3269 E3/4 Lower South China Sea, Singapore OPTICIAN [South China Sea]).

Obviously, with such an efficient transport system in place, there would have been no technical obstacle to moving food from surplus to deficit areas. But use of the line also needs to be considered. According to an unconfirmed Chinese intelligence report of late 1944, owing to the movement north of fifty thousand Japanese troops from Saigon to Hanoi, all civilian traffic on the line was suspended through September 7, 1944 (NAA A3269 G5/4 [South

China Sea, South China, French Indochina and North] SHARK). Whatever the veracity of that report, it does fit generalized accounts contending that the Japanese military subordinated use of the line to military needs, both before and after the March 9, 1945 *coup de force*. Undoubtedly, the Allies were also acting on this kind of assessment in targeting the Trans-Indochinois line.

There is also some conflict in Allied intelligence reporting. A report from September 1944 indicates that American bombing and strafing attacks destroyed or damaged several bridges on the northern sector of the north-south rail line, resulting in dislocation of transport services. The tenor of this account is confirmed by an October 10, 1944, report citing the "poor condition" of the track, making possible a maximum of four thousand tons of cargo monthly and with possibilities of repair "negligible." But we know that different sectors of the line were not subject to irreparable damage (Saigon-Danang-Ninh Binh), just as repair and, undoubtedly, porterage were also ways around the problem. According to an intelligence assessment of January 1945, the Japanese army had demanded of the French (still technically in charge of the line) that six pairs of trains per week should run between Saigon and Danang, with one train a day running in both directions from Viet Tri (northwest of Hanoi) to Lao Cai (at the Vietnam terminus of the Haiphong-Kunming line) (NAA A3269 G5/4 [South China Sea, South China, French Indochina and North] SHARK). This assessment suggests that there was no breakdown in the rail transportation system at this stage, and there is no reason why rice could not have been entering this traffic if there had been the will.

By November 29, 1944, however, traffic over the railway bridge at Ninh Binh had been stopped by aerial bombing, with two railway cars destroyed. The following day the railway was again damaged at Phu Ly. It is fair to comment that if these two sections of the line had not been speedily repaired, then traffic in and out of the southern Red River delta would have been drastically interrupted. Especially, as discussed in a following chapter, these were critical weeks when the administration depended absolutely on rail traffic to resupply food needs in the north. Much, of course, would also have depended on nonrail transport from Phi Ly to local markets and the administration and distribution of rice within the deficit zones. Summarizing, we can state that with the famine crisis beginning to bite, rail traffic was still reaching Ninh Binh from Danang via Hue, Vinh, Dong Hoi, and Thanh Hoa, without major interruption (NAA A3269 G5/4 [South China Sea, South China, French Indochina and North] SHARK).

US bombing of the rail line may not have been the critical factor in starving the north of southern rice, especially as it appears that north-south communication was not completely ruptured in the run-up to March–April, the peak of the northern famine, but combined with attacks on coastal shipping, it did not make life easier for the concerned Japanese or French authorities dealing with transport and food issues. While we do not have a complete log of American bombing targets over Vietnam, railway lines may not have been the main target alongside military and industrial centers, as with Hanoi and Haiphong.

Urban Bombing

For a time, as Mickelsen (2008) argues in a rare study of Allied bombing of Vietnam during the Pacific War, the Americans were diverted from the main mission by acts of "vengeance" against the Vichy French who betrayed downed American aviators. Head of French military forces in Vietnam (and secret Gaullist collaborator), General Eugene Mordant was convinced that the Fourteenth Air Force had deliberately bombed Hanoi in December 1943 and again in April 1944, in retaliation for Decoux's policy of surrendering downed American fliers to the Japanese. Mordant's fears were reinforced by a warning from Fourteenth Air Force commander Claire Chennault that all the major towns in northern Vietnam would be bombed if similar incidents occurred in the future.

Notably, on December 10 and 12, 1943, Hanoi (and not the usual target of the nearby Japanese airfield at Gia Lam) had been attacked for the first time, causing 1,232 casualties and 500 deaths (or, in other reports, 1,377 dead, mostly from collapsed houses and shelters). On April 8, 1944, Hanoi was hit again by the 308th Bomb Group (H) when the Yersin hospital complex was targeted, leaving 46 civilians dead with 141 wounded in Vietnamese and Chinese residential areas. In February 1945 the French authorities in Tonkin also put in place a special schedule of indemnities for localities suffering bombardments, pledging relief within fifteen days, but only for places twice bombed. Bac Ninh, which had been bombed July 1–15, 1944, met that criteria (AOM RS Tonkin 1B/96, RS Allimand à Santé, Hanoi, Feb. 23, 1945).

The state of mind of the population of Hanoi is expressed in a rare firsthand report from late 1944. Taking the form of a letter written by a Vietnamese schoolteacher, Pha Ngoc Thai, to a provincial councilor, the author explains that the situation in Hanoi and the Red River delta had become more exasperating by the day owing to the bombings. In Hanoi, air raids alerts were a twenty-four-hour occurrence. "We can't do anything, we spend our time running to the air raid trenches. People flee at the first signal." The delta population had also been informed of the dangers of remaining in certain locations. Co Bi (Gia Lam), Pho Ly, and Nam Binh are all mentioned. "Everyone is afraid, because of the memory of the December 10 and 11 bombardments last year." All the roads were crammed with carts and *pousse-pousse* transporting furniture and runaways. Likewise, the tramways were bursting with evacuees. As explained, the majority of the inhabitants of Hanoi had relocated to villages in Ha Dong (to the southwest) (AOM RS Tonkin 1B 13434, Nov. 29–Dec. 31, 1944).

According to a French military source, on February 7, 1945, China-based American Superfortress aircraft made Saigon their target. Flying above the clouds and visually sighting their targets, their object was the navy arsenal. However, bombs fell on the military barracks and a hospital, killing 31 Europeans, including three French officers and 24 soldiers, along with 110 locals. The French vehemently protested the raids to Washington via the head of the French naval mission to the United States. Also, as reported, five downed American aviators rescued by members of the Resistance in the Saigon region on January 12 for dispatch to China had been apprehended by the Japanese (SHD GR 4 Q 45 Indochine 1943–1948 Major-Général Défense Nationale, Paris, Feb. 22, 1945). Again, on June 12, 1945, thirty-one B-24s bombed Saigon-Cholon, leading to 425 French and Vietnamese deaths, including many prisoners at the central prison (among those who did not escape) (FIR, no.11, June 1–15, 1945, Far Eastern Bureau, New Delhi). Phnom Penh was also targeted with civilian casualties. Such raids halted only with Japan's capitulation, although leaflet distribution flights announcing Japan's surrender continued, as did some search flights (ONI Weekly 2439, 4, 34, Aug. 22, 1945).

Whether or not these raids were actually a case of "vengeance," the American message was made very clear. As General Mordant informed Paris on March 2, 1945, the Americans intended to bomb all lines of communications in Tonkin and Annam. The destruction of four large bridges north and south of Vinh two days earlier was a case in point. In the event of a protest lodged to the Americans, he plaintively advised, let it be known that "the attacks are not justified by the situation" (SHD GR 4Q Indochine 1943–1945 tél., à GUGON, Paris, March 2, 1945).

Yet there was also cooperation between the French military mission in Kunming and the Americans. According to a US State Department source, between March 12 and March 28, 1945, American planes based in China had accomplished twenty-four (unspecified) missions in Indochina at the specific request of the French military resistance. Separately, another thirty-four missions accomplished one hundred sorties, including twenty-five bombing runs and seventy-five reconnaissance flights. However, it is unlikely that French military command in Kunming was calling down bombing raids on urban targets or even infrastructure. Rather, the French requested American assistance in the evacuation of French refugees, presumably those arriving in extremely remote locations in southern Yunnan across the border with Indochina following the Japanese coup. As testament of this element of cooperation with the Gaullist Resistance, and for his part in conducting this "particularly difficult" mission, General Chennault of the Fourteenth Air Force was duly awarded a French Légion d'Honneur (MAE AOI 49, "Action Alliée Clandestine, Note," Paris, April 16, 1945).

The following month witnessed even greater French-US cooperation. Up to April 25, the Fourteenth Air Force had flown 61 missions consisting of 184 sorties at the specific request of the Free French, including the dropping of supplies to French Resistance forces (one sortie dropped six thousand pounds of supplies). Negotiations were then under way as to dropping clothing, rations, and small arms to isolated groups behind Japanese lines so as to facilitate their entry into China (MAE AOI 50, E 166-11, Paris, May 3, 1945). Even so, French Resistance forces bewailed the general lack of American cooperation in this area.

As Mickelsen (2008) explains, neither did Americans control the skies over Vietnam. Facing down both Vichy antiaircraft batteries and Japanese fighters, the Americans suffered 414 casualties in the course of these missions alongside a host of downed fliers. For instance, in late 1943, three B-24 Liberators were shot down in a single raid over Haiphong by thirty-five or more Japanese fighters. Downed American fliers continued to be detained and placed in captivity right down until the Japanese surrender. While it appeared to the Vichy French authorities in Hanoi that they were being punished by the Americans for turning over downed fliers to the devices of the Japanese, the Resistance was also running an underground escape network and incurring severe risks. As alluded to, Viet Minh assistance in rescuing more than one American pilot would help cement a cooperative relationship between the OSS and the Viet Minh.

Admiral William Halsey's Third Fleet

Notably, on January 12, 1945, a US task force under Rear Admiral Gerald F. Bogan, part of Admiral William Halsey's Third Fleet, struck the Indochina coast. US T-38 aircraft attacked four large enemy convoys off the Vietnam coast (location and destination unclear), sinking twenty-five vessels and severely damaging another thirteen. Among the losses was the French light cruiser *Lamotte-Picquet*, a strategic Vichy asset in defeating the Thai navy at Koh Chang in the Gulf of Thailand on January 17, 1941. Shipping losses along the coast were reported as heavy, just as port arrivals in Saigon-Vung Tau began to trend downward. The French announced their losses while the Japanese remained silent. Altogether destroying 110 Japanese planes and sinking 44 ships, raids conducted by Halsey's Third Fleet inflicted one of the heaviest blows to Japanese shipping in the war. As naval historian Koburger (1997, 15) points out, these actions effectively put an end to major maritime traffic along the Indochina coast.

More than achieving naval supremacy, the Halsey raids also—ambiguously—sent a political message to the Japanese high command, namely that an American invasion of Indochina was imminent and that the French could no longer be trusted to remain passive. Tønnesson (1991, 172–73, 190, 201) argues that Japanese military fear of American invasion prompted the high command to accelerate plans for Operation Meigo. He also establishes a causal link between the Halsey raids and the March 9 coup. Because Roosevelt followed developments in the Pacific through his reading of Magic translations, he clearly knew of the impending coup. Tønnesson (2002, 22) concedes, however, that the evidence remains speculative as to whether Roosevelt actually ordered the raids, even if they did reflect his desire to liberate Indochina from French "colonialism."

FRENCH MISGIVINGS: THE WRITINGS OF PAUL MUS

In line with de Gaulle's March 24, 1945, declaration, and against the intense diplomatic background of Free French lobbying with Washington, French planners took stock of their naval and military assets—badly wanting. Deepening their cooperation with the British in India, as with training and logistics, and falling in line with Mountbatten's Sri Lanka-based SEAC, charged with taking the Japanese surrender in Indochina south of the sixteenth parallel, the French set up their military and political headquarters in Kandy under General Jacques Philippe Leclerc, the "liberator" of Paris from the Nazis. Not only was France determined to restore a version of the colonial status quo in the wake of the Japanese surrender, but it was also adamant in gaining Allied acceptance as a belligerent against the Japanese. To this end, France would duly take its place among the Allies at the formal Japanese surrender ceremony of September 2, 1945, on the USS *Missouri* in Tokyo Bay and at the ensuing Tokyo War Crimes Trials.

One who departed from the received French wisdom, albeit from a position sensitive to Vietnamese history, was Paul Mus (1902–69), variously director of EFEO in Hanoi, head of the psychological warfare section of the Resistance for the mission in Indochina (January–March 1945), and political adviser to General Sabattier (April–May 1945). On August 1, 1945, during a period in Paris when he served on de Gaulle's Comité de l'Indochine, just weeks prior to joining Leclerc in Kandy as political adviser, Mus penned a thirty-point memorandum—a virtual position paper—on the way ahead, evocatively titled "Note sur le Crise Morale Franco-Indochinoise." Consigned to French archives, the document entered print only in recent times (Chandler and Goscha 2005). Necessarily, my offering is highly select, with an emphasis on Mus's rare understanding of Vietnamese nationalism and sense of the French loss of the "mandate of heaven" to the Japanese.

"It is clear," Mus wrote, "that, in effect, our relations with the Indochinese and, above all, with the Vietnamese in 1945 are disappointing and difficult."

As he recalled the period prior to the Japanese *coup de force* of March 9, Paris had played a waiting game. But over a much longer time frame:

> We hitherto had growing pains, and this was grasped much more early and completely by the Indochinese elite than by us. During this period too many colonials were insensitive to the malaise and to the onset of new revolts such as signaled by Yen Bai, Thai Nguyen, among others, including those from an even earlier age.

In reflecting on the scientific and educational advancement of the Vietnamese, he wrote:

> The patent fact, at least from the viewpoint of Western civilization, and by the standards with which we hold ourselves, is that we can say that Indochina has reached its majority. But not a quantitative majority on the educational level or by the modern productivity of the masses. . . . On the contrary, what we can recognize is a qualitative majority. In effect, . . . [Vietnam] has already produced a sufficient number of brilliant individuals who can play an equal and sometimes even better game than the metropolitan French [whom] they emulate. Among them are jurists, clinicians, engineers, teachers, amply demonstrating a modern aptitude.

Of the Indochinese masses and, above all, the Vietnamese population (nineteen million out of twenty-three million), he pointed out, they draw their history from a "substantial and healthy foundation":

> In adapting to the modern world they do not build upon a void. . . . Isn't it normal and desirable in these conditions that the major qualitative elements, such as inspired by our education, should be extended generally so that their compatriots can likewise benefit from the system of which they have been principal beneficiaries?

As to "the very particular nature of Vietnamese nationalism," Mus obviously offered a thoughtful and nuanced understanding.

> This nationalism, which is sometimes repudiated, exists, and is singularly tenacious. Taken alone, it is elusive. Granted that it is fashioned by history, it is by origin and nature above all ritual and social. It is neither aggressive or militarist, at least in the form in which it has largely spread among the masses. Politically, it is not exacerbated, at this level, by any irredentism. It is not haunted by any clear image of a glorious lost national history, such as represented by the conquest of neighboring countries over long time. It is not that Vietnamese nationalism is philosophical by nature, but in its moderation has no prior vocation. For example, the history of conflicts between Vietnamese and Cham

> people conforms to this understanding where, in the natural course of things, one among two expansive communities eliminated the other by arms.

Turning to the weight of Chinese tradition, Mus continued:

> But on the northern side, the incessant contact with a measured and prestigious neighbor has ended by modeling its national character. The Chinese preponderance that translates alternatively by subjection or by the simple vassal status has never entirely left it free from the allures of nationality vigorously asserted, even though powerfully impregnated with the cultural imitation of the master or suzerain. It is a small common merit that has been preserved under these conditions, not only a national temperament with its own social force but even under these borrowings of over 2,000 years, this Vietnamese "resistance" is essentially unbending. It has resulted in a nationalism deeply entrenched in the soil, limited only by the open sky.

In trying to pinpoint the Vietnamese essence emerging out of this history, Mus returns to the idealized model of the Vietnamese village, such as constructed before him by fellow EFEO scholar Pierre Gourou:

> In sum, what the Vietnamese have preserved across the vicissitudes of their history is a community of blood, of language, of sentiment, comprising a vital milieu enduring over long time. . . . For whoever is familiar with these people, the background of this state of things, the more or less unconscious but concrete model of this ideal community, is the village. This is the form in which the Vietnamese socializes and is the basis of its patriotism.

On the question of sovereignty, Mus turns to the metaphysical, namely the rise and fall of dynasties, as with the notion of loss of the "mandate of heaven." Apparently repeated in a number of texts, Mus's analogy of the Japanese intervention and the loss of mandate of heaven has been much critiqued (Chandler and Goscha 2005). But it is also true that Mus was in Hanoi the very day that the French lost power (FitzGerald 1972, 86; Chandler 2009, 166).

> Above this actual molecular structure sits the clear and effective notion of the monarchical state otherwise anonymous in the larger sweep of the history of the Vietnamese nation. But from its origins, and especially from the 13th century, the imitation of Chinese institutions is also there, leaving its mark. In medieval China, taken as a model, the feudal phase of the Warring Kingdoms is largely forgotten. Power is exercised according to state ritual. The sovereignty is of cosmic essence. The source of its authority is the order of the universe, ruled by astrology and numbers, magic diagrams, etc. Temporal power is but a projection on earth by the intermediary of the dynasty as indicated by the destiny of this

supernatural norm. It is from this that flows the theory of royal power, essentially universal, establishing a right to rule, neither dynastic, racial, national or personal, but cosmic and rational. Translated into the rich and invasive ceremonial of the state religion, these conceptions have had profound reactions upon the popular mentality and have oriented the communal political sense in the Far East towards forms which often disconcert us. A magical virtue is imagined behind each dynasty. When the virtue is exhausted, the dynasty falls. No recourse to temporal political arts can rescue it. This is the principle recognized in revolutions, and it is that which gives it its ineluctable character. Such a theory assures obedience, the "divine right" of a dynasty such as endures but is not created again. Between people and them, a bond of blood for the better and worse, such as obtains in other lands; a cyclic conception. . . . Even in modern Asia, it is impossible to grasp the movement of public opinion and of local history outside of its references. One is unable to even take into account the various experiments of this sort of political world; a civilian authority proves its legitimacy by its success. That is the touch-stone of "virtue." Everything that goes against it is rebellion, from the instant when a "virtue" imposes itself to the end. The contrary case is rebellion.

Turning to the perennial revolutionary identification of the enemy, Mus offers emic Vietnamese understandings of the Japanese *coup de force* (actually referring to March 9, 1945):

> A study of the uses of the Vietnamese word "*giao*" which means enemy but above all "pirate" would be very instructive in this regard. Everything that Tonkin understood by an immediate American intervention, that is to say towards March 11, led to the Japanese being denominated "*giao*," but after March 12 they became the Japanese saviors "*ong nhat*." Their virtue had risen temporarily.

Mus also sought to answer a very traditional question that actually was in the throes of subversion at the hands of the Viet Minh: "In what way does Vietnamese nationalism flow from the elite to the masses?" On the complex impact of the Japanese occupation on the elite, he wrote that Japan sought to reclaim the economic and military potential of the country without any recognition of the "paternalistic" French contribution to the country:

> To employ French vocabulary, they reclaimed from Admiral Decoux a heavy industry and even an Indochinese Saint Cyr at Dalat. It was not just a fantasy of the elite but the first alignment of the politics of modern nationalism. Formerly closed off from the world, the world came to find them. In this regard, we must increasingly address the demands of the local masses behind this elite of which we presently have representatives in Paris.

As Mus conceded, the French poorly understood how the Indochinese community in France was actually linked by bonds with its country. As he noted, some were young when they arrived in France and were out of touch with recent events, though also sensitive to avoid being labeled "collaborators or quislings."

Mus was also one of the more serious critics of de Gaulle's Declaration of March 24, 1945, calling for the creation of an "Indochina Federation" under France but still maintaining the tripartite division of Vietnam. As he observed, prior to the Japanese coup, one part of the Vietnamese population at least was satisfied with the relationship between Indochina and France, as measured by the distance they kept from Vichy and could otherwise relate to the Free French concept of a new regime free from foreign subjection. However, as he continued:

> The speech made by the General on the occasion of Vietnamese New Year has produced in this regard a particularly displeasing impression. It expounds uniquely upon two themes, respectively: "our dear Indochina" and "our faithful Indochina" only holding out for our return. Nothing here reflects the political, military, or moral drama which evolves towards the crisis that we know. Nothing, for example, leads me to suggest whether or not the Chief satisfied the French community that further deaths will be prevented. Nor the famine menacing hundreds of thousands of Vietnamese in Tonkin and north Annam. Nothing indicates that he has grasped the evolution of a spirit which can be called national, the shock of foreign invasion . . . such as with the perception of a national structure that could have provided the means of defense. The Declaration of March 23 [*sic*] came after the coup, confirming these doubts, yet setting the background for the division of the Vietnamese nation into three parts along lines envisaged by the French administration, but not in line with history outside of the French presence in the Far East.
>
> It is with sincerity that the Vietnamese revolutionaries shot dead by the Vichy regime in Saigon cried out "Vive le Viet Nam; Vive de Gaulle."

In other words, the struggle against fascism won the admiration of the Vietnamese masses (and the Communist Party), but that support did not necessarily translate into an easy acceptance of the colonial status quo. Especially, as Mus cautioned, it sidestepped the crucial Vietnamese concern for unity of the nation. Turning to likely Vietnamese responses to a return to French rule, especially after France had failed to prevent a Japanese invasion, he wrote:

> The Indochinese paid and still pay too dearly for the fact that they have been administered as a colony along 19th century lines to accept for long time to be administered by the Ministry of Colonies. This is the thesis and we have responded by appearing to localize. It is not just intellectual advocacy but the awakening of a national sentiment, calling upon a consciousness on its own soil and answering back to the brutal invasion which we did not prevent. (AOM

Indochine/NF/1219, "Note sur le Crise Morale Franco-Indochinoise," Captain Paul Mus, Paris, Aug. 1, 1945)[3]

Still, Mus was employed by the French state and was prepared to play his part, albeit in a new government that was prepared to acknowledge the kind of advice he had just tendered and, moreover, one that was prepared to reinvent itself. Notably, Mus was with Leclerc on the USS *Missouri* on September 2, 1945, to receive the Japanese surrender for France prior to assuming the role of political adviser in Admiral Thierry d'Argenlieu's office, once established in Saigon. In this capacity Mus acted as an official French interlocutor with Ho Chi Minh and, for a spell, joined French forces in the southern delta (Chandler 2009, 170). Alienated from the French establishment for his contrarian views, Mus "defected" to academia in the United States in 1950–51. At Yale University and through his publications, Mus also became an influential commentator on the expanding "Vietnam war." Patently, as explained above, Mus, was far ahead of his colleagues in understanding the cultural complexities and psychology of Vietnamese responses to the Japanese invasion, the cosmic significance of the notion of the fall of the mandate of heaven, the looming famine, and, little comprehended in French circles, the notion of nationalism and a united Vietnam, wielded with such success by the Viet Minh.

It is somewhat more controversial to suggest, however, as with Archimedes Patti (1980, 188–89), that the "unsophisticated masses" saw the act of abdication by Emperor Bao Dai as sanctioning the Viet Minh to inherit the mantle of imperial power, especially, as discussed in chapter 7, as there were many extenuating circumstances surrounding the "August Revolution."

CONCLUSION

As revealed, Allied responses to Japan when defeat at home appeared inevitable were played out in distant capitals, whether Washington, London, Algiers, Calcutta, Kandy, Kunming, or Chongqing, bringing together a host of politicians, generals, and leaders. Crucially, at the Potsdam Declaration meeting, Truman, Churchill, and Chiang Kai-shek capped this process. Closer to the action, Ho Chi Minh and Vo Nguyen Giap would also enter the stage. So, in turn, would certain of the *eminence gris* of militarist Japan, such as identified by the Tokyo War Crimes Trials. As with most of the actions of World War II, ordinary people hardly mattered. With the example of Saigon under the Popular Front in mind, it makes us wonder about how the niceties of city hall politics and electioneering can be blown away by naked ambition and ruthless power plays such as those unleashed by Nazi Germany and its Asian allies.

But Allied coordination was not unproblematical, especially given conflicted relations between French and Chinese and even French and Americans, just as visions of a future Indochina and its carving up were various in the run-up to taking the local Japanese surrender. US bombing of military and—perchance—civilian targets over Hanoi and Saigon between 1943 and 1945 may not at the time have signaled a harbinger of things to come. But, as with the firebombing of cities in Germany and Japan and before it, the Japanese bombing of urban populations in China, so the American conventional bombing of urban targets in Vietnam signaled a decisive shift in the willingness to shrink the line between military and civilian combatants, virtually changing the rules of warfare. Particularly in the Indochina theater, the US bombing also compromised the ability of Vichy France to transport rice and other food supplies.

The incremental slide in position of the United States from support for anticolonialism to containment of global communism also served to heal the breach between the French provisional government and what it believed were selfish US interests in backing a Viet Minh takeover. But, as exposed by Paul Mus among others, the major contradiction for the French was that between its own ambitions, written in stone in the March 24, 1945 Declaration, and the mass aspirations of the Vietnamese people for unity and the capture of that spirit by an armed minoritarian faction called the Viet Minh. As Mus acknowledged, having lost face to the Japanese in a virtual "loss of the mandate of heaven," France faced an uphill task in mounting its colonial restoration, no matter the imperative and the merits. But not even Mus predicted a Viet Minh takeover within days of the Japanese surrender nor the prospect of the communists winning popular legitimacy amid a subsistence crisis created by the famine and subsequent flood of late August 1945.

Although it is beyond the scope of this book, from small beginnings, as with the OSS, or from even such commercial operations in French Indochina as Caltex and Texaco, American involvement in Indochina underwent a steady progression. Even alongside Chiang Kai-shek, US president Roosevelt and his successor, Truman, were kingmakers in postwar Indochina. And even when France won its grudging diplomatic support from Washington as to drawing the line on a determinedly communist northern Vietnam, so it increasingly became beholden to American lend-lease and, in the defense of Dien Bien Phu, looked to significant American logistical and material support. As exposed in a following chapter, the Allies did not plan for a worst-case humanitarian disaster. Still, the intelligence strongly pointed to the need for urgent food supplies, not just to succor occupation forces but to cope with a phenomenal breakdown in subsistence on the part of the starved and wretched inhabitants of the northern delta.

NOTES

1. The development of Gaullist and British policies over Indochina from the fall of France in 1940 to the Japanese surrender has been tracked by a number of authors from both British and French sources (Dennis 1987; Dreifort 1991; Thomas 1997; 2000).

2. For this and other detailed logs of Japanese shipping losses inflicted by US sea and, with less detail, air power, see Cressman (1999).

3. Author's translation from original (faded) archival document. For the full text of the Mus document in French, see Chandler and Goscha (2005, 310–14).

Chapter 7

The "August Revolution" of 1945 and Its Defense

The rise and triumph of the Viet Minh in northern Indochina is often seen as against all odds, especially alongside Chinese-backed Vietnamese nationalist forces. We should also understand that emerging in 1941 as a broad front, the Viet Minh had no monopoly on anti-French, anti-Japan appeal but was one of several groups active in the rugged Guangxi-Yunnan borderland. Emerging by 1944 as a proto-anti-Japan resistance army, the Viet Minh had eclipsed, although not entirely abandoned, the older ICP networks. Controversially, in this new role it also received vital American intelligence assistance. But having seized power in Hanoi in August 1945, whether as revolution or a coup, as sometimes debated, the Viet Minh were also obliged to face down a range of threats, not only from domestic rivals and enemies but also from the Nationalist Chinese and their protégés. To win legitimacy, the fledgling Democratic Republic of Vietnam (DRV) was not only obliged to protect the population but also to feed them. Whether or not the Viet Minh successfully portrayed themselves as agrarian reformers, we certainly need to know how the ragtag guerrilla army could so quickly win mass support, not only from its elite intellectual cadre but also from the ethnic minority heartland, where it launched its army and, crucially, from townsfolk and rural dwellers across the nation. Terror alone cannot explain Viet Minh recruitment success. To be sure, as Lockhart (1989, 105) has asserted, the Great Famine "helped focus support for the Viet Minh."[1]

This chapter divides into five parts. First, it traces the birth of the Viet Minh Front (May 1941) and its activities in the Viet Bac zone. Second, with particular reference to French sources, it examines the "famine" rebellion in Thai Nguyen (November 1944–February 1945), Viet Minh exploitation, and French rationalizations. Third, it traces the Viet Minh rise to power in northern Vietnam both prior to and after the Japanese *coup de force* of

March 9, 1945, also backgrounding support from the American OSS. A fourth part turns to Annam in the revolution, including the quixotic role of Emperor Bao Dai. The chapter concludes with a brief discussion of the Nationalist Chinese intervention under General Lu Han and the role of the Dong Minh Hoi (DMH).

BIRTH OF THE VIET MINH FRONT (MAY 1941)

With his return from Moscow in 1938 and visit to the Chinese communist wartime capital of Yan'an, Ho Chi Minh embedded himself with the CCP in Kunming and, in February 1939, also accepted an assignment at Henggang in Hunan Province involving the joint training of CCP and Nationalist Chinese troops. In September, he then moved between Guilin and Longzhou in Guangxi in a failed attempt to contact ICP members. During a visit to Chongqing, the now veteran revolutionary made contact with Zhou Enlai, then serving as CCP liaison chief in the Nationalist Chinese wartime capital. Importantly, he also made contact with ICP members in exile. In February 1940, he also visited Kunming as well as bases along the Yunnan railroad, returning to Kunming in late May 1940 and meeting up with such ICP veterans as Pham Van Dong and Vo Nguyen Giap prior to returning to Guilin (Duiker 2000, 236–38).

By this stage, Ho Chi Minh had obviously gained a global picture of the terrain and the competing nationalist parties, including the VNQDD, as well as the strength of the enemy. With great circumspection he had reintroduced himself back into the domestic ICP networks. In turn, the ICP leadership circle, including future Viet Minh military strategist Vo Nguyen Giap, had become increasing cognizant of the efficacy of Maoist-style guerrilla warfare. Learning of the June 1940 defeat of France and the advent of Vichy, important discussions were held in Guilin, Chongqing (with the CCP) and Kunming as to the selection of a base area and the timing of an uprising (Duiker 2000, 242–43). Undeniably, the voice of Ho Chi Minh was heeded in these discussions. As discussed below, the Vietnam border with southern Guangxi would prove to be better sited than southern Yunnan.

To comprehend the birth of the Viet Minh front in an obscure ethnic minority backwater of northeast Vietnam in May 1941, we require some knowledge of the complex ethnic demography of this zone. Almost from its inception, the Viet Minh recognized the strategic importance of the highlands to the success of the revolution. The future "Viet Bac" liberated zone, or the forested and mountainous northeastern provinces of Tonkin coming under the sway of the Viet Minh, was also known to the French as the Second Military Region, the site of past battles with highland-based rebels. The highland bases offered shelter to retreating lowland rebels and ready access to the Chinese border. But it was Cao Bang, contiguous with Guangxi and accessible to Yunnan, that first emerged as an ICP base.

Emergence of the Cao Bang Sanctuary

On February 8, 1941, following a thirty-year absence from his homeland, Ho Chi Minh (still going by a pseudonym and unknown to French intelligence) reentered Vietnam from Guangxi, settling in a grotto in the hamlet of Pac Bo (Ha Quang District, Cao Bang Province), just across the Chinese border (Vietnam 1979, 23–24) and today a national monument. As Brocheux (2007, 69) observes, then as now, Pac Bo was an ethnic Nung hamlet some thirty kilometers from Cao Bang and close to the Chinese border. Across the border in China, just prior to his personally moving return to Vietnam, Ho Chi Minh and his group had settled into two Zhuang-Nung villages whose population had supported the Chinese communists since the 1920s. Remote from the lowlands and shielded by rugged terrain, Cao Bang was also devoid of natural resources and supplies of food except that cultivated locally or foraged from the forest. It also shared propinquity with an equally remote part of Guangxi in China. In other words, it fitted the geography of a borderland guerrilla rear base.

With the Nung closely related to the Tay (Tho) and both groups closely related to the Zhuang minority of southwestern China, Tay and Nung speak the same language and share cultural practices, and both groups cultivate irrigated upland rice (Hoang Nam 2008, 9). Together, the Tay and the Nung were then the largest ethnic groups in the Viet Bac, albeit with extensive cultural and historical ties with the lowland-dwelling Kinh (M. Elliott 1974, 4). As revealed in table 7.1, the percentage of Tho (Tay) in the so-named Viet Bac or First and Second Military Regions far eclipsed those of other ethnic groups. Only Mon Cai revealed a significant percentage of "others." Kinh

Table 7.1. Ethnic Minorities of the Viet Bac Region, 1938–39

Locality	*Total Population*	*Tho (Tay) or Nung*	*Other*
First Military Region			
Mon Cai	88,500	62,500	26,000
Lang Son	151,200	144,200	7,000
Second Military Region			
Cao Bang	173,500	163,500	10,000
Bac Can	54,300	51,700	2,600
Total	467,500	421,900	45,600

Source: MAE AOI 68, "Note sur les Minorités Ethniques," Conférence de Dalat, May 9, 1946.

were undoubtedly few on the ground in these mountain provinces during this period.

Between May 10 and May 19, 1941, at the Pac Bo-Cao Bang location, in his capacity as Comintern representative, Ho Chi Minh hosted a congress of the eighth plenum of the ICP to approve the formation of a new united front to resist both the French and Japanese. Among those attending were the "veteran" ex-ICP cadres Hoang Van Thu, Phung Chi Kien, Truong Chinh, Pham Van Dong, and Hoang Van Hoang (Vietnam 1979, 27). Launched on May 19, 1941, under the golden-starred red flag, this new front was named the Viet Nam Doc Lap Dong Minh Hoi, also known as the Viet Minh or the Independence League.

Notionally embracing a number of smaller nationalist parties, it was clear that the dominant strand was controlled by ex-ICP cadre, with Truong Chinh, future DRV ideologue appointed secretary general, and other senior positions occupied by former ICP members. Importantly, however, Marxist rhetoric stressing the struggle against feudalism was toned down to emphasize patriotic slogans revolving around "national liberation" or "national salvation" fronts (*Pentagon Papers* 1971, book 1, part 1.B, B-22–23, 1971).

Prior to his absence in China, as discussed below, Ho Chi Minh spent about one year in the Cao Bang sanctuary, including a spell from April 1942 in a new base in Lan Son, a village in the same province but farther from the Chinese border. By 1943, three of the nine districts of Cao Bang province were entirely under communist control. As Brocheux (2007, 75) comments, such activities indicate that the Viet Minh base area, now dubbed the Viet Bac, was expanding.

Vo Nguyen Giap would also step to the fore following the decision made at the Pac Bo conference to link up a corridor between the Cao Bang and Bac Son-Vo Nhai bases. Notably, Giap was deputed to accomplish his work, albeit in the face of French forces who also went on the offensive. With Ho Chi Minh out of the scene, Chu Van Tan's forces began filtering back in late 1942–early 1943. At the Lung Hoang conference in January 1943, Chu Van Tan, Vo Nguyen Giap, and Pham Van Dong again came together to strategize on opening the Co Bang-Bac Son-Vo Nhai corridor (Elliott 1974, 20).

According to an official source, on February 28, 1943, an expanded central committee was convened in the hamlet of Vong La in Phuc Yen Province to define a new strategy (even though the ICP standing committee was still based in Hanoi). The conference decided to broaden the national united front against the "Japanese and French fascists," to set up an Anti-Japanese Democratic Front, to enter into alliance with Gaullists in certain circumstances, and to win over anti-Japanese Chinese (Vietnam 1979, 44–45).

The linkup with the two provinces was achieved only in March 1945 when units of Giap's forces and those of Chu Van Tan met at Cho Chu in Thai

Nguyen (Elliott 1974, 22–24), an event leading to the formation of the Vietnam Liberation Army. As the official history records, the juncture of the two forces entailed a southern march and a northern march. In August 1943, Giap worked south from Cao Bang to Thai Nguyen. On his part, minority General Chu Van Tan moved north from Bac Son to Cao Bang, creating a corridor through the province and linking up with the China border. By late 1943, French forces were active in confronting rebel actions in this sector, effectively igniting the guerrilla war (Vietnam 1979, 56–57).

Ho Chi Minh in China (1942–44)

The years 1942–43 were obviously a period of great flux for the Viet Minh, especially given their geographic fragmentation, poor communications, and the incarceration of their leading light. Entering Guangxi on August 13, 1942, Ho Chi Minh was arrested in a border town by local Nationalist Chinese authorities and, on August 29, dispatched to Guilin via Tsing Si, arriving in mid-October. In rather heroic but somewhat obscure circumstances, he survived confinement in thirty successive prisons for a period of fourteen months. It was in these circumstances that he composed his prison diary, romantic prose-poem works in classical characters (Vietnam 1979, 57). Following numerous interventions by Vietnamese nationalists to the Chinese authorities, as well as by the ICP to the Soviet Union, Ho was transferred to Liuchow in Guangxi in May 1943. Although released from prison nine months later by the Chinese warlord General Zhang Fakui, he was ambiguously installed as leader of the KMT-controlled DMH. No longer incarcerated, he was still under the surveillance and political guidance of General Zhang, who had taken into hand a mission to see through Vietnamese independence under Nationalist Chinese auspices. There were then six hundred Vietnamese in Liuchow along with some twenty Vietnamese leaders of parties and groups. On August 10, certain of these leaders formed the DMH. Having excluded ICP and Viet Minh members (active inside Vietnam as well as in Guangxi and Yunnan), leaders of the new party included some members of the Liberation League, the Japanese-sponsored Phuoc Quoc, the VNQDD, and some Chinese nationalists. Meanwhile, Ho was allowed to join the DMH. By March 1944, however, the DMH elected membership revealed a slight VNQDD prominence over Phuoc Quoc with two ICP members included (Chen 1969, 55–83).

As a French intelligence report confirms, General Zhang also offered hospitality to the Indochina communists at training camps in Guangxi and Liuchow, alongside members of the Phuoc Quoc. Though their goals may have been different, the report contended, this cohabitation offered enormous advantages to the Viet Minh. Notably, armed and provided with funds by the Chinese, they were able to mount cross-border attacks, especially as Chinese territory offered perfect sanctuary for these raiders. From the outset of its creation, the Viet Minh successively launched propaganda in the mountainous northeastern zone of Tonkin, such as the distribution of tracts, acts of terrorism, assassinations of indigenous notables, and attacks on French police and military posts. By working among the ethnic minorities of this region they sought to create a favorable climate for recruitment of new members and to create a territorial base inside Indochina (MAE AOI 162 "Biographie d'Ho Chi Minh" établi par F.O.M. ca. 1/9/49).

As French intelligence summarized, not only had the Chinese Nationalists given exile to Vietnamese agitators fleeing Indochina but, since the Japanese coup of March 9, 1945, sought to use these agitators to advance their own goals in Indochina. As far as the French side was concerned, Chinese Nationalist government collusion with the VNQDD and the DMH was proven. This was demonstrated by the presence of the headquarters of the two anti-French parties in southern China. Vietnamese living in north China were also supported and funded by the KMT, just as the leading lights of this party frequently attended reunions of the former (AOM Indo NF 134/1217 "Agissements Chinois . . . en Indochine"). Yet French intelligence still failed to track Ho Chi Minh's presence in China, much less pin down his new role alongside his captors.

Ho Chi Minh's Return from China

Arriving back in Vietnam in October 1944, following his two years' absence in China (explained away as "seeking foreign assistance"), Ho Chi Minh intervened in a party decision to stage a rebellion in the Cao Bang base. According to an official history, he argued that the time for a national uprising was not ripe, thus saving Cao Bang from certain destruction. Looking ahead to military solutions, he gave instructions to set up an armed force. Headed by Vo Nguyen Giap and coming into being in Nguyen Binh district in Cao Bang on December 22, 1944, the brigade-level force was soon tested in battle, notwithstanding its ostensible political orientation (Vietnam 1979, 63–64).

Not without insight, as Chen (1975, 34) observes, and impressed by what he saw in Yan'an on his way back home from Moscow via Xian in 1938, Ho Chi Minh began to lead his revolution in Pac Bo in 1941 along Maoist lines (See Duiker 2000, 230–31). Understanding the parallels in the rural-regional situation between China and Vietnam, Ho Chi Minh sought to make systematic use of this advantageous situation. But while the Viet Minh embraced the Chinese revolutionary formula comprising a party, an army, and a united front, there were many home-grown features in the Vietnamese generation of people's war, especially the high reliance on the ethnic minorities, not only in hosting a rear base but also in carrying the guns.

REBELLION IN THAI NGUYEN (NOVEMBER 1944–FEBRUARY 1945)

One of the most significant though understudied preludes to the Viet Minh insurgency, as mentioned, was the rebellion of November 1944 breaking out in Thai Nguyen and Tuyen Quang, two mountainous provinces, respectively, north and northwest of Hanoi, and later extending to Cao Bang, or what the French called the Second Military Region, as mentioned, a vast mountainous zone contiguous with the border of Guangxi. According to Hanyok (1996, 104), drawing on US Navy communication intelligence (COMINT) intercepts of Japanese high-frequency radio reports sent from Hanoi to Tokyo, the rebellions could be directly linked with French policies that aggravated famine. French agents were purportedly gouging the peasantry with unfavorable rates of exchange, and much of the rice crop was being expropriated by the Japanese. The famine-like conditions that had persisted for over a year were further aggravated by a drier-than-usual rainy season followed by a colder-than-average winter which had seriously reduced the rice crop in Tonkin.

To recapitulate, Japanese agricultural policy in Tonkin had been to supplant rice crop agriculture for industrial crops such as flax, jute, and castor beans. Through their actions, the Allied air campaign had cut off north-south heavy transport, thus isolating Tonkin from the rice basket of southern Indochina. By Tet 1945, as described in chapter 8, famine would be taking its devastating toll on Vietnamese in the geographically most vulnerable parts of Tonkin and northern Annam, with at least one thousand a day dying at that juncture. Also, as Hanyok (1996) argues, the Viet Minh continued to exploit the famine, "the engine of their popularity among the Tonkin peasants." Rice had risen in price 1,000 percent over March, out of reach for the majority. The Viet Minh then commenced to seize Japanese-controlled warehouses to distribute rice to the starving peasants. Taking advantage of the situation, the Viet Minh set up local people's committees backed by locally raised peasant units.

All together in this affair, around six thousand to seven thousand peasants armed with crude weapons launched into rebellion in Thai Nguyen, possibly under Viet Minh instigation. The French responded by dispatching a battalion of legionnaires, subsequently reinforced by a further two battalions along with artillery and tanks. Neither side seems to have prevailed, with the French suffering desertions (of Vietnamese rifle companies) owing to Viet Minh propaganda and the rebels dispersing into the forest zone. As recorded by the Japanese, the rebellion made a big impression on the nationalists. Apparently, Decoux himself coordinated military actions (Hanyok 1996).

Drawing on scattered French military intelligence records on the rebellion in Thai Nguyen and Cao Bang between November 1944 and March 1945, a picture of determined and desperate struggle of a marginalized and miserable group emerges. According to a DGER source, the leader of the Thai Nguyen rebellion, a certain Nong Van Cuu (Gung) (until his surrender on December 8), headed a band of thirty-one rebels, with a former *ly truong* or mid-level administrator heading a band of seventeen, not all of them armed. French operations mounted against the rebel base camp in the Hang Co caves on November 26 netted "various communist documents" along with a five-tonne stock of paddy. At that point, thirty-three individuals were arrested. A subsequent operation recovered a stock of fifteen tonnes of paddy along with more documents. By December 15, sixty-eight rebels had been arrested, seven were killed "in operations," and two surrendered. Through December, these bands launched attacks on villages, leaving a trail of deaths and decapitations. By the end of the month, following French repressions, two bands remained; one comprised twenty persons armed with spears along with one hundred women and children camp followers, while another band of one hundred was seen as losing all momentum or moving in the direction of China (MAE AOI 261, BR No. 943/EO, DGER, Jan. 29, 1945). It is hard to conceive this rebellion as having any communist connection aside from the incriminating documents, yet neither could the French prevail in their military efforts.

Operating out of a cave headquarters in the Hoa An region through late November–December 1944, the Cao Bang rebels were also on the offensive, attacking villages and French military posts, as with the attack on Phai Khat military post in Nguyen Binh on December 25 by eighty well-armed rebels wearing fake military uniforms. The following day, in an attack on a *garde indigène* post (Nga Nhan), they made off with forty rifles along with ammunition. On November 27, 1944, the French took the initiative, arresting a rebel ex-*tirailleur*. In an early December firefight at Hoa An, including use of hand grenades on the part of the rebels, paddy and weapons were seized. Toward the end of December, a French patrol came under automatic weapon fire and grenade attack near the Chinese border. At this point, it appears, the Japanese took an interest in the rebellion, dispatching one Lieutenant Abe of the Hanoi *gendarmerie* to Thai Nguyen to gather intelligence in the Dinh Ca region. Meantime, the Japanese intelligence command in Haiphong sent one of its informers into the "troubled region" to gather information on the "communist uprising" (MAE AOI 261, BR No. 943/EO, DGER, Jan. 29, 1945).

From this description, it is hard to believe that this ragtag army was the nucleus of the future Vietnamese People's Army. Yet the attack on the Phai Khat post on December 25, 1944, by a rebel group disguised as colonial police is actually memorialized in an official Vietnamese memoir. Drawn from an oral account, it relates how the captured weapons from this victory were sufficient to equip half a platoon. The ruse of disguise was replayed successfully on December 26 in the attack on the Nga Nhan post, twenty-five kilometers from Phai Khat. As described in reverent tones, these were the actions of the first platoon of the Vietnam People's Army, numbering just thirty-four members. Including Tay, Nung, Dao, and other minority peoples alongside Kinh, the platoon was officially formed at a ceremony held under the red and gold-star flag on December 22, 1944, in Sam Cao forest, Nguyen Binh District, Cao Bang Province and was witnessed by members of the Cao Bang–Bac Can–Lan Son committee. Armed with primitive weapons, the platoon also handily wielded a US submachine gun obtained from Kunming (Vietnam 2009b, 4–9). Still, it is seductive to believe that this early wave of rebels in Thai Nguyen were driven by hunger and oppression rather than guided by incomprehensible ideology, though it is also easy to see how their grievances were manipulated.

Within six months (early June 1945), the embryonic Viet Minh formation (so described by French intelligence) had morphed into an armed force of five thousand rifles holding out in the Cao Bang, Bac Kan, and That Khe area in Lang Son Province. Viewed as avoiding full-on conflict with the Japanese, the Viet Minh forces, in fact the putative Vietnamese People's Army, worked to swell their ranks by encouraging desertions from the *tirailleurs*, actually in competition with their rivals, the DMH. According to the French report, "They avoid all actions against the Japanese but form a wall which virtually prevents the collection of information" (MAE AOI 161, BR, No.219 MO/R "Activité du Viet Minh dans le 2ième Territoire Militaire (Cao Bang)," June 4, 1945). As explained below, the armed capacity of the Viet Minh was also considerably boosted by assistance and training provided by the American OSS.

French Rationalizations of the Rebellion

According to General Sabattier writing from Chongqing in May 1945, the French had erred since 1940 by failing to pay attention to rising "troubles and agitation" in Tonkin, tending to view them as a *mal endemique* (endemic evil) worthy only of surveillance and not remedy. It would appear that the French first deployed ethnic Rhade rifle companies in the zone northeast of Nan Cham on the frontier with Guangxi. However, in November 1944, a European battalion was also dispatched to Thai Nguyen, where the revolutionaries had assassinated guards and villagers. As French intelligence recorded, for a period of three months following on from the Japanese *coup de force*, the rebels had extended their activities to the west and southwest of Cao Bang. The situation then became so serious that it necessitated the deployment of numerous Garde units along with two battalions. At the time of the Japanese coup, a second battalion was then en route from Lang Son to Cao Bang (AOM Indo NF/134/1167–68 "Note pour le Gouvernment," Sabattier, Chungking, May 28, 1945).

Relating the events and military responses from September 1944 effected in the Second Military Region also encompassing Cao Bang, Sabattier confirmed the political as opposed to purely military character of these incidents. He then sought to exploit the prospect of an impending Japanese defeat. In other words, the French now sought to win Viet Minh cooperation in order to jointly resist the Japanese and to persuade the Viet Minh to drop their policy of opposition to the French to be rid of the Japanese. Certain second-echelon communist leaders had been approached, but they also proved capable of soon breaking their promises. Drawing in all these sources of information and contacts, the French military command concluded that "the interests in this game were multiple," especially as "the strings were pulled by numerous irresponsible individuals and organizations, under diverse influences, of which the Japanese were not stranger." To complicate matters, the rebel groups in the countryside included not only dedicated communists and nationalists but also adventurers and those fleeing from justice. In a word, Sabattier summarized, the single common theme among these individuals was "discontent" (AOM Indo NF/134/1167–68 "Note pour le Gouvernment," Sabattier, Chungking, May 28, 1945).

As Sabattier continued, in an atmosphere where French sovereignty was subject to ridicule on the part of the rebels, the small indigenous officials, otherwise pro-French, were assassinated along with their families. On the other hand, subject to terror and suffering at the hands of the rebels, the peasantry was likewise reticent to supply information and even displayed hostility. Adding to the complexity of the situation was clan and ethnic rivalry, arms, and opium trafficking, occurring with an atmosphere of "denunciations and terror." As Sabattier lamented, "We could have taken stronger military action and we also considered political means, but in dealing with these so-called chiefs we faced deception after deception. Every time we are in contact with a chief, he becomes like a silhouette and disappears like a phantom into the fog until disappearing completely. Happy for those who could prevail over the revolutionary propagandists of the Second Military Region" (AOM Indo NF/134/1167–68 "Note pour le Gouvernment," Sabattier, Chungking, May 28, 1945).

Since the March 9 event, Sabattier continued, an alternation had been characteristic in the relations between French troops and the revolutionaries of the Cao Bang region. "Certain of these revolutionaries have assisted us, and certain have attacked us with full force. It seems that, after we are assisted, then we are attacked. But, in point of fact, it should be recognized that Japanese intrigues have fully developed; they are like an arrow directed against us."

Sabattier also predicted that Japan would seek to raise an Indochinese army, although he understood that recruitment would be fraught with difficulties (AOM Indo NF/134/1167–68 "Note pour le Gouvernment," Sabattier, Chungking, May 28, 1945).

By February 1945, with the onset of winter, the rebels began to leave the forest zone owing to lack of food and cold weather. According to Hanyok (1996, 105), this rebellion neither figures in French or Viet Minh histories, with the Viet Minh tracing its armed rebellion back to actions against two French posts in December 1944. As surmised, the rebellion could have occurred spontaneously and outside of Viet Minh auspices, or it was disavowed by the Viet Minh owing to its failure.

Yet another French intelligence source is more affirmative in the way of directly connecting the embryonic Viet Minh and the Thai Nguyen rebellion, especially after Ho Chi Minh's release from prison in Guilin (in August 1944). As stated, Ho Chi Minh did not work for twenty years as a revolutionary only to see the Chinese replace the French as colonial overlords but, immediately on breaking with the DMH, crossed the China-Tonkin frontier with a group of 760 partisans, "where he sought to capitalize upon the Thai Nguyen insurrection (November 11, 1944 and onward) . . . of which causes are obscure and which would hinder him in extending his influence throughout this region." As stated in chapter 6, during this period, Ho Chi Minh made several journeys to China (Yunnan and Guangxi), including a stay of six months in Kunming meeting up with his "revolutionary school" comrades (or ex-ICP veterans) (MAE AOI 162 "Biographie d'Ho Chi Minh" établi par F.O.M. ca. 1/9/49).

According to Sabattier, these were truly little-known events at the time outside of official circles, especially as Decoux was not in communication with the provisional French government. While Sabattier confirms the role of communist organizations in these rebellions, he also highlights a long tradition of instability in this region. While both Sabattier and such modern interpreters as Hanyok acknowledge Japanese manipulation of the rebellions, Sabattier is silent on the underlying causes that plausibly linked the unrest to socioeconomic discontent stemming from food shortages and the looming famine.

THE VIET MINH RISE TO POWER

As an underground organization during the Japanese occupation, it remains to explain how the Viet Minh emerged as an entirely coherent armed organization at the point of the Japanese surrender, even if it did not have a monopoly on the anticolonial nationalist movement, widely contested by many factions, parties, and individuals. While the southern-based Viet Minh had to face up to a variety of religious sects, nationalists, and Trotskyists, the shadow imposed over the Viet Minh in the north was China and the interest of the Nationalist Chinese. Ho Chi Minh himself was trapped in this contradiction, especially during his period of captivity. Yet as viewed through the eyes of American intelligence, even though Ho Chi Minh had been installed as leader of a rival organization, the KMT-controlled DMH, he still retained his Viet Minh leadership in this dual arrangement. As explained below, the DMH acquired modest political significance in Vietnam only after Chinese Nationalist forces occupied Tonkin in late 1945, leaving the Viet Minh as "the only effective and extensive resistance movement" on the inside (Pentagon Papers 1971, Book 1, Part 1.B, B-22–23).

Using declassified Magic documents (see US Government 1978), Hanyok (1996, 103) has offered a checkered picture of the Viet Minh in the twelve-month period prior to its meteoric rise to power in Hanoi. In April 1944, Japanese sources revealed the existence of a communist group with an office on Tienstin Road in Hanoi, possibly an ICP branch, which issued a regular periodical, *Viet Lap* (Independent Vietnam). Some instances were recorded of communist propaganda work of both an anti-Japanese and anti-French cast. Japanese sources also revealed that the communists of Thai Binh region had recovered from earlier suppression. Notably, as mentioned, in the spring of 1944, Ho Chi Minh staged his return from Jingxi County, across the border in Guangxi, along with Vo Nguyen Giap. Whether or not they managed to keep a lid on rebellions deemed premature is unclear, however.

Meanwhile, from late November 1944 to early January 1945, the French also mounted a major campaign to eradicate the Viet Minh threat by mounting a wave of arrests in such diverse locations as Cao Bang, Bac Giang, Bac Ninh, and Nghe An. In Thanh Hoa Province eight Viet Minh militants were arrested, including a key leader wanted since 1941 (MAE AOI 49, BR, Activité des groupements Indochinoise anti-française depuis la fin Nov. 1944).

But the Japanese military takeover of March 1945 and the internment of the French garrisons, with the exception of the flight to Yunnan of French forces under General Alessandri, left the field open to the Viet Minh in the northern highlands. Accordingly, the Viet Minh moved rapidly to seize power in the Viet Bac (Cao Bang, Bac Can, Lang Son, Ha Giang, Tuyen Quang, and Thai Nguyen Provinces). By June 4, 1945, a liberated zone had been set up by Ho Chi Minh covering the six provinces plus adjacent areas in Bac Giang, Phu Thu, Yen Bai, and Vinh Yen. The Army of National Salvation and the Vietnamese Propaganda and Liberation Army were merged, becoming the Liberation Army (Elliott 1974, 25).

According to American intercepts of Japanese radio transmissions, the Viet Minh carrying out acts of "terrorism" in Hanoi and in the countryside mounted an active campaign to interrupt Japanese rice requisitions and to thwart the collection of farm taxes. Large-scale Japanese operations against the Viet Minh got under way on June 20, 1945, in the attempt to subjugate the Thai Nguyen and Bac Kan areas. Meanwhile, the Japanese began to arrest Viet Minh and nationalist suspects. While some hundreds of people in Hanoi, Haiphong, and the Nan Dinh regions were swept up in these arrests, the greater part of the communist leadership escaped the dragnet. Among those arrested were members of Bao Dai's government, including cabinet members, some of whom were seen as having connections with the Viet Minh (Magic 1207, July 15, 1945). American intercepts also reveal that in June 1945, the Japanese Twenty-First Division launched attacks against Viet Minh positions in Thai Nguyen and Bac Kan, just as the Viet Minh tied down Japanese military units on the border regions. According to Hanyok (1996, 107), these were more than small-scale skirmishes. As evidence, he offers the case of the July 19 Viet Minh attack on Tan Trao, a small valley lying between mountains and jungles in Son Duong District, forty kilometers from Tuyen Quang town and two hundred kilometers from Hanoi, involving a force of five hundred and leaving fifty Japanese dead. Nevertheless, the Viet Minh also liberated a number of interned French civilians and escorted some of them to China and safety.

Nevertheless, French sources are not so sanguine as to Viet Minh combativeness against the Japanese enemy. In fact, they are dismissive. In this view, following the Japanese takeover, Ho Chi Minh never measured up directly against the Japanese except rhetorically. Moreover, to take power, he avoided all acts of hostility toward Japan, just as the Viet Minh and Japanese were in conversations up until the day of their capitulation. Notably, in early January 1945, a "neutrality agreement" had been undertaken to help secure the Viet Minh "liberated zone" in Thai Nguyen. French sources claim that such opportunism redounded on French efforts. "With the exception of agent Bernier, all other French agents in situ or arriving by parachute were blocked by the Viet Minh from entering into actions against the Japanese." According to the French report, not only had the Viet Minh greatly benefited from American OSS assistance in the form of weapons and matériel, such as discussed below, the equipment was mostly used against the French (MAE AOI 162 "Biographie d'Ho Chi Minh" établi par F.O.M. ca. 1/9/49). The only exceptions to Viet Minh reticence to confront the Japanese were the attack on Tan Trao/Tam-Dac on July 16 (19), 1945, the assassination of a Japanese officer at Phu Tho; and the so-called Cho Chu affair of August 1945, an attack on the Japanese fort in Thai Nguyen (Bartholomew-Feis 2006, 206).

There is no question as well that the Viet Minh leadership were carefully monitoring broader political events surrounding the war, namely the German Instrument of Surrender of May 7, 1945, the role and international status of the Soviet Union, the progress of the Allies in the Pacific War, and, crucially for the future of postsurrender Indochina, the Potsdam Declaration of July 26, 1945, where it was decided to temporarily partition Indochina at the sixteenth parallel. No less important, the Viet Minh also anticipated the imminent defeat of Japan, although the actual event and its timing obviously took them by surprise. But they were prepared. As mentioned, Ho Chi Minh himself undoubtedly learned of such epic developments as the dropping of the atomic bombs over Hiroshima (August 6, Tokyo time) by word of mouth from the OSS or over OSS-supplied radio. In any case, the news galvanized the Viet Minh under Ho Chi Minh to convene on August 13 at the then densely forested Tan Trao base (ahead of the Imperial Rescript of Surrender of August 15) to draw up a National Insurrection Committee along with an immediate call to arms (Patti 1980, 134).

The Viet Minh and the Great Famine

As the Vichy administration well knew during its dying days in Hanoi, not only did the shadow of a Japanese takeover darken the skies, but the Viet Minh and its propagandists were already sapping away at French prestige and even challenging French authority in the mountainous north. For example, at the height of the famine, and to the great alarm of the authorities, on February 9, 1945, *quoc ngu* posters were discovered in the reading room of the Bibliothèque Pierre Pasquier in Hanoi, calling on the student population to rise up. Signed off by one Duong Duc Nien, a doctoral student who had fled to the mountains, the posters also bore the imprimatur of the Viet Nam Dan Chu Dang (Democratic Party of Vietnam), a Viet Minh affiliate. As the French police observed, this was the first recorded example of Viet Minh print propaganda discovered in Hanoi (AOM RS Tonkin *IB 424–25, Services de Police, Hanoi, Feb. 16, 1945).

Viet Minh Exploitation of the Famine

In January–February 1945, the French establishment in Hanoi became increasingly anxious as to the potential of the Viet Minh to exploit the food-famine crisis. As the key individual commanding information collected from provincial officials, Resident Superior Chauvet of Tonkin was expressly requested by General Mordant to offer his opinions. Mordant, in turn, represented the Conseil de l'Indochine (Indochina Council), the highest-level official French policy-making body in Indochina. Without mincing words, as Chauvet warned, a "very violent discontent" had already emerged in Tonkin, particularly in the provinces where the harvest was poorest. This discontent was being exploited by agitators, whether communists, xenophobes, or nationalists, "and we can expect bloody incidents in the weeks to come." The communists, he asserted, were on the point of preparing an uprising. Having been "tracked without mercy" for the preceding four years, they were not going to capitulate anytime soon, he advised, unless measures of clemency could be brought into play (which he favored). Otherwise, they could not ignore the contradiction or negative comparison between the French Indochina regime and the metropolitan provisional French government (which included members of the Communist Party) (AOM RST *IB 424–35, Hanoi, Jan.–Feb. 1945).

Elaborating, Chauvet revealed that all his residents had reported "an undeniable dissidence in Tonkin." Possibly running against the official consensus, he argued that the causes of the discontent were not necessarily of a political nature but, rather, stemmed from economic causes. Accordingly, he advised, the administration should make distinctions between those suffering from the crisis and those better off. Notably, agricultural producers did not take kindly to the multiple administrative obligations imposed on them in the course of their daily life, as with paddy procurements, prioritized cultivations, and so on. More generally, for the peasant cultivators of Tonkin living from the soil, scarcity and famine were not novel. But in the provinces of Nam Dinh and Thai Ninh, such discontent was real. At the same time, all those individuals on fixed salaries, such as workers and coolies, also suffered from the growing food crisis owing to the rising cost of living. In both cases, discontent was not new, but it was aggravated by the abnormal economic situation in Tonkin (AOM RST *IB 424–25, Hanoi, Jan.–Feb. 1945).

As Chauvet continued, from the time of his taking up office (ca. mid-1944), he had sought to dissipate discontent by all means possible. Although the peasant cultivators may have disagreed, he claimed to have worked to make their burden lighter. For instance, he sought to diminish the area given over to prioritized cultivation such as with castor, peanuts, and Japanese jute to augment the price paid to the producers and to diminish the *écart* (gap) between the latter and the free-market price. Moreover, he had lightened the paddy levies by thirty-one thousand tonnes in Nam Dinh and Thai Binh or the zones devastated by the October 1944 typhoons. He also claimed to have regularized peasant obligations and burdens by driving out the multiple abuses and embezzlement of all kinds as well as reducing the margins collected by the intermediaries. Meanwhile, he had strengthened all economic services in the protectorate with a view to focusing on economic issues. To this end, he had created a special agricultural inspectorate. With respect to the salariat, he had increased their rations, including those of families evacuated to the countryside. Added to that, he had taken all measures possible to prevent the price of rice rising further (reaching 280–300 piasters a quintal in Hanoi). Reverting to Malthusian language, he restated the problem as one of food needs of a rising population in Tonkin outstripping production, aggravated by the isolation of the country and the lack of financial means on the part of the population. Finally, he explained his efforts at procuring rice from outside, including China (AOM RST *IB 424–35, Hanoi, Jan.–Feb. 1945).

It would seem that, humanitarian relief aside, Chauvet and the administration were also concerned to maintain public order at any cost. As Chauvet declaimed, "There is no doubt that the current discontent is exploited by agents of disorder." It would be astonishing if they (the communists) were not behind it. Such exploitation could lead to serious popular movements among the disaster-stricken and miserable population in Tonkin. In other words, they could become "political subjects." "As the man in the street in Hanoi well knows, he is malnourished and poorly clothed and submits to his condition like millions of humans in the world—as a direct or indirect consequence of the turmoil which shakes the entire world." But still wedded to the notion of a passive, conservative peasantry, Chauvet continued, "He is skeptical at any amelioration that might occur in the event of trouble or a change of authority." "Naturally timorous, much suffering would have to take place for him to throw off his reserve." "I confirm that the work of agitators especially in the high and middle regions of Tonkin, an area where absolutely no susceptible economic reason exists to invoke anti-French propaganda, could very well facilitate secret activities, given the isolation of this region and the character of its population" (AOM RST *IB 424–35, Hanoi, Jan.–Feb. 1945).

Needless to say, Vietnamese historians have labored to fill in several gaps in the history of the period between the onset of the famine and the August Revolution, especially in the way of inserting a role by the communist underground. For instance, according to an official source, on March 10, 1945, the Nguyen Hue Party Committee directed the Third Salvation Army and local self-defense fighters in an uprising in Tuyen Quang Province. The following day, the "Ba To" uprising took place in Quang Ngai. And, in the face of the famine, the central standing committee issued the instruction "to destroy paddy stores to cope with starvation." Also, as mentioned, on May 15, 1945, a ceremony was held in Dien Bien Thuong, Cho Chu, in Thai Nguyen Province, to unify the Vietnam Salvation Army and the Vietnam Propaganda and Liberation Army into the Vietnam Liberation Army under the command of Vo Nguyen Giap, Tran Dang Ding, and Chu Van Tan (Vietnam 2009b: 12–13). Still, much remains obscure in this highly schematic official account.

Japanese–Viet Minh Cooperation

According to French sources, even prior to the arrival of Chinese troops and even during their tenure, the Japanese had supplied weapons to the Viet Minh. French intelligence believed it was possible that extremely large quantities of arms were transferred, including stocks of French weapons seized after the Japanese military coup. In any case, groups of well-armed Japanese continued to struggle either alongside the Viet Minh or semiautonomously. More generally, Japanese officers, junior officers, and rank and file took their place in Viet Minh military schools serving as instructors and even dressing in Viet Minh military uniforms. Others were embedded within units and, in one case, even headed a Viet Minh unit. Certain military insignia worn by the Viet Minh were actually Japanese, just as the utilization of arms was of Japanese inspiration. Certain Japanese sought to camouflage their presence by masquerading as "new Vietnamese," such as by wearing local dress and cohabiting with Viet Minh. While some had fled Vietnam, still others had local wives and even children and fully intended to stay on. Among them were many "Formosans" even further assimilated among the indigenous people and without slacking off in their propaganda output in favor of the Viet Minh. Japanese advisers also assisted in the preparation of anti-French press and radio propaganda. As identified, the head of propaganda in Hanoi within a dedicated Japanese support section was Komatsu Kiyoshi, a French-speaking literati boasting a prewar acquaintance with André Gide, future French Prime Minister Georges Bidault, and André Malraux. Reportedly he was also in communication with the Americans, Major Archimedes Patti included (AOM NF 138–39/1258; Goscha 2002). Basically this was correct. Back in Japan, Komatsu published widely on his Parisian literary connections and political activities in support of North Vietnam (Vinh Sinh 2002). It is a fact that in both northern and southern Vietnam, large numbers of Japanese deserters, especially from among the *kempeitai*, would also throw their support to the anti-French Viet Minh cause at the moment of the Japanese surrender.

The OSS and the Viet Minh Dalliance

Evidence of active OSS complicity with the Viet Minh prior to the Japanese surrender is offered by the case of agent Laurence Gordon, the Anglo-Canadian former director of Caltex in Indochina, who, from his base in Kunming, had made transfers of a million Chinese dollars (three hundred thousand piasters) a month to the Viet Minh through 1944. He also supplied radio equipment along with an American operator in Pac Do, a region off-limits except for the Americans, as well as several hundred weapons, including submachine guns. French intelligence also believed that the Americans had made a deal with the Viet Minh regarding future economic advantage (AOM Indo NF/134/1217 Agissements Americains contre le rétablissement de la gouvernment Français en Indochine). Such communication was also known as the GBT network, after the initials of the key three members. G stood for Gordon, B stood for Harry V. Bernard, another staff member of Caltex, and T stood for Frankie Tan, a Chinese American (see Bartholomew-Feis

2006, chap.4). According to Thomas (2000, 951), Gordon had been recruited and trained by British SIS (Secret Intelligence Service) staff in New Delhi. Locally, the GBT group fell under the coordination of Chiang Kai-shek's operational director, Admiral Yang Hsuan Chen, though the British had also encouraged OSS chief Donovan to liaise with Gordon.

In the spring and summer of 1945, following the Japanese coup, both the OSS and the Anglo-American GBT group started to give serious consideration to entering into intelligence-sharing cooperation with the Viet Minh. Initial support for this venture came from two members of the GBT group, namely Frankie Tan and the Hong Kong–born Mac C. Shin, who had fled the Japanese occupation of the British colony. In April 1945, Tan and Shin flew from Kunming to a point north of Cao Bang. With a Viet Minh escort, they crossed the border, meeting up with Ho Chi Minh in the caves of Pac Bo, a Viet Minh base just inside Vietnam. Together with Ho Chi Minh they then trekked to the main Viet Minh guerrilla base in Tan Trao, a remote ethnic minority village some hundred kilometers north of Hanoi, arriving the following month (Bartholomew-Feis 2006, 158–68).

In turn, the Tan/Shin mission opened the way for the arrival of the larger—and better-known—OSS Deer Team. In June 1945 they were joined by the first OSS officer, Dan Phelan (as discussed below), but it wasn't until mid-July that the main OSS operation began. At that time, a group of OSS officers under Major Allison Thomas, code-named "Deer Team," parachuted into the Viet Minh base, part of the Air Ground Air Services (AGAS)/GBT–Viet Minh intelligence collaboration. Active through July–August, Deer Team supplied the Viet Minh with substantial amounts of modern military equipment and began training them in advanced combat tactics and weapons operations (Patti 1980, chap. 11; Bartholomew-Feis 2006, chap. 7).

Meeting Lieutenant Charles Fenn between March 17 and March 25, 1945, Ho Chi Minh accepted joint Viet Minh–OSS cooperation inside Vietnam. On May 9, 1945, writing from a base area, Ho Chi Minh sent a handwritten letter to Fenn thanking him for his support in training Viet Minh radio operators "in the common struggle against the Japs." Pointedly, he also added a salutation of respect for Chennault (See Duiker 2000, 330). On his part, Fenn also received an appreciative letter from Ho Chi Minh dated June 9, 1945, again praising the work of the two agents and requesting Fenn to pass on to him a package of Allied flags sent to a contact point in Kunming, namely the "Indochina cafe" (Fenn 2004, 198). In fact, it was Fenn, accompanied by future DRV Prime Minister Pham Van Dong, who had introduced Ho Chi Minh to Chennault (Patti 1980, 58, 545n). The admiration was mutual. With his eventual departure from the OSS, Fenn (1973), a future Ho Chi Minh biographer, was suspected by French intelligence of setting up in Hong Kong with the intention of launching a Viet Minh information bulletin.

At this point, OSS operative Archimedes Patti stepped into the picture. Making direct contact with Ho Chi Minh on April 27, 1945, at a remote village near Jingxi, Patti learned of the dire situation in northern Vietnam stemming from the famine and was offered documentary evidence by Ho in the form of photographs to prove it (Patti 1980, 83–85).[2] As historian Bartholomew-Feis (2006, 176) interprets, Patti's superiors urgently wanted hard intelligence and, for Patti, the Viet Minh networks appeared to fit the bill. In any case, at the time of this encounter, the Viet Minh and the AGAS-Fenn group were already working in close cooperation and already shared a presence in the Viet Bac. They were joined in mid-June by agent Dan Phelan, who arrived by parachute. On May 16, the youthful and headstrong Major Allison Thomas would be commissioned to head Deer Team. Although she finds it questionable in retrospect, Patti came around to the view that Viet Minh objectives of seeking American support in their endeavor to win an independent Vietnam did not conflict with American policy. Having surveyed the remnants of France's colonial army scattered over southern Yunnan, Patti did not look with confidence on French resources, quickly hitting a "sour note" with French intelligence chief Jean Sainteny.

On July 16, 1945, dramatically stepping up OSS–Viet Minh cooperation, an advance OSS Deer Team party under Major Thomas with the French-speaking Défourneaux as deputy, along with one French agent and two pro-French Vietnamese, parachuted into the Tonkin border region at Tan Trao (Kim Lung). There, they met up with the AGAS team and their Viet Minh associates, Vo Nguyen Giap and Ho Chi Minh included. With the unwanted French agent evicted by the Viet Minh, the Americans carried on weapons supply and training with their new allies. In a notable humanitarian action, OSS agent Paul Hoagland administered medicine to Ho Chi Minh, then undergoing a serious bout of malaria (Bartholomew-Feis 2006, 207–8).

With the war against Japan coming to an end, the Viet Minh–ICP staged a "strategy conference" held at the nearby village of Tan Trao August 13–15 (Bartholomew-Feis 2006, 213). The following day, the Viet Minh convened the so-called National People's Congress, also approving the yellow star on a red background for a flag, along with an anthem. Undoubtedly, at this juncture, Ho Chi Minh learned himself via US radio of the dropping of the atomic bombs on Hiroshima and Nagasaki and the crucial information as to the Japanese surrender. With the congress over, Deer Team, Vo Nguyen Giap, and the Viet Minh contingent departed in the direction of Thai Nguyen, the Défourneaux group taking a different route. Thomas, who had accompanied a Viet Minh group, joined in and, possibly contrary to orders and logic, helped to plan an attack on the Japanese position at Thai Nguyen (Cho Chu) seeking their surrender. Although something of a sideshow compared with events unfolding in Hanoi, the Thai Nguyen battle was symbolically important for the

Viet Minh and Giap, with Ho Chi Minh also making a brief visit to the liberated town (Bartholomew-Feis 2006, 222–24). Remaining until September 9, Deer Team with two hundred trained and well-armed guerrillas had advanced practically as far as Hanoi (Patti 1980, 197–98).

Meantime, in Chongqing, French diplomats and military personnel worked hard to gain American assistance to remove certain of their assets to Hanoi the moment Japan surrendered. In fact, at the San Francisco Conference (April 26–June 26) the US formally informed French Foreign Minister Georges Bidault that French sovereignty over Indochina would be acknowledged (see Dommen 2001, 96). Precisely, on August 11, Paris instructed its representatives in Chongqing to request General Wedemeyer (in writing) to supply an aircraft to be placed at the disposal of the French mission in Kunming. The French team was slated to arrive in Kunming on August 16. The French side understood that winning American support for this mission would not be easy. As acknowledged in Paris, Wedemeyer had already refused point blank to help move French troops to northern Indochina (AOM Indo NF 327/271 tél., Chungking, Aug. 11, 1945).

The Viet Minh Triumph (August–September 1945)

Famously, on September 2, 1945, in Hanoi's Ba Dinh Square, Ho Chi Minh proclaimed the independence of Vietnam before a crowd of five hundred thousand, uttering the words, "All men are created equal; they are endowed by their Creator with certain inalienable Rights; among these are Life, Liberty, and the pursuit of Happiness." Noting that this immortal statement was made in the Declaration of Independence of the United States of America and noting the Declaration of the French Revolution of 1791 on the Rights of Man and Citizen, Ho Chi Minh also pointed out that for the previous eighty years, the French colonial regime had abused the standard of "liberty, equality and fraternity," violated the Vietnamese fatherland, and oppressed Vietnamese citizens. He also blamed France for delivering over the country to the Japanese "fascists" with the result that from the end of 1944, under the double yoke of France and Japan, "from Quang Tri province to the North of Viet Nam more than two million of our fellow citizens died from starvation" (Fall 1967b, 141–42). As Bartholomew-Feis (2006, 242–43) conjectures, having sounded out a "sheepish" Patti as to the text of the declaration, Ho "the master manipulator" was thus able to inveigle the American into endorsement of Vietnam's independence from the head of the American mission. This may be true, but Ho Chi Minh was also determined to stamp Vietnam with an independent imprimatur separate from that future communist China or the Soviet Union.

More generally, the French acknowledged and let it be known to wartime Allies that the postsurrender interregnum in northern Vietnam had developed into a confused situation in which more or less improvised groups sought to take power under the name of the Viet Minh in order to win Vietnamese independence. As well recognized by French intelligence, at the heart of the Viet Minh stood a communist organization. In this light, Paris also made it known that it could not prejudge sentiments of the rights of the Indochinese people as to self-government at least until it had made a deep investigation of the situation subsequent to the French restoration. The lack of capacity of the so-proclaimed Hanoi government in coping with food supplies and transport was well recorded.

On the other hand, according to a Vietnamese source, fearful of a French return, the sudden Japanese surrender forced the Viet Minh to accelerate its plans. At the Tan Trao conference of August 13–15, 1945 (now dubbed the National Congress of People's Representatives), Pham Van Dong made the opening speech, announced the agenda, and introduced Ho Chi Minh as none other than the veteran revolutionary Nguyen Ai Quoc. Ho Chi Minh and Truong Chinh also made declarations in support of a general uprising (Vietnam 2009b, 15–16). This they achieved in a number of cities across Indochina within two days of the Potsdam Declaration. In Hanoi, a political action committee was formed to coordinate with the Bao Dai government. In the event, the Viet Minh seized power in Hanoi on August 19. By August 23, the Viet Minh were in power in Hue and, as discussed below, had established the Executive Committee of the South Vietnam Republic. Even so, as discussed below, power in Hanoi was also briefly contested on August 17.

Responding to news of the atomic bombing of Nagasaki on August 9, Nguyen Khang, chairman of the Hanoi revolutionary military committee, still out of contact with the Ho Chi Minh group then meeting at Tan Trao (on August 13), prepared for the eventuality of staging an insurrection. Having secured a meeting with Bao Dai's representative in Hanoi, the *Kham sai* (Viceroy) Phan Ke Toai, he rejected an invitation to join Bao Dai's independence government. With Tan Trao approval to mount an insurrection forthcoming, on August 17 Nguyen Khang rallied his committee forces in downtown Hanoi at the very moment that the Tran Trong Kim administration staged a mass meeting of civil servants (Patti 1980, 164).

According to a French source composed sometime after the event, in the run-up to the Japanese surrender, the Viet Minh stepped up its political work, even infiltrating the administration and police in Hanoi, and was thus poised to intervene at the moment of the Japanese surrender. At this time, the DMH and VNQDD were still back in China and would not enter Vietnam until the arrival of the Chinese Nationalist troops mandated by the Allies to take the Japanese surrender. In the meantime, the Japanese created a "zone of insecurity" to deliberately exclude the French while leaving the "quisling" Tran Trong Kim and other Vietnamese officials in place. Crucially, on August 12, a senior *kempeitai* official entered into discussions with the Viet Minh and the pro-Nippon government in Hanoi regarding scenarios for a Viet Minh takeover of power. On August 17 in the Place de Théâtre in Hanoi, fronting the opera house, a meeting convened by the (pro-Imperial-Japanese supported) Comité de Fonctionaires, or "civil service committee," was witnessed by an impressive crowd. The stage was shared by the Japanese and the pro-Nippon government, otherwise branded by Vietnamese sources as a "sham 'independence' administration to welcome the allied powers." As reported by Resident Superior Paul Chauvet (albeit under house arrest), suddenly a well-organized band seized the stage, drove off the speakers, and acclaimed the rally in the name of the Viet Minh, then "a little-known name." The game was played. All the levers of control, notably the police and *garde indigène*, fell without opposition into the hands of the insurgents. "In effect, it is well evident that, without the complicity of the Japanese who disposed the totality of arms and the material resources, the men of the Viet Minh, inferior in number and above all military means, would not have been able to affect a *coup de force*" (MAE AOI 162 "Biographie d'Ho Chi Minh" établi par F.O.M. ca. 1/9/49). Having edged the Bao Daists off the podium, in front of a crowd of some two hundred thousand, the imperial flag was lowered and the Viet Minh flag raised. Basically this coup was achieved by subverting and disrupting a countermeeting organized to rally support behind the (Japanese-supported) Kim Hue government.

As Patti (1980, 165) underscores, this was the first public and unopposed meeting of the Viet Minh as a political force. The Hanoi City Committee then planned for a full insurrection on the same day. The residence superior was occupied and Bao Daists ousted. With the insurgents gathering weapons, numbers of Bao Daists rallied to its cause as the days proceeded. Japanese guards backed away when the committee members/Viet Minh stormed the Garde Indochinois security division, taking more weapons. Under Japanese guard, the Banque de l'Indochine premises, the governor's palace, and Japanese garrisons still eluded the committee, but other strategic buildings yielded to Viet Minh control. At that moment, Giap, Colonel Thomas, and Deer Team were still battling the Japanese at Thai Nguyen down from the mountains. In other words, the seizure of power in Hanoi was a bloodless affair, the city having liberated itself. There was no (armed) coup (except that achieved in front of the opera house).

By August 20, 1945, swathes of northern Vietnam had fallen into the hands of the Viet Minh (People's Revolutionary Committee) while awaiting the arrival in Hanoi of Ho Chi Minh. Within the week, on August 29, the triumphant revolutionaries announced the formation of a provisional government of unity, with Ho Chi Minh appointed as president of the council, Vo Nguyen Giap, interior, Pham Van Dong, finance, Chu Van Tan, national defense, and

Phan Ngoc Tach, the Saigon medico-revolutionary, health, among others. Several days later, Ho Chi Minh took over the leadership of the provisional government surrounded by faithful Moscow returnee lieutenants, several neutral personalities, and people of different political tendencies otherwise designed to give the communist regime a democratic veneer (Patti 1980, 165). A week after the Viet Minh seized power, two Liberation Army detachments comprised of "Viet Bac" minorities also marched in Hanoi (Elliott 1974, 25).

As Bartholomew-Feis (2006, 237) embellishes, although Viet Minh radio had called to "launch the insurrection," the message was received only in Lang Son, Cao Bang, and Ha Giang. Even so, as with the case in Hanoi, local committees reacted in line with the evolving situation, marching on government offices, detaining mandarins, installing Viet Minh flags, and so on. As explained below, the contagion spread south as well, with one hundred thousand peasants marching on Hue on August 23 and Bao Dai renouncing the imperial throne.

With the French restoration of power successfully accomplished in Saigon on the heels of the arriving British SEAC mission, the checkmate of the French by the Viet Minh in Hanoi was total. As revealed by a French intelligence assessment of August 23, 1945, transmitted by General Leclerc, the senior French military official in Vietnam with his base in Saigon, an attempt by a French naval force to proceed by the maritime route to Hanoi was blocked by the "revolutionaries." Taken prisoner, the French personnel were forced back to Haiphong, still under Japanese "protection." The report also noted "very serious floods" cutting road communication in the delta as well as the rail link between Haiphong and Viet Tri. With the port of Haiphong "unusable," only Hong Gai and Cam Pha were accessible. In Leclerc's spare and stark words transmitted to an undoubtedly perplexed and unbelieving Parisian official audience, "The Viet Minh have taken power in Hanoi." The population is "reserved" (MAE AOI 28 tél., E165-2 "Resumé de Situation," Leclerc à d'Argenlieu, Aug. 23, 1945).

In actuality, they were also starving to death. As an official history offers, with Ho Chi Minh newly arrived in Hanoi (albeit secreted in a house in Hang Ngang Street) and chairing the first meeting of the central standing committee, the revolution had triumphed, but an administration remained to be created. According to an official source, "Water was rising in all rivers. The dike system, which had not been attended to by the colonialists, was broken in a number of places. Rice fields were flooded in several provinces of Bac Bo or northern Vietnam. "Starvation which had caused the deaths of millions of people was again threatening the life of Vietnamese. A host of new tasks confronted the revolutionaries" (Vietnam 2009b, 23). At the inaugural session of the provisional government on September 3, Ho Chi Minh also instructed the council of ministers to "launch a production drive to fight famine." Pending the anticipated arrival of the maize and sweet potato crop within three or four months, the president ordered a general fast once every ten days with rice distributions to the poor, a message duly amplified and published in the pro-Viet Minh *National Salvation* newspaper in the capital (Vo Nguyen Giap 2010, 31; Ho Chi Minh Museum). We will return to the question of food supply and the September 1945 flood and consequences in a following chapter.

Jean Sainteny's Arrival in Hanoi

As described, the Viet Minh takeovers were hardly smooth and were even aborted in the south. To degrees, the Japanese kept order or worked tacitly with the Viet Minh to achieve the same. Unlike in the south, the French were still interned in Hanoi by the Japanese, and the Chinese troops had yet to arrive. The Viet Minh immediately launched an anti-French campaign doing such things as blacking out French-language signboards and destroying statues and other French or colonial symbols. Just as Hanoi and other centers were festooned with anti-French slogans, so the tricolor was nowhere to be seen. The red flag with the yellow star now flew over the cities of the three regions of Vietnam.

Working out of Calcutta and Kunming, the French response to the Japanese surrender was swift, albeit severely limited by resources and within the terms dictated by the Allies. Mounting long-range flights from Calcutta, by mid- to late August the French had accomplished parachute landings in Saigon (one, involving Jean Cédille); Vinh (two), with one reserved for Hue; Sept-Pagodes (one); Pakse and Thakek in southern Laos (one each); and Hanoi (one, involving Pierre Messmer). Both Jean Cédille and Messmer bore official accreditation as the Provisional Government of the French Republic "commissioners" (AOM Indo NF 337/2711, Grandfils, DGER à Comité l'Indochine, Aug. 28, 1945).

Arriving at a secondary airport near Hanoi on August 22 along with Patti's OSS team, Jean Sainteny and party literally fell into the hands of Japanese "protectors." Arrested as soon as they disembarked, they also regained their liberty as well. To Sainteny's chagrin, the Japanese in Hanoi refused to deal with him on the grounds that France was not represented at the Potsdam Conference. Certainly, the reception could have been worse, especially given Sainteny's ambiguous status, just as the risks and stakes were high. The French team had radio-transmitting capability, but their messages were controlled by the Japanese. In one of these messages, Sainteny had made known that the situation was "serious" (AOM Indo NF 337/2711, Grandfils, DGER à Comité l'Indochine, Aug. 28, 1945).

At that time, senior French generals along with troops were still imprisoned in the Hanoi citadel. This raised fears for the French that the Viet Minh would release them and then hold them as hostages. Initially, grave fears were also held for "Commissioner" Messmer, who, having parachuted into the Hanoi area, had fallen into Viet Minh hands, albeit well treated. The Cédille team arriving in Saigon was described as in a similar situation to Sainteny in Hanoi. The pro-French Prince Savang in Luang Prabang was under French guard as a precaution against Chinese occupation. The French commando Fabre along with a force of 130 men was on the verge of entering Vientiane. Two Direction Générale des Etudes et Recherches (DGER) French intelligence officers were arrested by the Japanese at Lang Son. More generally, French forces in China were blocked from entering northern Indochina by the Nationalist Chinese Third and Fourth Territorial Armies. As correctly surmised, the British were placing greater priority on the liberation of Singapore than on Saigon. At that point (August 28), French intelligence learned that Saigon would be occupied by the British-commanded Indian Twenty-Sixth Division (AOM Indo NF 337/2711, Grandfils, DGER à Comité l'Indochine, Aug. 28, 1945).

Livid at the American complicity with the Viet Minh, Sainteny continued to pour scorn on the Patti group, a theme that appears as a leitmotif in French intelligence documents. For example, as late as October 1945, the French embassy in Washington was instructed to brief the American State Department that Indochina was "outside of the American zone of action and that French opinion was very disturbed by the actions of certain American representatives." According to French information, American representatives in Hanoi still refused to occupy the Vinh camp where numerous French were detained by the Viet Minh. Meanwhile, American officers who had parachuted into Laos favored disarming French troops under the pretext that international accords did not allow direct French occupation (a reference to the controversial actions by Raven mission under Captain Aaron Banks). Moreover, Nollday, an American OSS agent based in Thailand, had favored the Free Lao (Lao Issara) Party (MAE AOI 34 tél., Paris, à Ambass. France, Washington, "Attitude des représentants americains en Indochine," Oct. 1945).

As future French high commissioner for Indochina, Thierry d'Argenlieu (1985, 49) wrote in his memoirs, "The first Yankee emissaries were dogmatically—naively anti-colonial, often manifesting without measure or nuance their ideological sympathies as spokespersons convinced of the right of the Annamite people." Archimedes Patti even attended a Viet Minh flag-raising ceremony. Dommen (2001, 123–24), sharply critical of the actions of individual OSS members as with the Raven mission in Laos, is actually fulsome in praise for Patti, not only in handling a complex and dangerous brief but also for his "objective" assessment of Viet Minh immaturity and communist inclinations. Patti also showed deference to Bao Dai in Hanoi, suspecting that he had been forced to abdicate. As Bartholomew-Feis (2006, 237–41) allows, Patti also cabled his concerns to Kunming over Viet Minh government plans to nationalize the Banque de l'Indochine and the Yunnan railroad, among other utilities. More or less, Patti's reports to Kunming mixed concern with the "party state" developing in Hanoi and his undisguised pleasure at seeing the French nixed. But whereas the OSS in the north had credibility or, as Bartholomew-Feis (2006, chap.7) emphasizes, were actively used by the Viet Minh provisional government to enhance their democratic or international credentials, the constellation of political forces in the south, namely the French on the heels of the British, offered no such political space for the nationalists.[3]

But as far as the French were concerned, the Japanese surrender signaled a return to the legal status quo and the restoration of French sovereignty. As Dommen (2001, 114–15) emphasizes, the main actions by the Viet Minh in August were directed against representatives of the emperor and the imperial government, as with the *Kham sai* in Hanoi. Rather than dislodging the French (the Japanese had accomplished that), the Viet Minh liberation committees replaced imperial authorities wherever they had the strength. In making this point, Dommen is arguing that rather than usurping power from the Japanese, as Ho Chi Minh contended in his declaration of September 2, the Viet Minh had actually usurped power from the imperial government, "the legal representative of the Vietnamese people in the absence of French sovereignty." It is not just semantics, he implies, but the Viet Minh action better fits the description of *coup d'état* than revolution, as would appear to be the case with the Japanese "coup" against the French.

ANNAM IN THE REVOLUTION

Following the Viet Minh seizure of power in Hanoi on August 19, 1945, developments in Hue also entered a crucial stage. Officialized history of the Viet Minh takeover in Hue prefers to trace back Viet Minh preplanning to January 1945, namely the action of a special envoy of the Annam Party Committee in passing on a copy of the Viet Minh constitution to the Hue Party Committee. In this narrative, on May 23, during a secret meeting on boats moored in the Cau Mai lagoon, preparations for insurrection were discussed. Yet such seems improbable given the strength of Japanese forces, Tran Trong Kim "government" units, and pro-Japanese paramilitary units in and around Hue. However, there is no question that with Thua Thien province as the nucleus, the Viet Minh attracted increasing numbers of adherents, students, and civil servants among them, and kept up low-key actions such as the seizure of Japanese rice junks. The insurrection, however, was not launched until the propitious and strategic day of August 15 in Thua Thien and Hue under the leadership of one To Huu, president of the Insurrection Committee. The

Japanese-installed Tran Trong Kim administration was persuaded to resign. At this juncture, officers of the Bao An (security police) and cadres of the military school went over to the Viet Minh. Still, the French sought to mount their restoration and were infiltrating agents through Laos or parachuting into Thua Thien. On August 23, with crowds massing, the Insurrection Committee sent an ultimatum to Bao Dai, calling on him to abdicate in favor of the Viet Minh. That afternoon, To Huu proclaimed before a crowd of 150,000 the end of the monarchy and the dawn of the republican era under the Viet Minh. Obviously keeping a low profile, the Japanese command were, in this account, informed the following day (Hong Thy and H.N. 1975, 58–62). Dated August 25, Bao Dai's abdication rescript was posted outside the palace and cabled to Hanoi, Saigon, and every major local province (Dommen 2001, 109). Bao Dai's abdication ceremony took place on August 30 in front of the Ngo Mon gate, with the last of the Nguyen kings surrendering his golden seal along with the jewel-encrusted sword, the regalia of the kingdom, to the delegation of the Vietnam Democratic Party from Hanoi which came to receive them.

In Lockhart's (1989, 140) account, "Ba To" (Quang Ngai–based guerrilla units) mobilized in the countryside for a march on Hue. On August 22, Bao Dai received a telegram from Hanoi requesting him to abdicate. In the absence of Tran Trong Kim or any ministers, the emperor found himself in total isolation as tens of thousands of pro–Viet Minh elements massed in the streets of the imperial capital. A radically new imagining of Vietnam outside of Japanese auspices and outside of imperial conceptions was about to crystallize, but would it be by revolutionary putsch or by the stroke of a pen? Dommen (2001, 111–13) adds a more skeptical note, especially questioning the degree of voluntarism on the part of Bao Dai, as private citizen, in delivering up his seal to the Viet Minh, not to mention his actual knowledge of the Viet Minh and even Ho Chi Minh and the nature of the obviously stage-managed abdication ceremony reenactment where the imperial flag was lowered and the Viet Minh flag run up. In this interpretation, the text of Bao Dai's proclamation was altered to include a Viet Minh invitation to form a cabinet. Lockhart (1989, 140) aptly—and correctly, in my estimation—describes Bao Dai's August 30 abdication as "the most central event in modern Vietnamese history," especially as it lent legitimacy—at least as viewed in Hanoi—to the country's first republican government on a national scale.

The "southward" movement of the Viet Minh subsequent to the August Revolution was confirmed in an August 24 message sent by the Japanese embassy office in Saigon to the Japanese adviser at Hue. As stated, the Viet Minh were "very active," especially north of Quy Nhon, at Tam Quan, and at Quang Nai and all places south of Hue in the zone designated for British occupation and where guerrilla war was at that time being carried out against Japanese forces (Magic 1252, Aug. 29, 1945). Following Lockhart (1989, 139–40), this

Saigon City Hall with statue of Ho Chi Minh in the foreground.
Major site of political struggles during the 1930s and again in August–September 1945.
Source: Author, 2012.

would be a reference to the Ba To guerrillas who had been propagandizing and mobilizing in preparation for marches on the cities, including the imperial capital. But officialized Vietnamese histories also elaborate on the dispatch of northern military units south with the first southbound unit leaving Hanoi by train on September 26. Arriving in Vinh, this detachment doubled its strength, adding a company from Thanh Hoa and two others from Nghe An. Others joined up with the Ba To guerrillas, still others joined the fight in Nha Trang,

Phan Thiet, with others arriving in Bien Hoa to join the Saigon battlefront (Vietnam 2009b, 58–59).

Late in August 1945, Independence League (Viet Minh) representatives told Japanese ambassador Yokoyama in Hue that a certain understanding had been reached with the United Nations as to independence. But while the Viet Minh League did not expect to make progress by way of negotiations, it held the "trump card of a nationwide people's rebellion." Early in September, clashes occurred in Hue between French and Vietnamese. These were contained by the Japanese. As of September 3, however, clashes became a daily occurrence led by popular elements wielding both arms and bamboo spears. In response to the charge by Yokoyama that such demonstrations were counterproductive to the Viet Minh's cause, the local leadership blandly replied that the demonstrators could not be controlled (Magic 1278, Sept. 24, 1945).

Shortly after the August Revolution, the future South Vietnamese strongman Ngo Dinh Diem was detained by Viet Minh fighters in central Vietnam. Prior to being held in a secret mountain location, he was taken to Hanoi in early 1946 to meet Ho Chi Minh, who offered him a position in his Viet Minh unity government. As Miller (2004, 438) interprets, Diem pursued the offer only because his request to control certain aspects of policy was rebuffed. Contrary to Diem's obfuscations surrounding this period, French intelligence records that he maintained contacts with the Viet Minh for at least the ensuing two years in the hope that he could split the Viet Minh leadership, events and issues closely followed in Nam Bo (Cochinchina). But while pursuing a *pas de deux* with the Viet Minh, Diem was also flirting with anticommunist alliances and groups.

Bao Dai in the Revolution

As discussed in chapter 6, the Japanese-sponsored Tran Trong Kim government brokered major symbolic and administrative changes in the conception of Vietnam, radically breaking with the treaties entered into between France and Hue. Bao Dai appeared to be reacting to events otherwise brokered by the Japanese, but he was also an actor. On August 18, 1945, still as emperor of Annam, Bao Dai dashed off a message to provisional government of France President Charles de Gaulle (albeit apparently unanswered), speaking as a "friend rather than a head of state." Allowing that the French had likewise suffered over "four deadly years," he advised that the Vietnamese, with a history of twenty centuries and a glorious past, could no longer support foreign domination. Prophetically, he stated, "Even if you were to arrive to reestablish a French administration here, it would no longer be obeyed; each village would be a nest of resistance, every former friend an enemy, and your officials and colonists themselves would ask to depart from this unbreathable atmosphere." His message was clear: recognize Vietnamese independence, and "renounce any idea of reestablishing French sovereignty or administration here in whatever form it may be." As the Pentagon Papers commented, in any case the message was moot because within a week, Bao Dai would cede his powers to the DRV (Pentagon Papers 1971, B-30, Origins of the Viet Minh).

Contrary to his analysis of the August Revolution in Hanoi, Dommen (2001, 113) concedes that events in Annam truly appeared to constitute a revolution. Not only had Vietnamese been deeply shocked to see the French dislodged from the apex of power where they had stood over the past eighty years, but under the Tran Trong Kim government, Vietnamese now commanded the highest positions. And, as mentioned, all visible symbols of France, statues, street names, and so on were destroyed. While Ho Chi Minh's declaration of independence did not acknowledge Bao Dai or Tran Trong Kim, he did echo, however, the substance of Bao Dai's stated rejections of France.

Terror and Control

Sometimes described as a virtual bloodless putsch or coup occurring in a power vacuum, the August Revolution was not entirely bloodless either before or after the event. Another strand of writing emphasizes the terror dimension of the Viet Minh takeover (the work of Fall and of Duiker). According to French sources, since taking power the Viet Minh had committed various crimes in both northern and southern Vietnam. These allegedly ranged from pillage, arson, arbitrary arrests, tortures, thefts, murders, or the "full gamut of horrors committed by bandits without scruples." Victims showed no discrimination, with women, children, and men snatched from their homes. They counted missionaries, religious figures, doctors, indigenous notables, peasants, and *lettrés* "who, though thoroughly patriotic disapproved of the Viet Minh excesses." Victims also included Vietnamese married to Europeans and indigenous merchants who sold to Europeans. Setting aside the kidnappings, murders, and mutilations of September 23, 1945, committed in Saigon, a reference to the Cité Herraud massacre, victims in the north included one dozen Europeans killed in Hanoi at the end of August 1945 (AOM Indo NF/134/1217 Preneuf, 2éme Bureau, "Atrocités comises par le Viet-Minh," Saigon, Jan. 18, 1946).

However, as Lockhart (1989, 115) argues, rather than forcing control over the population, the Viet Minh sought to mobilize and organize them. Commencing immediately after the March 9 Japanese takeover, as the French administration started to crumble, the Viet Minh orchestrated attacks on provincial rice stores accumulated for collection by the Japanese army. Some of these military rice stores contained one hundred tonnes, even one thousand tonnes. One of Lockhart's sources lists up to ninety such attacks across seventeen northern provinces. As Lockhart (1989, 117–19) embellishes, outside the Viet Bac region, where there was no regular Liberation Army, the act of attacking rice stores—symbols of enemies of the people—on the part of local "national salvation units," as in Bac Giang province, actually helped to crystallize the development of "people's armed forces." With attacks on rice stores continuing in the northern regions, they also spread to the central regions by April and May, thereby enhancing the capacity of the Viet Minh to mobilize and organize greater numbers of people.

But the Viet Minh also had the numbers as well, having rapidly expanded since the Japanese capitulation. Emerging as a Quan Giai Phong, or Liberation Army, its ranks were stiffened by a number of ex-*tirailleurs*, albeit under the command of the guerrilla comrades-in-arms of Ho Chi Minh. From the moment of the Japanese capitulation, as signaled, Japanese auxiliaries joined the People's Army as military instructors. But with a large rank-and-file membership of very dubious quality, the Quan Gia Phong was not an impressive force. Matters changed with the creation of the truly National Army (Quan Quoc Gia) and, from November 1945, with an expanded recruitment of rifle company veterans under a National Salvation Front. At the same time, "undesirable elements" were eliminated while an intensive induction and training program was mounted for younger recruits. Meantime, Tu Ve, or self-defense groups, were established in all regions as National Army reserves but with certain ones formed as guerrilla units and others serving police functions. At this time, ten military regions embracing north and central Vietnam were established. By December 1945, the Quan Quoc Gia comprised a force of twenty-eight thousand, including four thousand ex-Japanese and two thousand ex-guerrillas, swollen also by various subaltern cadre. Vo Nguyen Giap assumed the role of DRV minister of defense (SHD GR 4Q 45, "Note de Renseignements: L'Armée du Viet Minh," Sept. 11, 1945).

THE DRV AND THE CHINESE–DONG MINH HOI CHALLENGE

As Lockhart (1989, 146–47) argues, contrary to the view that the fledgling DRV government lacked unity, alongside the decentralized nature of local activists and military units an autocratic center also existed. While the new regime obviously faced disorder and challenges, it quickly set in place a structure. From September 2, 1945, the DRV ruled through thirteen ministries and with former emperor Bao Dai serving as supreme political adviser. In a sense, Lockhart continues, DRV centralism followed colonial and even precolonial practice where power was concentrated, culminating in the person of the president. But in a quick succession of revolutionary decrees, former

French offices were abolished and replaced by a parallel system of "people committee" and "resistance committee" with an "ascending succession of supervisory agencies from village to national level." He also finds it paradoxical that alongside this show of "democratic centralism," it was truly in the regions where enthusiasm for the goals of the revolution reached new heights (and excesses), especially after August 1945. Although the British, French, and Chinese invasions would interrupt the Viet Minh state-building project, Hanoi's command over propaganda was both unrelenting and far reaching in socializing the new revolutionary values.

The Chinese–Dong Minh Hoi Challenge

Commencing in late August 1945, a total of two hundred thousand Chinese Nationalist troops under the overall command of Kunming-based General Lu Han entered Vietnam, one column arriving at Lai Cai and marching along the Red River and another column (the Sixty-Second Army Corps) entering from Guangxi via Cao Bang and Lang Son. They did not, of course, all arrive simultaneously. Haiphong and Nam Dinh were occupied on September 26 by elements of the Sixty-Second Army, and by October, ninety thousand troops had entered northern Indochina (SHD GR 4Q 45 Indochine 1943–48; Sainteny 1953, 143).

From all accounts, the Chinese troop arrival was a disorderly affair accompanied by many acts of disobedience and considerable plunder, including supplies of rice. With VNQDD troops in train, Cao Bang town was destroyed and Lau Cai occupied (Vietnam 2009b, 42–43). According to David Marr (2010, 139), within two days of his arrival in Hanoi, Lu Han extracted an agreement from Ho Chi Minh whereby he accepted inflated Chinese currency in the purchase of local rice to feed Chinese occupation forces. DRV agents then visited the delta, awarding rice quotas for Chinese consumption. Meantime, Chinese agents leaned on the French in Saigon to make up the shortfall. Such a view is contradicted by Vo Nguyen Giap (2010, 48–52), who rationalizes that although under duress from the Chinese command, Ho Chi Minh actually drew the line at supplying scarce rice at a time when the people were starving. It is hard to reconcile these views but, objectively, there was hardly a spare grain of rice left in the delta at this stage.

As French military historian Teulières (1978, 38–42) explains, with the support of Colonel Hsiao Wen heading up the political section of the Nationalist Chinese command, Lu Han sought to take into hand various parts of the country, transforming northern Vietnam into a veritable "chessboard of feudal politics." Arriving in Hanoi on September 11, Lu Han dislodged Sainteny and staff and set up headquarters in the former governor general's palace. French sources confirm that the arrival of Chinese troops in Hanoi was followed by abuses of all kinds. On September 20, French citizens were expelled from their homes otherwise subject to looting. The French consulate at Longzhou, sixty miles from Lang Son, was also looted. Meantime, Chinese troops committed a massacre of members of the recalcitrant Tho minority in the Lang Son region.

More generally, following the Japanese surrender, the Nationalist Chinese sought to prevent French troops under General Alessandri from entering Indochina. According to Sainteny (1953, 153), troops under Colonel Quilichini had been blocked by DMH elements from entering the Dien Bien Phu area. More than that, the Chinese worked to permanently install their own forces in both northern Vietnam and Laos. It was only after a high-level *démarche* from the French government to Chinese counterparts that General Alessandri even received an authorization to enter Tonkin to witness the Japanese surrender.

The Japanese Surrender Ceremony

It is with some sense of symbolism that the Chinese Nationalists chose the Puginier Palace as the site for the Japanese surrender ceremony held on September 27, 1945. To the disdain of the French, the tricolor was not displayed alongside other Allied flags at the ceremony. Although invited to the ceremony, General Alessandri declined to be present owing to what he considered derisory seating arrangements that relegated him to the margins. As voiced by d'Argenlieu to the Chinese government, there were three elements of concern. The first concerned the expulsion of Sainteny from the governor general's palace by Lu Han on September 12 and the French demand for its immediate restitution. Otherwise, the Puginier Palace was viewed by the French as symbolizing the federal capital of all Indochina (including zones south of the sixteenth parallel), and they had a point. Undoubtedly, the distinction was lost on the Chinese, just as the French vainly sought to restore the legal status quo. The second complaint concerned participation in the actual Japanese surrender ceremony. As d'Argenlieu argued, the Chinese pretext that only the Potsdam Declaration signatories (United States, United Kingdom, and China) merited such honor could not be sustained, especially as General Leclerc had attended the Japanese surrender ceremonies in Tokyo and was a signatory. France demanded that the Chinese forces in Laos disarm both Viet Minh and Japanese forces and put an end to this situation. Part of the problem was the disproportion of Chinese occupying forces versus the small number of Japanese. Whereas the British had deployed one division in southern Vietnam restricted to Saigon and its neighborhood, the Chinese had deployed four divisions, not only in Hanoi but throughout Tonkin, northern Laos, and northern Annam (AOM Indo NF/134/1244 d'Argenlieu, "Memorandum . . . Chinoises en Indochine," n.d.).

Up until this time, the French presence in Tonkin had been little more than symbolic around the figure of Jean Sainteny with both the Viet Minh and the Chinese entrenched in Hanoi (Sainteny 1953, 143–59). But changing circumstances in China presented France with an opportunity. Notably, Lu Han's forces were urgently required in Manchuria as Chiang Kai-shek and communist forces began to face off in the north. Likewise, the Viet Minh sought to play the French card to rid the country of the mistrusted historical enemy, the Chinese. Two accords were central to this sweeping change on the geopolitical chessboard. The first was the Sino-French accords of February 28, 1946. The second was the March 6, 1946, accords between the Viet Minh and the French (also known as the Sainteny–Ho Chi Minh accords) (Teulières 1978, 38–42). At this point, some of the three thousand French troops that had fled to China after the Japanese coup started to return to northwest Vietnam, raising the stakes for the outbreak of conflict.

CONCLUSION

The Viet Minh triumph in Hanoi in August 1945 was obviously a very checkered affair. Notwithstanding tactical support rendered by the OSS, it was a military-political coup rather easily accomplished in the face of Japanese capitulation and even cooperation, especially as French forces were either interned in Hanoi or in disarray in Yunnan. The August Revolution as a takeover of state power could be rationalized in line with Leninist dogma on revolutionary takeover, but it was also highly circumstantial, especially alongside Chinese ambitions and colonial firepower once it was readied. In fact, the short-lived Franco–Viet Minh détente of March–November 1946 evolved out of this vulnerability. By entering into an agreement with the French in March 1946 as to a cohabitation in Hanoi and Haiphong, the Viet Minh could also buy time and see the exit of the threatening Chinese presence.

But as a combined political-military coup by a dedicated Leninist organization married to an embryonic guerrilla army, the August Revolution also fell into the mold of a Maoist-style insurgency with its successful and tested reliance on a rugged mountainous rear base, its dependence on the long-oppressed ethnic minorities of that region, the skilled use of propaganda, and in line with the overall thesis of this work, the desperate economic condition of the peasant masses of the Red River delta, who, in the throes of an epochal natural disaster, had nothing to lose by throwing in their lot with the anticolonial party.

Although reserving a detailed analysis of the Great Famine for chapter 8, we have seen in the Thai Nguyen rebellion of late 1944 a virtual rehearsal for the August Revolution if we are to read it as the collective action of desperate, rice-starved peasants in seizing rice and territory outside of government control. Sustained Viet Minh propaganda backed by actions in the way of seizure of grain stores in the wake of the Japanese surrender undoubtedly also confirmed in the eyes of millions the terminal end of the hydraulic pact with France as custodians. While the earlier Bac Son communist uprising in Tonkin in late September 1941 also involving some ethnic minorities might have stood outside this analysis, we can nevertheless also see in this event an early Viet Minh understanding of the importance of inaccessible base areas populated by historically marginalized and oppressed ethnic minority populations, ripe for leadership and political direction.

It cannot be overstressed that whereas from its inception the ICP had focused on the victims as well as beneficiaries of colonial capitalism, whether as peasant-farmers in the rice surplus producing zones of the two deltas and in central Vietnam or even the urban proletariat and intellectuals, under the conjuncture presented by the Japanese occupation a radical new conception of guerrilla warfare took shape. In this vision, as carried forward by such military planners as Vo Nguyen Giap and the ethnic minority general, Chu Van Tan, the revolution would work from the periphery to the capital, a strategy that would again be unveiled during the war of national resistance following the French reoccupation of Hanoi, down until the epic Battle of Dien Bien Phu.

Viet Minh actions in Hue did resemble a classic revolution of the masses with the ancient capital as the symbol and the defection of the monarch accomplished against embedded local interests and local French armed resistance. Yet because of the comparative isolation of Annam and the ease with which the French could control the coastal littoral and port cities, the outcome was also more contested. Although space precludes analysis, the Annam model of local armed Viet Minh uprisings was also applied by the Viet Minh in Laos and Cambodia in the wake of the Japanese capitulation but without much success, owing to the almost exclusive Vietnamese character of the uprisings and a fairly cool reception on the part of local communities. By contrast, the southern Viet Minh faced a vastly different political and social environment compared to their comrades in the north, with their large rear base in southwestern China alongside tactical, albeit opportunistic, support from Nationalist China and even the American OSS. The southern reality was also a product of Japanese manipulation of anti-French nationalists, in part matching the heterogeneous character of social-religious demography but also in line with urban realities in Saigon, where the ICP never had a monopoly of power or ideas.

NOTES

1. The "August Revolution" leading to the proclamation of the DRV on September 2, 1945, has rightfully attracted a volume of scholarship, ranging from an earlier generation of French scholars, as with Devillers (1952) and Mus (1952), and participant accounts, as with d'Argenlieu (1985), Sabattier (1952), Sainteny (1953), and Patti (1980), to such works by Vietnam specialists as Chen (1969), Tønnesson (1984, 1991, 2010), and Marr (1997, 2013), including military analyst Lockhart (1989). Needless to say, the event and its background also fit into a carefully constructed officialized Vietnamese narrative.

2. Now lodged in the Archimedes L. Patti Papers, Special Collection in the University of Central Florida, Orlando, the graphic photographs are actually among the few that remain of the Great Famine. Certain of them have been printed, such as in Bartholomew-Feis (2006, 31).

3. Events in Saigon have been well covered in a number of standard histories (e.g., Neville 2007). On the OSS in the south, see my "Origins of the American War in Vietnam: The OSS Role in Saigon in 1945," *Asia-Pacific Journal* 19, no. 3, May 9, 2009.

Chapter 8

The Great Vietnamese Famine, 1944–45

Reaching its zenith in March–April 1945, there is no question that the mortality stemming from the Great Famine lasting from October 1944 to May 1945 eclipsed in scale all human tragedies of the modern period in Vietnam, even if the absolute number of deaths remains disputed.[1] Allowing the contingency of natural cause as a predisposing factor for mass famine, this short chapter revisits the Great Vietnamese Famine of 1944–45 in light of flaws in human agency as well as destabilization stemming from war and conflict. While I downplay the issue of impacts of the famine in deference to seeking cause—in any case a subject worthy of much closer attention—the human suffering of the famine has not been effaced by time. As mentioned below, it was recorded in Hanoi newspapers of the time. It survives in local memory. It has been fictionalized by Vietnamese writers, and it is firmly emblazoned in official Vietnamese history.[2]

Gabriel Kolko (1985, 36) is one who has appreciated the political importance of the famine in preparing the ground for the revolution that followed, observing that the communists broke open the rice stores to avert famine. Stein Tønnesson (1984) has also highlighted the famine setting in which the Viet Minh launched themselves to power. Nguyen Khac Vien (1975, 92–95) affirms that it was the Viet Minh who took the lead in calling on the peasants to resist orders to plant jute and led opposition to the forced sale of rice, terming this a joint French-Japanese oppression. This view is not contradicted by Patti (1980, 133), who argues that the unplanned effects of Viet Minh seizures of paddy stocks provided relief from the famine as the price of rice fell; identified the Japanese and French as the common enemy; encouraged people to organize for self-defense; highlighted the importance of organized resistance; and recruited for the Viet Minh. Lockhart (1989, chap. 4) has gone further in directly linking Viet Minh recruitment and popular mobilization with the famine. For his part, Marr (2013, 320–21) has emphasized the role of the nascent DRV state in taking charge of grain procurement and distribution and in desperately working to prevent a recurrence of the terrible famine.

But, as replayed in an epilogue, why is it important now to apportion cause for the famine, or even blame? I would argue that the Great Vietnam Famine of 1944–45 is at least one of the underwritten tragedies stemming from the Pacific War. Outside of Vietnam, very few dedicated articles or studies have sought to contextualize this event from either the side of Vietnamese history or the side of Japanese and/or French and American responsibility. No doubt a court of law would seek to distinguish between deliberate policy, benign neglect, and/or the unanticipated consequences of social action. But rather than pinning blame as with a court of law or a war crimes trial, what I seek here is closer to a truth commission–style investigation that precisely seeks to uncover a number of thinly veiled truths that could possibly stimulate even further research, not only on war and memory issues related to the famine but also in the field of famine prevention.

To a large extent, the Great Famine of 1944–45 arose out of a set of circumstances and fairly well established vulnerabilities such as those backgrounded in chapter 1. Put another way, a series of natural events impacting the Red River delta region was bound to impact food security during this period, especially given other external factors. Even so, to replay Nguyen-Marshall's (2008, 36) objections, we should be cautious as to the "food-availability-decline theory" under which all in the affected areas suffer equally. In line with Amartya Sen's (1981) "entitlement" approach to famine, temporary food shortage alone cannot explain why some people starve while others in the same region do not. As with the experience of earlier floods and droughts in Vietnam (not to mention other case studies), the effects of famines are not indiscriminate, as certain categories of people have proved better able to cope with such factors as rising prices of rice and access to alternative sources of nutrition and assistance. To this end, we should seek an understanding of the early signposts of the impending disaster as well as the mitigating factors put in place by the state to satisfy the entitlement of victims if that was the case. Contrariwise, it could also be significant if the state failed to redeem the "hydraulic pact" with the population.

This chapter divides into six sections. A first backgrounds the preludes of the Great Famine from its origins with the crop failures of late 1944. The question of failure in the face of warnings is discussed in a second section. A third section offers examples of individuals coping with adversity. A fourth section discusses crisis management by the French in Tonkin, including rice stores, social relief measures, and the dispatch south of relief junks. Another section deals with the Japanese takeover and the failure of famine management. A final section reflects on the social impacts of the famine.

PRELUDES TO THE GREAT FAMINE

Unquestionably, there is merit in a multicause approach to the famine. But from a food security perspective, we should not neglect to examine harvest conditions alongside natural events in the lead-up to the Great Famine. Researching from a range of colonial sources, Nguyen The Anh (1998a, 215) points out that food scarcity and hunger were already the lot of Tonkin as early as 1943, but the mediocre harvest of the following year brought the region to the brink of disaster. First, the crop harvested in the fifth month of 1944 yielded only 655,000 tonnes of paddy, or 154,000 tonnes less than the corresponding harvest of 1942. Tonkin already required emergency assistance if it was to survive until the harvest of the tenth month. But at the moment when supplies were exhausted, the region was hit with major typhoons (three striking the coastal regions between May and September 1944) and with "tidal waves of rare violence" that flooded and destroyed a large part of the autumn rice crop. Famine was already rife, with entire villages sometimes perishing. The crisis was further aggravated by a long, cold winter of "nearly unprecedented severity" preventing the cultivation of secondary crops.

The Typhoon Regime of 1944

As Le Manh Hung (2004, 254) summarizes, the crops first failed in Tonkin in spring 1944 with drought and insects reducing the output of the fifth-month harvest by 10 percent compared with the previous year. Then a series of typhoons, including the typhoon of October 1944 hitting Nam Dinh and Thai Binh, damaged the tenth-month harvest, causing a serious food crisis. He also adds that beginning in late 1944, famine broke out in Nghe Anh and Ha Tinh, where, according to a French archival source, twelve persons a day were dying and where in hundreds of villages children were being sold for about twenty piasters. On December 9, 1944, the newly formed Conseil de l'Indochine (Indochina Council) met to discuss the famine, yet nothing much was done to address the problem. As discussed below, no decision was made to reduce taxes or obligatory sales of rice (although Japanese pressure was also there). The council did extend the rice ration in the towns, allowing each adult to purchase ten kilograms a month at a controlled price, but this measure hardly helped the rural peasantry who commenced flocking to the cities in search of sustenance.

In the wake of typhoons of July, September, and October 1944, the hydraulic pact once again kicked into action. For example, dikes damaged by the typhoons of July and September 1944 in Quang Yen, near Haiphong on Ha Long Bay in the lower delta, received special funding for repair works from the Banque Provinciale de Credit Agricole (AOM RST NF *IB 92 Allimand à Quang Yen, Jan. 13, 1945). Funding for repair work for dikes damaged in the particularly vulnerable maritime province of Nam Dinh by the typhoons of October 1944 took the form of an emergency allocation of five hundred thousand piasters to prevent further disaster and costs likely to result from the onset of the next rains (AOM RST *IB4 494–56, Chauvet à Contrôle Financier, Hanoi, Feb. 10, 1945).

The impact of the typhoons is well captured in a first-person account from an individual named Duy Hoa residing at Phat Diem in Ninh Binh. Writing on February 2, 1945, he explained how his region had been "*essuyé*" (wiped out) by two typhoons and two floods in the course of the year. "The rice buds had scarcely formed when they came under prolonged inundation, leading to the complete loss of the harvest. . . . We have not seen a flood of such size for 10 years," he exclaimed. Noting that the harvest at Ham Dinh and Phat Dien had been completely lost, "no reserve of rice exists." As he explained the peasant-producer dilemma or trap in the face of official rice procurement demands, "to reap the rice fields we have to pay 40 piasters for labor costs but we also have to deliver a quintal of rice (100 kg.) to the administration. Nothing out of this remains for our consumption." Moreover, those who lack grain, as demanded by the *quan phu* (chief of prefecture), are obliged to purchase it on the market to meet the delivery requirement. "For my part," he continued, "I paid 250 piasters for a quintal of paddy and received 19 piasters in return." Obliged to purchase two quintals of paddy at 500 piasters to redeem the demand, all his efforts were focused on finding this money. Although personally hard pressed, "for those who cannot deliver up the quantity of rice demanded by the administration, they are also vulnerable to having their lands and property confiscated." Then there was the paddy collector who also exploited them. Then awaited the final trap. As explained, "With rice selling at 2 piasters a box, we are obliged to expend 3 piasters a day to satisfy our hunger, bur rice on the market is also scarce" (AOM RST *IB 218/425 Resident Ninh Binh, Feb. 2, 1945). Squeezed on both the production and consumption side, there was clearly no way out for the indigent peasant of Ninh Binh.

The famine then spread north from Ninh Binh, sweeping the densely populated lower delta or maritime provinces of Nam Dinh, Thai Binh, Hung Yen, and Ha Dong. According to Nguyen The Anh (1998a, 217), citing a Vietnamese newspaper source in Nam Dinh, out of an estimated 1,259,734 inhabitants, 646,147 were estimated to have starved to death. By mid-April 1945, the total number of victims in Nam Dinh and Thai Binh may have reached 467,000. As Le Manh Hung (2004, 254) clarifies, it was precisely in these provinces where dependence on the tenth-month harvest was greatest for survival, just as typhus then made an appearance. By Tet (lunar New Year, February 1945), the famine was already widespread, reaching its peak during the armed Japanese takeover of March 9 and continuing until late May.

ANTICIPATING THE FIFTH-MONTH 1945 HARVEST DEFICIT

As the authorities well knew, the specter of famine during Tet 1945 and the long *soudure* period was only a rehearsal for the devastation that would follow with the predictable failure of the upcoming fifth-month harvest of 1945. The prospects of a fifth-month failure were, in fact, outlined by the resident superior in his missive to the governor general of January 20 to justify emergency transport planning. As he pointed out, the deeply cold and lingering winter had already frozen many rice seedlings. Normally, the tenth-month harvest would carry the population through to July, but not only was this harvest delayed by one month, Tonkin was already experiencing a food deficit. Just to cover the upcoming needs for July, an additional seven thousand tonnes had to be reserved to feed the disaster-stricken provinces, including the towns and cities (AOM RST *IB 218/425 Chauvet à GG, Hanoi, Feb. 20, 1945).

As a French intelligence report corroborates, notwithstanding various administrative measures put in place, in May 1945 the delta provinces were struck by a famine of calamitous proportions, leaving between five hundred thousand and six hundred thousand victims. If the harvest of the fifth month had been handled in the summer, it declared, then the base price for rice would have decreased below the threshold of 250 piasters (presumably a more affordable level). But all economic regulation had been abolished, and the black market had taken over. Rather than blaming the French, it was the passivity of Japanese-backed regimes in the face of the crisis that aggravated the problem (AOM SLOTFOM NTCIP, "Le Viet Minh L'Action de la Chine et de Japon dans la Formation et son Accession," Paris, Aug. 7, 1946).

Also looking back at the flow of events following from March 1945, a French report of September 1945 asserted that "the Vietnamese masses started to suffer from a consecutive famine on heavy rice requisitions effected by the Japanese," and the neglect (effect) caused the catastrophic flood in eight delta provinces at a time when all reserve stocks were exhausted. Over a six-month period, the masses had to fend for themselves in the total absence of established traditional authorities, officials, and elites. Pointedly, this report added, such conditions contrived to fire up the revolutionary ferment of the Viet Minh (SHD GR 4 Q 45, "Les Evénéments au Tonkin entre la Capitulation Japonais et l'arrivé des Troupes Chinoises," Paris, Sept. 1, 1945).

As the key French actor in handling the crisis up until the Japanese military takeover in March 1945, the forty-year-old Paul Chauvet appears to have been well chosen, at least from a French administrative perspective.[3] Assuming the important office of resident superior of Tonkin in late 1944 in the wake of a roulette of Vichy predecessors at a time when Decoux began to put out feelers

Tonkin (North Vietnam), Provincial Boundaries

to the Free French, the governor general might also have seen in Chauvet a strategic individual at an undeniably critical juncture in French colonial history.

The question of early warning of disaster is also important. We recall that the delta was hit by a disastrous typhoon and flooding in August–September 1944. But there is also a sense that provincial reporting to the *comité des céréales*, or "grain board" (such as established by Decoux in December 1942), its executive organ, the Comptoir des Céréales, or "grain agency," which held a monopoly on purchase of paddy crops, and/or coordination between the provincial residents and the resident superior answering to the governor general was in serious need of overhaul. We recall as well that these were not normal times given the diversion of food to industrial crops, including jute, peanuts, and cotton, and the diversion of paddy for distilling, as mandated by the Japanese authorities. Compulsory deliveries, levies, and taxes were other burdens imposed on the peasant-producer.

Up until the crisis, it appears, there had been no surveys as to the sustainability of the levy system from the peasant-producer perspective. Increasingly, speculation and the hoarding of rice led to an unsustainable cost of living for large sections of both the rural and urban populations, an obvious warming signal as well. A finely honed system of ration cards introduced by Vichy, with special privileges for French and the official class, also called into question the critical nutritional needs of the masses, who, falling through the cracks of the colonial welfare system, were pushed back into the hands of the village collectivity and traditional authority. Obviously there was little here to suggest "entitlement" of the indigent in either the Japanese or French scheme, but at the same time, only state macromanagement, as with price controls, could turn the situation around.

Less prosaic warnings also took the form of rural-urban migrations as traditional coping measures broke down and desperate peasants started to invade district capitals as scavengers. Hanoi was not spared. As signaled in an official report, the arrival in Hanoi in early January 1945 by boat and rail of numerous destitute people from the provinces had led to a surge in begging and theft. Certain people were in such a dire physiological condition that they died in the street within hours of arrival (AOM RST *IB/93 Chauvet to Residents Hai Dinh, Thai Binh, Jan. 15, 1945). Still, as yet, there was no mention of death from epidemic disease, though the threat of disease contagion was also obviously in mind with respect to the urban areas.

Responding to the Tenth-Month Harvest of 1944

In many ways, the tipping point in the crisis was the tenth-month harvest of 1944 which, because of the August–September typhoons and flood damage, was bound to yield a reduced harvest. Obviously, data collection was at a premium. It appears that prior to this event, the reporting mechanism of the provincial administrations had been carried on in a fairly ad hoc way, leaving a serious gap in knowledge at the center. In the event, the acting resident superior (Allende) set down new setup instructions for reporting on the tenth-month harvest of 1944, namely by seeking information from provincial merchants and acting on this information via telephone or telegram. Such entailed (a) sending weekly reports to the Comptoir des Céréales of the tonnage of paddy remaining in each province; and (b) reporting to the *comptoir* on the third and eighteenth of each month the total past fifteen days of deliveries made. As specified, the first telegram should indicate the tonnage harvested in the course of the campaign and the date, multiplied by the tonnage delivered (AOM RST *IB 379 1892, Allende à Residents, Jan. 1945). At least, in theory, a standardized data collection system was in place, but did it work in a situation where every day counted and where the fixed delivery system was still in place?

Ongoing Japanese Military Demands and Burdens

The question of ongoing Japanese military demands on diminishing supplies of rice is a difficult area to investigate in the absence of incriminating Japanese documentation. Very little information on Japanese military procurement enters the pages of the resident superior's archive, simply because it was not his remit. In any case, the interface between the resident superior and the Japanese civilian authorities was via the Bureau des Affairs Japonaise. In this bizarre cohabitation, it often appears that the two administrations ran in parallel, although there were still rules of engagement, apparently.

But alongside "standard" rules on Japanese rice procurement as worked out by Vichy-Japanese conversations, in the weeks leading up to Operation Meigo, Japan moved a large number of forces into northern Vietnam from China. For example, according to the account by Di Ho, an indigent but literate farmer from Phat Diem in Ninh Binh, in the early stages of the famine, Japanese soldiers arriving from Thanh Ho descended on Phat Diem during a market day, stripped the place of rice and other goods, loaded the goods on lorries, and departed without paying a sou (AOM RST *IB 18/425 Résident Ninh Binh, Di Ho à Nguyen Ba Hung, Feb. 2, 1945). Undoubtedly, these were thin pickings, but if these acts were replicated in market towns across the delta—and there is every reason to believe that this was standard practice on the part of the newly arriving troops—then the impact was simply deadly.

Stresses in the Levy System

Notably, in a rationalization of January 22, 1945, designed to overcome problems within the grain board in Tonkin, Chauvet delegated the inspector of administrative affairs, Domec, to coordinate activities of the Comptoir des Céréales (AOM RST *1B92, Hanoi, Jan. 31, 1945). As the following example reveals, the inspectorate operated right down to the *phu*, or lowest administrative level. To wit, in early January 1945, the *phu* of Kim Son in Nam Dinh became an object of close inspection following the typhoon and rains. First the area was visited by a Vietnamese inspector and then by the resident, leading to a meeting with officials, big landowners, and members of the Rice Office to evaluate the productivity of rice fields. The result was a decrease in the levy for the *phu* of Kim Son (from 2,145 tonnes to 1,586 tonnes) and a modest decrease in the levy for the *phu* of Yen Khan, also hard hit. Overall, the province of Nam Dinh was assessed at 4,000 tonnes for general supply and 1,180 tonnes for official use and for certain collectivities (AOM RST *1B 92 GG, Hanoi, Jan. 13, 1945). Obviously, this was a crushing levy by any standards, and the "gracious" remission accorded would have offered little solace to the peasant-producer already at a subsistence threshold. Still, there is no sense that Chauvet sought to completely do away with the levies, even if he sought to fine-tune the system or mitigate the burden.

Micromanagement of the Crisis

Several themes emerge from the Tonkin residence archive as to the micromanagement of the crisis, namely strictly controlling leakage of paddy from the procurement regime and the need to reprovision the deficit delta provinces with whatever surplus existed in the more provident provinces. For example, in February 1945, Chauvet issued instructions to the resident of Thai Nguyen Province ordering him to go ahead with procurements of rice and paddy, whether on behalf of the army or whether to help make up for the rice deficit of the delta provinces. But in stressing the need to avoid price rises, he also ordered that details on all purchases be provided to the *comptoir*, that all merchants prove their official status, and that all exports of paddy from the province be strongly forbidden, down to the tiniest amounts (AOM RST *IB/96 15415, Chauvet à Résident Thai Nguyen, Feb. 1945).

Rumblings of Peasant Discontent

As discussed in chapter 7, rebellion had already broken out in the rugged terrain around Cao Bang and Bac Giang northeast of Hanoi, led by shadowy bands mostly attacking the French along with Vietnamese collaborators rather than Japanese adversaries. Then, on January 12, 1945, Resident Superior Chauvet reported on a "very violent discontent" in rural Tonkin, particularly in the provinces where the harvest had been very poor, cautioning against "communists, xenophobes and nationalists." More than that, as he predicted, "bloody incidents were to be feared in the coming months." In that, he was correct (AOM RST *IB 424–425 Chauvet à GG, Hanoi, letter no 38-s/AP of Jan. 12, 1945).

Striking a bold position, or at least sensitive to the political risks of failure, Chauvet counseled Decoux to lessen the burden on the peasant. "I advise you to diminish to the maximum the area of priority cultivation, notably peanuts and castor beans. Restrict to the maximum the extended plantations of Japanese jute, and sensibly augment the administrative price paid to producers in a fashion to diminish the enormous gap which exists between the farmer and the free market." As he pointed out, the peasant producers of Nam Dinh and Thai Binh had been squeezed by all kinds of embezzlement which burdened them and reduced their margins to the profit of intermediaries. He also advised an increase in official rations to hardworking government staff otherwise vexed by adverse public opinion (AOM RST *IB 424–425 Chauvet à GG, Hanoi, letter no 38-s/AP of Jan. 12, 1945). The following month, Chauvet also removed the requirement that cotton cultivators must sell their output to the government (Marr 1997, 32).

Price Rises

But all these measures, actually sweeping in their design, had not stopped the price of rice from incrementally rising. The situation was unlike that in Nghe-Tinh in 1931–32, where the price of rice fell in line with state intervention in the market with an injection of new supplies. According to Jordan (1996, 49), writing of the famine of northern Europe of 1315–22 that affected thirty million people, high prices force consumption among the vast majority of people downward to more modest levels and keep it there, so that available resources are more slowly depleted. But if the population is already subsisting at or near the threshold of biological survival, then the case for stabilization breaks down. As Jordan concludes on a philosophical note, "It should be evident . . . that the price levels of staples, primarily cereals, were critical, not only to the overall functioning of the economy, but also in more subtle ways than we might have supposed to the health or apparent health of the population." Notwithstanding the remove in time and space, the basic economic logic of price-supply equilibrium also held in northern Vietnam at this time of crisis.

The price of rice in Hanoi then reached $380 a quintal (or five times or more the going price in some rural areas) (Marr 1997, 32). News of the looming tragedy such as conveyed by clandestine military sources was also received by French circles in Chongqing. Writing from Hanoi on February 23, 1945, General Mordant confirmed that the economic situation in Tonkin–northern Annam had become "very grave" owing to the shortage of rice, the price varying between four hundred and five hundred piasters for one hundred kilograms (MAE AOI 29 tél. Chungking, Feb. 26, 1945). As Le Manh Hung (2004, 242) points out, food and clothing prices occupied the most important part of the family budget in Vietnam. Although vegetable prices remained mostly constant, just about everything else (rice, meat, fat) tripled in price between March 1943 and May 1944. The main cause of inflation, he explains, was the vast increase in the amount of money in circulation between 1942 and 1944, increasing at an annual rate of almost 100 percent but not matched by the total quantity of goods for sale.

COPING WITH ADVERSITY

We have precious few firsthand accounts of famine survivors, much less of victims, but the following account by a certain Nguyen Van Nghia of Quang Yen Province, northeast of Haiphong and taking the form of an intercepted letter, is entirely illustrative of the misfortune of millions, yet he was also the privileged holder of a ration card. As he wrote to his friend, "You know better than others that my salary scarcely suffers me to pay for basic foods to eat. My ration card allows 40 kg. of rice a month. I consume 60 kg. of rice a month. I pay for the missing 20 kg. on the black market at $3.50 a kg. For this reason I have to engage in business; otherwise, I'll die of hunger, not to mention my family who await my support" (AOM RST *IB 18/425 Résident Quang Yen, Feb. 1945).

Another intercepted letter of February 1945 sent by "Thuan" of Haiphong to the editors of *Tin Hau* newspaper in Hanoi waxed analytical on the multiple causes of the crisis that had already sent the price of rice to $320 a quintal. In this account, speculators spread false rumors with a view to exploiting a credulous public. The harvest in the maritime provinces had been destroyed by typhoons. Rich people were in competition with each other to stockpile rice. Farmers no longer placed their rice in the marketplace. Communications between north and south had become increasingly difficult. Even though the administration had taken measures not to alarm the population, had sought to drive out hoarders, had issued new ration cards, and had placed restrictions on restaurants, rice smugglers employed every ruse at their disposal to evade the law (AOM RST *IB 18/425 Résident Haiphong, Feb. 2, 1945).

Social Welfare Measures

As Nguyen The Anh (1998a, 218) acknowledges, the Vichy authorities did offer certain relief measures commencing in January 1945, as with the setting up of a mutual-aid committee for Tonkin with the needs of distressed persons in mind. As Chauvet informed the governor general in early February 1945, "In order to mitigate to the greatest degree possible the critical situation in which we find ourselves from the point of view of food, especially as it affects the people of Thai Binh and Nam Dinh, I have requested the Residents to organize soup kitchens and to distribute rice and cash to the most needy inhabitants, right through the *soudure* [the inter-harvest gap]." Accordingly, the provincial committees of mutual aid and social assistance should liaise with the *chefs de province* to realize an elaborate assistance program. Given the deficient budget, he continued, "I authorize Special Provident Funds, such as falls under the decree of July 1935 pertaining to disasters. I suggest that 250,000 piasters be made available under this disposition" (AOM RST *IB 494–56 Chauvet à GG, Hanoi, Feb. 9, 1945).

Diet, Food Consumption, Rationing, and Other Ameliorative Measures

Food consumption was another matter. Poor and plenty went together up to a certain point, such as invoked in Seung-joon Lee's (2011) analysis of food supply in Republican China. As Marr (1980, 135) explains, to reduce the risk of famine the French introduced ration cards (especially to the official and urban classes), set official market prices, and bought up large quantities of food to sell as needed. In mid-1943, the monthly per capita rice rate in urban areas was set at fifteen kilograms per month, dropping to twelve kilograms at the end of the year. After the Japanese *coup de force*, the Japanese declared a seven kilogram ration per month (although in reality less). To be sure, as Marr (1980, 135) declaims, this was a "situation ripe for economic speculation, pilfering, corruption and potential disaster."

Working with the mayor of Hanoi, Chauvet sought to control the ostentatious consumption of food in Hanoi's many French and local restaurants. From December 4, 1944, the sale of bread was restricted exclusively to holders of a "carte de rationnement européene," though evasions were observed on the part of a number of Vietnamese bakeries and, no doubt, clients. Decrees of January 6 and February 10 restricted the number of dishes on offer in hotels and restaurants and their opening times (AOM RST *IB4 94/95/96, Chauvet à Maire, Hanoi, Feb. 10, 1945). But this was the unreal world of the urban privileged classes and salariat. While people in this class were supplementing their diet with corn, manioc, sweet potatoes, beans, or black-market rice, the malnourished people of the delta, already habituated to scavenging for rodents and insects, were facing down starvation.

As well understood in humanitarian situations, it is usually the most vulnerable members of society who are the first to suffer. We need much more documentation, but it would appear that children figured among those in this category. Although highly prized in Vietnamese society and in normal times already engaged in a range of family or household economic activities in a rural setting, in a time of crisis they could also impose an impossible burden on family income/subsistence. In such circumstances there may have been a trend—even a survival necessity—to transfer children to the care of others or even, as a last, desperate choice, to abandon them. The tragedy of the situation was hinted at in December 1944, when Chauvet became alerted to the presence of abandoned children in Hanoi, a clear sign of social breakdown that can only be linked to acute distress. Acting on the initiative of a church organization that sought to create a 250-bed refuge in the suburbs, Chauvet requested a government subvention of 250,000 piasters, generously indicating that the administrative status of the institution could be settled at a future date (AOM RST *IB 92 Chauvet à GG, Hanoi, Jan. 2, 1945).

Crackdown on Speculators and Fraudsters

Likewise, the administration sought to crack down on fraud, especially the role of middlemen in gouging the indigent peasantry, as it would appear that such practices were rampant. Speculation for private gain, shortchanging the official Comptoir des Céréales, and general fraud were all targets of this policy. Both the price of rice as well as its quality was at issue. In a celebrated case in Nam Dinh, where eleven rice merchants were fined, the guilty sought to defend their actions by arguing that the poor quality of rice was as received from the *hang sao* (paddy huskers) and that they were punished because of the faults of others. Such a defense led the *Tin Moi* editorialist to query, "Well, why didn't they check the rice at reception?" (AOM RST *IB 1B 13434 Résident France, Nam Dinh, Dec. 19, 1944). As Gourou (1955, 473), explains, the *hang sao*, numbering some thirty-seven thousand and particularly numerous in Hai Duong province, performed the vital work of transforming paddy into rice suitable for human consumption. As it appears, they also took their cut.

In January–February 1945, Chauvet indicated that he had cracked down hard on speculators and hoarders, sending defaulters to a work camp, including the wife of the vice president of the Hanoi Grain Board along with the president of the Haiphong branch. Other dossiers were being examined, albeit allowing tolerance of petty customs infringements, such as with small alcohol and salt smugglers (AOM RST *IB 424–425 Chauvet à GG, Hanoi, Jan–Feb. 1945).

Misery in Thai Binh

With the maritime zone the most severely hit by the late 1944 typhoons, it would have appeared obvious to the authorities that Thai Binh and Nam Dinh were the provinces most vulnerable to harvest losses in the tenth month. Such deficits were indeed confirmed. Virtually an island bounded by three rivers, low lying Thai Binh, as with the neighboring province of Nam Dinh to the south, then—as now—are densely populated and intensively cultivated zones. Abutting the Gulf of Tonkin, both provinces are also highly susceptible to typhoon and/or flood damage. As the resident of Thai Binh made it known, the number of victims in need of support numbered four hundred thousand, or one-quarter of the population of the province. In the single circumscription of Kien Xuong, with a population of 250,000 (also worked over by political agitators), the harvest had been next to zero. In Nam Dinh province, the harvest yielded only thirty-five thousand tonnes versus an average yield of ninety thousand tonnes. As evaluated by the Indochina Rice Office, the total deficit of paddy stemming from the failed tenth-month harvest was on the order of five thousand tonnes, revealing a "massive reduction" in supply in Tonkin. In Hanoi, as reported, the number of persons dying from hunger had increased tenfold over several weeks (late January–early February 1945) (AOM RST *IB/96 18/425, Chauvet à GG, Hanoi, Feb. 20, 1945).

Landlocked Hai Duong Province in the central southern delta also stood out during the early stages of the crisis as a place where rice speculators threatened to derail the best-laid plans. As the resident at Thai Binh revealed on January 21, 1945, merchants and even individuals arriving from the coastal province of Thai Binh extended their activities through all the markets in Hai Duong Province and, to a lesser extent, in Hung Yen (another landlocked province forming the eastern gateway to Hanoi), buying up all the locally produced rice. In order to attract these purchases, itinerant merchants (*ramasseurs*) preyed on small vendors, provoking a steep rise in the local price wherever they operated, an increase which had immediate repercussions in surrounding villages. Although Thai Binh Province was included in a zone where circulation was free (suggesting that private trade was restricted in other zones), it appeared that massive purchases by certain individuals weighed heavily on a "nervous" market. The resident requested permission to intervene by controlling the massive entry of outsiders into Hai Duong arriving via Ninh Giang District. As he elaborated, "It is not exactly a question of forbidding the circulation of small merchants but, rather, stopping individuals who buy at any price." In one case, an individual had obtained an authorization from the grain board to buy up to two hundred tonnes of paddy from the end of December and successfully purchased all the rice brought to markets frequented by such intermediaries (AOM RST *IB 92 Résident Thai Binh à Résident Hadong, Hung Yen, Jan. 21, 1945). From this distance it is hard to identify which social elements facilitated the pernicious actions of rice speculators, but it certainly smacks of government malfeasance at the provincial level.

Describing the local scene as a site of "misery," in late February Chauvet entered into a verbal duel with the resident of Thai Binh on how to manage the crisis, now slipping out of control. First, he wished to know whether peasant farmers of Thai Binh still had the wherewithal to proceed with seed purchase. Then he excoriated the official for not replying to his earlier request with precision as to local peasants' financial means. As he declaimed, "The 400,000 people of your province are in urgent need of assistance. But you have not even offered exact information as to the food situation in your province; you have simply made an appeal for assistance." In no uncertain terms, he continued, "I cannot dissimulate in underscoring that you have not offered timely information on the deplorable state of the harvest in certain circumscriptions of the province which you administer." "In sum," Chauvet scolded, "you were late in reporting upon a difficult situation in your province, especially after the harvest was underway." Without beating around the bush, Chauvet then set down the measures to be taken. First, restitute the three-thousand-tonne levy to the people of the worst-afflicted zone, a measure which should enable them the means of survival for one month. Second, redistribute the four thousand and eventually five thousand tonnes of rice still blocked in your province, which should be able to tide the population over until the beginning of May. As for the timing of this distribution, allocate one thousand tonnes at the end of February, three thousand tonnes at the beginning of April; and several hundred tonnes for provincial works employing healthy labor and as supplement rations. As Chauvet explained, he was "examining" the possibility of reducing to three thousand tonnes the amount required to deliver to the Comptoir des Céréales at Nam Dinh otherwise fixed at four thousand tonnes. Third, according to the rhythm of rice arrivals from Cochinchina, he was prepared to offer aid in proportion to needs in Nam Dinh ("but unlikely to be large"). Fourth, he granted thirty thousand piasters for soup kitchens (AOM RST *IB 424–425 Chauvet à Résident Thai Binh, Feb. 23, 1945).

We wonder whether this exchange was a clash of egos or a case of paralyzed bureaucracy, especially as Chauvet virtually conceded all the demands made by the resident of Nam Binh, who appeared to have sulked or retreated in the face of inaction on the part of Hanoi. The telephone appears to have been working, and they had been talking. It appears that the resident wished to do away with the iniquitous levy altogether, whereas Chauvet was defensive about this burden, albeit depending on information and circumstances. More is the regret that the hapless population of Nam Binh could not have been granted redress immediately when the crisis broke or at the first signs of harvest failure and not the Ides of March or, actually, February, the tragic Tet of 1945.

CENTRAL-LEVEL CRISIS MANAGEMENT

There is no doubt that, once in the driving seat, Resident Superior Chauvet sought to galvanize the lower echelons of the administration into action, although he was not about to lift the Japanese-imposed levies either. On January 8, 1945, Chauvet issued new instructions to all residents with respect to procedures to follow on data collection and sharing which is regarded as the harvest campaign. It is surprising, however, that no such measures were in place. Were his predecessors complaisant in this regard? First, he requested weekly reports to be submitted to the grain board as to the tonnage remaining in each province owing to lack of transport. Second, he requested the residents to cable the grain board their data on the third and eighteenth of the month of the total harvest for the preceding fifteen-day period. In other words, he sought province-wide data for fifteen-day periods on all rice harvested (paddy) in tonnage, indicating first or second harvest if applicable (AOM RST *IB 92 Chauvet à Résidents, Jan. 8, 1945).

On the same day, Chauvet also authorized the president of the grain board to confront holders of nondeclared stocks of paddy. Once uncovered, such stocks were to be reserved for "our primordial needs," especially in taking into account the "difficult provinces" where the stocks had yet to be distributed. As Chauvet, remarked, "It was a case of offering relief to the poorest inhabitants of the region" by taking it away from "the most culpable and delinquent," even if this meant using repressive measures against defaulters (AOM RST *IB 92 94/05/06 Chauvet à Résident Hadong, Jan. 8, 1945).

Reporting on the food situation as it stood in the height of winter in 1945, as Chauvet declaimed, "The economic situation is known to you. If the Tonkin peasant of certain overcrowded regions is unfortunate and undernourished in normal times and only receives half the ration of rice necessary, the present situation is of particularly grave character." Owing to the rigorous and delayed cold season prevailing that winter, he noted, many of the seedlings had been frozen. Not only was the current harvest affected by a month's delay, but the month of July would have to be covered by the harvest of the tenth month of 1944. Even so, he continued, "one must anticipate a deficit in the production of paddy." With a view to needs, Chauvet specified, "We thus foresee a need for 7,000 tonnes supplement (for the July consumption), for the disaster-struck provinces and towns and with arrivals from the Cochinchina rail line to cover the soudure." Once again, he declared, "I advise that the quantities collected for the harvest of the 10th month, even if everything goes well, will not even cover urban consumption (Hanoi-Haiphong) on the actual basis of need (monthly ration of 9 kg. per person) which, until June, should include all supplies arriving from sea and rail used to supply deficit provinces." Concluding this dispatch, he wrote, "The imperative to cover the month of July will require 7,000 tonnes of these arrivals which should be augmented to the maximum to avoid a reduction in supply to the needy provinces" (AOM RST *IB/96 18/425, Chauvet à GG, Hanoi, Feb. 20, 1945).

Rice Stores

The practice of storing rice has a long history in Vietnam and in other cultures, so the state-level management of rice stores should not necessarily be controversial. Even so, the diversion of rice for noncivilian use in Indochina entered postwar propaganda recriminations. There is reason to believe that, ahead of the Japanese *coup de force*, elements of the French military had been discreetly creating rice stockpiles. We can assume that the Japanese military in Indochina at large did so in an even more systematic fashion, especially as it prepared for the contingency of a feared American invasion.

Obviously, the stockpiling of rice outside of the purvey of the grain board undermined the best reporting and contingency planning by diminishing the availability of rice entering the ration system or even the marketplace. Our data on rice stores is deficient, but we know that the grain board managed at least a dozen, if not dozens, of stores across Tonkin, including urban areas. For example, storehouse no. 7 in Hanoi held fifty-one tonnes of rice in December 1944. By January1945, this figure had been increased to 794 tonnes. At the same time, storehouse no. 9 held 1,200 tonnes. Typically, the rice was placed in separate lots, each indicating weight and the date the rice entered the store. The quality of the rice was another question. Frequently, as noted, the rice held in no. 9 was unfit for human consumption. Ideally, the rice would remain in store only for a period of between three and six months, pending replenishment of stock, but this requirement had obviously been breached to the detriment of rice quality. To remedy the situation, as Chauvet ordered, it was imperative to conduct regular checks of the storehouses to monitor condition and especially to check against excessive moisture. He now required the grain board to draw up monthly tabulations for each *magasin*, including such vital data as warehouse number, surplus stock from the first day of each month, the previous month, and the date of entry of the oldest stock. He requested the president of the grain board and the secretary general to sign off in person on the records and not some "subaltern irresponsible official" not held accountable for his decisions (AOM RST *1B 93 Chauvet, note, Jan. 19, 1945). This was strong language and an important administrative check, suggesting a record of mismanagement of the storehouses or worse.

On January 31, 1945, Chauvet set in motion a meeting that would bring together all the key administrators of the worst-affected provinces, namely Nam Dinh, Thai Binh, and Bac Giang. As he inferred, coordination was lacking between the local cereals section of the economic services and the grain board. Rightly, he pointed out, the *chefs de provinces* lacked a big-picture view of the generalized problems facing Tonkin, "of which only the centralized services of the Resident Superior and myself" have full knowledge (AOM RST *IB 92 Chauvet à GG, Hanoi, Jan. 31, 1945). Undoubtedly, Chauvet was correct in that he alone commanded a big-picture view and—so we could say—the buck literally stopped with him (and his distant Japanese counterparts who seemed only to react to events rather than guide them when it came to public administration or social needs of the population).

In a rare communication on military rice stores entering the Tonkin archive, Chauvet made it known to the resident of Son La that he had received instructions from the military authority of its intention to create food stocks, especially paddy, on the right bank of the Black River as well as in the town of Son La. As explained, these depots would serve to supply army units operating in these areas "in line with the evolution of the political situation." Chauvet duly gave him the go-ahead along with guarantees of protection in the event of "serious and exceptional problems" (AOM RST *1B 424–426 Chauvet à Résident, Sonla, Feb. 12, 1945). While, as Chauvet well knew, the military were preparing for the imminence of a Japanese military takeover, he might also have had in mind the prospect of Viet Minh orchestrated attacks on the rice stores, because that is precisely what was already transpiring in certain locations.

Mobilizing the Junk Fleet

Importantly, in mid-January 1945, Resident Superior Chauvet set in motion a number of key decisions as to a new—desperate, actually—logistics operation to rescue the population of northern Vietnam. The fate of millions was in his hands. As he informed the governor general on January 20, the merchant marine was preparing the imminent dispatch from Tonkin to Saigon of oceangoing junks, each over twenty tonnes in capacity, to lade rice for the return journey north. Included were a small number of larger-capacity junks charged with lading both rice and sugar (crystallized and red). With Danang as a staging point, the junks would return to Nam Dinh or other lower delta ports. In stressing the urgency of the situation, as Chauvet pointed out, "If the Tonkin peasant of the overpopulated regions is unfortunate and undernourished in normal times and receiving scarcely half the necessary amount of rice needed to survive, then the present situation is of particularly serious character" (AOM RST *IB 9218/425 Chauvet à GG, Hanoi, Feb. 20, 1945). In the meantime, he sought to gather more complete information on river junks as well as oceangoing junks, their numbers, and their capacities.

As Chauvet clarified, although the largest part of (southern) rice stocks had already been dispatched to Danang by junk and rail, it would be highly desirable that the larger, oceangoing junks be commissioned to transport the near totality of the Cochinchina rice directly to the north, especially as Annam had already sent its own fleet of oceangoing junks south to load rice. Relative to Annam with its well-endowed fleet, Tonkin was disadvantaged, especially as transport statistics for January 1945 revealed that the dispatch of rice for the grain board in Tonkin reached only 1,630 tonnes versus 2,277 tonnes for Annam. To compensate, approximately two-thirds of rice sent by rail from Saigon should be earmarked for Tonkin, with one-third dedicated for Annam. As Chauvet further pointed out, the tenth-month harvest for 1944 was abnormal "and does not even cover urban consumption" (fixed at nine kilograms monthly per person through June), even allowing for the amount expected to arrive by rail and junk. Just to cover the rice needs for the month of July required a total of seven thousand tonnes which had to be augmented to the maximum to avoid reducing supply in the worst-affected provinces (AOM RST *IB 9218/425 Chauvet à GG, Hanoi, Feb. 20, 1945).

As the situation evolved, the colonial administration declared the transport of rice as virtually the number one priority. Both rail and maritime transport were still considered viable at this stage. Given that transport by sea was less rapid than by rail, the governor general requested that all nonindispensable traffic be rejected and that all other demands for transport be justified unless urgent. Right off, he commanded the dispatch of 170 tonnes of value-added food (rice flour, maize flour, salted fish, etc.) to be consigned north by rail.

Given the needs of Tonkin for rice, the figure of one thousand tonnes of rice as registered in February represented a minimum figure. Allowing that a range of smaller junks (under twenty tonnes) had already been dispatched to collect rice stored at Danang, it was now imperative to deploy junks of over eighty tonnes in capacity to satisfy the "vital economic interest." Anticipating a timely delivery of the rice, Chauvet also looked to provincial distribution and transportation pending its arrival. To this end, he earmarked one hundred tonnes of rice for Lang Son and another one hundred tonnes for Phu Lang Thuang (AOM RST *IB/ 98 Chauvet à Services Economique, Hanoi, Feb. 20, 1945).

On February 22, Chauvet sought weekly updates on the economic needs of the residents of Vinh, Thanh Hoa, and Nam Dinh. With respect to Vinh, he sought vital data on the tonnage of rice arriving from Cochinchina on the account of Tonkin, the total amount of rice freighted by rail or junk, the total tonnage exported per week, and the quality of stock held in Vinh on account of Tonkin. From Thanh Hoa, he sought information on the total quantity of rice entering the harbor, the weekly amount, and the quality. Similar information was also demanded from Nam Dinh (AOM RST *IB/98 Chauvet à Services de Céréales, Hanoi, Feb. 22, 1945).

As colonial sources confirm, by late February a small number of junks had sailed south to take on rice stored at Ben Thuy on the Ca River, near Vinh. These junks included dedicated oceangoing junks belonging to the customs service, including one already sent from Ca Cha to Ben Thuy, with other junks commissioned to haul rice from Ben Thuy to Nam Dinh and Ben Thuy-Haiphong (AOM RST 1B/9 Allimand à Douanes et Régies, Hanoi, Feb. 26, 1945). In a letter of February 28, Chauvet also confirmed that under the auspices of the merchant marine, the junks were already under way and the actual purchase of the rice by credit duly arranged. Notably, the Saigon Committee for Cereals had agreed to dispatch ten thousand to fifteen thousand tonnes by sea, with the maximum of tonnage of rice reserved for Nam Dinh and Haiphong (AOM RST *IB 92 18/ 425, Chauvet à GG, Hanoi, Feb. 28, 1945).

Accordingly, Chauvet drew up a schema of needs by affected province in Tonkin. These requirements were (in tonnes), Nam Dinh, nine thousand; Thai Binh, four thousand; Ninh Binh, one thousand; and urban and collective centers, seven thousand—or a total of twenty-one thousand tonnes. Added to this were local purchases, 1,600 tonnes and arrivals by rail, 6,000 tonnes, or a total of 7,600 tonnes. This added up to a grand total of 13,400 tonnes. Chauvet also drew up a strict distribution timetable with the rider that food supply had to be given the highest priority so that the arrivals would not take place later than the dates indicated (AOM RST *IB 92 18/ 425, Chauvet à GG, Hanoi, Feb. 28, 1945).

In this plan, consumption for March–April (9,000 tonnes) would be covered by local purchase (1,600 tonnes) and rail arrivals (6,000 tonnes), or a total of 7,600 tonnes. Also, in this timetable, it was deemed imperative that maritime deliveries arrive before March 15 (4,400 tonnes), before April 15 (1,500 tonnes), and before June 15 (7,500 tonnes), or a total of 13,600 tonnes. As Chauvet warned, "The most critical period for the population of the disaster-stricken provinces will be March 15 to the end of the month of May" (AOM RST *IB 92 18/ 425, Chauvet à GG, Hanoi, Feb. 28, 1945). (See table 8.1.)

Although February was outside of the typhoon season, we have to consider the logistics of junk transport. Traditionally, the official grain junks servicing Hue followed a Chinese astrological calendar governing departures, one month down, and one month up (see Woodside 1971, 140). In the best of conditions, a return journey from Haiphong or even from Danang to Saigon could take many weeks. Setting aside unfavorable winds and currents, a range of hazards awaited Chauvet's junks as well, namely Allied attacks and piracy. And even having arrived south in Danang or Saigon, the junks also faced the unexpected administrative vacuum preceding out of the Japanese military takeover. What went wrong with Chauvet's timetable? Well, we don't know. Chauvet himself shared the fate of his countrymen following Operation Meigo, the abrupt Japanese military takeover of March 9, 1945. While, as Marr (1997, 63) points out, middle- and lower-level French officials remained at their desks, it is also clear that top-level French management was out of the picture.

A Warning to the United States

US bombing of the Red River delta also roused the concern of the Gaullist French head of mission and intelligence unit (M5) in Kunming, Major Jean Sainteny. Sainteny's history lesson/warning of July 1945 in the form of a letter directed at the US Air Force and the Washington government could not have been better timed. Describing himself as *chef d'escadrons* (squadron leader) and *chef de la base de Kunming*, Sainteny warned that not only was the delta population in the throes of a devastating famine, but survivors were

Table 8.1. Resident Superior Chauvet's Timetable for Famine Relief for Tonkin, 1945 (by Month), in Tonnes of Rice Imported from Cochinchina

	March	*April*	*May*	*June*	*July*	*Total*
Nam Dinh	2,000	2,600	2,500	1,500	500	9,100
Thai Binh	1,600	2,400	0	0	0	4,000
Ninh Binh	0	500	500	0	0	1,000
Cities	0	0	0	0	7,000	7,000

Source: AOM RST *18/ 425, Resident Superior Chauvet à Gouverneur Général, Hanoi, Feb. 28, 1945.

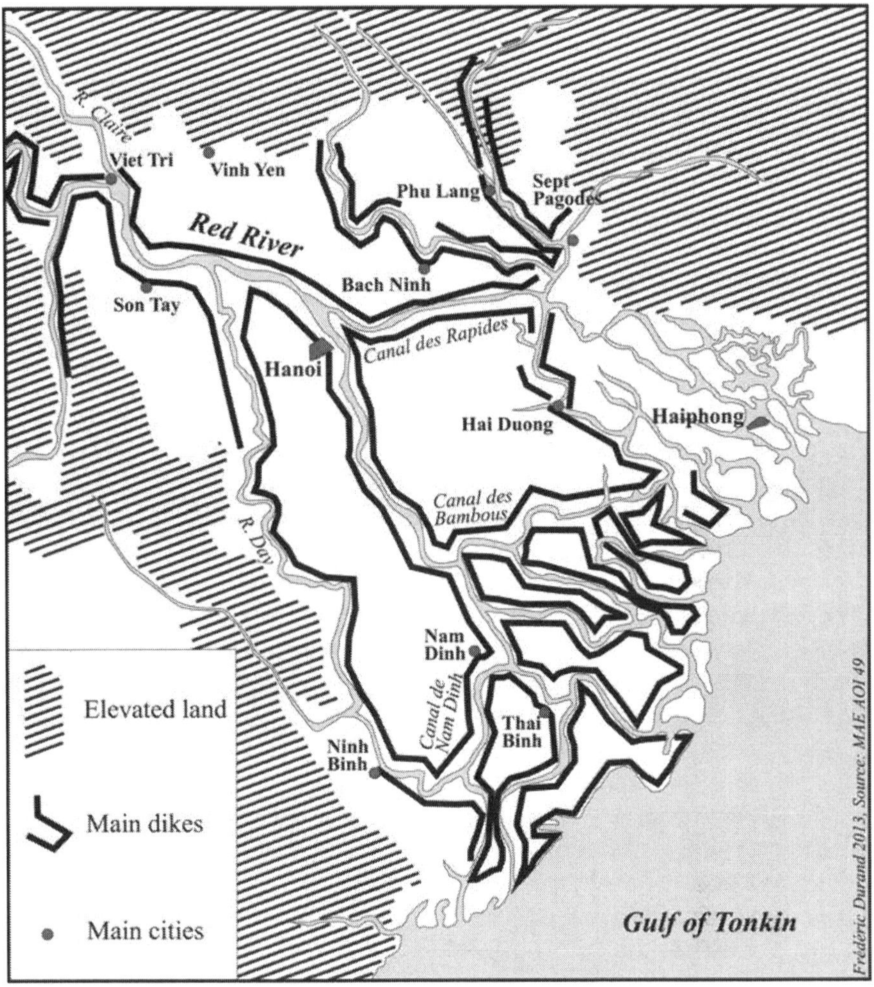

Red River Delta Dikes Deemed Vulnerable to American Wartime Bombing, Jean Sainteny, Head of Free French Intelligence, Kunming, China, July 1945

also hostage to virtual elimination through flooding and disease. As Sainteny well understood, further bombing damage to the dikes at this critical juncture would impose a devastating blow on even famine survivors, along with untold numbers of others.

Besides pointing out the extreme population density of the northern delta, the French intelligence chief also recorded that reaching back to the eleventh century under the Ly dynasty, a system of dikes along the Red River and its tributaries had reached a length of nine hundred kilometers by 1940. Owing to French hydraulic works, the total volume of water contained by these dikes reached twenty million cubic meters, rising to eighty-five million in 1940. While the best opinion of hydrologists held that it was a mistake on the part of the French to perpetuate and develop this system of dikes, he asserted there was no turning back, short of evacuating eight million people from the delta. Nevertheless, since 1926, the accomplishment of this "stupendous work" had prevented a recurrence of major flooding. (That was not exactly true because the floods of 1937 and 1944 severely tested the system.) A major consequence of the dike system was that the river "exhausted its bed," meaning that for most of the year the water level was higher than the delta. Supported by a network of master dikes alongside lesser dikes, vast sunken *casiers* (polders) lay embedded behind earthen walls. The largest of the polders in the central delta were partly bounded by the Canal des Rapides and Bambous, respectively. Such was the delicate hydraulic balance that the water did not even flow into the sea. This Sainteny illustrated with a detailed map. The master dikes were capable of containing a flood of 13 meters with the maximum high of 12.40 meters reached in the flood of March 12, 1940. The rupture of a single dike could flood an entire compartment; a dozen breaches could submerge the entire delta. The flat terrain offered no refuge. It could be taken for granted that the specter of cholera would appear after the flood and, with even greater consequence, famine. As Sainteny explained, all the locals upheld a perfect understanding of the vital need to protect the dikes. At the time of floods, the entire population, from the mandarins to the most humble, worked day and night to consolidate the barrage against a suspected breach. In the Annam penal code, the death penalty was imposed on those who defaulted on the maintenance of the dikes. As Sainteny wrote, "While we are in charge, constant surveillance is necessary; the least défaillance (failure) could bring about a catastrophe" (MAE AOI 49 "Note au sujèt des digues du Tonkin," Sainteny, PAC/TQ/6 Mission Militaire Française de Kunming, July 15, 1945).

To make his point, Sainteny offered the single example of the actions of the US Fourteenth Air Force during the preceding autumn. In seeking to destroy the Ham Rong/Ham Hong (dragon jaw) bridge (ten kilometers north of Thanh Hoa), the dike on the right side of the Song Ma (Ma River) was damaged by bombing.[4] Then, as now, the strategic Thanh Hoa bridge allowing both road and rail traffic served as the key intraregional communication link connecting the southern perimeter of the Red River delta with northern Annam. In November 1944, following a "sudden and unexpected" flood (a reference to the impact of the typhoon of that month), the dikes gave way at this location. The northern part of Thanh Hoa Province was submerged for ten days and the harvest destroyed. Normally an exporter of rice, the area was subject to a famine which took several thousands of victims. As Sainteny well understood, as a consequence of the rupture in communication links between northern and southern Vietnam, Tonkin could not easily be reprovisioned with rice from outside, that the flood of August took a great toll on the tenth-month harvest, jeopardizing the upcoming fifth-month harvest, that the northern delta area was producing only 60 percent of its rice requirements, and that the people of Tonkin were undernourished (MAE AOI 49 "Note au sujèt des digues du Tonkin," Sainteny, PAC/TQ/6 Mission Militaire Française de Kunming, July 15, 1945).

The gravity of the situation was initially conveyed on August 1, 1945, by the French military mission in Kunming to the commander of the US Fourteenth Air Force (Chennault) and repeated on August 7 by the French embassy in Washington in a *démarche* to acting US secretary of state Joseph C. Grew. In the event, Grew duly informed the secretary of state that serial bombardment of the dikes in the Red River delta—as evidently contemplated by US military planners—would cause "formidable danger to the population of this area." This was no understatement. At risk were the lives of eight million people in densely populated land crosscut by dikes built up over the centuries (SWNCC, 35 Crew to Secretary of State, Aug. 6, 1945). Ironically, the question of bombing of the dikes was revisited by Pentagon planners in the 1960s, just as nuclear options were weighed in some quarters.

There is something of a disconnect between Sainteny's report of mid-July 1945 and the reality of famine, which had already struck in the delta, in part as a consequence of earlier bombing of vital infrastructure. Even if he was short on local details, his big-picture view of the general vulnerability of the delta to repeated shocks, manmade or natural, along with his warning to the Fourteenth Air Force was not misplaced, and perhaps in this light he might be held as a protector of the Vietnamese people from an even greater calamity, even if it remains to establish whether or not the US actually had further plans to bomb the dikes or associated targets at that time (as they certainly did twenty years later). Certainly there were no other voices on the French or American side making these bald and shocking facts alive.

With the discussion weighted on top-level famine management concerns, the data is far less revealing of local impacts. Still, in the following pages I seek to tease out the actual consequences of Chauvet's orders and instructions, at least as carried through following the Japanese takeover and the installation of the "puppet" Tran Trong Kim administration in Annam, revisiting the question of overall social impacts of the famine in a final section.

THE JAPANESE TAKEOVER AND THE FAILURE OF FAMINE MANAGEMENT

Did the junk fleet even arrive back in northern Vietnam? If so, was there any administrative structure still in place that was capable of receiving and distributing the rice? Were the Viet Minh capable of filling this vacuum? Doubtful.

Still, the Japanese stepped into the shoes of the French administration. To wit, the existence (and nonarrival) of a fleet of one hundred junks was revealed by a communication of April 26 between Nishimura, the top Japanese civilian official in Hanoi, and Ambassador Yokoyama in Hue. As Marr (1997, 101–3) explains, various reactive and ad hoc measures were taken to release rice stocks and to locate the missing shipments. In the event, the junk fleet bringing relief only began to arrive in the north in late July, "by which time the immediate crisis had passed." Why was this? Marr does not exactly explain the delay at the southern end but does reveal that certain of the junks had been robbed for want of guards, while other junks had been commandeered by the Viet Minh in Quang Ngai, and other cargoes spoiled, but this cannot be the entire explanation. Looking back at Chauvet's timetable, all the deadlines were missed, from the expected rail arrivals necessary to tide the population over for the months of March–April, not to mention the gap created by the delayed arrival of the junk fleet, through April–July, as the famine ran its course. Perhaps even the departure could have been hastened, as every day delayed led to an exponential increase in fatalities. If Resident Superior Chauvet and his circle did not suffer some sense of *crise morale* for the tragedy to follow, then it would be surprising. It was not just a case of failed humanitarianism but a derailed logistics operation that was overwhelmed by political events.

Undoubtedly the Japanese handling of the Great Famine in the period between the March 9, 1945, military takeover and the August Revolution is the least well documented. No scholar to my knowledge has discovered or exploited Japanese-language documentation on this period, and we may well ask why, unless the answer is that the concerned authorities simply shredded documents to avoid incrimination. As a result, the investigator into these terrible months has little to go by aside from the usual propaganda flourishes. But it was also the period when mortality rates increased exponentially with the failure of the 1945 fifth-month harvest, as earlier predicted by the French administration. It was also the tipping point for the Viet Minh in winning the battle for hearts and minds, to parody the language of Americans in the Vietnam War some fourteen years later.

As Marr (1997, 100) acknowledges, although they also opened the floodgates on famine victims entering Hanoi, the Japanese ignored the famine for at least two weeks following the coup. Meanwhile, Nishimura ordered a reversion to 1944 rules on the compulsory sale of rice. Neither, for that matter, could we expect any sense of urgency on the waterfront in postcoup Saigon (or Danang) at a time when the junks should have been lading rice for the return journey.

A little over a month after the military takeover, and with the French administration interned, as Radio Saigon blandly reported, "The last season in Tonkin and north Annam has been insufficient owing to lack of water and the food situation in these regions is greatly insufficient (three words missing)." The inhabitants of the eastern part of Tonkin and the northern part of Annam are in a "very difficult situation." As the broadcast continued, listeners heard that Minoda Fujio, the Japanese-installed governor of Cochinchina, had recently authorized the creation of a comité de secours (mutual-aid committee) for northern Indochina (headed by an evidently pro-Wang Jingwei eminence from the Chinese community). Concluding, the broadcast intoned, "The Japanese authorities will do all possible to participate in relief works and distribute rice among the unfortunate population" (MAE AOI 26, DGER; Marr 1997, 100). Obviously there was much understatement and obfuscation in this broadcast, as propaganda and misinformation still ruled the airwaves.

Three weeks later, the DGER learned from Radio Saigon that because of bad harvests, the food situation in Tonkin and north Annam was "critical," and heard of reports of drought in Luang Prabang. Acknowledging the creation of the mutual-aid committee, the DGER advised, "The precarious means of transport renders the results doubtful" (MAE AOI DGER à Comité de L'Indochine, no. 112, Paris, May 18, 1945). Tragically, as it played out, the DGER assessment was correct. The famine continued until June 1945 before ending completely (though the struggle over rice could hardly have stopped that abruptly, as demonstrated below).

Crisis Management under the Tran Trong Kim Administration

With the advent of the Tran Trong Kim administration, installed in Hue on April 17, 1945, the Japanese authorities agreed to give up the system of compulsory deliveries. They also canceled all the former stipulations concerning paddy and rice. They then turned on speculators, using such threats as the death penalty and temporarily reducing the price of rice in Hanoi from six hundred to four hundred piasters per quintal. Under the new dispensation, only the administration was authorized to buy rice or paddy directly from the producer but offered some flexibility for small quantities to expedite the provisioning of individuals. As Nguyen The Anh (1998a, 218–19) concedes, in theory, the situation of farmers should have improved through an overhauling of the system of prices paid to producers, five times higher than paid under the previous regime. Relief was also brought to small farmers through Emperor Bao Dai's decree of May 3, 1945, allowing a moratorium to debtors on agricultural loans. The question of relief from the south was also revisited by the equipment minister, Nguyen Huu Thu, who traveled to Saigon in June 1945 to negotiate with the Japanese the details of rice transport from south to north. The question of migration by northerners to the south was also discussed. An active press campaign in the south also raised awareness as to the needs of the north, kicking off a mutual-aid committee and "a veritable upsurge of national solidarity" over the relief issue. Certain junk traffic might have been restored. These measures, in conjunction with some alleviation of the famine following the gathering of the harvest of the fifth month, allowed a temporary reprieve to the crisis. With the introduction of free food distribution, the price of rice also fell. As Nguyen The Anh (1998a, 218–20) allows, the Tran Trong Kim administration and Vietnamese in general were actually more proactive in managing the crisis than the French or the Japanese, although the Japanese were still the masters of the overall situation. In any case, the respite would be short-lived.

SOCIAL IMPACTS OF THE FAMINE

For an event of biblical proportions, surprisingly very little documentation on the actual famine and suffering it caused remains. We simply lack a province-by-province or town-by-town accounting of mortality, including victim vulnerability by age and gender, especially as not all suffered equally. As studied by Dikötter (2010, 245–63), this was definitely the case in China during the Great Leap Forward famine with regard to children, women, and the elderly. We also need to know more about village abandonment, rural beggary, vagabondage, and rural crime such as studied by Jordan (1996, 97, 115) with reference to the great famine that struck northern Europe in the fourteenth century.

Strange Diet

The same applies to "strange diets," or the attempt by victims of famines to make up the loss of regular food by recourse to such items as plants, bark, leather, cloth, grubs, and, in extreme cases, cadavers (although some of this behavior is recorded in press accounts and even novels about the event in Vietnam, themselves recreations of some version of popular memory).

Although we lack basic information on deteriorating diet on an individual level such as would enable us to construct a chronology as the famine ran its course, one report of December 1944 from Nam Dinh, the province at the vortex of the Great Famine, is revealing. Writing well before mass starvation set in, an anonymous Vietnamese editorialist of the Hanoi newspaper *Tin Moi* (Dec. 6, 1944) observed, "We Vietnamese must have a strong stomach capable of digesting bad rice mixed with paddy and stones and bits of brick, provided that the rice is well chewed." Seeking to expose the actions of fraudulent rice merchants, the writer also allowed that local Europeans were also obliged to eat the same low-quality fare. Even following complaints, the quality of the rice remained the same, mixed with paddy and broken grain (AOM Tonkin *IB 13434 Résident France, Nam Dinh, Dec. 19, 1944).

Another French report of early February 1945 from Thai Binh, then experiencing a 75–90 percent crop failure of the tenth-month 1944 harvest, found the peasantry reduced to scavenging "anything they can eat." We are not offered details on diet, but some survived on a kind of "paddy porridge," or porridge made from unhusked paddy, grilled to turn it into balls of flour that were in turn mixed with water to produce a rice porridge (AOM RST *IB 18/425 "Rapport d'inspecteur du Thai Binh," Feb. 3, 1945). Obviously, subsidiary crops were missing from this diet, as one Duy Hoa, a literate peasant from Ninh Binh, complained in a private letter, "Nothing remains for our consumption, we lack potatoes and maize. We have only a single bowl of rice. But when the soudure arrives, where shall we find rice to survive? Having lost our harvest, the administration has no pity on us" (AOM RST *IB 218/425 Résident Ninh Binh, Duy Hoa letter, Feb. 2, 1945).

Next to rice, corn was a backstop in the peasant diet and often grown as a supplementary crop on more hilly ground or outside the delta. But as the food shortage began to bite, even the export of maize across the Annam boundary was proscribed by a law of December 11, 1944, although manioc, another staple in times of stress, was not controlled. In early 1945, Thanh Hoa province was identified as having a small exportable surplus of two hundred tonnes of maize, and this amount was tapped for "sale" in Nam Dinh to the "poorest" inhabitants of the province. As Chauvet commented, although this quantity of corn was relatively small, its appearance on the marketplace in Nam Dinh would help to stabilize the price of rice during the Tet season. The need to keep up food supply to the most vulnerable regions was to be encouraged (AOM RST *IB/98 Chauvet à GG, Hanoi, Feb. 1, 1945). In normal times, Tonkin also produced a corn surplus, so the need to outsource corn to Annam also raises the question of why corn was not available in Tonkin, unless it too had been sidelined in the push to grow jute and other industrial crops.

As the famine progressed, starving people resorted to eating a "strange diet," including bran, "cattle cake," vegetables, banana bulbs, hibiscus leaves, meat, and fish when available. But according to Pham Cao Duong (1985, 182), these foods lacked the necessary nourishment, with most of the famine victims succumbing to beriberi. Cannibalism then made an appearance. Citing Vu Quoc Thuc in *l'Economie communaliste* (1951), he writes that as early as December 1944, long lines of famished peasants entered Hanoi, Haiphong, and Nam Dinh, leaving the sidewalks strewn with beggars and corpses. In heavily hit Nan Dinh and Thai Binh Provinces, certain villages were nearly abandoned.

Interviewed for an international television series in 1981, Tran Duy Hung, a former medical student in Hanoi requested by Ho Chi Minh to serve as mayor of Hanoi, offers possibly the most authentic account of the famine as it played out in the capital. Describing the situation of Tet of 1945 and the desperate inrush into Hanoi of starving masses from such provinces as Nam Dinh, Thai Binh, Thanh Hoa, and Hung Yen, he relates:

> But before they managed to arrive in Hanoi they had already spent many days on the road, carrying each other along the way, without anything to eat. The grown ups were carrying their children in baskets. By that time, at least 40,000 starving poor peasants in our estimate arrived in Hanoi to beg for food and to wait for handouts, for alms. We called it alms at the time.
>
> They were lying about all over the streets, except for the streets where the French residences were. They lay on the pavements. And it was a particularly cold year that year. But at that time we could not do everything to help them. Not only that the French did not organize any hunger relief, but the Japanese specifically forbade us to carry out any hunger relief effort of our own.
>
> But even if the French had wanted to organize some hunger relief, they would not have been able to obtain any rice anyway. Hanoi was full of agonizing sights at the time. People dug into the garbage dumps in order find any edible thing at all: Banana peels, tangerine peels, discarded greens and vegetable, and so on. They also ate rats. But this was not enough to keep them alive. Therefore, we witnessed a lot of heart rending scenes.
>
> Every morning when we opened our door, we saw five to seven corpses of people who had died the night before. At that time I was already a doctor but I was also a Boy Scout master. Hence, I and others organized the boy scouts to get rice from their families to give out to the hungry people in a marketplace. But this really did not help that much. There were just so many starving people and they just dropped dead everywhere. So we had to organize teams to pick up the corpses and buried them (Tran Duy Hung 1981, translation as given).

Le Manh Hung (2004, 253) also offers a firsthand report by a French official of April 1945 on the "starvation roads" of living corpses flocking to provincial towns and cities, saying they were such that they made one feel "ashamed to be a human being." Heat loss and progressive malnutrition sapped away at the miserable population. Typically, in famine situations, not all die of hunger; there are secondary causes as well, such as dysentery, fever, and typhus. But it is striking as well that mass epidemic is not mentioned here or in the literature as a major cause of death.

The Specter of Epidemic

It is probably not inconsequential that Louis Pasteur remains an icon in postrevolutionary Vietnam (for example, Pasteur Avenue in Saigon today), especially as the French brought to bear their scientific and medical knowledge on basic health, disease control, and especially control of epidemics, which, as intimated, have a long and devastating history in Vietnam and were not completely eliminated during colonial times. As Hanoi was alerted in early February 1945, *la peste* (plague) had been detected in south Annam, understood to have been transmitted through sacks of rice sourced from Cholon. This was potentially a worst-case scenario. Rats were identified as the carrier, and the instruction went out immediately to take measures against the introduction of rats into northern Vietnam through rice transport. In practical terms, every rice sack had to be examined at the moment of unloading, whether by train or by junk. Sailors and junk personnel showing signs of illness had to be hospitalized immediately (AOM RST *IB 424–425 Chauvet à Résident Maire, Hanoi, Feb. 10, 1945).

As far as is known, these control measures worked, and plague did not reach northern Vietnam (although we have noted the presence of typhus). In any case, the role of disease in aggravating the Great Famine is an underresearched area. But weakened by lack of calorific intake, diarrhea, and dehydration, many more died in such circumstances. Lingering in a weakened condition for weeks, debilitated by "strange diet," and fatally deprived of caloric intake, the victims quickly succumbed to starvation. In other words, mortality peaked at the end of the cycle necessary to sustain life. At least this is the broad clinical pattern on mortality as elaborated by Dikötter (2010, 274–86) with respect to China's Great Leap famine and entirely applicable to the Vietnam case.

Why would Vietnam be spared a major epidemic at this juncture, given a historic prevalence of epidemics accompanying famine events? Granted that the Great Famine was, after all, a starvation event, recovery following a devastating demographic decline was remarkably rapid, suggesting administrative intervention in the way of successful disease control. In contrast to famines arising from conflict situations, public administration infrastructure was intact in Tonkin, even through the Japanese military occupation. The American bombing aside, it was not a direct war zone. It remains to be studied, but public hospitals along with health and quarantine services continued to function to the extent that they could cope. Corpses were collected in the streets of Hanoi in the interest of disease control and, presumably, communal-level authorities disposed of the dead, just as the living adopted a range of coping mechanisms in part habituated by past experience of such events. Even so, a cohort of survivors among youth, especially, would have borne the effects of malnutrition throughout their life cycle.

CONCLUSION

For the people of the Red River delta and even parts of north-central Vietnam, the timing of the Japanese military coup of March 9, 1945, was a disaster. It could not have been worse. Threat of famine was not an unknown event; it was omnipresent in certain zones, especially after droughts and floods, it had been mitigated in 1937–38 with diligence on the part of the administration, and there were many finely honed coping mechanisms applied by local hamlets and communities since time immemorial. But in late 1944–early 1945, as we have seen, the crisis became one of a generational or even millennial order if viewed over the long-term period. Why was this? Even setting aside demographic pressures, massive Japanese grain exports or stockpiling in Saigon, and Allied interdiction of rail communication, the ability of a peasant-producer in rural northern Vietnam in 1944–45 to sustain a livelihood was threatened by a series of externally imposed impositions or shocks. Alongside the familiar and resented head taxes and other imposts was the rice levy. For those on the brink of subsistence—the mass of peasant-producers, already pushed to the wall by floods and typhoons of 1944—the levy was the last (rice) straw. But even where a surplus could be diverted to the marketplace, speculators and opportunists moved in by diverting rice to an illegal black market, further driving up prices and sinking even those with fixed incomes—the petty salariat, the day workers, and others. As seen, many among the most indigent and vulnerable—and they included women and children—began turning up in the streets of provincial towns and even Hanoi. For them, begging, scavenging, theft, and even brigandry were the only response. Viet Minh recruitment arising out of the famine is another story. At the end of the day, Chauvet's tight logistics rescue operation failed. His actions and responses were not necessarily bad or ill judged, and certainly his was not just another tightfisted remedial welfare operation. Humanitarian concerns were uppermost in the planning of the rescue operation, even allowing that some broader sense of colonial noblesse oblige was also at play. No less, Sainteny's concerns were for the millions (and French honor). Notwithstanding different perspectives, undoubtedly both individuals knew that the real winner emerging from this tragedy would be the Viet Minh.

Although Hanoi, together with a number of independent researchers, remains equivocal in apportioning blame to both French and Japanese, it has to be said that French and Japanese motives in stockpiling rice differed in fundamentals and answered entirely different needs. It also has to be said that even if northern Vietnam had become increasingly dependent on imports of southern rice over the previous two decades, France and the Pasteur Institute can hardly be blamed for the demographic increase in the north. The wild card in this equation was, of course, the US recourse to bombing in Indochina that often did not discriminate between civilian and military targets. As mentioned, the Americans were warned by the French of the consequences of destroying dikes in the north at this juncture. The other somewhat inexplicable—although believable—act was the willful destruction of rice stocks at war's end by the Japanese military.

If the law of unintended consequences has to be spelled out, then it is clear that continued rice requisitions demanded by the Japanese and implemented and monitored by the local Vichy French administration in the absence of optimum distribution mechanisms, alongside siphoning off of surpluses in a situation of administrative breakdown and even semianarchy after the ill-timed Japanese coup, magnified the impact of the disaster. Human failure and agency combined to betray the people of northern and north-central Vietnam. Affirming the thrust of Sen's general arguments, food distribution mechanisms broke down, not in a situation of absolute scarcity as in some conflict situations, but in an environment where all the warning signs pointed to the urgent need for administrative action, in the case of Vietnam, moving surplus rice north from the Mekong delta. More than that, more rational and humane policies directed at northern Vietnam would have seen more land under rice cultivation, less rice diverted to industrial alcohol and other products, corn and other crops planted and reserved as a backup, fewer forced deliveries, greater availability of food crops in the marketplace, and the rational and humane use of stockpiled rice.

NOTES

1. According to Le Manh Hung (2004, 256), the earliest estimate was in May 1945 when the imperial delegate in Hanoi requested mortality statistics from all the Tonkin provinces. Altogether 380,069 deaths from starvation were recorded from twenty provinces and 20,347 dead from illness. From a range of official and other sources, as David Marr (1997, 104) concludes, the death toll probably reached one million, or 10 percent of the population of the affected area perishing in a five-month period. Citing a Northern Committee report of November 1946, Marr (2013, 330) suggests one million died in the north and 300,000 in central Vietnam, with 11,458 victims of the August 1945 flood. Ngo Vinh Long (1991, 129) offers that two million people died in Tonkin alone during the few months from the end of 1944 to the early part of 1945. Bui Ming Dung (1995, 575–76), who sampled a range of sources, estimates between one and two million victims.

2. Personal accounts of the famine have been collected, such as Van Tao and Furuta Motoo, eds., *Nan doi Nam 1945 o Viet Nam: Nhung Chung tich lich su* (1995). Ngo Vinh Long (1991), Pham Cao Duong (1985), and David Marr (1997; 2013, chap. 6) have all offered partial translations or word pictures of the scope of the famine. A French eyewitness account of the famine in Hanoi is found in Perkins (2012, 135–50). Notwithstanding these accounts and studies, it appears to me that the actual impact of the famine and its geographical impact is the least well researched aspect.

3. A graduate of the Ecole Coloniale, Chauvet entered service in Indochina in 1927–28. Besides a spell as *chef de province* in Sa Dec and military service in Tonkin from 1941 to 1942, he served as resident of Lang Son and, prior to taking up office as

resident superior in Hanoi, served as head of political affairs under Decoux 1942–44. Not only did Chauvet survive the Japanese occupation, upon repatriation to France in late 1945, he reentered colonial service in Africa, rising to high office. Dying at the age of 103, he definitely outlived all his contemporaries from Hanoi days (with the possible exception of General Giap).

4. As a footnote to the above, the target of a Viet Minh attack in 1945, the Ham Rong bridge, was rebuilt between 1957 and 1964 and personally inaugurated by Ho Chi Minh. Oblivious to Sainteny's 1945 warning, from March 1965 the bridge became the target of practically unprecedented US bombing against a single target. But it was not until 1972 that major result was achieved against the heavily defended bridge. This was by the pioneering use of laser-guided bombs dropped by Phantoms of the Eighth Tactical Fighter Wing based at Ubon Airbase in Thailand. All told, the assault on Ham Rong bridge is simply staggering in the annals of war. On the US side, 873 sorties led to the acknowledged loss of eleven aircraft and the downing of 104 US pilots. (See http://en.wikipedia.org/wiki/Thanh_Hoa_Bridge.)

Epilogue

The famine crisis did not end abruptly with the political events of August 1945 but reached a new peak with the Great Flood of August–September of that year. Likewise, the returning French were confronted with the question of food supply, just as the Allies leaned heavily on France to yield Indochinese rice to meet a regional shortfall. This short epilogue offers, first, a reprise on the extended famine, including the new emerging contestation over rice supplies among the French, the Viet Minh, and the Nationalist Chinese. It then seeks to address the issue of attribution of blame. It ends with a broad-brush panorama of postrevolutionary trends in land reform and food security in North Vietnam.

THE GREAT FLOOD OF AUGUST 1945 AND THE EXTENDED FAMINE

From the point of view of food security, the Viet Minh August Revolution of 1945, leading to the DRV proclamation of independence the following month, was not exactly propitious, and we wonder how the Viet Minh coped with the situation. Coming at the height of the rainy season and with vast sections of the upper delta underwater, the food situation was on the verge of disaster, with one-third of the prospective November crop destroyed (Marr 2013, 321). According to Viet Minh estimates, the 1945 autumn harvest was poor and hardly sufficed to feed eight million persons for three months. To avoid nationwide starvation, the DRV government launched an all-out campaign against famine. The entry of 152,000 Nationalist Chinese army personnel into northern Indochina to accept the Japanese surrender increased the difficulty of food supply. As explained below, the problem was only gradually alleviated with the arrival of supplies from Saigon, though, as Chen (1969, 133) contends, the French also tried to delay shipments to the north.

The period after August 1945 presents the researcher with the greatest lacunae of information, whether French or Viet Minh. What is known is that on top of the April 1945 famine, the already desperately vulnerable people of the Red River delta were threatened with another disaster, namely flood. Certain scattered information entered Allied intelligence, such as the telegraphic French consular report of August 29, 1945, on the highland province of Cao Bang, recently occupied by Chinese Nationalist forces, remarking that "Paddy has been prematurely cut by the Japanese and the harvest definitely ruined by the floods" (MAE AOI 49 tél., Pechkoff, Tchongking, Aug. 29, 1945). The gravity of the situation was also carried in a stark US State Department report of September 13, 1945, monitored by the French: "A very serious famine threatens immediately the population of Tonkin owing to a the flooding of the Red River. The people have already consumed their seed rice" (MAE AOI 49 tél., Bonnet, Washington, Sept. 13, 1945 "Menace de famine au Tonkin").

As witnessed by Jean Sainteny (1953, 71, 74), who, as mentioned in chapter 7, flew into Hanoi from Kunming on August 22, the delta was covered by an "immense lagoon" from which certain isolated villages protruded above the water. The Red River was at its maximum of 12.40 meters, with the Banc de Sable village submerged. As Nguyen The Anh (1998a, 220) summarizes, during the second fortnight of August 1945, torrential rains raised the Red River to 12.68 meters in Hanoi (actually peaking at 14.43 meters), the highest ever recorded. There were considerable breaches in the dike system, and floods submerged newly planted paddy fields in Ha Dong, Bac Ninh, Son Tay, Phuc Yen, Vinh Yen, Hai Duong, Ha Nam, and Thai Binh Provinces. Floods covered 330,000 hectares of the tenth-month rice, which would represent a loss of 510,000 tonnes of rice. Prices again skyrocketed, leading to a return of widespread famine conditions and, as indicated, with people in certain provinces consuming their remaining rice seed. With its population of two hundred thousand, this time around Hanoi was itself the stage of the famine.

While flooding in the delta also inundated rice fields, leading to loss of the upcoming harvest, the impact did not rest there. As Jordan (1996, 529) found from his historical studies on famine, floods also destroy local transportation and distribution networks alongside markets. No less obviously, floods sweep away domestic animals, including pigs, chickens, and other domestic birds. They devastate coastal and riverine fishing—fish ponds, fish traps, or aquaculture. Although writing of Europe, Jordan also noted the devastating impact of flooding on salt production and distribution. The August floods also took a huge toll on water buffaloes, vital in the rice fields, along with beef cattle (Marr 2013, 331). Doubtless as well, northern Vietnam suffered these impacts, such as shortages of salt used for the production of *nuoc mam* and as a general food preservative.

As told by Marr (2013, 320–22), immediately following independence celebrations, President Ho Chi Minh placed mass hunger at the top of his list of state priorities. Launching a rice collection campaign on October 11, he called on all classes to collect and contribute rice, literally a mass exercise in national sacrifice in the interest of survival. Although initially experimenting with free-market economics on the grounds that famine was threatening, over the following weeks a raft of state controls were reimposed, such as bans on exporting food crops.

The dire situation confronting the newly installed communist government in the north is further brought into relief by a letter dated November 23, 1945, one of a small series penned by Ho Chi Minh, signing himself as president of the provisional government of the DRV and addressed to US president Harry S. Truman. However, while Ho Chi Minh's cable was received by the US State Department, it was neither passed on to the president nor acted on (Duiker 2000, 330). Slightly edited for typos and telegraph conventions, it read:

> For strictly humanitarian reasons I beg to call your Excellency's attention to the following. During Winter 1944 and Spring 1945, 2,000,000 Vietnamese died of starvation owing to the starving policy of the French who seized and stored to rottenness all rice available. In Summer 1945 three fourth(s) cultivated land submerged by flood followed by drought five sixth(s) normal harvest lost. Presence of Chinese occupation army increases number of people to be fed with stock already insufficient. Besides transport of rice from Cochinchina is rendered impossible by French-provoke(d) conflict. People begin starving and casualties are increasing every day. Provisional Government of Vietnam Republic has done everything possible under above-mentioned circumstances. We are facing imminent catastrophe unless great world powers and international relief organizations bring us immediate assistance. Therefore I earnestly appeal to your Excellency to accept my hearty and anticipated thanks.
>
> Respectfully, Ho Chi Minh (Duiker 2000, 330; letter reproduced without comment)

Setting aside the question of blame, Ho Chi Minh's letter does bring into relief the enduring nature of the famine through late November 1945, especially aggravated by the summer 1945 flood. It was also a plea for humanitarian intervention, and more's the pity it was not heeded. He may also have been reflecting on the plight of the northern provinces that had escaped the August floods. Here, a drought in September–October caused crops to wither and, in the absence of relief, led to death from starvation of several tens of thousands (Marr 2013, 322).

Emergency Food Relief

Jean Sainteny, who set up a virtual one-man French bureau (Commisariat de France) in Hanoi in September 1945, also found himself charged with the well-being of the French civilian and military population, including food supply. As he wrote, at a juncture when northern Vietnam was suffering "its most murderous famine in history," food supply for the French and local people was his most pressing concern (Sainteny 1953, 128). As witnessed in Hanoi, the price of rice spiraled from five to even nine piasters a kilo. Whether direct witness or not, he also reported that driven by famine and the failure of the harvest of the tenth month, starving peasants arriving in Hanoi simply died on the streets, facts corroborated by Tran Duy Hung (1981), among others.

Once established in Saigon, the French did seek to ameliorate the food shortage in the north, deemed in one British report to still be critical "owing to a partial failure of the rice crop due to flooding." In late October–early November 1945, a French ship (the *Kontum*) loaded nin thousand tonnes of rice in Saigon for Haiphong, expecting to return with urgently needed coal for the Saigon power station (NAA MFA 1838/14 Part I, cablegram, Dept. External Affairs, Nov. 3, 1945 from Secretary of State for Dominion Office, London). Exclusively earmarked for the food relief of the French population in Hanoi, the consignment was initially considered vulnerable to a Viet Minh boycott (as the Viet Minh controlled the local rice supplies). While air supply was feasible for medicine and milk, it was not considered appropriate for the supply of rice. Organized by the French Office de Ravitaillement (or supply office), the shipment was, necessarily, in coordination with the Chinese authorities who controlled Haiphong port and who alone had the means to transport the rice to Hanoi. But with the arrival of the ship at the end of November, one thousand tonnes of rice were "abandoned" (or diverted), while fifty tonnes were seized by the local Yunnanese commander. Another fifteen tonnes were appropriated by his interpreter owing to the "blackmail" of his security detail. The transport of the balance of rice to Hanoi was not without difficulties and subject to various thefts by the Chinese, further shrinking the volume. The arrival of the remaining rice at the Hanoi quayside was greeted with wild excitement by the Vietnamese, but it would take five more days of "discussions" before the remainder of the consignment was delivered to the French-controlled citadel (SHD GR4 Q5 Indochine 1943–48 "L'Occupation militaire de l'Indochine au Nord du 16ème parallele après la capitulation Japonaise"). In the event, it was only through American and British intercession that the Chinese seizure of the rice was "unblocked." Making an exit through Haiphong harbor and loaded with vital coal for Saigon, the *Kontum* was sunk by a Japanese mine (Sainteny 1953, 130).[1]

At the end of January 1946, another French merchant marine convoy arrived at Haiphong with rice for both the Chinese and the French. Running into a similar set of problems, the rice—or what remained of the consignment—only arrived in Hanoi one month later. According to a French account, the dispatch of rice to Hue, Vinh, and other centers was even more difficult, certain areas not receiving food relief until March 1946. The blame for all these logistics problems was squarely placed on the Chinese army, which helped with neither transport nor security nor assistance such as "one had the right to expect of an Allied nation" (SHD GR4 Q5 Indochine 1943–48; Sainteny 1953, 130). The thirty- to forty-day lapse of time between the arrival of the French in Saigon and the first dispatch of rice north may have been unconscionable for some, but there were also serious logistics issues at stake, not the least the semianarchy in the south.

By early May–June 1946, according to Marr (2013, 327), signs of a favorable harvest were evident. The DRV policy of planting yams, corn, and beans paid off, largely averting the fear of famine before the coming June harvest. As also described by Marr (2013, 330), the evolution of a coherent "rice system" by the DRV authorities went through some trial and error (not excluding Haiphong, where Chinese merchants ran their own show). As he concedes, "problems associated with the command economy were already surfacing." Notably, famine was still claiming some twenty thousand lives during the first half of 1946, with masses of the population reduced to eating one meal a day.

Setting aside the agency of the DRV state—many of the old French-trained bureaucrats remained in place—and the people themselves, such as emphasized by Marr, some consideration should also be given to the broader question of postwar rice supply, especially as the French commanded the lion's share of rice sourced from the southern delta and especially given that rice supply became a highly politicized issue.

International Claims on Vietnam's Rice

As intimated, the struggle over rice did not end with the Viet Minh takeover in August 1945 or the Japanese surrender but entered a new phase just as the British-led SEAC mission in the south and the arriving OSS and French representatives in Hanoi stared down a humanitarian crisis that had both urban as well as rural consequences. As well acknowledged by Ho Chi Minh, the arrival of Nationalist Chinese forces under Lu Han merely compounded the food crisis, especially as they laid claims on finite sources of rice in competition with locals while also making claims on rice controlled by the arriving French in Saigon.

But, as Singapore-based SEAC was quick to realize, the postwar food crisis touched not only Vietnam but also parts of India, Malaya, Java, and China, including Shanghai and Hong Kong. To this end, the Singapore branch of the Combined Food Board sought to take stock of regional supplies of rice with a view to their rational distribution. France was also party to the dictates of the Food Board, and the record illustrates a few of the political tensions behind the postwar politics of rice.[2] More generally in the immediate postwar period, the broad South, East, and Southeast Asian area, as with Bengal, northern Vietnam, Indonesia, China, and Japan, all faced critical problems of food supply and distribution. As the Singapore *Straits Times* (March 2, 1946) editorialized on the role of the board, "Without its sanction no nation can import substantial quantities of foodstuffs, and it is in a position to direct that producing nations should export specific percentages of their outputs to specific countries." As the paper also cautioned, the "poker bidding" aspects of the situation must not be overlooked in view of conflicting demands and statements.

Conflicting views also emerged between SEAC (Lord Killearn) and d'Argenlieu and his circle. At the March 1946 Food Conference, held in Singapore, the SEAC representative for Indochina (Lieutenant Colonel Kirkwood) reported that the famine situation in northern Indochina continued, with April and May predicted as "danger months." Rice could not be exported from the south until June, and the French required transport assistance (T. Smith 2007, 91). This assessment was not out of line with the grave apprehensions expressed by Ho Chi Minh in his November 1945 letter to Washington. Even so, some skepticism was raised as to this assessment. Notably, SEAC political adviser in Saigon E. W. Mekleireid, who visited northern Indochina at the time, failed to confirm famine reports that the French had issued, noting that the locals had increased production of maize and potatoes (Smith 2007, 91). Bereft of all outside assistance, as Marr (2013, chap. 6) elaborates, by this stage it is certainly true that the survivors were making concerted efforts to cope.

As Nguyen The Anh (1998a, 223–24) has outlined, by the end of 1945 the fledgling DRV claimed that the harvest of the winter of 1945 took place under favorable conditions and the harvest of the fifth month of 1946 produced a yield sharply superior to the prewar period, or equivalent to 2,592,000 tonnes of basic foodstuffs. Whatever the veracity of this figure, after November 1945 the French were supplying twenty thousand tonnes of rice per month to northern Vietnam, in large part needed to feed the Chinese army of 180,000 troops. While it is true that by the spring of 1946, people were no longer dying of starvation in Vietnam, fear of a reversion to famine, as discussed below, also caused the DRV to set in abeyance its struggle against "feudalism," waiting until 1953 to launch its radical agrarian reforms.

French pledges at Singapore (April 1946) were not met, and the French withdrew their representatives from the July liaison meeting (Smith 2007, 90). Notably, in March 1946, the UK representative of the Food Board made claims on twenty thousand tonnes of rice in Saigon for SEAC purposes, along with surplus maize. But, as François de Langlade of the Paris-based Comité de l'Indochine informed Saigon, the first priority was to meet rice needs in Tonkin, and in any case the maize in storage in Saigon was not fit for human consumption. Defensively, he pointed out that SEAC no longer controlled Indochina and that just as Britain placed priorities on its own territories, so did France. Moreover, as he wished it known, surplus rice accumulating from the forthcoming harvest would be absorbed by metropolitan France (MAE AOI 331, 1944–55 tél., Comité de l'Indochine à Haussaire Indo Saigon, March 25, 1946).

Otherwise, the two priority destinations for Indochinese rice were the French Indian Ocean territory of Réunion and French colonies in India. In July 1946, the SS *Albert Calmettre* embarked from Saigon with three thousand tonnes of rice destined for Réunion, contracted to return with three thousand tonnes of red sugar. In mid-1946, Paris instructed Saigon to focus its attention on French India, where "famine threatens." Accordingly, of the seven thousand tonnes of rice earmarked for French colonies, Paris ordered the urgent dispatch of five thousand tonnes of rice to Pondicherry (otherwise denied rice relief by the British). China, namely T. V. Soong's representative in Saigon, also began to lean on the French for rice supply. D'Argenlieu agreed and contracted to deliver five thousand tonnes to China, but with a catch, namely that it be tied to the Chinese troop withdrawal from northern Indochina (already the subject of major French diplomatic negotiations also involving the Viet Minh). A first tranche of rice for China (5,000 tonnes) was delivered to Shanghai in August 1946, with a second (3,700 tonnes) under way in September (MAE AOI 331 1944–55).

In mid-1946, Paris agreed to release an exportable surplus of twelve thousand tonnes of Indochinese rice. With board agreement, this amount was allocated accordingly, namely, 5,000 tonnes to SEAC, 500 tonnes to Shanghai, and 6,500 tonnes to the French colonies. Of the surplus of 150,000 tonnes anticipated from the new harvest, 5,000 tonnes would be sent to China. A maximum of two thousand tonnes of rice was allocated to the First Chinese Army in northern Vietnam (in line with the Chinese evacuation timetable). With good reason, Paris also warned that the mobilization of rice opened the door to speculation in this commodity (MAE AOI 331 1944–55 Haussaire Indo Saigon à Comité Indochine, June 26, 1946).[3]

Certainly there were hard choices, although the needs of northern Vietnam were still regarded as primary. In mid-1946, d'Argenlieu delivered six thousand tonnes of broken white rice to the UN Relief and Rehabilitation

Administration (UNRRA), with the former Japanese stock of maize confirmed as nonconsumable. The impact of famine on the political situation in Indochina was also uppermost in d'Argenlieu's thinking. As he made known to British officials in September 1946, "Communism was after all the greatest danger and the failure to improve material conditions would play straight into the hands of the communists" (Smith 2007, 91).

According to Jacques Meyrier, France's ambassador to China who had earlier negotiated the evacuation of Chinese forces from Indochina, it had to be conceded that notwithstanding genuine transport delays in evacuating all elements of the Chinese Fifty-Seventh Division from northern Vietnam, China kept to its bargain. He felt that any foot dragging on delivering the remaining tonnage of rice would not be well received by Nanjing at a time when China was coming around to a more favorable disposition vis-à-vis France. Otherwise, it would be "dangerous" to use rice as a weapon for political pressure (although that was precisely what was happening). Meyrier instructed Paris, "Do not place obstacles in the way of export of rice to China" (MAE AOI 331 1944–55 Meyrier, Nankin, tél., Sept. 2, 1946, Paris).

At the Rice Board meeting in Singapore of November 12, 1946, France made it known (presumably on the basis of harvest predictions) that it would command an (exportable) surplus of two hundred thousand tonnes of rice for 1946 to be distributed according to the following formula: French colonies, thirty thousand tonnes; China, thirty thousand tonnes; Malaya, fifteen thousand tonnes; Hong Kong, fifteen thousand tonnes; British India, ten thousand tonnes; and SCAP, ten thousand tonnes. At least another ten thousand tonnes remained at the discretion of the French authorities. In adding SCAP to this list, Paris also wished its diplomats to make it known that the sooner Thailand relinquished its occupation of the rich Cambodian rice-growing provinces of Battambang and Siem Reap and facilitated their retrocession, the sooner France would have even more rice to dispose.

The Rice War in the Southern Delta

The "rice war," of course, continued inside Indochina. French investigative journalist Jacques Despuech is one who identified the struggle over the western Mekong delta region between the French and the Viet Minh in the early postrestoration days. Producing 1.5 million tonnes of rice a year, the southern "rice bowl" still managed to produce an annual surplus of one million tonnes. Obviously, these facts were not lost on the Viet Minh, who took it upon themselves to organize the transport of rice from the western Mekong delta to different regions in order to supply their troops and, second, to export quantities of this rice to neighboring countries in exchange for arms and war materials. They also collected taxes on harvests at the rate of thirty Banque de l'Indochine piasters a quintal. All up, in 1948, the Viet Minh collected five hundred million piasters (8.5 billion francs) from the rice trade alone in southern Vietnam, alongside salt, pepper, and fish procured from Cambodia (Despuech 1953, 132–33).

In the event, French pledges of further rice deliveries to Malaya in early 1947 could not be matched. With the Viet Minh surrounding Saigon, supplies of rice reaching the market declined (Smith 2007, 93). By the end of 1948, the French anticipated a surplus of four hundred thousand tonnes of rice, the results of a good harvest and an extension of the cultivated area. Even so, and suggestive of the "rice wars" being fought out in the Mekong delta, only seventy-five thousand tonnes were expected to be actually delivered to Cholon by the first trimester of 1948 owing to "logistics problems." This tonnage was earmarked for the French Union, including metropolitan France (MAE AOI 331 1944–55 tél. High Comm, Nov. 25, 1948, Affaires Etrangère). Nevertheless, the French kept up deliveries of Indochinese rice to UNRRA (representing French annual contributions to this UN mission). The squeeze on rice deliveries also impacted price, with the price of rice doubling in the course of 1946 and trebling between February 1946 and February 1948 (Smith 2007, 98).

Needless to say, just as the Viet Minh diverted rice away from the Cholon marketplace, so the French stepped up their efforts to control the distribution of rice harvested in the southern delta. Despuech asserts that the Viet Minh cached millions of tonnes of stocks of rice in the delta to prevent their discovery by French Union troops. As such, the stocks became the property of the Viet Minh government, which bought the harvest from the concerned cooperatives charged with maintaining the stocks. But while collecting tax in Banque de l'Indochine piasters, the Viet Minh paid for rice in "Ho Chi Minh money," otherwise "not inspiring much confidence." Meanwhile, the DRV piasters fluctuated according to the local value of rice which, by 1946 onward, became subject to extreme inflation. Not surprisingly, DRV officials sought to reclaim up to 60 percent of their salaries in rice (Despuech 1953, 131–33).

French intelligence reports consistently reveal that rice, gold, and opium were all traded by the Viet Minh for weapons and matériel during this period, especially across the frontier with China. We should also acknowledge that the post-1946 French reoccupation of the northern delta region was not only a question of control of territory and people but also a contest with the Viet Minh to control the rice (and opium) harvest. The history of the French war in the north down until and even following major defeat in the isolated mountain valley of Dien Bien Phu in March–May 1954 was in large part about control of the delta, its population, and its rice, just as various French military figures (such as General Jean de Lattre Tassigny) sought by all means possible, including manipulation of the Catholic bishoprics, to build defensive lines of block houses and, through a ratcheting up of counterrevolutionary violence, to retain control over this vital space.

THE ATTRIBUTION OF BLAME

Firsthand accounts, novels, and works of scholarly reconstruction have all helped build up a picture of the Great Famine. Still, it was never subject to any "truth commission" inquiry. nor for that matter, did it enter the casebook of war crimes investigators, whether in Saigon or at the Tokyo War Crimes Trials. Though Viet Minh accounts are not shy on apportioning blame, they are short on documentation, no doubt a result of the confusion and semianarchy that reigned in the wake of the Japanese surrender. Seemingly, from the Japanese side, military-linked companies included, they simply shredded documents to avoid incrimination, just as the French high-level record simply goes blank after the Japanese armed takeover in March 1945.

While responsibility for the Great Famine remains controversial, there is no question that the Viet Minh derived maximum propaganda advantage from the tragedy. According to Marr (1997, 109), in the immediate aftermath of the tragedy, famine survivors most readily blamed the French still in charge until March 1945 and were less inclined to blame the Japanese. No blame was attributed to the Allied forces in destroying infrastructure or the Viet Minh who were supporting Allied actions. Also, as mentioned, the DRV Declaration of Independence of September 2, 1945, specifically cited both French and Japanese actions, namely: "[From 1940] our people were subjected to the double yoke of the French and the Japanese. Their sufferings and miseries increased. The result was that from the end of last year to the beginning of this year from Quang Tri province to the north of Vietnam, more than two million of our fellow citizens died from starvation" (Chen 1969, 337, app. 2).

But the French did not let the blame question rest there. Just ten days later, on September 12, Paris reacted to the DRV allegations that the French were responsible for the April 1945 famine and the deaths of two million people by preparing a set of counterarguments to be broadcast over French radio. First, as announced, it was under the Japanese occupation that rice was massively requisitioned and stocks run down during the intraharvest *soudure* period. Second, war destroyed the transportation system. Third, the area under rice cultivation was diminished, owing to the Japanese push to plant jute, vanilla, and peanuts. Fourth, owing to the Japanese pillage of large estates, the harvest of the tenth month of 1944 was already two hundred thousand tonnes in deficit. Up until the March 9 Japanese *coup de force*, the French had worked assiduously to expedite rice to the famine-threatened areas of Tonkin. However, after the military takeover and with the famine reaching a critical stage at the end of April 1945, the French could hardly be expected to exercise duties otherwise delegated to Japanese and "inexperienced" Vietnamese (MAE AOI 49 "Note à DGER," Paris, Sept. 12, 1945).

As a postwar French report expanded, owing to the shortfall in the tenth-month 1944 harvest, the (Vichy) French administration had built up reserve stocks in each province. However, the Japanese drew down on most of these stocks while reducing rice production and the area under cultivation owing to a switch to industrial crops to service their own requirements. In defeat, the Japanese removed rice stocks and threw them into the Mekong River at Thakek and Paksane in southern Laos. This vandalism condemned thousands of Indochinese people to die of famine. The harvest of the tenth month of 1945 revealed another compromise, owing to the floods that ravaged Red River delta rice fields and causing major losses of life. While the postwar French administration in central and southern Vietnam exercised protective measures by provoking or encouraging "disorder and pillage," the "provisional government" (the DRV) "hampered French government assistance in these regions." Accordingly, "It is they who should be held responsible for launching the famine as much for its aggravation and continuing disorders" (AOM Indo NF 134/1219 Direction d'Information, "Les Japonais et leurs collaborateurs sont responsible de la famine," n.d.).

According to a French military intelligence report, albeit written sometime after the events, "The Vietnamese masses began to suffer from consecutive *dissete* (shortages) owing to heavy procurements of rice effected by the Japanese and the *incurie* (mismanagement) which followed the catastrophic flooding of eight provinces of the Tonkin delta without any existing stock in reserve." Over the following six months, the situation was further exacerbated by the collapse of all established authority, traditional authority included, and by the failure of administrators and elites. "All this," the report continued, "prepared for the reception of revolutionary ferment and in the working up of xenophobia" (SHD GR4 Q5 Indochine 1943–48 "L'Occupation militaire de l'Indochine au Nord du 16ème parallele après la capitulation Japonaise"). In other words, as this report implied, the Viet Minh turned a dire situation to political advantage.

One searches in vain for self-examination on the side of the French in handling the famine crisis, but Paul Chauvet, whom we have portrayed as the top concerned French official in Hanoi, did in fact offer some telling counterfactuals in an address of late January–early February 1945 to leading policy makers (the Indochina Council). Anticipating mass starvation as it played in out in the weeks to come along with social breakdown and Viet Minh exploitation, Chauvet stated, "I simply regret the true nature of our preoccupations such as expressed by the heads of administrative services in not having been able to recognize earlier on and [even having] been privy through secondary considerations [the need to meet the shortfall in rice].” Nevertheless, he continued, “once the Indochina Council made the decision to quickly redress the penury of rice, then new attempts were made to achieve this goal.” In a startling revelation of administrative lapses reaching back to January 1945, Chauvet declared: The railway could have dumped all the first-, second-, and third-class passengers and given priority to rice. The army could have dispatched its convoys of lorries to Saigon to fetch the rice. The railway could have delivered several thousand tonnes to Tonkin to stabilize the “nervous market” during the “delicate” *soudure*. In a virtual declaration of defeat, as Chauvet acknowledged, the act of calling on the merchant marine to lend its junks and personnel to fetch the rice was “just possibly our final effort” (AOM RS Tonkin 1B 424–35 Chauvet à GG, Hanoi, Jan–Feb. 1945). Though Chauvet was careful to shift the blame from himself and, by innuendo, to attribute shortcomings to lower-level officials, his analysis was undoubtedly correct. There is just a touch of pathos and helplessness in this otherwise brief but revealing account from the inside at a juncture of the crisis where death from starvation was all around but possibly as well, not all was lost, just—and a very big caveat—if the administration (and the Japanese) were galvanized into rapid and coordinated action.

Seeking the Truth

Contrary to the view that the French and Japanese, and perhaps even the Americans, all shared responsibility for the tragedy such as appears in a number of official Vietnamese and other writings, Bui Ming Dung (1995, 573–18) makes the argument—and I agree—that the Japanese exacted rice not only for their local use or exports to Japan alone but for other parts of the empire, even at the height of the starvation. At the heart of Dung’s analysis is a refutation of certain of the more enduring attributions of causes of the famine. First, he dismisses the argument that Tonkin (as opposed to Annam) suffered a subsistence crisis (Tonkin rice production exceeded that of Annam, while demographic increase was greater in Annam than Tonkin). Second, he refutes the arguments of certain Japanese interlocutors (General Tsuchibashi Yuichi included), who asserted that bad weather or typhoons were the single determinant factor. Third, inflation, he argues, hit urban rather than rural dwellers harder. Fourth, to the extent that the French were active under Japanese duress, that role, of course, ceased abruptly after March 9 with the Japanese seizure of direct power. Nor does he find the French complicit in the making of the famine. To the extent that the French implemented policy changes, they were ordered by the Japanese to meet Japanese, not indigenous, demands. Fifth, notwithstanding American bombing, the transport system did not entirely collapse; it was simply reoriented to Japanese military use (rice transport took less volume than other commodities). Sixth, the Japanese forcibly introduced not only jute but cotton, vegetable oil plants, and other industrial crops in northern Vietnam at the expense of maize, rice, and other food crops. Maize also began to supplant rice in exports to Japan (and the Philippines) in 1945, although rice was also exported to other places during this year. Seventh, the Japanese stockpiled rice (in Saigon harbor and even in rural Laos) right up to the point of their surrender. Finally, overarching all considerations, the export of Indochinese rice to Japan and the empire appears to have been a Japanese policy from the outset. Additional to this list, we should not neglect the role of Japanese *kaisha* in facilitating and profiting from this system, as with the well-documented example of Mitsui Bussan Kaisha (BEI 1944).

As a truth-seeking exercise, the work of Japanese Vietnam scholar Furuta Motoo (1998) is outstanding. Between 1992 and 1995, Furuta joined a Vietnamese research team conducting a virtual retrospective mortality analysis of the Great Famine, eventually published by the Vietnam Research Institute of History in 1995. Based on household survey and interviews conducted at twenty-five sites in northern Annam and Tonkin (including ethnic minority hamlets, hamlets in the middle reaches of the Red River delta, hamlets with handicraft industries located near big cities, and nonagricultural and agricultural hamlets), the team found that losses were most heavily concentrated in the densely populated Red River delta, characterized by agricultural hamlets that had very small amounts of arable land. Of the twenty-five sites surveyed, Furuta offers detailed data on two hamlets, namely, Luong Phu in Thien Hai District in Thai Binh Province, and Phuong Thong hamlet in Phu Tien District in Hung Yen Province. In Phu Luong (with 286 families surveyed), famine deaths had begun to occur by January 1945, with surviving residents reporting that the famine peaked between January and May, when the spring harvest took place, and that famine conditions continued for several months. Among his important findings were that economic factors sharply separated the fate of families. Notably, he found that ownership of arable land (especially more than one *mau*) mitigated the effect of the famine, whereas the death rate for landless peasants reached 53.3 percent. Among other occupational categories, fishermen were extremely vulnerable, possibly because the peak of the famine occurred outside the season for gathering shrimps and crabs. By contrast, carpenters fared better with their larger market and savings. From his survey of Phuong Thong hamlet he concluded that out of 792 individuals in 153 households surveyed, 180 people died, or 22.7 percent of the total population. Again, families holding private land fared better. By contrast, families holding no arable land suffered an overall death rate of 63.9 percent. Although Phuong Long hamlet was poorer than Luong Phu hamlet, it suffered fewer overall deaths. This he attributes to the proximity of a jute factory that brought in some extra income.

From another background, Japanese social activist and journalist Saotome Katsumoto researched and published a dedicated book on the famine titled (in Japanese) *A Record of the Starvation of 2,000,000 in Vietnam: 1945 under Japanese Occupation* (1993). Also one of Japan's leading peace education activists and writer-thinkers on "antiwar thought," Saotome begins this work by relating his own experiences of wartime rationing in Tokyo, explaining that supplies for children were far from a priority during the war years. The lack of rice in wartime Japan to feed children sets the stage for the discussion of Vietnamese hardships. He then tells how rice taken from Vietnam and consumed by Japanese civilians precipitated famine that possibly claimed two million lives. As Mathew Penney (2005) explains, Saotome's research also helped him "to understand the true form of the 'Greater East Asia Co-Prosperity Sphere' that Japanese militarism had built up in Indochina." In the 1980s, Saotome condemned Japanese war atrocities in the same terms as the American bombing of Tokyo. Overall, as Penney explains, he seeks to stimulate his audience to think about the issues of agency in war, about victims and assailants, and, in part, to inspire reflection on Japan's prosperity and place in the world. As Saotome (1993, 180) concludes, "I hope that this book will help us consider the human condition from the past to the present and into the future."

Inter alia, Saotome (1993, 146) offers official DRV famine mortality figures collected from an on-the-spot survey conducted in 1964 exclusively for the period covering late 1944–early 1945 in eight (of the seventeen) districts making up present-day Nghe An province. These districts were selected on the basis of having the highest mortality rates in the province. Included is Nam Dan district, itself comprising thirty villages (including Ho Chi Minh's natal village of Kim Lien). Altogether, 263 villages were investigated. The total number of deaths was recorded as 42,670. The total number of families lost to famine was 2,280. In Nam Dan District alone, 1,129 individuals perished and 33 families were lost. Furuta and Saotome, respectively, cannot offer absolute mortality numbers, but their respective village researches are entirely illustrative of the bigger picture. Summarizing, Saotome (1993, 163–67) finds four causes for the famine. First are the typhoon and floods of autumn 1944 as well as damage caused by cold weather. Second is interruption to north-south communications as well as sea routes by Allied bombing. Third are (Japanese) demands to convert rice and maize fields to jute. Fourth is the Franco-Japanese system of forced delivery/purchase of rice.

LAND REFORM AND FOOD SECURITY IN NORTH VIETNAM

More generally, land reform measures kicked off immediately after the August Revolution, as with the reduction of land rent and usurious interest rates and a decree on agricultural taxes becoming the centerpiece of the social revolution then unfolding in North Vietnam. French plantation owners were immediate losers, alongside other "enemies," but big landlords also came under pressure, more especially as land tax collection kicked off after the November 1945 rice harvest (Marr 2013, 333, 351).

Duncanson (1968, 173), who served with the British Thompson counter-insurgency mission in South Vietnam, may be only partly correct in asserting that, compared to China, land reform had not been a (dominant) ICP or Viet Minh slogan up until this point. (It was an issue in 1930–31, and it was revisited by Truong Chinh and Vo Nguyen Giap in their investigations into the peasant problem.) Still, according to Kahin (1987, 40–41), throughout 1946–47, the party opposed any land reform policy likely to drive landlords into the French camp, though in fact, many landlords, including those who had joined the revolution, became collaborators. Accordingly, through 1949, the party's strategy was to cajole peasants and landlords into joining an inclusive united front. After that date, the party took a firmer line, giving poor peasants first priority in land redistribution. But most land formerly owned by collaborators or French and redistributed during this period was actually in South Vietnam, not in the north.

But the war of "national resistance," following the breakdown of the entente with the French in March 1946 and the reversion to guerrilla warfare, also raised the critical issue of food supply for both Viet Minh partisans and the general population outside of the French-controlled zones. From pen portraits and black-and-white photographs, we gain some picture of the tremendous adversity faced by Ho Chi Minh and his followers in the Viet Bac region—forced to grow their own food, forced to cope with wild animals, and obliged to frequently relocate their abode and gardens to elude the French. Here we see Ho Chi Minh tending corn, here we see the Vietnamese leader fishing in a mountain stream, here we see partisans eating a frugal meal. As the concerned French General Raoul Salan (1975, 83) pointed out, armed resistance would have been futile without a well-worked-out economic plan on behalf of the guerrilla to ensure recruitment, supply, and survival. As he remarks, "From the beginning, the economic struggle was the major concern and leitmotif of the Viet Minh leadership." As a people's army, by necessity they recruited from the peasantry, thereby withdrawing vital labor from the rice fields required for transplanting, harvesting, repairing dikes, and so on. As Salan continues, it is fair to say that the only way that the chronic food crisis in the Viet Bac could be overcome for the Viet Minh was to win control over supplies in the southern delta and in Cambodia. Yet despite all adversity, the Viet Minh did not starve. This owed to their careful attention to complementary food supplies, the exploitation of dry-field rice through attention to fertilizer, productivity, and rational use of manpower.

In large part inspired by China's land reform of 1946–53, the key ideologue involved in driving land reform in the north was Truong Chinh (1977). Couched in Marxist rhetoric, his ideas are presented in a series of essays written between 1949 and 1954. Obviously, landlords were targeted as the enemy, but determining people's class status was also a delicate issue and seen as the key to successful mobilization for land reform. The binding question in this ultraleftist program was whether to confiscate, requisition, or forcibly purchase land for redistribution to peasants. Leftist impulses also had to be reined in, as with a stated prohibition against wanton killing or destroying cultural artifacts. Rather, as a concession to the legacy of history, December 12, 1953, was made the starting point for determining landlord status. In a complicated formula involving rich, middle, and poor peasants, even a poor or landless peasant who had come onto additional land or draft animals could be reclassified as belonging to the upper stratum (Truong Chinh 1977, 528).

Obviously, these loose guidelines were subject to different interpretations locally (as, for example, in handling the ethnic minorities). Neither was land reform smooth in North Vietnam, especially as the war continued, and many excesses proved counterproductive. In fact, Truong Chinh's land reform was a disaster and was acknowledged as such by the party (as with the Giap report of October 1956 on "errors"). Following the formal land reform campaign launched at the end of 1953, most villages in North Vietnam were subsequently covered from mid-1955 to mid-1956. This final year was also the most radical period, with many peasants falsely labeled as landlords and subjected to the confiscation of their land. Evidence also suggests that the land reform program was accompanied by the massive uprooting of people, the victimization of innocents, and the recurrence of famine (1954–55), leading to a substantial number of deaths. Many "class enemies" were executed, though perhaps not the huge numbers later claimed by some. As Duiker (2000, 446) embellishes, "For the first time since the Nghe-Tinh revolt, the Party had decided to unleash the specter of class warfare in the countryside." In the latter half of 1956, the party recognized that it had made serious errors, and a campaign to correct the errors lasted until 1958 (see Hoang Van Chi 1964; Moïse 1983).

Needless to say, the perception of land reform in North Vietnam as a disaster was mirrored in Western intelligence and media reporting, although the worst excesses were undoubtedly over by the early 1960s as a number of hydraulic programs came to be established with or without fraternal socialist cooperation. For instance, a rare Western visitor to Thanh Hoa Province in the early 1960s, the pro-Hanoi Wilfred Burchett (1966, 17) explained that although the village he visited had been receiving a state rice subsidy up until 1961, benefiting from irrigation waters supplied by the Ban Thac dam as well as the use of organic fertilizer, it was soon able to repay the state with a surplus harvest. He also described the use of electric pumps much debated by French engineers but not widely implemented. Whereas Chinese and Soviet engineers assisted the fledgling DRV in the early decades with dike repair, the World Bank, the Asian Development Bank (ADB), and UNDP among other donors have, in turn, built on the legacy of essentially the French system of hydraulic controls. In Gilard's (2006, 49) estimate, through their good works, they have further reduced the risks of major inundation to a probability of 0.4, or once every 250 years.

On the downside, however, salinity rates have risen in the lower Mekong, linked with global warming and rising sea levels. Listed by the World Bank today as among the countries most threatened by rising sea levels, water levels in coastal Vietnam are expected to rise twenty to thirty centimeters in the next few decades. In April 2011, saltwater at four parts per thousand reached as far as fifty-six kilometers inland, damaging crops and livestock. Today a region of seventeen million people, the entire lower Mekong is threatened with seawater invasion, forcing people to switch crops and innovate. Likewise, drinking water has to be fetched from increasingly higher reaches of the river owing to salination (Gillet 2011).

The Doi Moi Era in Vietnam

With time, the "green revolution" would also arrive in northern Vietnam (much later in Laos), increasing yields, productivity, and rural incomes, albeit not outside of party control. Today, as described by Gilard (2006, 45), the entire northern delta resembles a vast "polderized" space around which is circled a network of tributaries and branches of the Red River, some of them artificially created by human intervention, assuring the passage of water between the upstream basin and the maritime outlet. At the heart of each polder exists a network of canals ensuring such functions as irrigation and drainage, connected with an external hydrographic network by a complex system of water gates and pumps. Villages, comprising several thousand inhabitants, tend to be situated on the older, established levees or branches of the river. Population density is greater where the agricultural potential is also better. The agricultural cycle follows cultural and seasonal rhythms. Rice cultivation is complemented in the slack seasons by horticulture, maize, mulberries used for silk, and the keeping of pigs or cattle. Maintaining the system of dikes reaching 2,300 kilometers in length remains a state concern, but sea wall protection against saline encroachment brought by frequent typhoons could also be a local obligation. As suggested, Vietnam has not been alone in managing its hydraulic culture, including the problems of flood control, agricultural extension, and rural development.

Although post-1975 collectivization never reached the same level in the southern delta as in the north—and with some areas entirely left out of this program—the south today has undergone a series of transformations, including land expropriation and redistribution along with the settlement of landless farmers and former soldiers. However, the reverse trend ushered in by *doi moi*, or economic reform, seriously undertaken from the early 1980s, also led to decollectivization and the eventual end of state farms in 1987. This period also witnessed a progressive shift toward double- and even triple-cropping (although at this writing triple-cropping is not being encouraged). Today, "floating rice" remains but a small percentage of that grown in colonial times. Where Chinese brokers once tendered credit and commanded the harvest, today local "village people's committees," producer committees, or other parastate agents are in charge of the implementation of policies defined by the state hydraulic services. As Le Meur and colleagues (2005) point out, the 1990s liberalization in Vietnam did not by any means weaken the role of the state over agriculture, as in support of "development" such as the construction or maintenance of canals or dikes; organizing migration; defining agricultural choices (double- or triple-cropping); securing the institutional environment (issuing land titles, water contracts); or resolving disputes.

Reforms associated with *doi moi* did not solve all problems in the agricultural sector, especially in the north. In June 1988, the chief of the Communist Party of Vietnam, Nguyen Van Linh, was forced to concede that notwithstanding economic reforms already in train, Vietnam's economy had collapsed. Several months before this admission, Vietnam had appealed to the international community for food relief to stave off famine threatening an officially estimated three million people in the north. Such was brought into high relief when, in early 1988, Vietnam urgently requested donations of fertilizer, insecticide, and food from the international community. Despite the reforms, the country was then unable to feed itself. Population growth of more than 2 percent per annum outstripped food production. This translated into an extra million mouths a year to feed out of a population of sixty million. Bad weather, drought, disease, and infection, it was feared, would take their toll on the 1988 winter–spring crop in northern Vietnam. At first Hanoi sought international assistance to meet the near-starvation needs of four to seven million people in the north. Beggars, and even corpses, began turning up in the streets of Hanoi. By early June, as harvest began, Vietnam dropped its famine claim, reporting higher-than-average rice yields. Nevertheless, as UN agency reports then cautioned, the food crisis was thought likely to continue to at least 1990. In the interim, malnutrition was seen as likely to prevail, especially in the north. Relative to the south, buffered by more fertile lands and relatively efficient private farms, the north was also handicapped by larger-scale state-run collective farms (although it should also be mentioned that southern agriculture was then under considerable stress) (Gunn 1988, 378–79).

With a population of 87,840,000 (World Bank 2011), Vietnam is the seventh most populous country in the world. Following *doi moi*, Vietnam has shifted from a primarily agriculture-based economy to a multisector economy promoting industrialization, with the share of agriculture reduced to 21 percent of total GDP. Paddy rice production is still the major agriculture activity in the country and, in the interests of food security, the national land use plan of 2008 prescribes that at least 3.8 million hectares of land be set aside for the purpose of producing paddy. In fact, because of competing claims on land use, the land area under paddy has decreased from 4.2 million hectares in 2000 to 4 million hectares in 2009. Poverty rates have decreased across these years, and productivity of many staple foods has increased significantly since 2000. However, displacement and resettlement due to hydropower development is another factor in causing transitory or chronic food insecurity for affected families in more vulnerable slope areas (Pham Huu Ty et al. 2011, 24).

Consistent with its "productionist revolution," for the 1989–11 period, Vietnam exported more than 83.6 million tonnes of rice worth more than twenty-five billion US dollars and had an export figure for 2011 of 7.1 million tonnes of rice (rising from 4.69 million tonnes in 2006). In 2012, a conference organized by the "people's committee" of Dong Thap Province, bordering Cambodia, complained that rice production in the southern delta focused on output and quantity and had not been accompanied by good planning and identification of markets. There were too many growers, most of them operating on a very small scale. There were also too many intermediaries involved in rice production and consumption. There were still too many postharvest losses and a low rate of mechanization. There was also agreement that the Cuu Long (Mekong delta) should follow large-scale production models in order to facilitate the building of rice brands, especially for higher-end rice. As also noted, the southern delta had nearly 1.8 million hectares under rice cultivation, accounting for 53 percent of the country's paddy yield and 96 percent of its rice exports (*Viet Nam News*, April 2, 2012, 14). Although Vietnam now trails Thailand as a leading rice exporter, we are struck that certain of these complaints are reminiscent of those identified by the colonial Rice Board.

One lesson from our study on food sufficiency in the face of demographic increases and other challenges is to suggest that there is never cause for complacency. Even setting aside environmental factors, as Khong Dien (2002, 145) has pointed out, owing to demographic increase, the trend in Vietnam from 1940–80 witnessed a 34 percent decline in average rice share per capita, although it recovered in the 1990s. As Dien remarked, this instability shows that food output increase has not always corresponded with population increase. Undoubtedly, this understanding still holds, just as pressure on arable land, as with urbanization and other developments, saps away at Vietnam's total rice hectarage. Such understandings lead us to suggest that regional food sufficiency will always be a problem, leaving planners hostage to a range of natural and human conditions, even if good yearly surplus yields also exist.

NOTES

1. To place these figures into perspective, Hanoi city alone was then consuming 4,500 tonnes of rice a month (Marr 2013, 326), alongside the needs of other cities and regions.

2. Established in June 1942 and seated in Washington, the Food Board comprised the US secretary of agriculture, representatives of the British Ministry for Food, and, subsequently, Canadian counterparts. For the 1942–46 period it served as "the supreme Allied body for the planning of food supplies," and with the United States and Canada as the major suppliers of food, the board sought to harmonize potential supplies and their transportation among the Allied members. Stretched to the limit in servicing European food needs, the question of supply was also dogged by the food catastrophe in India (the Bengal famine) and heavy demands from SCAP in Japan as well (Rolls 1956).

3. At this point, the French Ministry of Foreign Affairs sought local information on rice distribution accomplished by France in Tonkin and north Annam, including transport and relations with SEAC and China. Regrettably, the dossier, if at all answered, remains empty in the MAE archives (Langlade, tél. Mar. 27, 1946).

Glossary

F = French
J = Japanese
V = Vietnamese

an sat (V): Judge.
bang ta (V): Mandarins with police powers.
bo chanh (V): Treasurer.
chi (V): Ruling.
co mat vien (V): Privy council.
corvée (F): System of impressed labor.
dien chu (V): Big landlords.
du (V): Proclamation.
garde indigène (F): Native guards, literally; French militia.
hang sao (V): Paddy huskers.
huyen (V): District or subprefecture (several cantons).
kaisha (J): Companies.
kham sai (V): Imperial delegate.
kinh luoc su (V): Viceroy.
linh (V): Vietnamese soldier.
lua chien (V): Winter harvest.
lua mua (V): Harvest of the season.
ly truong (V): Mid-level administrator.
mau (V): Measure for rice fields (approx. one-third hectare).
nan doi (V): Famine.
nha que (V): Rural dweller.
nom (V): Chinese language.
phu (V): Prefecture.

phu doan (V): Governor.
quan an (V): Magistrate.
quan phu (V): Chief of prefecture.
quoc ngu (V): National language.
rai (*ray*): Slash-and-burn land (swidden).
sapeque (F): Copper-zinc coin issued by the French.
soudure (F): Dry period between two harvests.
ta dien (V): Tenant farmer.
tong duc (V): Provincial governor.
tri huyen (V): Subprefect.
tri phu (V): Prefect.
Tu Ve (V): Self-defense group.
tuan phu (V): Mandarin or head of small province.
tuan vu (V): Mandarin or head of large province.
Viet Khieu (V): Overseas Vietnamese.
xa (V): Rural commune.
xu uy (V): ICP term meaning "commune of the country."

References

Archives

France

Centre des archives d'outre-mer, Aix-en-Provence (AOM)
Nouveau Fonds, Indochine (NF)
Fonds Ministériels (formerly Rue Oudinet, Paris)
Fonds Indochine, Résidence Supèrieur Tonkin (RST)
Service de liaison avec les orginaires des territoires français d'Outre-mer (SLOTFOM)
Ministère des affaires étrangères, Archives Diplomatiques, Paris (MAE)
Fonds Asie Océanie 1944–1955 Indochine (AOI)
Service Historique de la Défense (SHD), formerly Service Historique de l'Armée de Terre, Vincennes (SHAT)
Fonds GR 4 Q 1, 2, 45 Indochine 1943–1948 Major-Général Défense Nationale
Fonds Indochine sous-serie 10H

Other

Diplomatic Record Office of the Ministry of Foreign Affairs, Tokyo (MOFA)
Japan Center for Historical Records (JACAR). National Archives of Japan. http://www.jacar.go.jp/english/index.html.
National Archives of Australia, Canberra (NAA). http://www.naa.gov.au.
Public Record Office, London (PRO)
Public Record Office, Hong Kong (PRO HK)
Kweilin Weekly Intelligence Summary (KWIZ)
Ho Chi Minh Museum—BaoTang Ho Chi Minh (Ho Chi Minh City)
Vietnam Center and Archive (Pike Collection). http://www.vietnam.ttu.edu/.

OFFICIAL SOURCES

US Government. 1942. "Stragetic Survey of Indochina." OSS/State Department Intelligence and Research Reports, Washington, DC, March 14.

———. 1943. *Peace and War: United States Foreign Policy, 1931–1941*. Washington, DC: US Government Printing Office.

———. 1947. OSS Documents Relating to OSS Activity in French Indochina (Reel II). OSS, Part II, "Postwar Japan, Korea and Southeast Asia." Department of State, August 2, "Biographical Information on Prominent Nationalist Leaders in French Indochina."

———. 1949. "Political Alignments of Vietnamese Nationalists." Washington, DC: Department of State, Division of Research for Far East, Office of Intelligence Research.

———. 1978. *The Magic Documents: Summaries and Transcripts of the Top-Secret Diplomatic Communications of Japan, 1938–1945*. Washington, DC: US Department of Defense.

———. Office of National Intelligence Weekly.

Vietnam. 1978. *An Outline History of the Vietnam Workers' Party, 1930–1975*. Hanoi: Foreign Languages Publishing House.

———. (1972) 1979. *History of the August Revolution*. 2nd ed. Hanoi: Foreign Languages Publishing House.

———. 2008. *Reminiscences of Ho Chi Minh*. Hanoi: Gioi Publishers.

Vietnam. 2009a. *Ho Chi Minh's Life and Cause*. Hanoi: Gioi Publishers.

Vietnam. 2009b. *The 30 Year War, 1945–1975*. Hanoi: Gioi Publishers.

NEWSPAPERS

La Dépèche Colonial (Saigon)
L'Echo Annamite (Saigon)
La France Indochine (Saigon)
L'Humanité (Paris)
L'Impartiel (Saigon)
L'Indochine (Saigon)
Le Jeune Annam (Saigon)
La Lutte (Saigon)
L'Opinion (Saigon)
Le Tribune Indochinois (Saigon)
Saigon-Moi (Saigon)
Straits Times (Singapore)
Tin Hau (Hanoi)
Tin Moi (Hanoi)
Viet Nam News (Ho Chi Minh City)
Vietnam-Presse (Saigon)

WORKS

Aldrich, Richard. 2000. *Intelligence and the War against Japan, Britain, America and the Politics of the Secret Service*. Cambridge: Cambridge University Press.

Andrew, Dudley, and Steven Ungar. 2005. *Popular Front Paris and the Poetics of Culture*. Cambridge, MA: Harvard University Press.

Andrus, John R., and Katrine R. C. Greene. 1944. "Recent Developments in Indo-China: 1939–43." In *The Economic Development of French Indochina*, edited by Charles Robequain, 351–89. London: Oxford University Press.

Anon. *Rapport de la Commission Superiéur du Digues*. Hanoi, 1896.

———. 1911. *Rapport de la Chambre de Commerce de Hanoi et de Nord Annam*. Hanoi-Haiphong: IDEO.

———. 1926. *M. Varenne et la presse indochinoise (extraits de L'Indochine* Républicaine*)*. Hanoi: Express, 1926.

———. 1931. *Riziculture en Indochine*. Hanoi: IDEO.

———. 1946. "Millions Die in China's Famine (photographs by George Silk)." *Life* (May 13), 29–34.

———. 2010. Revolutionary History. http://www.revolutionaryhistory.co.uk/.

Ballard, G. 1935. *Le problème du riz en Cochinchine*. Paris: Société d'informations économiques.

Bartholomew-Feis, Dixie. 2006. *The OSS and Ho Chi Minh: Unexpected Allies in the War against Japan*. Lawrence: University Press of Kansas.

Beau, Paul. 1908. *Situation de l'Indochine française de 1902 à 1907 (Rapport par Beau, gouverneur général)*. Saigon: M. Rey.

BEI (*Bulletin Economique de l'Indochine*). 1944. Hanoi: Service de la statistique générale.

Bernal, Martin. 1981. "The Nghe-Tinh Soviet Movement 1930–1931." *Past and Present* 92 (Aug.): 148–68.

Bernard, Paul. 1932. *L'Indochine et la crise, le problème du riz*. Saigon: Aspar.

———. 1934. *Le Problème économique indochinois*. Paris: Nouvelles Editions Latines.

Borton, Lady. 2010. *Ho Chi Minh; A Journey*. 2nd ed. Hanoi: Gioi Publishers.

Bose, Sugata. 1990. "Starvation amidst Plenty: The Making of Famine in Bengal, Honan, and Tonkin, 1942–44." *Modern Asian Studies* 24 (4): 699–727.

Bouvier, René. 1937. *Richesse et Misère du Delta Tonkinois*. Paris: Imprimèrie Tournon.

Brocheux, Pierre. 1977. "L'implantation du mouvement communiste en Indochine française: Le Cas du *Nghe-Tinh* (1930–1931)." *Revue d'Histoire Moderne et Contemporaine* 24 (1): 49–74.

———. 1995. *The Mekong Delta: Ecology, Economy, and Revolution*. Wisconsin Monograph No. 12. Madison: University of Wisconsin–Madison Center for Southeast Asian Studies.

———. 2007. *Ho Chi Minh: A Biography*. Cambridge: Cambridge University Press.

Brocheux, Pierre, and Daniel Hémery. 2009. *Indochina: An Ambiguous Colonization, 1858–1954*. Berkeley: University of California Press.

Bruneau, Michel. 2005. "From a Centred to a Decentred Tropicality: Francophone Colonial and Postcolonial Geography in Monsoon Asia." *Singapore Journal of Tropical Geography* 26 (3): 304–22.

Bruzon, E., and P. Carton. 1930. *Le climat de l'Indochine et les typhoons de la mer de Chine*. Hanoi: Imprimèrie d'Extrême-Orient.

Bui Ming Dung. 1995. "Japan's Role in the Vietnamese Starvation of 1944–45." *Modern Asian Studies* 29 (3): 575–76.

Burchett, Wilfred G. 1966. *Vietnam North: A First-Hand Report*. London: Lawrence & Wishart.

Castagnol, E. M. 1930. "Monographie agricole de la province de Nghê-An." *Bulletin Economique de l'Indochine* 33 (Nov.).

Césaire, Aimé. 1955. *Discours sur le Colonialisme*. Paris: Présence Africain.

Chan Lau Kit Ching. 1999. *From Nothing to Nothing: The Chinese Communist Movement and Hong Kong, 1921–1936*. Hong Kong: Hong Kong University Press.

Chanda, Nayan. 1993. "India in Indochina." In *Indian Communities in Southeast Asia*, edited by K. S. Sandhu and H. Mani, 31–45. Singapore: ISEAS.

Chandler, David P. 2009. "Paul Mus (1902–1969): A Biographical Sketch." *Journal of Vietnamese Studies* 4 (1): 149–91.

Chandler, David F., William R. Roff, John R.W. Smail, David Joel Steinberg, Robert H. Taylor, Alexander Woodside, David K. Wyatt 1987. *In Search of Southeast Asia. A Modern History*, rev. ed., ed. David Joel Steinberg, Honolulu: University of Hawaii Press.

Chandler, David P., and Christopher E. Goscha, eds. 2005. *Paul Mus (1902–1969): L'Espace d'un Regard*. Paris: Les Indes Savante.

Chassigneux, Edmond. 1913. *L'Irrigation dans le Delta du Tonkin*. Paris: C. Delagrave.

Chen King C. 1969. *Vietnam and China 1938–54*. Princeton, NJ: Princeton University Press.

———. 1975. "Some Comparisons between the Chinese and Vietnamese Revolutions." *Asian Profile* 3 (3): 227–41.

Chonchirdsin, Sud. 1999. "The Indochinese Congress (May 1936–March 1937): False Hope of Vietnamese Nationalists." *Journal of Southeast Asian Studies* 30 (2): 338–46.

Claval, Paul. 2005. "Colonial Experience and the Development of Tropical Geography in France." *Singapore Journal of Tropical Geography* 26 (23): 289–303.

Cleary, Mark. 2003. "Land Codes and the State in French Cochinchina c.1900–1940." *Journal of Historical Geography* 29 (3): 356–75.

———. 2004a. "Ecological Setting of Southeast Asia." In *Southeast Asia: A Historical Encyclopedia from Angkor Wat to East Timor*, edited by Ooi Kin Geat, 453–59. Santa Barbara, CA.: Clio Press.

———. 2004b. "Monsoons." In *Southeast Asia: A Historical Encyclopedia from Angkor Wat to East Timor*, edited by Ooi Kin Geat, 908–9. Santa Barbara, CA: Clio Press.

Cook, Megan. 1977. *The Constitutionalist Party in Cochinchina: The Years of Decline, 1930–1942*. Clayton, Vic., Australia: Centre of Southeast Asian Studies, Monash University.

Cooke, Nola, and James A. Anderson, eds., *The Tongking Gulf Through History*, Philadelphia, PA: University of Pennsylvania Press, 2011.

Cooke, Nola, and Li Tana, eds. 2005. *Water Frontier: Commerce and the Chinese in the Lower Mekong Region, 1750–1880*. Lanham, MD: Rowman & Littlefield.

Cotter, Michael G. 1968. "Towards a Social History of the Vietnamese Southward Movement." *Journal of Southeast Asian History* 9 (1): 12–24.

Coulet, G. 1928. "Bonzes Pagode et Société sécréte en Cochinchine." *Extrême-Asie*, Nouvelle Série, no. 25 (July): 7–13.

Cressman, Robert J. 1999. *The Official Chronology of the U.S. Navy in World War II*, Annapolis. Md: US Naval Institute Press.

Dang Quang Tinh. 1999. *Viet Nam Country Report 1999*. Asian Disaster Reduction Center (ADRC), Kobe, Japan. http://www.adrc.asia/countryreport/VNM/VNMeng99/Vietnam99.htm#_Toc494263605.

d'Argenlieu, Thierry. 1985. *Chronique d'Indochine, 1945–1947*. Paris: Albin Michel.

Decoux, Jean. 1949. *A la Barre de l'Indochine: Histoire de mon gouvernement général, 1940–1945*, Paris: Plon.

Despuech, J. 1953. *Le Trafic de Piastres*. Paris: Deux Rives.

Detwiler, Donald S., and Charles Burton Burdock, eds. 1980. *War in Asia and the Pacific, 1937–1949*. 15 vols. New York: Garland.

Devillers, Philippe. 1952. *Histoire du Viet-nam de 1940 à 1952*. Paris: Editions du Seuil.

Dennis, Peter. 1987. *Troubled Days of Peace: Mountbatten and Southeast Asia Command, 1945–46*, New York: St. Martin's.

Dikötter, Frank. 2010. *Mao's Great Famine: The History of China's Most Devastating Catastrophe, 1958–1962*. New York: Walker.

Dion, J. n.d. *Histoire de Slotfom*. n.p.

Dommen, Arthur J. 2001. *The Indochinese Experience of the French and Americans: Nationalism and Communism in Cambodia, Laos, and Vietnam*. Bloomington: Indiana University Press.

Dreifort, John E. 1991. *Myopic Grandeur: The Ambivalence of French Foreign Policy Toward the Far East, 1919–1945, Kent,* OH: Kent State University Press.

Duiker, William J. 1976a. "The Red Soviets of Nghe-Tinh: An Early Communist Rebellion in Vietnam." *Journal of Southeast Asian Studies*, 4 (2): 186–98.

———. 1976b. *The Rise of Nationalism in Vietnam 1940–41*. Ithaca, NY: Cornell University Press.

———. 1996. *The Communist Road to Power in Vietnam*. Boulder, CO: Westview.

———. 2000. *Ho Chi Minh*. New York: Hyperion.

Dumont, René. (1935) 1995. *La Culture de Riz dans le Delta du Tonkin*. Paris: Société des Editions Géographiques. Reprint, Patani: Prince of Songkla University.

———. 1997. *Famines, le retour*. Paris: Politis-Arléa.

Duncanson, Dennis J. 1968. *Government and Revolution in Vietnam*. Oxford: Oxford University Press for the Royal Institute of International Affairs.

———. 1974. "Ho Chi Minh in Hong Kong, 1931–32." *China Quarterly* 57 (Jan.–March): 84–100.

Durand, Frédéric, Frédéric Fortunel, and Pham Viêt Hà. 2005. "La Question foncière dans les dynamiques rurales du Centre Viêt Nam." In *Agriculture, environenent et sociétés sur les Hautes terres du Viêt Nam*, edited by R. De Koninck, F. Durand, and F. Fortunel, 121–58. Toulouse: Editions Arkuiris; Bangkok: IRASEC.

Elliott, David W. P. 2006. *The Vietnamese War: Revolution and Social Change in the Mekong Delta, 1930–1975*. Pacific Basin Institute Book. New York: M. E. Sharpe.

Elliott, Mai. 1974. *Reminiscences on the Army for National Salvation: Memoir of General Chu Van Tan*. Data paper no. 97. Ithaca, NY: Cornell University Southeast Asia Program, 1974.

Encyclopaedia Britannica. "Haiphong Cyclone." http://www.britannica.com/EBchecked/topic/1483619/Haiphong-cyclone.

Fall, Bernard B. (1967a) 1985. *Hell in a Very Small Place: The Siege of Dien Bien Phu*. Philadelphia: Lippincott; New York: Da Capo.

———. 1967b. *Ho Chi Minh on Revolution, Selected Writings, 1920–66*. New York: Praeger.

Fenn, Charles. 1973. *Ho Chi Minh: A Biographical Introduction*. New York: Scribner.

———. 2004. *At the Dragon's Gate: With the OSS in the Far East*. Annapolis, Md. Naval Institute Press.

Féray, Pierre-Richard. 1979. *Le Viêt-Nam au xx siècle*. Paris: Presse Universitaire de France.

Feyssal, P. de. 1933. *L'Endettement agraire en Cochinchine*. Hanoi: IDEO.

FitzGerald, Francis. 1972. *Fire in the Lake: The Vietnamese and the Americans in Vietnam*. New York: Little, Brown.

Furuta Motoo. 1998. "A Survey of Village Conditions during the 1945 Famine in Vietnam." In *Food Supplies and the Japanese Occupation in South-East Asia*, edited by Paul H. Kratoska, 227–338. Basingstoke: Macmillan.

Furuta Motoo and Van Tao, eds. (1995) 2001. *Nan doi Nam 1945 o Viet Nam: Nhung Chung tich lich su*. Hanoi: Nha Nam.

Gaudal, André. 1947. *L'Indochine en Face du Japon*. Paris: J. Susse.

Gauthier, J. 1930. *Digues de Tonkin, travaux de défense contres les inondations*. Hanoi, Imprimèrie d'Extrême-Orient.

Geertz, Clifford. 1963. *Agricultural Involution: The Processes of Ecological Change in Indonesia*. Berkeley: University of California Press.

Gendre, Claude. 2009. *Le De Tham (1846–1913): Un résistant Vietnamien à la colonisation française*. Paris: L'Harmattan.

Gibbons, William Conrad. 1986. *The U.S. Government and the Vietnam War: Executive and Legislative Roles and Relationships, Part 1: 1945–1960*. Princeton, NJ: Princeton University Press.

Giebel, Christoph. 2004. *Imagined Ancestries of Vietnamese Communism: Ton Duc Thang and the Politics of History and Memory*. Seattle: University of Washington Press.

Gilard, Olivier. 2006. "Risques d'inondation dans le delta du fleuve Rouge: De la nécessité d'améliorer leur prise en compte dans le processus d'aménagement du territoire." *Hérodote*, no. 121/2: 42–54.

Gillet, Kit. 2011. "Rising Seas Menace Vietnam's Rice Bowl." *Guardian Weekly*, August 26, 10.
Goscha, Christopher E. 1999. *Thailand and the Southeast Asian Networks of the Vietnamese Revolution, 1885–1954*. London: Routledge.
———. 2002. "Belated Allies: The Technical Contributions of Japanese Deserters to the Viet Minh (1945–1950)." In *A Companion to the Vietnam War*, edited by Marilyn Young and Robert Buzzanco, 37–64. London: Blackwell.
Gourou, Pierre. 1931. *Le Tonkin*. Paris: Exposition Coloniale Internationale.
———. (1936) 1955. *Les Paysans de delta tonkinois. Etude de geographie humaines* (*The Peasants of the Tonkin Delta: A Study of Human Geography*). Vol. 2. Paris: Editions d'Art et d'Histoire. Reprint, New Haven, CT: Human Relations Area Files.
———. (1940) 1945. *L'Utilisation du sol en Indochine française* (*Land Utilization in French Indochina*). Paris: 1940. Reprint, Washington, DC: Institute of Pacific Relations.
Greenland, D. J., ed. 1997. *The Sustainability of Rice Farming*. London: CABI; Manila: IRRI.
Gunn, Geoffrey C. 1985. "Reinterpreting Cambodian History: New Light on the Origins of Communism in Southern Indochina (1927–39)." *Kabar Seberang*, no. 16: 25–64.
———. 1988. *Political Struggles in Laos (1950–1954): Vietnamese Communist Power and the Lao Struggle for National Independence*. Bangkok: Duang Kamol.
———. 1990. *Rebellion in Laos: Peasant and Politics in a Colonial Backwater*. Boulder, CO: Westview.
———. 1998. *Theravadins, Colonialists and Commissars in Laos*. Bangkok: White Lotus.
———. 2009. "Origins of the American War in Vietnam: The OSS Role in Saigon in 1945." *Asia-Pacific Journal* 19-3-09 (May 9). http://www.japanfocus.org/-Geoffrey-Gunn/3137.
———. 2012. "From War Claims to Reparations: France, Japan and the 'Vietnam War.'" *Tonan Ajia Kenkyu Nenpo* (Southeast Asia Research Center) 53: 1–36.
Hammer, Ellen. (1954) 1966. *The Struggle for Indochina*. Stanford, CA: Stanford University Press.
Hanyok, Robert. 1996. "Guerillas in the Mist: COMINT and the Formation of the Viet Minh, 1941–45." *Cryptologic Quarterly* 15 (1): 95–114.
Harrison, James P. 1989. *The Endless War: Vietnam's Struggle for Independence*. New York: Columbia University Press.
Haseman, John B. 1978. *The Thai Resistance Movement during the Second World War*. DeKalb: Northern Illinois University Center for Southeast Asian Studies.
Hémery, Daniel. 1975. *Révolutionnaires Vietnamiens et Pouvoir Colonial en Indochine: communistes, trotskystes, nationalistes à Saigon de 1932 à 1937*. Paris: Maspero.
———. 1981."Tha Thu Thau: L'itinéraire politique d'un révolutionairre vietnamien pendant les années 1930." In *Histoire de l'asie du sud-est, révoltes, réformes, révolutions*, edited by Pierre Brocheux, 193–222. Lille: Presse Universitaires de Lille.
Henry, Yves. 1932. *Economie Agricole de l'Indochine*. Hanoi: Exposition Coloniale Internationale de Paris.

Henry, Yves, and Maurice Devisme. 1928. *Documents de démographie et riziculture en Indochine*. Hanoi: Bulletin économique de l'Indochine.

Higham, Charles. 1989. *The Archaeology of Mainland Southeast Asia, from 10,000 BC to the Fall of Angkor*. Cambridge: Cambridge University Press.

———. 2002. *The Early Cultures of Mainland Southeast Asia*. Bangkok: River Books.

Hill, Kimloan. 2006. "Strangers in a Foreign Land: Vietnamese Soldiers and Workers in France during World War I." In *Viet Nam: Borderless Histories*, edited by Nhung Tuyet Tran and Anthony Reid, 256–89. Madison: University of Wisconsin Press.

Ho Chi Minh. 1979. *Ho Chi Minh: Partriotisme et Inernationalisme Prolétarien*. Hanoi: Editions de la Langues Etrangères.

———. 2010. *Carnet de Prison*. Hanoi: Gioi Publishers, 2010.

Hoang Cao Khai. 1915. *Memoire de S.E. Hoang-Cao-Khai, Les Inondations au Tonkin et Rapport Technique de m. l'Ingenieur Principal Rover*. Hanoi: IDEO.

Hoang Nam. 2008. *Les Nung au Viet Nam*. Hanoi: Gioi Publishers.

Hoang Van Chi. 1964. *From Colonialism to Communism: A Case History of North Vietnam*. New York: Praeger.

Hoang Van Dao. 2008. *Viet Nam Quoc Dan Dang: A Contemporary History of a National Struggle: 1927–1954*. Translated by Khue Huynh. Pittsburgh: Rose Dog Press.

Hodgkin, Thomas. 1981. *Vietnam: The Revolutionary Path*. London: MacMillan.

Hong Chuong. 1965. "35 Years of Brave and Glorious Struggle." *Hoc Tap* 1 (February): 36–44.

Hong Thy and H. N. 1975. "Old Hue: From the Origins to 1945." Hue: Past and Present. *Vietnamese Studies*, no. 37: 25–63.

Hue-Tam Ho Tai. 1983. *Millenarianism and Peasant Politics in Vietnam*. Cambridge, MA: Harvard University Press.

———. 1996. *Radicalism and the Origins of the Vietnamese Revolution*. Cambridge, MA: Harvard University Press.

———. 2010. *Passion, Betrayal, and Revolution in Colonial Saigon: The Memoirs of Bao Luong*. Berkeley: University of California Press.

Huynh Kim Khanh. 1982. *Vietnamese Communism 1925–1945*. Ithaca, NY: Cornell University Press.

Iioka Naoko. 2011. "The Trading Environment and the Failure of Tongking's Mid-Seventeenth Century Commercial Resurgence." In *The Tongking Gulf Through History*, edited by Nola Cooke, Li Tana, and James A. Anderson, 133–42. Philadelphia: University of Pennsylvania Press.

Jacobs, Seth. 2006. *Cold War Mandarin: Ngo Dinh Diem and the Origins of America's War in Vietnam, 1950–1963*. Lanham, MD: Rowman & Littlefield.

Jennings, Eric T. 2004. *Vichy in the Tropics: Petain's National Revolution in Madagascar, Guadeloupe, and Indochina, 1940–44*. Stanford, CA: Stanford University Press.

Jordan, William Chester. 1996. *The Great Famine: Northern Europe in the Early Fourteenth Century*. Princeton, NJ: Princeton University Press.

Kahin, George McT. 1987. *Intervention: How America Became Involved in Vietnam*. New York: Doubleday.

Khieu Samphan. 1979. *Cambodia's Economy and Industrial Development*. Data paper no. 111, Southeast Asia Program, Cornell University, Ithaca, NY.

Khong Dien. 2002. *Population and Ethno-Demography in Vietnam*. Chiang Mai: Silkworm Books.

Kiernan, Ben. 1996. *The Pol Pot Regime: Race, Power and Genocide in Cambodia under the Khmer Rouge, 1975–1979*. New Haven, CT: Yale University Press.

Kleinen, John. 2005. "Tropicality and Topicality: Pierre Gourou and the Genealogy of French Colonial Scholarship on Rural Vietnam." *Singapore Journal of Tropical Geography* 26 (3): 339–58.

Koburger, Charles W., Jr. 1997. *Naval Expeditions: The French Return to Indochina, 1945–1946*. New York: Praeger.

Kolko, Gabriel. 1985. *Anatomy of War: Vietnam, the United States and the Modern Historical Experience*. New York: Pantheon.

Lan, T. 2009. *Ho Chi Minh: Stories Told on the Trail*. Hanoi: Gioi Publishers.

Lebra, Joyce. 1977. *Japanese-Trained Armies in Southeast Asia*. Hong Kong: Heinemann.

Le Manh Hung. 2004. *The Impact of World War II on the Economy of Vietnam 1939–45*. Singapore: Eastern Universities Press.

Le Manh Trinh. 2008. "In Canton and Siam." In *Reminiscences of Ho Chi Minh*, 47–76. Hanoi: Gioi Publishers.

Le Meur, Pierre-Yves, Damien Hauswirth, Timothée Leurent, and Pascal Lienhard. 2005. *The Local Politics of Land and Water: Case Studies from the Mekong Delta*. 4 vols. Paris: Les Editions de Gret. http://regards.in2p3.fr/fiche.php?id=59437.

Lieberman, Victor. 2011. "Charter State Collapse in Southeast Asia, ca. 1250–1400, as a Problem in Regional and World History." *American Historical Review* 116 (4): 936–63. http://www.jstor.org/stable/10.1086/ahr.116.4.937.

Lockhart, Greg. 1989. *Nation at Arms: The Origins of the People's Army of Vietnam*. Sydney: Allen & Unwin.

Lotzer, Louis. 1933. *Monographie de la province de Vinh-Yên*. Hanoi: Imp. d'Extrême-Orient.

———. 1941. *La surpopulation du Tonkin et du Nord-Annam. Ses rapports avec la colonisation de la péninsule indochinoise*. Hanoi: Imp. d'Extrême-Orient.

Luong, Hy Van. 1986. "Agrarian Unrest from an Anthropological Perspective: The Case of Vietnam." *Comparative Politics* 17 (January): 153–74.

———. 2010. *Tradition, Revolution, and Market Economy in a North Vietnamese Village, 1925–2006*. Honolulu: University of Hawaii Press.

Marr, David G. 1971. *Vietnamese Anti-Colonialism, 1885–1925*. Berkeley: University of California Press.

———. 1980. "World War II and the Vietnamese Revolution." In *Southeast Asia under Japanese Occupation*, edited by Alfred W. McCoy, 125–58. New Haven, CT: Yale University Southeast Asia Studies, Monograph Series No. 22.

———. 1981. *Vietnamese Tradition on Trial: 1920–1945*. Berkeley: University of California Press.

———. 1997. *Vietnam 1945: The Quest for Power*. Berkeley: University of California Press.

———. 2010. "Vietnamese, Chinese, and Overseas Chinese during the Chinese Occupation of Northern Indochina (1945–1946)." *Chinese Southern Diaspora Studies* 4: 129–39.

———. 2013. *Vietnam: State, War, and Revolution (1945–1946)*. Berkeley: University of California Press.

Martinez, Julia. 2007. "Chinese Rice Trade and Shipping from the North Vietnamese Port of Hai Phong." *Chinese Southern Diaspora Studies* 1: 82–96. http://chl.anu.edu.au/publications/csds/csds2007/Martinez.pdf.

Marty, André Louis. 1933. *La Terreur Rouge en Annam (1930–1931)*. Vol. 5. Hanoi: IDEO.

McAleavy, Henry. 1968. *Black Flags in Vietnam: The Story of a Chinese Intervention*. London: Allen & Unwin.

McAlister, John T. Jr. 1969. *Vietnam: The Origins of Revolution*. New York: Knopf.

Mickelsen, Martin L. 2008. "A Mission of Vengeance: Vichy French in Indochina in World War II." *Air Power History* 55 (Fall). Available at http://www.thefreelibrary.com/A+mission+of+vengeance%3A+vichy+French+in+Indochina+in+World+War+II.-a0185247173.

Miles, Milton E. 1967. *A Different Kind of War: The Little-Known Story of the Combined Guerrilla Forces Created in China by the U.S. Navy and the Chinese during World War II*. Garden City, NY: Doubleday.

Miller, Edward. 2004. "Vision, Power and Agency: The Ascent of Ngo Dinh Diem, 1945–54." *Journal of Southeast Asian Studies* 35 (3): 433–58.

Moïse, Edwin E. 1983. *Land Reform in China and North Vietnam: Consolidating the Revolution at the Village Level*. Chapel Hill, NC: University of North Carolina Press.

Munholland, Kim. 2005. *Rock of Contention: Free French and Americans at War in New Caledonia, 1940–1945*. New York: Berghahn.

Murray, Martin. *The Development of Capitalism in Colonial Indochina (1870–1940)*. Berkeley: University of California Press.

Mus, Paul. 1949. "The Role of the Village in Vietnamese Politics." *Pacific Affairs* (September): 265–72.

———. 1952. *Viet-Nam: Sociologie d'une guerre*. Paris: Editions du Seuil.

Neville, Peter. 2007. *Britain in Vietnam: Prelude to Disaster, 1945–6*. London: Routledge.

Ngo Vinh Long. 1978. "The Indochinese Communist Party and Peasant Rebellion in Central Vietnam, 1930–1931." *Bulletin of Concerned Asian Scholars* 10 (4): 15–35.

———. 1991. *Before the Revolution: The Vietnamese Peasants under the French*. New York: Columbia University Press.

Nguyen Khac Vi. 1904. "Notes sur Différentes Variétiés de Riz." *Bulletin de Archives de l'Indochine* 7 (32): 867–75.

Nguyen Khac Vien. 1975. *The Long Resistance (1858–1975)*. Hanoi: Foreign Languages Publishing House.

Nguyen-Marshall, Van. 2008. *In Search of Moral Authority: The Discourse on Poverty, Poor Relief, and Charity in French Colonial Vietnam*. New York: Peter Lang.

Nguyen The Anh. 1985. "The Vietnamese Monarchy under French Colonial Rule 1884–1945." *Modern Asian Studies* 19 (1): 147–62.

———. 1992. *Monarchie et fait colonial au Viet-nam (1875–1925): Le crépuscule d'un ordre traditionnel*. Paris: Editions l'Harmattan.

———. 1998a. "Japanese Food Policies and the 1945 Great Famine in Indochina." In *Food Supplies and the Japanese Occupation in South-East Asia*, edited by Paul H. Kratoska, 208–26. Basingstoke: Macmillan.

———. 1998b. "The Vietnamese Confucian Literati and the Problem of Nation-Building in the Early Twentieth Century." In *Religion, Ethnicity and Modernity in Southeast Asia*, edited by Oh Myung-Seok and Kim Hyung-Jun. Seoul: Seoul National University Press. http://webcache.googleusercontent.com/search?q=cache:dIb5AxTtGNkJ:www.vninfos.com/selection/histoire/literati.html+Huynh+thuc+Kang&cd=7&hl=en&ct=clnk, accessed 2012.

Nguyen Ngoc Thi. 1973. "Revolutionary Upsurge 1930–1945." In *Saigon: From the Beginnings to 1945*, 62–93. Vietnamese Studies 45. Hanoi: Foreign Languages Publishing House.

Norman, E. H. 1975. *Origins of the Modern Japanese State: Selected Writings of E.H. Norman*. Edited by John W. Dover. New York: Pantheon.

Normandin, A. 1923. *La Question de Inondation au Tonkin et Ailleurs*. Cahier de la Société de Géographie de Hanoi, Quatrième Cahier. Hanoi-Haiphong: IDEO.

Osborne, Milton E. 1969. *The French Presence in Cochinchina & Cambodia: Rule and Response (1859–1905)*. Ithaca, NY: Cornell University Press.

Paterson, Thomas G., and Dennis Merrill. 1995. *Major Problems in American Foreign Policy*. Vol. 2, *Since 1914*. 4th ed. Lexington, MA: Heath.

Patti, Archimedes. 1980. *Why Vietnam? Prelude to America's Albatross*. Berkeley: University of California Press.

Penney, Mathew. 2005. "'The Most Crucial Education': Saotome Katsumoto and Japanese Anti-War Thought." http://japanfocus.org/-Matthew-Penney/1640. 2005.

[Pentagon Papers.] 1971. *The Pentagon Papers: The Defense Department History of United States Decision Making on Vietnam*. Gravel ed. Boston: Beacon.

Perkins, Mandaley. 2012. *Hanoi Adieu: A Bittersweet Memoir of French Indochina*. Hanoi: Gioi Publishers, 2012.

Peycam, Philippe M. F. 2012. *The Birth of Vietnamese Political Journalism*. New York: Columbia University Press.

Pham Cao Duong. 1985. *Vietnamese Peasants under French Domination, 1861–1945*. Center for South and Southeast Asia Studies, monograph no. 25. Berkeley: University of California.

Pham Huu Ty, Tran Nam Tu and Guus van Westen, et.al. 2011. "Food Security and Energy Development in Vientiane," *The Newsletter* (International Institute for Asian Studies), 58, Autumn/Winter, pp. 24–25.

Pike, Douglas. 1972. "North Vietnam in 1971." *Asian Survey* 12 (1): 16–24.

———. 1978. *History of Vietnamese Communism, 1925–1976*. Stanford, CA: Hoover Institution Press, Stanford University.

Ponchaud, François. (1976) 1978. *Cambodia: Year Zero*. New York: Holt, Rinehart and Winston.

Popkin, Samuel L. 1979. *The Rational Peasant: The Political Economy of Rural Society in Vietnam*. Berkeley: University of California Press.

Pouyanne, A. 1931. *L'Hydraulique agricole*. Hanoi: Bulletin Economique de l'Indochine.

Quinn-Judge, Sophie. 2003. *Ho Chi Minh: The Missing Years*. Berkeley: University of California Press.

Rice-Maxim, Edward. 1986. *Accommodation and Resistance: The French Left, Indochina, and the Cold War, 1944–1954*. New York: Greenwood.

Robequain, Charles. 1929. *Le Thanh Hoa, Etude Géographique d'une province Annamite*. 2 vols. Paris: EFEO.

———. 1935. *L'évolution économique de l'Indochine française*. Paris: Hartman.

———. 1944. *The Economic Development of French Indo-China*. London: Oxford University Press.

Rolls, E. 1956. *The Combined Food Board: A Study in Wartime International Planning*. Stanford, CA: Stanford University Press.

Rousset, Pierre. 1978. *Communism et Nationalism Vietnamien: Vietnam entre les deux guerres mondiales*. Paris: Editions Galilée.

Sabattier, G. 1952. *Le Destin de l'Indochine*. Paris: Plon.

Sainteny, Jean. 1953. *Histoire d'une paix manquée: Indochine 1945–1947*. Paris: Amiot-Dumont.

Salan, Raoul. 1975. *Indochine Rouge: Le Message d'Ho Chi Minh*. Paris: Presse de la Cité.

Saotome Katsumoto. 1993. *"2000000 nin" Gashi no Kiroku—1945nen, Nihon Senryou no moto de* [A record of the starvation of 2,000,000 in Vietnam: 1945 under Japanese occupation]. Tokyo: Otsuki Shoten.

Scott, James C. 1976. *The Moral Economy of the Peasant*. New Haven, CT: Yale University Press.

Sen, Amartya. 1981. *Poverty and Famines: An Essay on Entitlement and Deprivation*. Oxford: Oxford University Press.

Seung-joon Lee. 2011. *Gourmets in the Land of Famine: The Culture and Politics of Rice in Modern Canton*. Stanford, CA: Stanford University Press.

Shepherd, C., and A. McWilliam. 2011. "Ethnography, Agency, and Materiality: Anthropological Perspectives on Rice Development in East Timor." *East Asian Science, Technology and Society: An International Journal* 5 (2): 189–215.

Smith, Ralph B. 1969. "Bui Quang Chieu and the Constitutionalist Party in French Cochinchina, 1917–30." *Modern Asian Studies* 3 (2): 131–50.

Smith, Richard Harris. 1972. *OSS: The Secret History of America's First Central Intelligence Agency*. Berkeley: University of California Press.

Smith, Stuart Andrew. 2003. "Water First: A Political History of Hydraulics in Vietnam's Red River Delta." PhD diss., Australian National University.

Smith, Timothy O. 2007. *Britain and the Origins of the Vietnam War: United Kingdom Policy in Indo-China, 1943–50*. London: Palgrave Macmillan.

Tabuchi Yukichika. 1992. "Indochina's Role in Japan's Greater East Asia Co-Prosperity Sphere: A Food Procurement Strategy." In *Indochina in the 1940s and 1950s*, edited by Shiraishi Takashi and Furuta Mooto, 87–112. Ithaca, NY: SEAP, Southeast Asia Program, Cornell University.

Tanaka Yuki and Marilyn B. Young, eds. 2009. *A Twentieth-Century History of Bombing Civilians*. New York: New Press.

Tedral, Pierre. 1926. *La France devant le Pacifique: La Comédie Indochinoise*. Paris: Editions Vox.

Tessier, Olivier. 2011. "Outline of the Process of Red River Hydraulic Development during the Nguyen Dynasty." In *Environmental Change and Agricultural Sustainability in the Mekong Delta*, edited by Mart A. Stewart and Peter A. Coclanis, 45–65. New York: Springer.

Teulières, André. 1978. *La Guerre du Vietnam 1945–1975*. Paris: Lavauzelle.

Thaxton Jr., Ralph A. 2008. *Catastrophe and Contention in Rural China: Mao's Great Leap Forward, Famine and the Origins of Righteous Resistance in Da Fu Village*. Cambridge, MA: Cambridge University Press.

Thomas, Martin. 1997. "Free France, the British Government and the Future of French Indo-China, 1940–45." *Journal of Southeast Asian Studies* 28 (1): 137–60.

———. 2000. "Silent Partners: SOE's French Indo-China Section, 1943–1945." *Modern Asian Studies* 34 (4): 943–76.

Thompson,Virginia. 1937. *French Indochina*. London: George Allen & Unwin.

Thompson, Virginia, and Richard Adloff. 1953. "Cambodia Moves toward Independence." *Far Eastern Survey* 22 (9): 105–11.

Tønnesson, Stein. 1984. *The Outbreak of the War in Indochina, 1946*. Oslo: International Peace Research Institute.

———. 1991. *The Vietnamese Revolution of 1945: Roosevelt, Ho Chi Minh, and De Gaulle in a World at War*. Oslo: International Peace Research Institute.

———. 2002. "Franklin D. Roosevelt and the French Loss of Indochina, 9 March 1945." Paper presented at a symposium on the First Indochina War, Lyndon B. Johnson Presidential Library, Austin, Texas, November 1–3.

———. 2007. "Franklin Roosevelt: Trusteeship and Indochina." In *The First Vietnam War Colonial Conflict and Cold War Crisis*, edited by Mark Atwood Lawrence and Frederik Logevall, 56–73. Cambridge, MA: Harvard University Press.

———. 2010. *Vietnam 1946: How the War Began*. Foreword by Philippe Devillers. Berkeley: University of California Press, 2010.

Trager, Frank N. ed. 1959. *Marxism in Southeast Asia: A Study of Four Countries*. Stanford, CA: Stanford University Press.

Tran Duy Hung. 1981. Interview for series *Vietnam: A Television History*, episode 101, "Roots of a War." Antenne-2 France, Central Independent Television, WGBH. http://openvault.wgbh.org/catalog/vietnam-1937cc-interview-with-tran-duy-hung-1981.

Tran My-Van. 2005. *A Vietnamese Royal Exile: Prince Cuong* Đe *(1882–1951)*. London: Routledge.

Tran Ngoc Dinh. 1979. "Big Landownership of Cochin China under French Rule." *Nghien Cuu Lich Su*, no. 132 (May–June): 81–90 (English translation).

Trotsky, Leon. 1970. "The Chinese Revolution, Draft Program of the Comintern." In *The Third International after Lenin*. New York: Pathfinder.

———. 1973. "On the Declaration by the Indochinese Oppositions, 18 September 1930." In *Writings of Leon Trotsky (1930–31)*. New York: Pathfinder.

Truong Buu Lam. 1967. *Patterns of Vietnamese Response to Foreign Intervention: 1858–1900*. New Haven, CT: Yale University Monograph Series No. 11, Southeast Asia Studies.

Truong Chinh. 1977. *Truong-Chinh: Selected Writings*. Hanoi: Foreign Languages Publishing House.

Truong Chinh and Vo Nguyen Giap. 1974. *The Peasant Question (1937–1938)*. Translated and with introduction by Christine Pelzer White. Data paper no. 94, Southeast Asia Program, Cornell University, Ithaca, NY.

Van Tao and Furuta Mutoo. (1995) 2011. *Nan doi Nam 1945 o Viet Nam: Nhung Chung tich lich su* (Testimonies on the 1945 Famine in Vietnam). Hanoi: Nha Nam.

Vin Sinh. 2002. "Komatsu Kiyoshi and French Indochina." *Moussons*, no. 3 (June): 57–86.

———, ed. and trans. 2009. *Phan Châu Trinh and His Political Writings*. Ithaca, NY: Southeast Asia Program Publications.

Viollis, Andrée. 1935. Préface de André Malraux, *Indochine S.O.S.* Paris: Gallimard.

Vo Nguyen Giap. 2010. *Unforgettable Days*. Hanoi: Gioi Publishers.

Vu Quoc Thuc. 1951. *L'Economie Communaliste du Viet Nam*. Hanoi: Presses Universitaires du Vietnam.

White, Christine Pelzer. 1974. "The Vietnamese Revolutionary Alliance: Intellectuals, Workers and Peasants." In *Peasant Rebellion & Communist Revolution in Asia*, edited by John Wilson Lewis, 77–90. Stanford, CA: Stanford University Press.

Wong, Pak Nung. "Following the Grain: State Formation and Trans-National Grain-Trading Networks in the Philippines." *Journal of Contemporary Asia* 41 (4): 584–609.

Woodside, Alexander B. (1971) 1988. *Vietnam and the Chinese Model: A Comparative Study of Vietnamese and Chinese Government in the First Half of the Nineteenth Century*. Cambridge, MA: Harvard University Press.

———. 1976. *Community and Revolution in Modern Vietnam*. Boston: Houghton Mifflin.

World Bank. 2011. World Bank Indicators. http://data.worldbank.org/indicator.

Yoshizawa Minami. 1992. "The Nishihara Mission in Hanoi, July 1940." In *Indochina in the 1940s and 1950s*, edited by Shiraishi Takashi and Furuta Mooto, 9–54. Ithaca, NY: SEAP, Southeast Asia Program, Cornell University.

Zhou Xun, ed. *The Great Famine in China, 1958–1962: A Documentary History*. New Haven, CT: Yale University Press, 2012.

Zinoman, Peter. 2001. *The Colonial Bastille: A History of Imprisonment in Vietnam, 1862–1940*. Berkeley: University of California Press.

Index

About the Author

Geoffrey C. Gunn is a professor emeritus of Nagasaki University. With an interest in Indochina dating back to the "Vietnam War," he is also the author of *Rebellion in Laos: Peasant and Politics in a Colonial Backwater* (1996). More recently he has authored two world histories, namely *First Globalization: The Eurasian Exchange, 1500–1800* (Rowman & Littlefield, 2003) and *History without Borders: The Making of an Asian World Region, 1000–1800* (2011).